INDIA, DEMOCRACY AND DISAPPOINTMENTS

INDIA, DEMOCRACY AND DISAPPOINTMENTS

JOGINDER SINGH

GYAN

India, Democracy and Disappointments

Rs. 900

ISBN: 978-81-212-1040-9

Published in 2010 in India by
Gyan Publishing House
23, Main Ansari Road, Darya Ganj,
New Delhi-110002
Phones : 23282060, 23261060
Fax : 011-23285914
E-mail: books@gyanbooks.com
Website: www.gyanbooks.com

Lasser Type Setting by: Rudra Computer Graphics, Delhi
Printed at : Gian Ridhi Offset Printers, Delhi

Contents

Preface

A history of a Nation is a valuable guide to its past. But unless the events, as they happen, are recorded; they are later on bound to be garbled. Moreover, all history is a personal interpretation of the events by its authors. For the middle ages and the periods long gone by, there are hardly any reliable sources to discover, what really happened and why it was so.

With the arrival of the print media in a big way and the spread of computers, the entire spectrum for the writing, writers and fanning out has changed. This book is a compilation of my reactions to several events supported by references, which have happened in the country, in the first decade of 21st century. The book covers all aspects of Indian Life, be it corruption, bureaucracy, public expenditure, drugs problem, sting operations, freedom of Press, problems of ULFA/Bodos in the North East, terrorism in its various manifestations and its cost to the country as well as suicidal terrorism, criminalisation of politics, how good or bad is our governance and what can be done to improve it.

It also covers the organised crime and policing in the country. I have also ventured to write on the famous Italian Mafia in this book, as well on the racket in the transplantation of the organs, the role of Bollywood and black money. I have also covered sex, women and crime. A spicy specimen: "Sex has caught the imagination of kings and commoners alike since the time immemorial. Thrones have been lost and kingdoms bartered or sacrificed for women. Both in politics and crime, women have always been active. Whether it was legendary Helen of Troy or Ms Simpson, an American divorcee for whom Edward VIII gave up the British throne; from an illiterate girl to a lecturer, using sex for pelf or power is the common story."

Somehow we in India have been rather hypocritical about our interest in sex. All love triangles and quadrangles are centred over sex. Our leaders - at least some of them - "have been discreet in their affairs". A writer has to be extremely careful in writing, as he can be exposed to the libel suit.. I have tried to be as impartial as humanly possible in interpreting the events, happenings and the goings on in the country.

This book has been written with an idea, to serve as a wake up call to the rulers, in the interest of the common man, of which I am also one of them. The power to undo the past is denied to the man and only God can do it. The charm of this book lies in the facts and in the enigmatic lesson, it conveys, that irrespective of the promises of the rulers, irrespective of the party or parties, to which they belong, nothing has changed and yet everything is completely different. This book is different history. It is a guide to navigation in perilous times, which our country faces. It also reveals a little bit time gone by and shows who we are and why we are on the way we are.

The beauty of this book is that you can read any paragraph and still find something of use to provoke you to think.

1

Corruption: A Criminal Defiance on Nation

1. Corroded by Corruption the Nation that is People

1.1. A Foreword

Corruption is no stranger to our country. In fact, it is a well-known and famous resident. December 9 is observed as UN World Anti-Corruption Day. Citizens and organisations around the world use this day each year to highlight the issues related to corruption and how they affect the everyday lives of each and every one of us.

Transparency International also uses this day to highlight the work being done to fight corruption and reduce its impact around the world. But as far as our country is concerned, the day has come and gone, unsung, unnoticed and unheard. The indifference is due to the fact that people in our country have come to accept corruption as an inevitable part of their lives.

Our country has slipped again in the latest Transparency International rankings and is the 84th most corrupt country in the world. Indeed, the fight against corruption is not on the agenda of any political party. There used to be a time after independence when anybody suspected of being corrupt was looked down upon by the rest of the society. Nobody would socialise with such a person or like to be seen with him or her. But over a period of time, due to erosion in our value system and the lack of fear of punishment, those in positions of power have become increasingly corrupt and it is no longer something that is looked down upon.

Corruption in Government services is no more news in our country, unless someone 'big' is caught in a scandal. Government servants are generally considered corrupt by default with the odd exception here and there. It seems to have become a way of life and a part of our culture.

Indians have no option except to live with the reality of corruption which is equally rampant in both Government and the private sector. On the other hand, China has been able to reduce corruption considerably by promptly and sternly punishing the guilty.

What prevents crime in a society is the certainty of punishment, that is, if you are caught not only will you lose your job but also your old life and certainly your ill-gotten wealth. Unfortunately, there is no such fear in India. Laws exist only on paper and are there more to protect the corrupt rather than act as a deterrent.

As per present laws, no inquiry can even be started against an officer of the level of Joint Secretary and above in the Government without the permission of the Government. Even after an inquiry is completed, the sanction of the Government is required for filing a case in the courts. The rationale given for this is that decision-makers should have sufficient protection against arbitrary and whimsical action by investigating agencies.

Decision-makers in our country feel that they should be protected even if their actions are not able to stand the test of equity, justice and fairness. This is notwithstanding the Supreme Court order that corruption is not a part of the duty of any public servant and no permission or sanction is required for taking action against him or her.

More than that, the indifference of the Government in ensuring prompt justice by strengthening the judiciary is the biggest shield for the corrupt and the dishonest. According to the latest figures released by the Supreme Court, of the 16,158 sanctioned posts of judges in the subordinate courts, 3,239 are lying vacant. A whopping 2.6 crore cases are pending in the lower courts.

The 21 High Courts have 886 sanctioned posts of judges, of which 266 are vacant. In these courts over 38.31 lakh cases are pending. Presently, five of the 26 posts of judges in the Supreme Court are vacant. There are 49,346 cases pending in the apex court.

India's oldest pending case is 173 years old. It was first lodged in Kolkata when it was the administrative and commercial capital of India's British colonial masters. The case pertains to the ownership of thousands of acres of land, historic buildings and temples spread across north Kolkata. It has broken all records. In the late-18th century, British Governor-General Robert Clive had ruled that the property should remain in the custody of Raja Naba Krishna Deb, a major Bengali royal of the Sovabazar court. The only condition for the Raja's continued rule was that he pay a tax of Re. 1 a day — a duty still being collected by the Government.

Justice BS Chouhan, Chief Justice of Orissa High Court, adressing a seminar this year, said if the registration of cases were to be stopped and the process of disposing of the pending cases begun, then it would take 300 years to clear the entire backlog.

Corruption not only affects Indians, but also foreign firms wanting to do business here. Though our country is emerging as a destination for global investment, 38 per cent of over 5,400 company representatives surveyed by global consultancy firm Price water house Coopers said they were asked to pay bribes to get licences and orders over the past two years. Of those firms which had to contend with bribery in India, 66 per cent said they had lost to their competitors because of this factor.

Industrialists, businessmen and investors alone do not suffer. According to one report, Rs. 31,585.98 crore worth of wheat and rice meant for the poorest of the poor was siphoned from the public distribution system in 2006-2007. In this way, every year India's poor are cheated of 53.3 per cent of the wheat and 39 per cent of the rice meant for them.

Unless the menace of corruption is checked, the country will have to pay a heavier price than what it has paid so far. Corruption increases the cost of goods and services and leads to the poor sinking further into poverty.

Corruption can be eradicated when the punishment laid down by the law is severe. Officers involved in corruption must be dismissed immediately without waiting for the disposal of the cases, which can take anything from 10 to 15 years. This power is already vested in the Government. A nation can survive its fools, but it cannot survive corruption.

1.2. New Limits

India has done it again. It has not won an Olympic gold medal or made an invention or even discovered something new. It has retained its position as one of the most corrupt nations of the world. According to the 'Corruption Perception Index: 2004' released by Transparency International's India chapter, India is at the bottom of the heap with 55 most corrupt nations out of 146. Except a few media reports and discussions on some television channels, nobody or the Government has shown any concern for this downslide.

The result is, people now accept corruption as part of their lives. As an issue, corruption has ceased to matter in the elections-whether to assemblies or the Lok Sabha. The matter is raised by political parties only when they are themselves in the wilderness or short of new ideas. That is why, when the Government convened a meeting of former Chiefs of Defence Services to discuss security matters. However, the convention's attitude to corruption was exemplified in the adage, "Each man to himself, and God for us all."

The report of Transparency International indicates that Indians pay $5 billions, or Rs. 32,000 crore, in bribes every year. Allow me to add that this report only talks of the money paid by contractors to public servants including politicians and bureaucrats. This figure has been worked out on the basis of 10 per cent cut given by those who deal with the Government.

When I told this to a contractor, he laughed saying that if he paid only 10 per cent as "cut" (commission), he would not remain in business. Depending on the "honesty" of officials, he had to pay anything between 25 to 45 per cent as bribe. According to him, 10 per cent commission was a thing of the past and only "the honest" were satisfied with it. The days when babus were satisfied with a few token gifts on Diwali or New Year are gone. Today they demand cash in addition to gifts. At times the demands for items including television sets, refrigerators, music systems or jewellery is made well in advance.

A few years ago, the Central Vigilance Commission issued a circular banning acceptance of gifts. When I asked a senior officer if he was aware of this order and the extent to which it was followed, he chuckled and said, "Who will complain? Neither the giver nor the recipient is likely to make a complain. After all, where is the enforcement machinery?" I persisted, saying that the CVC expects officials to follow its instructions. His response was, such circulars existed a dime a dozen. In the absence of any regulatory mechanism, except the willingness showed by the official, the existence or non-existence of such orders did not matter.

The Government makes rules on the premise that the public is a thief. It creates a web of complicated procedures that give rise to corrupt practices. The other day, a television anchor told me about her own brush with the corrupt system. She wanted to purchase some property. Her identity card that indicated she was a mediaperson rescued her from the demands of bribery. At the time of registration, she was asked for a photograph of the registering officer. She said she had not brought her camera since she was not aware of such a requirement. At this she was helpfully told that she could get the same from the photographer outside the concerned office.

It cost her a tidy sum of Rs. 1200 for a photograph that would not have cost more than Rs. 100. Incidentally, the photographer had made copies of pictures of all the officers concerned. Indeed, it is a new modus operandi in which a photographer has become the medium to pocket bribes. A number of chartered accountants have been arrested by the CBI for acting as conduits of revenue officials either for settlement of cases or helping them in getting lucrative postings where they can line their pockets. If anything, corruption has grown at the retail level where public has to interact with the Government functionaries at all levels.

However, such corruption is not included in the survey conducted by Transparency International. According to another report, the price tag varies from person to person in accordance with his or her capacity to pay for the required Government service. These include obtaining ration cards, birth and death certificates, driving licenses, admission to schools and colleges, bank loans, customs, excise, income, sales or pollution tax clearances, lapsed insurance claims, admission to hospitals, and even Government or DDA accommodations. Monies are also exchanged if someone wants to escape the penalty for traffic violation, the examination system or even get married on the same day in a court. The list is illustrative and not exhaustive.

Another reason for the diffusion of corruption is lack of fear on the part of those indulging in it. The people have a right to know why those involved in high profile cases of corruption are always roaming free and calling the shots? The answer to this lies in the lack of political will to reform the criminal justice system. Also, the corrupt ensure that the whistle-blowers are taught a lesson of their lives. This has happened in a number of cases; for instance, the one involving National Highways Authority of India's engineer Satyendra Dubey, who was killed to prevent the exposure of corruption.

Corruption in our country is not a new phenomenon. There have been numerous surveys and cases that have revealed the widespread pattern of corruption prevalent in various Government departments. Corruption has been more than simply a problem for India. The national treasury is susceptible to rip-offs simply because there is so much money. The longstanding national policy has been to go slow if not exactly soft pedal the cases. Recently, the Supreme Court observed how efforts were being made to change the prosecutor in the Bihar fodder scam case and rightly found fault with the way things had been done under the influence of powerful politicians.

When it comes to rooting out corruption, irrespective of liberalisation or progress that is repeatedly claimed to have been made, nothing really changes. Charging a few politicians of corruption after they have learnt the ropes of wriggling out of cases on grounds of political vendetta does not make a difference.

Extortion, just like corruption, has neither disappeared nor reduced, but has grown more sophisticated with the help of lawyers and accountants. The reason for this malaise is that those at the helm are not always honest. However, they would not have been in power if they were not the sort of people they are. People often question what they should do to improve the situation and root out corruption. To this, Carlyle said: "Make yourself an honest man and then you may be sure that there is one rascal less in the world."

There is no doubt that the straight and the narrow path is the shortest route in both morals and geometry. It is also important for our rulers to realise that people are fashioned according to the examples they see. Laws, rules and edicts are less powerful than the models which Politicians exhibit. I think it is a matter of dishonour, ignominy and infamy to be branded as the 90th most corrupt country in the world. The responsibility for this situation, as well as for rectifying it, falls on Politicians who need not be reminded that example is the school of mankind and they will never learn at any other. Cicero said, "Be a pattern to others and then all will go well; for, as a whole city is infected by the licentious passions, and vices of great men, so it is likewise reformed by their moderation."

1.3. New Heights

The other day, I was talking to a senior Government official who lamented about the prevailing corruption culture in most public-dealing departments. Another gentleman standing by said; "Ours is new and a young democracy and it will take time to set the traditions of honesty and integrity." Another equally senior official said that our laws were too lenient for the corrupt and provided them all escape routes.

"Laws are like cobwebs where the small flies are caught and the great break through," said one of the seven wise men of Greece. This is confirmed by the latest CBI report which highlights the pendency of over 8,200 cases still awaiting punishment, because they are pending for want of completion of their trial. More than 2,276 cases have been pending trial in various courts all over the country for more than 10 years now. About 244 cases are pending trial for over 20 years. This figure also includes cases which are more than 25 years old. In 2006, 8,297 CBI cases were awaiting trial after completion of the investigations. The figure of pending trial cases was 6,898 in 2005.

In a country like India, which has over 1.90 crore public servants of the Central and State Governments, a few thousand cases do not make even a small dent in the massive problem of corruption. There are 438 cases in which charge-sheets have been filed and charges have not been framed by the designated courts for the last 10 years. High-level of corruption can be gauged from the fact that in 2006, CBI booked 1,917 cases against public servants from different Government agencies. Nearly half of the public servants (941) charged were gazetted officers, of whom 25 were of the level of joint secretary and above.

Out of the 1,156 cases registered in 2006, the highest was reported from the Customs and Central Excise Department (68), followed by the department of posts (57), railways (54), MCD (37). Another idiom brought to light in the CBI report is that the left hand often does not know what the right is doing. On the one hand, the Government has been talking of zero tolerance of corruption. On the other, 113 cases were pending at the end of 2006 for want of sanction for prosecution of corrupt public servants from different Government departments.

While replying to a question in Parliament on May 7, 2003, then Deputy Prime Minister LK Advani had said that out of the 186 cases pending against IAS and IPS officers till that time, the "overwhelming majority related to corruption charges". This number now, four years later, must be much higher.

On paper, corruption is a very high-risk activity. Officially, the CVC, other vigilance departments within Government organisations, the CBI, the anti-corruption bureaus of different States, CAG, etc., are there to check corruption. But in actual practice, the corrupt are protected through the subversion of the system from within.

The result is that corruption has become a low-risk, maybe almost no risk, and high-return activity. People naturally feel that the criminal justice system has failed the aggrieved and encouraged the corrupt. Cases are sought to be delayed for years under one pretext or the other till the impact of corruption gets diluted, or the case is forgotten.

Here is a case from Sikkim. On August 7, 1984, the CBI registered a case against an IAS officer and former Secretary, Rural Development of the State, for awarding contracts worth Rs. 1.62 crore to favoured contractors. The CBI filed a chargesheet in the same case on September 14, 1994, in the court of the Special Judge, Gangtok. But the official (who was charged, along with a former Sikkim Chief Minister) managed to delay trial by challenging the filing of the charges against them in the Sikkim High Court. On May 7, 2003, the High Court asked both the Secretary and the Former Chief Minister to face the trial for corruption.

A former Chief Excise Commissioner, Delhi, was arrested in 2001 for taking Rs. 10 lakh as bribe from Flex Industries. The CBI found Rs. 8 lakh in cash and bank deposits, two flats in Ghaziabad and a plot in Haryana, and 10 bank accounts.

A Chairman, Central Board for Excise and Customs, was arrested in April 2001 by the CBI for accepting Rs. 2 lakh as bribe through his son as the conduit, amassing ill-gotten wealth and helping a Chennai-based trader avail a Rs. 75 lakh duty drawback. A Commissioner (Appeals), IT, Mumbai, belonging to Indian Revenue Service, was caught accepting a bribe of Rs. 50,000 in 2002. Assets worth Rs. 2.1 crore were recovered from his flats in Delhi, Ahmedabad and Indore. One Punjab Public Service Commission Chairman was caught red-handed while taking a bribe of Rs. 5 lakh to promote an excise inspector to the Punjab Civil Service. The Vigilance Bureau unearthed ill-gotten wealth of Rs. 28 crore from him. The case has been pending trial for the last three years. He was not dismissed by the Government or impeached because he held a constitutional position. The delays have crippled the criminal justice system and made corruption now all pervasive.

Local self-governments in the form of Municipal Corporations are no better. The Municipal Corporation of Delhi (MCD) has the most dubious distinction. No less than the Deputy Chairman of its powerful standing committee was arrested by the CBI for accepting a bribe of Rs. 1 lakh from one of its employees. Corruption has become a way of life for most officials dealing with Government revenues or purchases.

Corruption is defined as the illegal use of public office for private gain. It hurts poor the most as it leads to the diversion of development-related funds into the pockets of the corrupt, the result being the undermining of Government's ability to provide basic services, besides feeding inequality and injustice, and discouraging foreign investment and aid.

Unfortunately, corruption is often highlighted only in monetary terms and never in terms of human sufferings it inflicts on the poor. Even in Delhi High Court, the MCD representative admitted that if the corporation starts taking action against the corrupt, nobody would be left to do whatever little they are doing.

Many a time it is asked whether there will ever be an end to the culture of corruption. The answer is "yes", but it requires a combination of law enforcement, stronger deterrence in the form of harshest possible punishments, greater economic freedom, transparency and prevention campaigns.

2. Corruption: Its Daring Nexuses, Criminality and Affliction

2.1. Politics and Corruption

Corruption in high places has regrettably become rather pronounced in the last few decades. It has become a part of Indian political culture. Major scandals that have surfaced from time to time include a number of defence deals such as Bofors and HDW submarine, Harshad Mehta securities scam (1992), the Jain hawala (1995), Urea import by National Fertilisers Ltd/Karsan (1995), JMM bribery (1996), the Sukh Ram telecom case (1996) and the Animal Husbandry scandal of Bihar (1996).

Corruption charges against several Chief Ministers including Mr. Prakash Singh Badal, Ms. J Jayalalithaa and Mr. OP Chautala, Ms. Mayawati, Mr. Bangaru Laxman, Mr. Dileep Singh Judeo as well as Mr. Natwar Singh are under inquiry. Granted that some allegations may have been wild and engineered by political rivalries, but in a majority of cases it cannot be said so.

Amassing of wealth by many politicians has gone beyond people's wildest expectations. Despite these scandals some political parties are even headed towards the alleged scamsters. Indeed, some have even come to power in certain States.

During electioneering, political parties promise the moons. Former BBC correspondent Mark Tully once said, "In India, what goes up comes down quite rapidly and, true to form, it wasn't long before the tempers aroused by the Tehelka scandal cooled, the excitement diminished, and the nation realised the revelation is not going to lead to any meaningful measures to curb corruption, let alone reform the administration which has been so porous."

We have a generous, pro-criminal and pro-accused criminal justice system, which is cluttered with cases. The following pendency of cases in several courts will give an idea as to why cases of corruption against people in high places drag on for years. The backlog of cases as on February 27, 2006, are in the Supreme Court was 33,635; in the High Courts, 33,41,040 and the subordinate judiciary, 2,53,06,458. Delay in verdicts also benefits high profile politicians. Surprisingly, the judiciary, too, has not remained immune from corruption. Former Chief Justice of India SP Bharucha once remarked that at least 20 per cent of judges are corrupt.

Addressing a conference of Chief Ministers and Chief Justices of the High Courts on March 11, 2006, the Chief Justice of India, Justice YK Sabharwal said, "The country's justice delivery system appears to be on the verge of the collapse... Not much has been done for the improvement of investigative and prosecution machinery. Significant suggestions, for separation of the investigative wing from the law and order duties and changes in the rules of evidence, still lie unattended... Public outrage over the failure of the criminal justice system in some high profile cases must shake us all up into the realisation that something needs to be urgently done to revamp the whole process, though steering clear of knee-jerk reactions, remembering that law is a serious business."

The truth is the entire criminal justice system is based on the premise that the people are willing to state the truth in a court of law under oath without bothering about their own safety or expenditure to be incurred or the time to be spent in giving evidence. This is apart from the harassment witnesses face from the defence. To cite a personal example, I once asked my wife to drop me to the nearest taxi stand, since the Government staff car did not come on time to take me to the airport. While returning home, her car was hit by a rashly driven bus. As I was away in Kolkata, I asked her to immediately report the case to the police. Although the mishap took place in 1979, the case came up after 16 years!

The defence lawyer for the accused asked whether her eyesight was ok, and whether she really knew driving - though she had been driving for 10 years before the accident occured - and why did she not take preventive measures to avoid the accident. In all this she had no help from the prosecutor. My wife told me that she was made to feel like an accused rather than a state witness.

It is precisely for this reason that nobody wants to be involved with the police or the criminal justice system. After undergoing an agonising experience, the witness is not compensated for the loss of the earning of the day. It is not surprising, then, that disinterested persons fight shy of extending a helping hand to police. At times, witnesses incur the wrath of hardened criminals and are deprived of their lives or limbs. The fact is the more high profile a case, the more the chances of harassment of witnesses.

There is every possibility of miscarriage of justice in the reluctance of the public to appear as a witness. It has happened in many high profile cases, where persons committing crimes have got away with it using either money or muscle power. More than that, the political class, irrespective of their parties, have a biradari, where they go out of their ways protect each other. In Uttar Pradesh, a Minister and an MLA were caught accepting bribe on camera. There was uproar in the political circles, surprisingly not on the corrupt practices but on the issue as to why had the sting operation been conducted.

Similarly, in Punjab, when a raid was conducted and a corrupt official was caught, the Minister protested as to why his permission was not taken before conducting the raid. In Meghalaya, the Community and Rural Development Minister, Mr Beckstar K Sangma, was removed from the Cabinet as he was accused in a multi-crore rupee Central funds fraud in the Garo hills.

Paradoxically, even after being convicted, politicians enjoy Government perks. After being convicted in a rape case, Forward Bloc MP from Purulia, Bir Singh Mahato sought the permission of the Supreme Court to attend the current session of Parliament. The apex court declined.

Despite the recommendations of several commissions and committees, no steps appear to have been taken by the Government to set matters right, by providing witnesses protection or introduce plea bargaining where an accused person to gets lesser sentence for truthfully confessing to his role in a crime.

Hopefully, our search for good governance will end in the 21st century. Excessive power with the rulers over the ruled is adding to existing corruption and inefficiency. The test of good governance is to maximise people's welfare, by providing an atmosphere where there is peace and order. There is no question of going soft on the criminals in any sphere of society. The Government should unleash the full force of the law and each one of the cases should be pursued relentlessly till they are adjudged.

Only then can we stand up and measure to Rabindranath Tagore's idea of a country where the mind is without fear and the head is held high.

2.2. Bureaucracy and Corruption

A raid conducted by the CBI in the third week of March on the premises of a former Chief Secretary of UP unearthed unaccounted wealth amounting to Rs 120 crore. The country's premier law enforcing agency declared that the official owned 42 properties in real estate that spread across three states in the names of his various family members. In addition to this the former civil servant was in the process of setting up a residential school for girls in Nainital. He also intended to bring Rs. 40 crore from abroad in order to convert black money to white.

It is a blot on of the country's system that such a person should have been allowed to reach one of the highest echelons of the IAS hierarchy. Moreover, it is not as if this official's misdemeanours were unknown to the people. In 1996, the UP IAS Officers' Association held a secret ballot to identify the three most corrupt officers in the State. The same official had reportedly figured in that list. In 1997, a delegation of IAS officers met the then Chief Minister of UP who belonged to the BJP and pleaded for an enquiry into the official's assets. However, no action was taken. A communication to then Prime Minister in regard to the four UP cadre IAS officers resulted in a secret probe which substantiated most of the charges against him.

Meanwhile, the NDA Government led by Mr Atal Bihari Vajpayee took over and directed the BJP Chief Minister to give his consent to a CBI inquiry. But the order remained unheeded. Later, two other chief ministers, one from the BSP and the other from the SP, came to power in UP. They extended similar protection to the official. In fact, one of them even managed to extend the latter's tenure. The State vigilance inquiry file was closed much against the wishes of the Central Government and the official was made the Chief Secretary of UP. It was only when a PIL was filed in the Supreme Court that those at the helm apprehended that the verdict may go against them. The official resigned from his post saying he did not want to cause further embarrassment to the Government because of the PIL.

It is obvious that by doing the bidding of four chief ministers, all of whom were from different political parties, the official not only survived but also thrived. Many would raise question as to what was the State's vigilance department doing all this time? Why did it allow such a corrupt functionary to roam free all these years? The fact remains that the vigilance set up, as it is constituted, is hemmed in by constraints. The present position of vigilance embraces the return of the infamous "single directive".

This provision in Section 6A of the CVC Act makes it obligatory for the CBI to secure prior approval of the Central Government before conducting any investigation under the Prevention of Corruption Act, 1988, if the allegations relate to an officer of the rank of Joint Secretary or above. The "single directive" was quashed by the Supreme Court in the Jain Hawala case filed by Vineet Narain in its judgment on December 17, 1997, on the basis of the argument that "every person accused of committing the same offence, is to be dealt with in the same manner in accordance with law, which is equal in its application to everyone".

It was a path breaking verdict and it restored a degree of fairness to the structure of governance which has all along sought to keep the rulers (politicians and bureaucrats) away from the regulatory mechanism. In order to ensure that bureaucrats get double protection, the CVC Act limits the area of selection of Central Vigilance Commissioner and Vigilance Commissioners to the retired bureaucrats and senior officers of public sector undertakings.

Another provision in Section 8 under the head "Functions and powers of the Central Vigilance Commission" requires the CVC to superintend the functioning of the CBI insofar as it relates to the investigation of offences under the Prevention of Corruption Act or an offence with which a public servant can be charged.

The CVC is authorised to give directions to the CBI under Section 4(1). The category of public servants that enjoy protection from investigation without the CVC's prior permission include members of All India Services serving as the Union and Group A Officers of the Central Government. Further, officers of the same level in public sector undertakings (as the Government may declare, by notification in the Official Gazette) would be immune to investigations without the CVC's permission.

The single directive that was declared unconstitutional by the Supreme Court in 1997 is back in the form of law. The new CVC law classifies the offenders on the basis of their status and is constitutionally a bad legislation. A PIL is pending with the Supreme Court. Incidentally, this law was passed unanimously by all members of Parliament -obviously because it facilitates the politician-bureaucratic nexus.

Sometime back the apex court held that citizens have the fundamental right to know the antecedents of their political representatives. Parliament unanimously introduced a provision to the effect that it is enough if the elected member furnish details about their assets to the Speaker. The new provision in Section 33 (B) of the Representation of People's Act declared that "no candidate shall be liable, to disclose or furnish any such information in respect of his election which is not required to be disclosed or furnished under this Act or the rules made there under". This provision had to come into effect notwithstanding any judgement or directive of the Election Commission to the contrary. The Supreme Court struck down the above provision on March 13, 2003, on the ground that the law violated fundamental rights of citizens guaranteed under Article 19(1) as interpreted by the court. The new CVC law stands on the same footing.

All talk of controlling corruption and breaking the bureaucrat criminal nexus is no more than delusion because it is not backed by political will. Corruption continues to thrive because we have an elaborate and deeply entrenched bureaucratic structure that has to be negotiated via a maze of complicated rules and regulation. According to Tacitus, a Roman historian, "The more corrupt the state, the more numerous the laws."

It is noteworthy that the least corrupt countries are the ones which have adhered to a transparent political and bureaucratic set up and a less intrusive government and with least rules and regulations. The countries that are well known for corruption have a burgeoning governmental set up with a plethora of rules, laws, quotas, prohibitions and regulations. States which repose faith in their people have a liberal outlook. On the other hand, the more rules a State has, the more scope there is for corruption and underhand dealings. Thus, in such places this malaise touches every aspect of the citizen's life.

Unfortunately, we have elevated Government to a level where all look up to it as a provider of solutions to the multitude of problems that the country faces. Also, Government is hardly the answer to dealing with corruption. In fact, it is the creator and instigator of the phenomenon. In order to reform the system, it is imperative that we create public opinion through pressure groups to drive home the point that it is time the system was transformed. One way of doing this is to ensure that the right to corruption free Government is made one of the fundamental rights in the Constitution. More, if each one of us resolves that regardless of the difficulties one faces, if one does not bribe Government functionaries, it will go a long way towards creating a system cleansed of this all-pervasive malaise. As Karl Kraus says, "Corruption is worse than prostitution. The latter might endanger the morals of an individual, the former invariably endangers the morals of the entire country."

2.2.1. The Challenge Exists

The Prime Minister of India, while addressing a conference of district collectors in the last week of May, 2005, said, "One major issue which has arisen is security of tenure of key functionaries like district collectors and superintendents of police... I do recognise (that) you are entitled to ask for this. No system in the government could deliver if people are changed without notice. Short tenure does not produce the desired results."

Expressing his concern over the frequent transfer of district heads, the Prime Minister added that no system could deliver if top civil servants were changed without notice. He frankly admitted that the Centre could not take up the issue on its own and had to work in tandem with the State governments. Mr Singh added, "I do propose to bring up this subject in the National Development Council as an integral part of improving the quality of administration and making it more transparent. It is necessary that our civil servants should be entitled to minimum security of tenure, so that they can be judged on the basis of tasks assigned to them."

It is an established fact that most transfer orders are given in order to place compliant individuals in key posts. They are expected to carry out the orders of the political executive which may not always be lawful. Today, transferring people to plum posts has become another industry. Ms Mayawati as the Chief Minister of UP created a record of sorts in 1997 when she transferred over 1400 civil and police officers in just six months of her reign. Mr Kalyan Singh transferred 521 officials in 1991-'92 and the Samajwadi Party Government headed by Mr Mulayam Singh Yadav issued transfer orders of 814 officials in 1993-'95. Again, till June 2002, during her stint as Chief Minster of UP, Ms Mayawati ordered transfers of about 300 IAS and IPS officers and 600 PCS officers in the first 21 days of her rule. This did not include the transfer of the Chief Secretary of the State.

All transfers are not done to ensure accountability or transparency in administration. A few years ago, a personal assistant of a Minister of State in the Finance Ministry was arrested by the CBI. He was charged with acting as a middleman who managed cash transactions as a price for transfer to a 'wet' postings. The easiest thing to do is to transfer an official for consideration, as it does not involve serious reading or application of mind, or for that matter, intelligence. Unfortunately in all this, the upright officers are ignored because it does not suit their unscrupulous superiors to have them around. However, the efficient but corrupt and obliging men are not shifted from their positions as there is a great demand for their services by all parties. These are the people who can combine acumen with shrewdness to gain wealth and other favours for themselves as well as their bosses.

Nobody can dispute the honesty and simplicity reflected in the lifestyle of Prime Minister Manmohan Singh. However, Mr Singh's problem is that being an upright politician, he is not manipulative. At times this leads to lack of political authority which is needed to bolster his stature as the country's Prime Minister. In the absence of this, his gentle hints and subtle insinuations are more often than not ignored.

India has been branded as the 83rd most corrupt country in the world. This dubious recognition reflects bad governance and unresponsive bureaucracy. Unfortunately, no Government, not even the present one, has shown a will to come down heavily on dishonest civil servants who have thrived regardless of which political party is in power.

From a Director General of Police or Chief Secretary of a State to even a District Magistrate, all are subjected to pulls and pressure. The officers are promised career advancement and preferential treatment in matters like promotion and postings if they fulfil the demands of the political executive. At the same time if they resist and do not comply with the orders of their masters, all chances of progress are lost.

While it is not always possible to penalise a government official according to statutory punishments under the Discipline and Appeal Rules without adequate proof and/or without following a prescribed procedure, it is not easy to subject him to administrative action by way of transfer or suspension on the basis of a complaint taken up for enquiry. (It happened to me as Director, CBI, as I had refused to compromise on the fodder scam case without any written order of the then Prime Minister).

No officer-apart from a few exceptions like the Director of the CBI-has a fixed tenure. This system of tenure was incorporated in accordance with a Supreme Court judgement. When a new Government assumes office, the first targets are the State and district police chiefs, chief secretaries and deputy commissioners of the district.

However, normal rules do exist for a minimum of three years in office. No bureaucrat can order his own posting. He is transferred following instructions of a competent authority, which-in the case of appointments in senior ranks-is generally a politician.

It is alright to announce a grand plan of Rs. 1,74,000 crore for development of rural infrastructure. The question is how much of it will actually be utilised for the intended purposes. Rajiv Gandhi had once said that out of every one rupee earmarked for rural areas, only 15 paise reach the intended beneficiary.

Given the plethora of scams everywhere, it is difficult to believe that things have not worsened. What the country needs is accountability and transparency in bureaucracy. However, this is resisted by the members of the bureaucracy themselves. Such reluctance to have a corruption-free system is not difficult to understand since bureaucrats too, are beneficiaries of a lawless system. Hence, the wide gap between ideals and reality.

The common man has a poor image of the bureaucracy. Few in our country would deign to believe that civil servants enjoy blemishless credibility. Despite Prime Minister's advice to have accountable Government machinery, the bureaucrats have the power to stymie whatever comes in their way of making a fast buck. Incidentally, nobody in the above Collector's Conference spoke of his own achievement in eliminating poverty and other socio-economic issues like education, health, employment and so on.

The general tendency among district collectors is to stay like laat sahibs in their respective districts caring the least about performance. Unlike in Government service, the jobs are not secure in the private sector; and an employee's retention depends solely on his performance. Certainly, if Government servant performs well, people go out of their way to press for his continuation in service at the given place in case he or she is being shifted.

It happened with yours truly when he was transferred twice from the post of District Superintendent of Police-Bidar; first to Bellary and later to Bijapur in Karnataka. The people, irrespective of their party affiliations, wrote to the Government stating in unison that no communal riot had occurred during my stewardship in the sensitive Bidar district, and that I should be reinstated. The Government took note of it and cancelled the transfer much to my regret as I was being moved to much bigger districts.

Ideally, bureaucrats should exhibit their willingness to work anywhere the Government posts them. Such a desire to work against all odds is shown only by the officers who are well known for their integrity and moral values. They should be upright, above board and eager to work without fear or favour. To work selflessly in order to serve people should be their motto.

Even if a government assures a civil servant posted in a region that he would enjoy a fixed tenure, it does not necessarily mean that the next government too would retain the same officer in that post. The present Government itself reversed the policy of the previous incumbent-which had given a tenure of two years to the Cabinet Secretary-when it transferred an existing official to an inconsequential post. It is time we remembered what Red Auerbach said, "An acre of performance is worth a whole world of promise."

2.3. Poverty and Corruption

The Government's claim that the economy is booming and poverty decreasing is sometimes deflated not by the Opposition, but the Government's own figures and analysis. All Governments claim to work for the uplift of the aam admi. But the reality shows a different picture. In our country, rural poverty has attracted greater attention than urban poverty, which merits equal attention.

Larger cities and metropolises — with the highest percentage of slum dwellers — are growing faster than the smaller towns. Incidentally, as the cities grow, so do the slums, the hotbed of urban poverty and vote-banks for politicians. But not all poor live in slums, as the urban poor population in the country is estimated to be nearly eight crore, while the slum population is roughly four crore.

According to the Report on Conditions of Work and Promotion of Livelihood in the Unorganised Sector, the first authoritative study on the state of informal or unorganised employment in India — compiled by the National Commission for Enterprises in the Unorganised Sector (NCEUS), a staggering 394.9 million workers, or 86 per cent of India's working population, toil in the unorganised sector.

Nearly 80 per cent of these workers are among those who live on less than Rs. 20 per day. Agriculture, the report found, was a fertile ground for poverty, especially for small and marginal farmers, 84 per cent of whom spent more than they earned and were often caught in debt trap. A large chunk of these 836 million Indians — 77 per cent of the country's population — is above the poverty line earning Rs. 12 per day.

What can Rs. 20 a day possibly fetch? It cannot even buy a person the things needed for his daily sustenance. Over 394.9 million workers (86 per cent of the working population) belong to the unorganised sector and work under "utterly deplorable" conditions with "extremely few livelihood options." They remain dismally poor, comprising largely Scheduled Castes, Scheduled Tribes, Other Backward Classes and Muslims, according to the report, "Conditions of work and promotion of livelihood in the unorganised sector". The report says that 88 per cent of the SCs and STs, 80 per cent of the OBCs and 85 per cent of Muslims belong to the category of "poor and vulnerable", earning less than Rs. 20 a day.

The report is based on Government data for the period between 1993-94 and 2004-05. A part of this period was ruled by the NDA Government, which claimed that India was "shining". The present Government, too, is raising the slogan, "Incredible India" to promote tourism. It forgets that there is nothing incredible about inviting foreigners to see Indian poverty.

In this country, poverty exists amid affluence, skyscrapers, latest cars and five star culture. In 1988, Rajiv Gandhi famously remarked that out of every one rupee provided by the Centre, only 15 per cent reached the intended beneficiaries. Since then, things have turned from bad to worse, with all kinds of scams being unearthed at regular intervals.

A substantial number of State and Union Ministers and other legislators have amassed money meant for people. Their banditry is bigger than infamous bandits'. There is no dearth of money for the poor but the state's inability to deal with the corrupt is a big roadblock.

The scams that have taken place in the country may have occurred at different points of time, but the basic objective of the accused has been to make as much money as possible out of the public projects. Nevertheless, the techniques that have been used as cover-up do not differ. Every successive scam generates better methods of cover-up. According to an estimate, the total amount of wealth of Indians, most of them politicians, in foreign bank accounts is placed at $410 billion. If this money could be spent on infrastructure, we would be a developed country. Our total budget accounts for $95 billion and the total amount needed for good industrial infrastructure development is $150 billion. This amount is equal to the cost of 366 nuclear reactors at the cost of $300 million each.

Corruption is the only factor keeping India, possessing rich natural and human resources, poor. It is a major destabilising factor. Most schemes like NREGA have built-in scope for corruption. In fact, no scheme ever stipulates the action to be taken against those who abuse or manipulate the law.

Not only the corrupt politicians, but Indian bureaucracy also has let the country down. The high level of corruption in the Government offices that deal with money and development schemes affects the poor by and large. Last year, public servants received Rs 21,068 crore in all as bribe, apart from the 'cut' from several Government schemes.

Between 1996 and 2000, the CBI and the Central Vigilance Commission investigated 13,265 individuals for corruption. Between 1998 and 2001, the CBI registered 2,256 cases under the Prevention of Corruption Act. Of these, 41 were from administrative departments, four were from the police and 23 from the revenue department. This is a drop in the ocean, as the total number of Government and public sector employees of State and Centre is 194 million.

Corruption in the bureaucracy has now come to be accepted as part of the machinery that governs India. Millions are at the receiving end of this phenomenon in their everyday lives, whenever they come in contact with any arm of the Government at any level anywhere in India. The classes of people who are affected include businessmen, investors — including foreigners — and foreign tourists. Unless corruption is checked, the vast majority of Indians, who are not in a position to bribe, will remain immersed in poverty. Any amount of funding to ameliorate their lot amounts to turning white money black. The courts are terribly overloaded due to the following pending data, as on February 27,2006 shows: Supreme Court 33,635, High Courts 33,41,040 and subordinate courts 2,53,06,458.

By delaying justice and by indulging in dilatory tactics, the corrupt get away with crime. Quick justice and reform in the criminal justice system are not the priority of any Government, though they all talk about "zero tolerance". If we can tackle corruption, we can tackle poverty.

2.4. Employment and Corruption

Concern has been expressed in some quarters over the trend of doctors leaving premier Government hospitals to join private ones. With more opportunities being offered by private players, since 1985-86, when private super speciality hospitals emerged, this trend has continued.

Some Government organisations are a reservoir of trained and expert manpower. Be it any sector the employees say they are the mainstay of Government and without them the regime will collapse. Whether it is the lower division clerk in education or census department, or a doctor, a policeman or a defence service officer all wants more and more compensations. Worse, such demands are never linked with performance and nobody talks about the incentives already given.

For instance, the housing facility or concession on travel given by Government is never taken into consideration. In the defence services - right from the jawan to the chiefs - all get ration for themselves, goods for use without taxes, travel by train or air at 50 per cent concession, Government accommodation at subsidised or nominal rent apart from leave travel concession. This is apart from a host of other facilities of working only for half a year. (A Government employee gets 30 days earned leave, 20 days of medical leave, 104 weeksend off, 12 gazetted holidays, two restricted holidays and 15 days of casual leave, in total 183 days in a year.)

Apart from that Government employees get full salary for one to two years for study leave in case they want to improve their qualification. On the contrary, a person in private sector gets only one day off in a week, and a few days of leave annually. He has to take care of his housing needs and other facilities. It is for this reason that Government jobs are so sought after. At the end of service a lifetime pension of 50 per cent of last drawn salary is also assured.

If the salary and perks given by Government or semi-government organisations are taken into account, the Government package turns out to be no less attractive. There is nothing wrong in seeking greener pastures. But the fact remains that when a person gets an attractive package to serve elsewhere it is the result of expertise or training gained on Government job.

Moreover, Government works in a system, and if the salaries in one segment are raised disproportionately it is bound to have a snowballing effect on other sectors. According to one assessment the daily expenditure of the State and Central Government on running the administration is about Rs. 2,500 crore. It turns into an astronomical figure by the end of the year. Whoever is being offered crores of rupees would obviously not stay even if he is given a few thousands extra. Also, the expertise still remains within the country and those who leave the medical or other professions do so at the fag end of their careers.

Anybody who has made a name for himself and has the skill will obviously leave if he or she is offered 10 or 15 times higher salary than what he or she is being paid. After all, nobody stays for the love of work or for the love of their colleagues. Moreover, there is hardly any profit in running community services like the provision of medical facilities by Government. Top institutes provide world-class services and charge a fraction of what the private hospitals or organisations do for providing similar facilities. Moreover, their services are open to the general public whereas a similar right cannot be exercised by the general public in respect of privately run hospitals, where the only motive behind running them is to make profit.

The question of brain drain has many angles. One of them is that of Indians going abroad after being educated in the country. The main reason is limited opportunities in our country where, according to the Government figures, there are 70 million educated unemployed. Our country produces approximately 60,000 computer science engineers every year. Obviously, the domestic market is not able to absorb such a large number. This leads to people migrating to places where there is demand for them, and where there are better opportunities available. In the end it all boils down to the simplest law of economics: The law of demand and supply.

The issue of "brain drain" is being discussed for over 30 years. Rajiv Gandhi, when he was asked why so many of the country's bright young people were leaving home for the West, replied: "Better brain drain than brain in the drain." This is something, which holds true even now.

Globalisation is a two-way process. We cannot be selective in this matter. At present there are about 17,000 Indian students in Britain and 80,000 in the US. Small wonder then the media today describes the US as a land of opportunities where Indian scientists and engineers have made it big. According to one estimate, the net worth of emigrants to the US from the IITs alone is $30 billion.

The United Nations Development Programme's (UNDP) Human Development Report 2001 estimates that India loses $2 billion a year in resources because of the emigration of software professionals to the US alone. It also revealed that around 100,000

Indians are going to make it to the US every year, the average cost of educating each of them being $300 to $500.

But the fact remains that now the world is open to Indians and Indian firms that were earlier inward looking. They are now being increasingly acquired by foreign concerns. Numerous Indian firms now have product development, technology processes and services that can compete globally. This is one of the less acknowledged consequences of globalisation. It means integration of domestic and world market for highly skilled individuals. Globalisation has bridged the gap between countries. The skills of an able doctor, a manufacturer, a trader or a good economist can be transferred across the globe as well as within the country. This is routine in IT, communication and other sectors in India where experts hop jobs from one firm to another.

The Indian Electrical and Electronics Manufacturers Association (IEEMA) has about 500 electrical and electronics manufacturers as its members with around 50,000 engineers working in these companies. Twenty per cent of the engineers consider leaving companies every year. It is the industry's task to recruit 10,000-12,000 engineers every year. About 7,000-10,000 engineers switch jobs after working for one to three years.

Many of these engineers flock to information technology and IT-enabled services industries. Others go for better prospects abroad. Ultimately it is the money, which makes the mare go. However, it is a stark reality that the 22 million Indians who have settled in 110 countries across the world have done so because they felt that they could not make their mark here or even eke out a decent living if they stayed in the country. If India's foreign exchange reserves are at over $130 billion, it is partly due to the contribution of brain shuffling rather than brain drain.

We should be proud of the achievements of our expatriate countrymen. The economy, notwithstanding the so-called brain drain, has received record returns of $10 billion through the multinational companies, foreign lenders and Indian diaspora who had invested in this country. Progress does require time, and as Martin Luther King Jr said: "As long as any Indian brain is used for the good of India, whether in India or elsewhere, it will be wrong to call it brain drain. Human progress is neither automatic nor inevitable... Every step towards the goal of justice requires sacrifice, suffering, and struggle; the tireless exertions and passionate concern of dedicated individuals."

2.5. Education and Corruption

The lure of money makes people do all kinds of things. Money gives and it takes. It makes honest men and knaves, fools and philosophers. Says Seneca: "Money does all things for reward. Some are pious and honest as long as they thrive upon it, but if the devil himself gives better wages, they soon change their party".

The Common Admission Test paper leak scandal once again proves that men are seldom innocently employed or self-employed when they are making money. CAT became a gold mine and made not only millionaires, but some billionaires. Unfortunately, the land of Ashoka and Buddha-Bihar-seems to have become fertile in giving birth to and then rearing scamsters. It is reported that such was the expertise of the leaker that one student who appeared for the examination in question, hoping to become a doctor, passed the same and made it to the first list. This, even though he failed his 12th standard (which he had thought he would pass)!

The nature of the scam can be seen from the fact that, in the 2003 CAT exam, nearly 600 of the 1,200 seats for medicine went to candidates from Bihar. For the first time in the 42-year-old history of the premier Indian Institutes of Management (IIMs), the CAT for the MBA programme was cancelled on November 23, because of the alleged leak of the question paper a few hours ahead of the examination. The question paper had about 150 questions running into over 40 pages. This has affected 1,27,000 IIM aspirants across the country, who had appeared for the examination from 26 centres. These candidates were competing for about 1,500 seats at the six IIMs. The same examination is to now be held in February 2004.

Studying in and passing out from the IIMs carry not only a lot of prestige, but also bring excellent placement and fat pay packages. Top graders got the following salaries last year: ISB, Hyderabad 16.5 lakh; IIM Bangalore 16 lakh; and IIM Kozhikode 15.2 lakh.

For placement year 2003, the average salary at IIM Bangalore was Rs. 6.11 lakh. The average salary for the 2003 batch was Rs. 6.2 lakh and Rs. 6.18 lakh for IIMs at Ahmedabad and Lucknow respectively. At IIM Kolkata, the 250-odd candidates found final placements within the first four days of the recruitment season. Not only the students studying at the IIMs but also the scamsters benefited.

The top kingpin of the racket is 'worth', roughly, Rs 100 crore. He, along with six others who have been arrested, has reportedly been involved in similar shenanigans with regard to the Bank's Probati-nary Officers and Medical Entrance Tests and other examinations. Reportedly, the scamster's asking rate for leaking various examination papers was Rs. 10-12 lakh for the MBBS examination. For the all-India medical PG, the rate was Rs. 12-14 lakh (higher for surgery, lower for anaesthesia). The CAT rate was only Rs. 5 lakh. Engineering was around Rs. 10 lakh. Of course, the money to be paid for services rendered could be negotiated.

Obviously a leak of this nature is no local and isolated incident. It would involve an organised, countrywide racket. Whatever has become public knowledge may only be the tip of the iceberg. The scam must have been going on for the past several years. Most people in the educational field in and out of Bihar seem to have been aware of it.

A few days ago, one of my fellow morning walkers wondered aloud rather uncharitably how it could be that a lot of Biharis-despite their State having numerous fake colleges and universities, hardly centres of excellence-had made it to top all-India colleges and services. He also said the maximum number of universities black-listed by the UGC were in that State. He asked how Bihar could be so disproportionately represented as job-holders all over the country. I told him Bihar also had produced Guru Gobind Singh, apart from national leaders like Jayaprakash Narayan. I also mentioned that there are bad apples in every State, so it would be unfair to single out Bihar, where there is acute poverty. Conceivably, the less privileged would do anything to get a job.

Unemployment in the country has created a situation that could best be described as "Ek anar, sau bimar". Whether jobs are sold by leaking exam papers, or by Public Service Commission officials, as it happened in Punjab and Maharashtra in 2001 and 2002, the effect is the same.

Such incidents reveal the hollowness of the claim that we have a foolproof and time-tested system, with adequate checks at every level. In fact, the publicity the CAT leak attracted is bound to affect the future of countless candidates. Many job recruiting agencies do not accept as gospel truth the degrees offered by some universities. The UPSC periodically publishes the list of many fake universities. The trouble is that neither the Government nor the affected institutions take such malfeasance seriously-all they do is take some token action. Crimes like evading taxes or copying or underselling or selling fakes are not reputation-tarnishers. The millions amassed via such malpractices are more than enough to buy 'respectability.'

The reality is that what has happened with the recent CAT question paper leak has been happening for a long time. A few decades ago, the CBI investigated a case involving a postal official working in Bihar. He had developed expertise in abstracting papers for the UPSC examination sent through the post. His close family members got top jobs in the country, courtesy his talents. He was prosecuted and sentenced.

Such prosecutions have hardly had any impact, since it takes a long time for trials to get over, what with postponed hearings and appeals. The goons, in fact, simply develop newer and better techniques to beat the system. In some places, there is outright copying by intimidating examiners; at others, it is done stealthily, with the examinees passing on slips or carrying written answers to possible questions into the examination halls. Even when invigilation is strict, bogus applicants send their examination forms along with genuine candidates and, in the normal course, get seats close by. The answer sheets of the dummy candidate are replaced/exchanged with that of the other candidate. At other places, examiners openly help the candidates for love or money.

We need to devise new methods to face the new challenges posed by crooks. A college Principal once told me that he had received a request from a State Minister to help a candidate to copy, which he had flatly rejected. He was threatened with dire consequences. A Vice-Chancellor of a prestigious university told me that he had also received a request for admission of a candidate from the highest quarters in the Government of India. When he regretted his inability to violate rules and norms, he was threatened with getting the sack. The threat could not be carried out under the rules straightway. By the time the exercise to axe him started, the Government had fallen and his job was saved.

Politicians are generally more concerned with saving their kursis than doing anything that rocks the boat. If there is a choice, many would prefer to be Ministers or holders of other important offices, rather than be morally right. It has been reported that the Ministry of Human Resources has set up a one-man Commission of Inquiry to look into the leak. It is represented by a retired Secretary, who earlier had got the sinecure of a CAG's job for six years after retirement.

Legally, the authority to investigate the leak of CAT examination papers should lie with the CBI. One only hopes that the appointment of a one-man commission is not used as the thin end of the wedge to foist IAS officers as heads on the prestigious IIMs. As it is, many retired or serving IAS officers are working as Vice-Chancellors, which has not resulted in any visible, appreciable improvement in the academic field. Let bureaucrats do their job and not dabble in the affairs of the IIMs or any other educational institution. Let them focus on improving the administration and leave academia to the academics.

As GF Train said, "There is no credit in knowing how to spell, but positive disgrace in being ignorant on that point. So there can be no credit in doing right, while it is infamous to do wrong."

2.5.1. An Example of Carrom Communication

The recent CBSE paper leak has brought into focus the ills that plague the examination system, including entrance tests for various courses. This is not the first scandal of its kind. The papers were leaked right under the nose of the Union Education Ministry. A five-member cartel was arrested for the CBSE Pre-Medical Test papers leak. The exam was slated for April 10 this year. The criminal gang used to demand money up to Rs. 10 lakh from the intended beneficiaries, for the test papers. An advance payment of Rs. 50,000 to Rs. one lakh was also required.

The complete payment was made only after the candidate confirmed the exam papers did carry all the questions leaked the night before. Students who desired to have the leaked test papers had to stay at the criminal gang's hideout till the examination day, that is, April 10, 2004, and proceed straight to the exam centres from there. When the police raided the house, they found eight boys and five girls, busy mugging the answers. Incidentally, the police discovered that most of the 13 students caught, were children of government officials and doctors.

The criminals were so bold that they had even placed advertisements in some newspapers in Rajasthan. Students and parents were asked to reach the specified house in Delhi to memorise the questions and answers. They were not allowed to take away anything in writing. Four of the seven parents contacted in Delhi were ready to pay money to secure a seat for their sons.

The other three contacted the accused through newspaper advertisements. The wards found at the place of the accused persons, belonged to officials working in MTNL, Delhi, Meteorological Department, and DDA, in fairly junior positions. How could they collect such huge amounts of money for payment, while working as supervisors or junior engineers, needs to be unravelled.

The gang conducted thorough research like big corporate houses and prepared a database on prospective candidates. The candidates were then contacted through various means. The modus operandi of the criminal gangs only confirms that such rackets have become more sophisticated with time. Such ventures also require the expertise of the underworld. In other words, this amounts to the criminalisation of our education system.

Around 2.4 lakh students appeared for the preliminary examination, which was again held on April 17 at 424 centres in 31 cities across the country. Of these, 75 were located in Delhi. The leakage this year reminds one of last year's CAT and CBSE pre-medical papers leaks. Like the CAT examination paper leak, this case also has been handed over to the CBI.

The arrest of half-a-dozen accused in Delhi is only the tip of the iceberg. Such leakages are coordinated on a national scale. Papers are sold to hundreds of aspirants in different centres all over the country. In 2003, CBSE premedical examination, questions papers were printed in Jaipur. These were sent to Canara Bank branches all over the country 15 days before the examination on April 27. Paper leak mafia identified a manager of a bank in Bokaro.

The manager procured the papers from the bank locker on receiving money in return. Unemployment is chronic in our country.

Each job has thousands of contenders. In such competitive times, each person seeks to gain an edge over the other. Once a person passes out from institutions like the IIMs and the IITs, his or her future is secure. Thus, the high demand for the entrance exam papers to these institutions. Even State Public Service Commission is not free from this malaise, as it happened in Punjab and Maharashtra in 2001 and 2002 respectively. Such occurrences reveal the hollowness of the system.

The real problem lies in the fact that neither the Government nor our politicians nor even those given the responsibility of safeguarding the integrity of the institutions, are concerned. There reactions are token. Soon, such incidents are forgotten. Cheating in examination is not considered a serious crime.

Hence, the culprits and the supervisors do not take the act of cheating seriously. The truth is, what has been revealed in the CBSE examination in April has been transpiring for a long time. A case investigated by the CBI revealed how a postal official, working in Bihar, developed an expertise in abstracting papers for top UPSC examination sent through post. His close relatives made it to the top in civil services through his malfeasance. He was later prosecuted and sentenced.

But such prosecutions do not have the desired impact, as these take a long time to be over. Considering the fact that money can be made through leaking examination papers, the sleaze experts develop newer techniques to beat the system. In many places, copying takes place with brazenness. Examiners are either intimidated or bought over with money. The net result is the same as the leakage of papers for CBSE or CAT examination.

Last year, Punjab Police busted a similar scam in which a politically well-connected rice mill owner was involved. A decoy, after a tip-off, was sent to him. The decoy struck a deal for getting the CBSE papers leaked a day before the entrance test for Rs. 11 lakh. The accused, after his arrest, made several disclosures including how he had been duping candidates for the past two years. He used to get a list of aspirants for PMT test from senior officials of the CBSE who were also involved in the scam.

The Jammu and Kashmir Vigilance Department too recently unearthed leakage of papers of last year's MBBS entrance test in the State. This fact came to light when the investigators were probing last year's paper leak of MD and MS entrance tests. Three accused in the MD and MS test paper leak told the investigators that they had sold papers of the MBBS entrance test, held on July 14, 2003, for lakhs of rupees. Investigators have also pointed out candidates who topped last year's merit list as beneficiaries of the leak. Parents of such candidates are also guilty as the students themselves would not be able to afford the cost of question papers.

The system of conducting examinations is becoming increasingly messy. Hardly a year passes without reports of one or the other examination not getting leaked. The Government sets up an Inquiry Commission or a inquiry committee which more often than not proves to be futile. Leakage of question papers strikes at the root of our education system. It renders any talk of academic excellence baseless. The Government should look into the matter seriously by setting up an appropriate inquiry authority.

Such a committee should have a representative of the investigating agencies, and not only educationists who are responsible for the mess. The examination system, as it is at present, is only a test of memory. It does not examine a candidate's knowledge or comprehension. There should be more objective content in examinations that test a student's aptitude on all criteria.

Moreover, those in supervisory positions should be held responsible for ineffective discharge of duties by the people working under them. Such people should be summarily dismissed. Unfortunately, there has been no political will to check the rot that has set in. It is time the executive showed that it intends to stem this decay. Says Falconer: "Do not talk about disgrace from a thing being known, when the disgrace is that the thing should exist."

2.5.2. Unfairness: The Doping in Education

The unabashed and blatant use of unfair means, both during examinations and in marking, is a shocking reminder of the fact that our educational and examination system has decayed. Recently, the police found an "evaluation centre" in a house in Agra, where minors and some youth were checking answer sheets of professional courses, including BBA, BCA, BPT, law from various institutes affiliated to the Chaudhary Charan Singh University, Meerut.

While some of those checking the answer sheets were class V and VI students, some others were graduates. None were either qualified or competent to check the answer sheets. The bogus evaluators were being paid up to Rs. 4 for each answer sheet.

According to the investigation reports, the criterion for allotting scores was the length of the answers, as well as the quality and dimension of the diagrams. Marks were also awarded as per the negotiations or the considerations paid for.

It appears the Registrar of the Chaudhary Charan Singh University was involved in the racket along with his son, who has since been arrested. The investigators recovered about 10,000 answer sheets from the house, while more were found dumped elsewhere in Agra. About 2,000 answer sheets of professional courses were discovered from a field near Agra.

The suspended Registrar seems to be an old hand in this game. He had earlier been suspended in 2001 in a similar case and an inquiry was ordered; but he wriggled out of all charges.

Our examination system is in a mess. The degree of intensity of using unfair means at examination centres is simply too high. This appalling situation is not a recent development. It has been there for the past many years. Now it is steadily eating away the vitality of education. Owing to this reason, education in our country has failed to serve its purpose.

In some places, education has been rendered redundant. Everybody - from students to invigilators and parents to teachers - go against examination rules. Whether it is primarily school or higher examinations like CAT or All-India entrance examination for post-graduate medical courses, which had to be cancelled in April 2006 by the Health Ministry, the same story of unfair practices continues. In the case All-India entrance examination for post-graduate medical courses, the Supreme Court ordered a CBI inquiry.

The situation in the education sector is grim. According to UNESCO, only 61 per cent children in India attend schools by the time they reach the age of 10. The drop out rate is 39 per cent.

The World Bank says that India is home to 25 per cent of the world's 104 million children who do not attend school. The increasing trend of using unfair means might have increased the literacy rate on paper, but it is of no use.

The deterioration in the education sector has been manifested by high-profile scams in the Punjab and Maharashtra Public Service Commissions. It is also reported that several private school founders, secretaries and headmasters just want a fairly good pass percentage of their institution. They work for monetary benefits and even promote mass copying. In fact, there is a price tag on copying, which is a good source of money.

An official, who did the checking in one State, observed: "More than 50 per cent students taking the exams were dependent on copying alone, for which they had paid heavy amounts to the school owners... In the several centres where the flying squad did not allow copying, the parents of students gheraoed the schools and demanded their money back as the promise made to them had not been fulfilled."

Fake universities and degrees have become a bane of the country. As IPS trainees, which I was in 1961, we had been taught law in the Training Academy, which was almost equal to LLB. But the law education and training did not confer any degree. I thought it would be a good idea to have a degree in law.

A few years ago, before my retirement, I saw an advertisement that ensured a law degree from a university. Without disclosing who I was, I wrote a letter to the advertiser that I was interested in doing law as a private candidate. I promptly got a letter written in poor Hindi that I was already late, but particular amount of money would ensure not only enrolment, but also my success in the examination.

A former Chairperson of the Union Public Service Commission told me that for the job of principal of a Government-run institution, he received applications from highly qualified candidates. One of them fitted the bill; but when interviewed, he could not answer even a single question, wherein he had reportedly secured 91 per cent marks. The chairperson became suspicious and asked the office to verify from the particular university whether the certificate was genuine. Finally, it was discovered that no such person was ever enrolled in that university.

There is no legal offence in copying during examination. Uttar Pradesh was the only State to have introduced a strict anti-copying law years ago. But the law was termed anti-poor. One political party had an election plank to nullify this law, if it came to power and it did so. In fact, by not strictly enforcing the anti-copying rule, the Government is doing a great disservice to the cause of education. No wonder even as per Government figures, the dropout rate of the stream of education of the students up to class VIII is 52 per cent. This figure reaches 63 per cent by the time students go to the 10th standard.

Where is education headed for? Does it serve any purpose to pass students with no knowledge in the name of Sarvshiksha Abhiyan? An organisation dealing with minorities' education has recommended that passing in English and Mathematics should not be compulsory up to certain classes. Does it mean that if we find some subjects difficult, we should dumb them? Instead of education for all, it appears that all campaigns for universal education have only aimed at generating figures that how many persons have been educated by their drive. It is neither spreading education nor even literacy.

The answer to these problems lies with parents, teachers and Governments. The parents should insist on their children to study, instead of depending upon their influence or money to get them through the examination.

The teachers should be accountable for ensuring fair means in the examinations. And the Government should not politicise the examination system.

2.6. Injecting Poison to the Veins of Development

It would be hard to find a country where politicians and bureaucrats are as corrupt and dishonest as they are in India. Of course, there is a tough competition among the States to outdo each other in corruption. In fact, some of them have been adjudged joint winners. Power once gained, whether political or bureaucratic, is used to dispense public funds for private purposes.

While international bodies like the World Bank are emphasising on weeding out graft, the Uttar Pradesh Government has set new standards in sweeping the issue of corruption under the carpet. It is to the credit of IAS officers of the UP cadre that they have been looking for those who are corrupt among them. The idea is to put these bureaucrats to shame in order to deter them from indulging in corruption in the future. Periodically, the association used to conduct a secret poll to look for 'black sheep' among themselves.

However, if anything, the result of their efforts has been quite the opposite. It has made the work of dishonest politicians easier, who are handed the list of the most corrupt officers. Such bureaucrats are in great demand everywhere because not only do they make a fortune themselves but also guide their masters into doing so.

The result of conducting such polls in selecting the top few officers for the badge of dishonour has had a contrary effect. Some of them who were voted most corrupt have ended up as chief secretaries of the states, which is the highest post a civil servant in any State can hope to reach. In August, the UP Government said in a statement, "It has been found after ascertaining the legal position that any voting conducted privately by a limited number of IAS officers to call other members corrupt is an act of misconduct."

I am not sure how, in the absence of the help that the UP IAS association was unwittingly giving to the politicians; to select the 'wrong men' for the right jobs, the politicians are going to manage. But politicians need not be disheartened by this thoughtless step taken by the UP Government, which will make it difficult to select the right man. The Central Vigilance Commission has released a list of names of tainted officers against whom cases were pending a few years ago. That list must still be valid for those who want to select such people for money making deals. As for the corrupt, they are past caring about their reputation and integrity thanks to the Government laying down rules, which make it difficult to nail the dishonest and prove them guilty. Article 311 of the Constitution, which gives protection to civil servants, has been enforced to absurd limits by all governments in connivance with devious bureaucrats. Such protection was considered necessary so that the bureaucrats could render their advice without fear and favour to their political masters. However, this has proved to be a bottleneck to get rid of the crooked.

The current system is a free for all with no check on those who want to make money by misusing public offices for private gains. Dacoits and criminals are having free run with many political parties supporting them. The famed bandit Nirbhay Singh Gujjar, who carries a reward of Rs. 2.5 lakh on his head, and is being chased by UP, Madhya Pradesh and Rajasthan Police, declared in a television interview that Mr Mulayam Singh Yadav was his mentor.

Indeed, in some States there is a major competition among political parties in recruiting musclemen, criminals and dacoits who are used to bully voters to win elections. With criminals ruling the roost in some political parties, and the Government imposing a virtual ban on exposing corruption among peers, the country has plumbed the depths of venality.

The UP Government, which describes exposing corruption as "an act of misconduct", is guilty of a greater misconduct. It is no less than keeping the masses in darkness. In fact, the UP IAS association needs to be complimented for taking this bold step though a similar campaign to identify the "three most corrupt IAS officers" on December 14, 1996, was grounded as the names were not made officially public. Of course, the media had publicised the result of the poll.

The World Bank has identified corruption as the single greatest obstacle to economic and social development. It undermines development by distorting the rule of law and weakening the institutional foundation on which economic activity depends. According to ongoing research at the World Bank Institute, "More than $1 trillion ($1,000 billion) is paid as bribes each year." As per another survey conducted in India, the common man pays bribes to the tune of Rs. 21,068 crore or about $4 billion a year for various public services. This fact has been brought to light by the report, 'India Corruption Study - 2005', released by Transparency International.

Corruption is a worldwide problem and not confined to India alone. It adds to the overall cost of development. Funds allocated for developmental are siphoned off by politicians and bureaucrats to line their pockets. In all this issues like reduction of poverty and inequality are neglected. World Bank Institute's research shows that there is "400 per cent governance dividend in controlling corruption and improving law and order". Incidentally, World Bank has already lent over $60 billion to our country and a part of the money has gone to each State including Uttar Pradesh.

Nobody, including the World Bank, will be overjoyed by the latest diktat of UP Government, which is to literally seal the lips of bureaucracy so that they cannot do anything to fight this menace. At a time when the Right to Information Act has been passed and the Prime Minister is talking about good governance and transparency, it should be considered anathema to put corruption under wraps by giving lame excuses.

Whatever the Government may say, citizens play no role in the fight against corruption. Corruption cases can be detected, handled, prosecuted or subjected to any other action only by the Government functionaries. The existing laws, which are against possession of assets disproportionate to known sources of income, are rarely if ever enforced by the Government departments.

Action against officials of the rank of joint secretary and above cannot be taken without the approval of the departmental ministry or secretary. If the person involved is at the highest level, forget prosecution nobody can even dare ask his permission for carrying out a simple investigation. This order of the Government has been challenged and the case is pending in the Supreme Court.

In this murky scenario, the entire fight against corruption has been given a go by. It is time to remind the Government and our people what Vanderbilt William said: "In any country where talent and virtue produce no advancement, money will be the national god. Its inhabitants will either have to possess money or make others believe that they do.

Wealth will be the highest virtue, poverty the greatest vice. Those who have money will display it in every imaginable way. If their ostentation does not exceed their fortune, all will be well. But if their ostentation does exceed their fortune, they will ruin themselves. In such a country the greatest fortunes will vanish in the twinkling of an eye. Those who don't have money will ruin themselves with vain efforts to conceal their poverty. That is one kind of affluence: The outward sign of wealth for a small number the mask of poverty for the majority, and a source of corruption for all."

2.7. Corruption: A Plunder on Economy

The Samajwadi Party (SP) in Uttar Pradesh came out with a video cassette featuring Ms Mayawati on March 3, 2003. The lady is seen asking party MPs and MLAs to divert some money from their constituency development funds to the BSP coffers. This alleged statement was made (and supposedly taped) on February 11, 2001, when Ms Mayawati was not UP Chief Minister. What she is alleged to have said is: "Every MLA gets (Rs) 75 lakh as his constituency fund. For MPs, the figure is two crore (rupees). Whatever work is carried out from this development fund, and how it's done depend on the MLA. So if you make five lakh out of this development fund, do not keep everything for yourself. Use four lakh for your constituency and give at least a lakh to the party. The same stands for MPs also. After all the BSP has made you an MLA or an MP. You should give something back to the party. Am I saying anything wrong?"

The entire Opposition in UP, led by the SP, served a notice of no-confidence on March 4 against the Mayawati Government. The no-confidence motion was defeated on the floor of the House on March 5 by a voice vote, without any debate. However, the level of mud-slinging in the war of words on that day reached the lowest ebb possible. There were reverberations of the day's incidents in the Lok Sabha, where it was charged that Ms Mayawati was "encouraging corruption", and her resignation was demanded.

There was also a demand for a CBI inquiry into the allegations of corruption. The CBI cannot take up the case on its own. It has to be referred to it by the State Government. Hence, it is doubtful Ms Mayawati will order an inquiry against herself. The lady has accused the SP of tampering with the video recording and using edited portions. "It has been edited out of context which alters the entire meaning of my speech," she said. Ms Mayawati has also ordered an inquiry into the money disbursed from the Chief Minister's discretionary fund during Mr Mulayam Singh Yadav's tenure from 1993 to 1995. An SP MP, on his part, said that "no other political leader in the world has been shown taking classes in corruption like Mayawati". He added, "If she has any morals left, she should immediately step down. She is the fountainhead of corruption, as has been proved in the video cassette." Another MP went further: "She has insulted all MPs by saying all dip into the MPLADS funds, and this includes the PM because he is an MP from her State. And if there could be a judicial inquiry into Tehelka, in which George

Fernandes was asked to quit despite (having) no direct link to the case, our tape is far more serious, as it shows Mayawati clearly asking for a cut from Government funds."

The unfortunate controversy, with the BSP and SP trading charges, merely highlights one of the ills facing this country. It is a fact corruption in our country, at almost all levels, has broken previous records and surpassed itself despite protestations to the contrary. Section 7, 8, 9 and 10 of the Prevention of Corruption Act would apply to the case in point, if the charges are proved in a court of law.

Section 8 involves taking gratification by corrupt or illegal means to influence public servants. This is punishable with imprisonment for a term not less than six months but which may extend to five years and also be liable to fine. It applies to anyone who accepts or obtains, agrees to accept or attempts to obtain gratification as a motive or reward for inducing-by corrupt or illegal means-any public servant, named or otherwise, to do or to forbear to do any official act, or-in the exercise of his official functions-to show favour or disfavour to any person. It would also apply to his rendering or attempting to render any service or disservice to any person with the Central Government, State Government, Parliament, State legislature, local authority, corporation or Government company referred to in a Section 2 clause, or any public servant, named or otherwise.

Whatever politicians may say against each other, the public perception is that most of them, cutting across party lines, are corrupt. A survey of Transparency International, a Germany-based NGO lends credence to this view. The NGO has classified India among the 30 most corrupt countries in the world in its "Corruption Perception Index (CPI) 2002", after carrying out an extensive survey in 102 nations. In the scale of 10, India had scored 2.7 (the higher the score, the less corrupt the country is) and stands 71st in the CPI, along with Russia, Tanzania, Zimbabwe and Honduras.

What is interesting is that there has been a slight decline in India's scores: In 1999, it was 2.9; in 2000, 2.8. There has been no change from the last year's figure. According to the report politicians, multinationals and the kickbacks that make the rounds between them are trapping whole nations in poverty and hampering sustainable development. Corrupt leaders and unscrupulous investors are obstacles to growth. Political elites and their cronies take bribes, which business people encourage to serve their own interests.

Politicians pay lip service to the fight against corruption, but they fail to act. They must clamp down on it so as to break the vicious circle of poverty and graft. Year after year, leaders make false promises about taking this combat further than it has gone before, especially when out of power.

So rampant is corruption that it is eroding even the institutions created for the protection and preservation of the Republic. Unless these tentacles are identified and eradicated through strong legislative, executive as well as judicial exercises, corrupt public servants will continue to paralyse the functioning of democratic institutions.

In a conference sometime ago on "Women in Urban Local Governance", organised by the Institute of Social Sciences and Centre for Sciences Humanities, it was revealed that women in politics are not very different from men. Women who replaced their husbands or male relatives are said to be more prone to corruption, as they have to maintain the same relations of "give and take" with contractors.

The great ruler, Sher Shah, once said, "Whoever has wealth, whether loyal or disloyal, can get his business settled as he likes by paying for it. But if a man has no money, although he may have displayed his loyalty on a hundred occasions or if he be a veteran soldier, he will never gain his end." What he saw as true of his times still holds good today. Edward Gibbon has said corruption is the most infallible symptom of constitutional liberty. Our politicians have bent and twisted the institutions of democracy to suit their particular genius for deviousness. This is more so in the era of coalitions, where political survival is considered more important that doing the right thing.

Governments complain about shortage of funds. Yet corruption remains a kind of random, unpredictable and arbitrary tax to be paid to get a sanction or some other favour from the powers that be. The primary source of bribes is black, unaccounted money and wealth acquired through illegal means. Corruption and black economy have derailed the country's development activity. Revenue flow to different segments of Governments has lagged behind expenditure. Consequently, they have gone bankrupt.

It is time to remind Prime Minister Atal Bihari Vajpayee that, on January 22, 2002, he reiterated his Government's commitment to put in place a new Lok Pal regime "with adequate powers to deal with charges of corruption against anyone, including the Prime Minister". Reminding the conference-which met after a gap of five years-that it was his Government's endeavour to "provide a clean, efficient, and transparent administration," Mr. Vajpayee declared that "the principle of zero tolerance would apply while dealing with corruption". A little more than one year is left for the Prime Minister to complete his term. And it still remains to be seen whether this cleanest of clean politicians will deliver on what he said, or whether his words were just another piece of political oratory.

2.7.1. Plunder Continues

It is a fact that Government employees are not involved in any production activity. They are still paid bonus-for doing nothing for which they have not already been paid. West Bengal spends over Rs. 920 crore per month on its 900,000 employees.

Tamil Nadu spends 94 per cent of its budget to pay salaries and wages. Yet there is hardly any tradition of work culture. If a person insists on punctuality and comes to office on time, he becomes the outcast. More often than not, he is shown the door or otherwise humiliated. Top political bosses do not want to crack the whip to enforce discipline. The result is that work culture comes to mean neglecting or not doing one's work. For these non-activities, there is no punishment. But one can get into trouble for doing one's job.

Consider the following facts to understand how the country's precious resources are being frittered away. Non-performing assets (NPAs) of banks and financial institutions (FIs) have touched a whopping Rs. 115,000 crore (approximately). Incidentally, the total amount of default on banks and FIs, as on March 31, 2000, stood at Rs. 79,185 crore. This figure has been growing. Out of NPAs related to banks, suits have been filed only in 4,303 cases for an amount of Rs. 24,727 crore. In the case of FIs, there are 1,166 cases involving an amount of Rs. 8,349 crore. The rise in bad debts is due to lack of will on the part of the Government. The Reserve Bank of India had announced a scheme of a one-time settlement to enable defaulters to pay outstanding dues on a simple rate of interest on the defaulted amount. It was hoped this would lead to the recovery of bad debts. The RBI, in a sugar coated review which did not appear to criticise any Government policy, said that though the scheme was doing well, recovery under it had fallen short of expectations. Most big defaulters were not interested in a one-time settlement, in the hope that they would get away with not paying at all.

Under the scheme, there is a provision allowing the defaulters to pay 25 per cent of the amount in one go and the rest over a period of one year. The banks would, however, charge an interest rate at the level of the prime lending rate (PLR) for the one year period. Big defaulters want more time under the one-time settlement.

Despite claims of downsizing the bureaucracy, in 1999-2000, nearly 84 per cent of the Government's spending-about Rs. 2,50,000 crore-was on its employees, as against about 76 per cent in the mid-1990s. The spate of scandals, like the one involving the former Chairman of the Punjab Public Service Commission and the allegations about the Haryana and Maharashtra Public Service Commissions - have brought into focus the issue of rampant corruption. Political parties talk about building a Ram temple or a mosque, or about the demolition of a mosque or church, but nobody talks about dealing with the menace of corruption.

The prevalence of corruption is a direct index of the state of affairs of good or bad governance. India is one of the most corrupt countries in the world, ranking 72 out of 91 in the Corruption Perception Index of the Transparency International, a Berlin based organisation. We are poorly governed, though we have copied the British system of governance which works on truth and honesty. Sadly, that system not only protects but also encourages corruption. The above scams have highlighted how constitutional bodies, which were designed to ensure fairness and probity in selection, have been compromised.

In fact, the British themselves were not sure whether the system they had bequeathed India was suited to the local genius and conditions. Sir John Malcolm, Governor of Bombay, observed in 1830 that, with the extension of the new laws, it had become very difficult to establish a system of good policing. The people for whom laws were framed came from different backgrounds, and had different characters and habits. They did not easily adapt to the new liberal laws. He also said: "The task of seizing the most notorious criminal is easy, compared to that of proving their guilt, according to the principles and the forms of our courts of justice. There is seldom that full evidence they require, and the consequence is the annual discharge of well-known plunderers, to recommence their career of guilt, and to take ample vengeance on those whom they suspect of having aided in their apprehension."

As there was no separation of judiciary and executive, and it was the responsibility of the latter to run the Government and maintain law and order, the British could work under the framework of the laws they framed. The judiciary up to the district level was subordinate to the District Officer and had to respect his wishes. In any case, corruption control was not a priority item on the British agenda. So they did not bother much about this aspect of administration.

The British Government's one aim was to maintain their rule by collecting taxes. This changed after Independence. People expected a corruption-free and people-friendly administration, not a bureaucracy that would prey on them. Yet today, in every sector, the system encourages corruption and poor governance, for the simple reason people do not stand up to it. Those who challenge neither dishonesty nor misuse of power are the very people who complain about corruption.

During my tenure as Director in the Commerce Ministry, some exporters complained about the heavy bribes they had to pay Inspectors to get consignments cleared. They also complained that, with Mr VP Singh as Commerce Minister, the kickbacks rate had increased. At my suggestions, Mr VP Singh, who later became Prime Minister, convened a meeting of the exporters. At the end of the meeting, I asked the Minister his views. He replied that the impression he got was that the exporters did not mind bribing; what they objected to was the steep rise in the rates due to the dangers involved. As Mr VP Singh was and is a man of integrity, it was certain that anybody coming in the vigilance net would face dismissal. So the Inspectors, not wanting to take any chances, wished to make as much money as possible.

I spoke about the same issue to a retired Home Secretary of the Government, asking him what could be done. He felt, as I feel, that unless the stress is laid on society's value system and the corrupt are openly shunned, the malaise will remain untreatable. He also said that when people like him and me joined service, we could hardly see any Government vehicles being put to personal use, for taking wives to markets and children to school. Today, misuse of the Government vehicles and telephones is not only accepted, it is also the done thing.

On one occasion, the CBI discovered that an official had made an organisation coming under his charge buy an additional air ticket along with his own ticket for official work. The destination was a place of pilgrimage. The Cabinet Min-ister in charge of the portfolio phoned to ask me to drop the matter, saying that everybody combined official work with personal matters. I told him that official work was fine with me, but I saw no reason for public money being spent on the wife of an official. The Minister said the officer would pay for his wife, and that the matter should be closed. I reminded him that he should have pulled up the official at the first instance, instead of approaching me. I told him that a wrong was a wrong, that we would send a report to his Ministry, and that it was for him to take cognisance of the lapse. An official communication is precisely what he did not want, since it would force him to take action. But I did not oblige him.

The trouble is, we lack role models the people and public officials can emulate. Only the corrupt and dishonest thrive under successive Governments, since the latter need their expertise in the collection of funds. It is important for our leaders to set high standards, so that others can follow. Without positive emulation, we sink into meanness, pettiness and mediocrity. Without it also, the country can achieve nothing excellent or great.

2.8. Health and Corruption

India remains the World Bank's single largest borrower. In 2007, it was the largest borrower from two World Bank institutions, accounting for $3.75 billion, or 15 per cent of their total lending as the Bank globally committed $34.3 billion. In 2005, the country borrowed $2.9 billion from the World Bank. However, for the second time in less than two years, the World Bank has levelled allegations of rampant corruption in implementing schemes with its money, which includes even those related to control of AIDS, tuberculosis and malaria.

A Detailed Implementation Review, launched by the World Bank in 2006 and supported by the Government of India, has found "significant indicators of fraud and corruption" that include "collusive behaviour, bid-rigging, bribery and manipulative bid practices".

World Bank President Robert B Zoellick has said, "This probe has revealed unacceptable indicators of fraud and corruption." In 2005, the World Bank's investigation into a reproductive and child health project found similar instances of corruption, including alleged kickbacks to Government officials. Following these findings, the Bank withheld funds worth nearly $2 billion meant for pending proposals in the health sector. The important cases highlighted in the report are as under:

- The Food and Drug Capacity Building Project (2003-08): The $54 million project was meant to upgrade food testing labs and technicians. The report alleges questionable procurement practices in contracts representing 88 per cent of value of equipment procured, shifting of bidding deadlines and favouritism, widespread deficiencies in delivery and installation of equipment in all 15 labs, besides discovering more than half of 282 equipment uninstalled or undelivered.
- The Orissa Heath Systems Development project (1998-2006): This $82.1 million project was the only State-level project that sought to improve the healthcare system in Orissa, which has the highest infant mortality rate in the country. The project, meant to renovate healthcare facilities, supplying additional medical equipment, was marred by fraud. As high as 93 per cent of the 55 project hospitals had problems like uninitiated or incomplete work, leaking roofs, crumbling ceilings and moulding walls and non-functional sewage system. Yet, all were given completion certificates. The report cited 17 equipments that violated technical specifications, including autoclaves that could explode and neonatal equipment, which lacked adequate electrical grounding, exposing babies and medical staff to electrical shocks.

• The Second National AIDS Control Project (1999 to 2006): This $193.7 million project aimed to reduce the spread of HIV infection in India and strengthen the country's capacity to respond to HIV/AIDS. The review found that selection and oversight of NGOs chosen for workshops and targeted interventions were corrupt. Procurement officials demanded and received bribes in exchange for awarding contracts. Several NGOs were not qualified to carry out HIV prevention activities and some did not even exist. They furnished false certificates to show their eligibility. Fraud was detected in 82 per cent of the 217 locally procured contracts.

• The Malaria Control Project (1997-2005): The $114 million project sought to assist the National Malaria Eradication programme by introducing effective mechanisms to control that disease. The review found bid-rigging, bribery, and collusion in procurement of medicine, bed nets and pharmaceuticals. The firms that debarred by the Bank for collusive behaviour in the earlier review, too, were found indulging in similar practices.

• The Tuberculosis Control Project (1997-2006): It was estimated that up to half of India's population was infected with TB and this $124.8 million project was meant to support the country's newly-launched DOTS programme. The review found collusion, fraud and corruption in 100 of 143 contracts.

The irregularities exposed in World Bank-aided health projects in India are only a tip of the iceberg. Regrettably, neither masses nor politicians feel outraged at the high level of corruption in the country. Regrettably, a survey has shown that Indians pay bribes worth more than Rs. 26,725 crore every year, though this figure could be much higher.

In India, public sector undertakings are often made to sing and dance to their Ministers's tune. But for the first time, the Chief Vigilance Commissioner in November 2003 complained to the Prime Minister that six Cabinet Ministers were allegedly harassing PSU chiefs for "personal favours". The PSU chiefs themselves made these complaints to the CVC. One PSU chief was reported to have complained that he was asked to get Rs. 20 crore delivered to his Minister's party office and when he refused, he was "denied" an extension.

Despite India claiming to become a new destination for global investors, 38 per cent of over 5,400 companies' representatives surveyed by global consultancy firm PricewaterhouseCoopers said they were asked to pay bribe to get licences.

It's a way of life for some Government officials to take bribe. Despite our talk about Indian culture, philosophy and time-tested spiritual values, how can we justify such corrupt practices? Poverty in India is wedded to corruption — in education or healthcare, roads or public distribution sector. Due to corruption, funds meant for development projects mostly end up in the pockets of custodians of public trust and money. This system has to go. But how does it go? It can go if there is a prompt justice system.

Chief Justice of India KG Balakrishnan observed in May 2007: "California's population is touching 38 million. In India, that's the number of cases pending in courts across the country." The Chief Justice also said that that India has only 12,000 judges — 2,000 short of the sanctioned strength. As a result, there are over 2.5 crore cases pending in lower courts, 37 lakh in High Courts and 46,000 in the Supreme Court.

"We need one judge for 500 cases to clear the backlog — that would mean 77,664 judges. At best, however, the judges' strength can be pushed up a few thousand more. We need more courts and more budget for the judiciary," Mr Balakrishnan said. Will the Government wake up?

3. Corruption in Data: a Conclusion

Wherever one looks one sees rampant corruption. In India there is no department which does not offer an opportunity to a person to make a climb from rags to riches. Revenue earning departments are well known for offering vast opportunities for corruption.

Despite the fact, that their top brass have been caught red handed while accepting kickbacks there has hardly been any decrease in corruption. The new entrants in services are as audacious and corrupt as their predecessors.

If any proof was needed of the massive scale of corruption in the country, it has been provided by the latest report of Transparency International. Its Corruption Perception Index, 2005, has placed

India in the 88th position among 159 nations. In 2005, India scored 2.9 on a scale of zero to 10, compared with 2.8 last year. It is hardly a consolation that Pakistan has been pronounced as almost doubly corrupt than India and ranked 144th most corrupt in the world.

The latest report by Transparency International, Asia-Insights & Benchmarks from Citizen Feedback Surveys in Five Countries, identifies high levels of corruption encountered by citizens attempting to access seven basic public services. In India, Pakistan and Sri Lanka, 100 per cent of respondents who interacted with the police during the past year, reported having encountered corruption. In Bangladesh, this figure was 84 per cent and in Nepal, 48 per cent.

Their experiences with the judiciary revealed that nearly all Indians, Sri Lankans and Pakistanis paid bribes. Judicial corruption was also significant in Bangladesh (75 per cent) and Nepal (42 per cent).

After the police and the judiciary, land administration has been identified as the next most corrupt sector across the region on the basis of the experiences of South Asian households. In Pakistan, 100 per cent of respondents who have dealt with the land administration authorities reported corruption. In Sri Lanka, this figure was 98 per cent. Land administration was somewhat cleaner in Bangladesh (73 per cent reported corruption), India (47 per cent) and Nepal (17 per cent).

The report also shows that even though public services should be made available freely, bribes and undue delays keep many from receiving them. It is primarily the poorest in society who suffer the most. The report also indicates that bribes are a heavy financial burden on the households.

Bribes have to be paid for availing all facilities be it health, education, etc. The survey report also revealed that bribes were extorted by public servants. Middle and lower level bureaucrats have been documented as the key facilitators of corruption in all sectors.

Another little noticed form of corruption in the country or where the Government money has been sunk, are the top 10 defaulters to the banking industry who owe more than Rs. 2,000 crore as outstanding dues against their names. Out of the top 10 defaulters, four belong to the steel industry notwithstanding the buoyancy in this sector with profitability of steel companies substantially improved. Apart from this the total non performing assets or bad debts with banks stand at about Rs. 55,000 crore.

In the last five years out of gross profit of Rs. 1,15,000 crore about Rs. 45,000 crore has been utilised for provisioning bad loans or writing off the money dues to the banks. In the last 10 years approximately Rs. 75,000 crore of bad loans have been written off. It is obvious that Government has been soft on all those involved in such transactions. The loser is the common man. It is pertinent to point out that all this money has been wasted on the well off sections of the country.

There are about 119 members in the present Lok Sabha who, according to their own affidavits, had some case or the other pending against them at the time of contesting elections. This is an increase from 40 in the previous Lok Sabha. The present situation has caused great disappointment among people. It is almost as if the problem of corruption in public life has become a non-issue.

The situation was projected by Lok Sabha Speaker Somnath Chatterjee while delivering the Bhim Sen Sachar Memorial Lecture: "Large sections of the people are greatly worried about the nexus between crime and politics as well as administration in the country. I am saddened to observe that politics in the country has to a large extent become criminalised and crime has become politicised."

The highest seats of power in the country have not remained untouched by corruption. Unfortunately, the corrupt today have lost the fear of facing ignominy after being charged with corruption. People now take duplicity in their stride to such an extent that violation of traditional ethics and principles has become acceptable to avoid pinpricks and confrontations.

The Santhanam Committed set up in 1962 to investigate into the causes of corruption and evolving remedies to stem the rising tide observed: "The advance of technological and scientific development has contributed to the emergence of a 'mass society' with a large rank and file, and a small controlling elite, encouraging the growth of monopolies, rise of a managerial class, and intricate institutional mechanisms.

The inability of society to appreciate an honest functioning social, political and economic process results in the emergence and growth of white collar and economic crimes. Corruption is a white-collar crime defying any permanent solution.

White-collar crimes have been jeopardising social and moral values. It is recklessly disrupting norms and rectitude. It has promoted hedonism, individualism that has supplanted traditionalism. Detestable competitive sprit to demonstrate affluence, living a life beyond means, living only for today and making the most out of it, an all round breakdown of family, societal, national discipline have all contributed towards mounting corruption, denying the underprivileged their legitimate share, making them poorer than before."

Election after election has produced fragmented verdicts with people known to have criminal records entering the legislatures and holding governments to ransom. There is flagrant violation of political norms. In fact, all political parties vie for with each other in fielding candidates who can win elections - their criminal records be damned. It is ludicrous to see people occupying positions of power, who are at the same time facing trials for corruption.

A standard argument is that these political worthies are presumed innocent till proved guilty. Regrettably, there is no national resolve or commitment to eliminate and wipe out corruption. The existing legal provisions need to be updated to bring about the preponderance of proof as sufficient, instead of proving the case beyond a shadow of doubt. At present, a number of cases end in acquittal due to technical reasons.

There is no reason why people who have been caught accepting bribes and who have assets disproportionate to their means of income should not be punished. There is a need to make the presumption of guilt more comprehensive at least in cases of corruption. Despite the directive of the Supreme Court there is no Whistle Blowers Protection Act, but only a lame duck resolution.

There is a need to bring about a comprehensive Whistle Blowers Protection Act. Corruption and bribery are not part of any Government servant's agenda. At the same time Government permission is required to book an officer of the level of Joint Secretary or above. Ours is the only country where such protection is extended to the corrupt or those suspected of corruption.

What can be greater indictment of the Government than Supreme Court's order to those at the helm in Uttar Pradesh to take action against the State's Chief Secretary?

Therefore, the law providing immunity to the civil servant needs to be scrapped. It is time we reminded the leaders of the country what President JF Kennedy said: "Take time to repair the roof when the sun is shining." It is too late now. But it is better to be late than never.

2

Corruption: The Fire Ground Under Every Step (Facets, Demi-gods and Combating Strategies)

Facets: Modes, Methods and Modalities

Making hey while the sun shines is an old saying. But in the present climate of raging corruption in the country, not only the authorities make hey (or money), but are also not hesitant to distribute a part of it to stay out of trouble.

Assam's Education Minister Ripon Bora was arrested, along with his two associates, by the Central Bureau of Investigation in June 2008 in Delhi while allegedly paying Rs. 10 lakh as bribe to an officer of the investigating agency. Mr Bora, a senior Minister, was a suspect in a murder case that was being probed by the CBI on the direction of the Gauhati High Court. The case pertained to the killing of tribal leader Daniel Topno, a candidate during the 1996 Assembly election, on September 27, 2000. Mr Bora was his rival.

"The Minister had approached the officer probing the case through a middleman for negotiating the outcome of the investigation," the CBI said. The officer to be bribed made a complaint and so a trap was laid.

Before any legal action is taken, it is the standard requirement in the CBI to get a formal complaint from the affected party or parties, even if he or she happens to be a CBI officer. This is the only way to set the law in motion.

There can be two types of corruption. One in which the bribe is demanded by a public servant; and, the other where bribe is offered to a public servant. In the case of a complaint where bribe is demanded, the complainant is asked to get the currency notes treated with a special powder and the serial number of notes is written down before the bribe is paid. Witnesses are procured in advance and they are so positioned when the transaction takes place that they can see the money being handed over and overhear their conversation between the complainant and the bribe-taker. After the transaction is over, the bribe-taker is arrested.

Where a bribe is being offered to a public servant and he has informed the CBI, even then the witnesses are called to witness the demand and passing of the money, so that when the case goes to the court, they can depose what they have seen. To maintain its credibility, the CBI gets witnesses from those Government departments that do not even have a remote connection with the people involved in corruption cases. In fact, the same witnesses are never used in other cases by the CBI. The advantage of this approach is that nobody can say that the same stock witnesses are being produced in all cases of the CBI.

Unfortunately, corruption in our country is going up with each passing day. As per the latest report of 'Transparency International', India is the 72nd most corrupt country in integrity and honesty in public administration in the world. It scores 35 marks out of 100. Under our laws pertaining to corruption, only a public servant can be guilty of corruption. Incidentally, MPs, MLAs and Ministers are also public servant and the same laws are applied to them as to the Government employees.

Corruption in public life has become so endemic that people have become cynical whether the Government is serious about eliminating and giving good governance to the people. There have been allegations against Orissa's Education Minister (denied by him) that the State Board of Secondary Education officials manipulated his son's marksheet. It is said that his son was allegedly given extra 124 marks in the last high school certificate examinations.

Another case, which was widely reported, is that of Union Transport and Shipping Minister TR Baalu, who has been charged of seeking favours for his family. Yet another case, which came up in Jharkhand High Court, is the alleged transfer of a Central Coalfields Limited to the north-eastern coalfields at the instance of a Union Minister, Mr Subodh Kant Sahay, who has been issued a notice by the High Court. The transfer has since then been stayed.

A detailed implementation review (DIR) report of the World Bank into the $ 76.4 million Orissa Health System Development Project (OHSDP), launched in 1998 and completed in 2006, said that the Health Minister and some officials had taken Rs 500,000 in bribes to give undue favours to a particular firm. The Minister has since denied the allegations. The State Government had earlier formed a three-member panel headed by the Chief Secretary to probe the corruption charges.

The system has already been ruined, with no will being shown by the Government to tackle the corrupt and dishonest. Recently, the Group of Ministers has rejected a proposal to do away with the need for Government approval to attach the property of tainted public servants to control corruption. On the contrary, it has decided that the investigating officer must take the prior Government sanction even to move the special judge for attachment of tainted property. The decision only represents one of many attempts of the Government to protect the corrupt and dishonest.

As per the CVC Act, no investigation or inquiry can be started against an officer of the level of Joint Secretary or above without the Government sanction. This was struck down by the Supreme Court in 1997, but was again introduced as a law. Even after such a sanction is received, which itself is doubtful, then sanction is needed to register a regular case. Again for prosecution in the court of law, formal Government sanction is legally binding. Even after this is done, the Government can always direct the investigating agency to withdraw the case from the court, as was done in the case of Captain Satish Sharma.

The people's exasperation on corruption has been best expressed by the Supreme Court: "Everyone wants to loot this country. The only deterrent is to hang a few corrupt persons from the lamp-post... The law does not permit us to do it but otherwise we would prefer to hang people like you from the lamp-post."

It is time to remind our leaders, what Theodore Roosevelt once observed: "We cannot afford to differ on the question of honesty if we expect our republic permanently to endure. Honesty is not so much a credit as an absolute prerequisite to efficient service to the public. Unless a man is honest, we have no right to keep him in public life; it matters not how brilliant his capacity."

1.1. Bribery: A Mire of Shush

I am an avid television viewer. The only trouble with watching TV serials is that there are far too many commercial breaks. But whenever Parliament is in session, especially debating sensitive matters or a confidence motions, there is nothing to beat this live, unrehearsed and quite often extemporaneous entertainment. The high TRP ratings for last week's televised debate in Parliament proves my point. But on the other hand with televised parliamentary sessions any gimmick can become a handy tool to drive home a point.

On July 22, one has to concede that a new low — or high, depending upon how you look at it — was established. Wads of currency notes were waved around with three BJP MPs claiming that it was bribe money offered to them to abstain from voting. Cash-for-vote is a new phenomenon after the cash-for-question scandal. Of course, in politics, as is in any other field, winning is all that matters. Nobody remembers the runners-up.

Money and politics are inextricably linked, not only in India but everywhere in the world. Despite the protests against the use of money to stay in power, this is not something new. Indeed, the quickest way to become rich in our country is through politics. The president of the Congress in 1962 had lamented that Congressmen who were paupers had become *crorepatis*.

A lot of din was raised in Parliament over the alleged inducements offered to some MPs either to abstain or switch sides. The protests are all very well, but do they translate into anything meaningful or is it only a drama to show to the people that the protesting parties are better than those in power? The correct course of action would have been to apprehend the person trying to bribe the MPs and hand him or her over to the police.

One by-product of the episode has been that most parties have gone on to expel members who did not adhere to the party's stand, including the political party to which the Speaker belonged. One wishes that the same amount of concern had been shown to tackle corruption in the country.

The latest Transparency International survey, that looked at corruption in India's school education sector, specially focussing on 'Below Poverty Line' households in rural areas, has thrown up even more scandalous conclusions than what we witnessed in Parliament. Its June 2008 report says that the survey, which covered 22,728 randomly selected BPL households across 31 States and Union Territories, revealed that a majority of those who paid bribes did so for getting their children admitted to schools or for getting their children promoted from one class to another. Issuing school-leaving certificates was another lucrative business for corrupt school authorities. However, the amount of bribe was the highest when it came for allotment of hostel accommodation.

According to the report, on an average a BPL household had to pay Rs. 171 as bribe in the last one year, mostly related to school education of their children. While looking at States with moderate or high corruption in the school education sector, the level of corruption in Bihar, Uttar Pradesh, Meghalaya and Goa was found to be "alarming".

Jammu & Kashmir, Manipur, Assam and Madhya Pradesh reported 'very high corruption' while Chandigarh, Delhi, Kerala, Tamil Nadu, Chhattisgarh, Rajasthan and Nagaland were put in the 'high corruption' category. Roughly, over Rs. 880 crore were paid in bribes by the BPL families in one year.

Also, Transparency International has ranked India at the 72nd position among 180 countries in terms of corruption. It also says that "maximum corruption takes place during Government procurements". For example, when the Government buys wheat or arms, or when public sector units procure raw material. This is also extremely difficult to quantify.

Even international organisations like the World Bank have exposed corruption in projects aided by them which are only the tip of the iceberg. Regrettably, neither the masses nor the politicians feel outraged at the high level of corruption that prevails. Another survey has shown that Indians pay bribes worth more than Rs. 26,725 crore every year; the actual figure is much higher.

In India, public sector undertakings are often made to sing and dance to the tune of the Ministers who are in charge. For the first time, the then Chief Vigilance Commissioner, in November 2003 complained to the then Prime Minister that six Cabinet Ministers were allegedly harassing PSU chiefs for "personal favours". The PSU chiefs had complained to the CVC. One PSU chief was reported to have said that he was asked to get Rs 20 crore delivered to his Minister's party office. When he refused to do so, he was "denied" an extension.

Despite India claiming to become a new destination for global investors, 38 per cent of over 5,400 companies' representatives, in a survey by global consultancy firm PricewaterhouseCoopers, said they were asked to pay bribe to get licences.

The people's exasperation on corruption has been best expressed by the Supreme Court, which has observed, "Everyone wants to loot this country. The only deterrent is to hang a few corrupt persons from the lamp-post... The law does not permit us to do it, but otherwise we would prefer to hang (corrupt) people from the lamp-post."

The more you read and observe about this thing called politics, the more you are likely to be convinced that each party is worse than the other. Truth is strictly optional in politics. The trouble is that laws are framed in air without consulting those who are either affected or who are charged with the duty of enforcing them. The result is that even those who are guilty are let off as they know their rights better than the ordinary citizens.

Justice Malimath, who headed a committee on reforms, says there is a need to concentrate on the rights of the victims. "The present criminal justice system has totally collapsed and is not acting as a deterrent for criminals... With the rate of conviction in criminal offences being low, there is very less risk factor for a person committing an offence. A national survey shows the conviction rate around seven per cent. So, 93 per cent get acquitted, resulting in criminals moving in the society without any stigma."

1.2. Bribery: Beyond Fatigue

The way the administrative machinery of the country is run has a vital bearing on its citizens. It is a test of the resolve of the

Government. In a clear reflection of how petty corruption is dogging the common man, this month 15 officials belonging to the New Delhi Municipal Committee were arrested for alleged bribery and running extortion rackets. Their arrests were effected as a result of a month-long sting operation to expose the protection racket operating within two kilometres of the nation's Parliament.

It appears that the accused were forcibly collecting sums of up to Rs. 30,000 as protection money from shopkeepers. In the event of non-payment they would harass the shopkeepers by confiscating their goods.

A good thing that is happening is that the common people are taking a pro-active role in conducting sting operations to fight corruption. Such a sting operation was conducted through the months of October, November and December of last year by a property dealer at 30 different points in Delhi in which over 100 traffic police personnel were caught on camera accepting bribes from blueline bus operators. The sting was conducted at busy traffic intersections with the help of some blueline operators who were being continually harassed by the traffic police for bribes. A Vigilance Branch probe established their identity and led to the suspension of 98 policemen including 11 sub-inspectors, 11 assistant sub-inspectors, 10 head constables and 66 constables. Apart from this 10 traffic inspectors are facing departmental inquiry in this connection.

The problem of petty corruption arises because there is significant power in the hands of petty law enforcement functionaries. At least in the national capital and in other big towns, there is a pro-active media to raise the issue and keep a check on the same. The farther a place is from the seat of power the more difficult it is to tackle this problem. Corruption or venal extortion has become a happy compromise due to compliance with outdated regulations. Every Government has talked of ending the 'Inspector Raj', but unwittingly every new law has added more inspectors to the already existing army of inspectors.

At a particular function after counting the number of functionaries I arrived at the conclusion that at least 35 different inspectors visit any industrial manufacturing unit. I was immediately corrected by an industrialist who said that the number was actually 65 with officers from health, electricity, labour, municipal, water, environment, sanitary, weights and measures, and many other Government departments.

In such a situation bribery has become endemic and is turning out to be the preferred mechanism of getting things done. It is so for the simple reason that filing complaints and seeking redressal of grievances is not only time consuming but one is not sure whether his or her efforts will actually fetch any response.

Some time back I visited a friend who is running a magazine. He operates out of an area which is both a market and a residential area. He told me that his workplace was sealed and that the people who had came to do the job did not accept that his magazine was registered with the Registrar of Newspapers. He said that he was now paying Rs. 1,000 per month for working out of his own house. I asked him as to why he did not complain. He said that if he spent his time in complaining and going to court, the final decision could take months if not years. He had a choice of either wasting his time on litigation or buy peace by paying Rs. 1,000 every month.

The problem in our country is that the size of the bribe goes up with the earning capacity of the entrepreneurs. The extent of bribery varies from place to place and from industry to industry. But the truth is that no matter what kind of a business you run, bribes stretch from the cradle to the grave.

People pay bribes in hospitals, to collect the body of a deceased relative from the mortuary, for garbage collection, to have clean drinking water, for getting their children admitted in good schools and for everything in between. These bribes have come to be hidden regressive taxes and have to be factored into a person's day-to-day expenditure. The rich and influential can sometime escape from this daily irritation but the poor have no choice but to part with a substantial portion of their income as bribes.

Transparency International has placed India two ranks lower on this year's Corruption Perception Index than it had in 2007. The only saving grace is that compared to its neighbours, India seems to have done well. Pakistan, for instance, is 140th on the list compared to India's rank at 74. Nepal and Sri Lanka are ranked at 135 and 96 respectively. China though is ranked one place above India. Another study by Transparency International and the Centre for Media Studies found that Indians believed the public services to be more corrupt than they actually are. The study focussed only on corruption experienced by the common man in interaction with Government departments. Citizens are not only served poorly by these bodies but very often have to pay bribes to get their work done.

Three-fourth of the citizens who responded thought that the level of corruption in public services has been increasing. One-third of them thought that both the officials concerned and the people know how much to be paid as 'extra' to get a job done. One-sixth of them said that users of Government services themselves are responsible for corruption. They were of the opinion that there is no active and sustained civil society movement against corruption and that efforts are sporadic, localised and short-lived and have never acquired the characteristics of a larger movement.

One-third of citizens affirmed that corruption is an obvious fact where both the givers and takers of bribes are familiar with the modalities. They also felt that it cannot be addressed only by reforms and by adopting technologies, although those things are the first order of initiatives that need to be taken.

The main causes of corruption are lack of transparency and accountability in the system, the absence of an effective corruption reporting mechanism and the lack of honesty among Government officials. Also, even if a person is caught, it takes ages to punish him or her.

If we want to end corruption the Government should outsource services wherever possible. Public service departments cannot cope with all the requirements of the people. It should purchase outputs rather than insisting on giving its inputs, which is not possible for it to do.

1.3. Delay: The Agony Prolonged

The Government has invested Rs. 4,27,102-crore in the past three years in public sector units, according to official data. The Government spending on PSUs was Rs. 1,34,766-crore in 2005-06; Rs. 1,44,279-crore in 2004-05; and, Rs. 1,48,067-crore in 2003-04.

According to a report of the Ministry of Statistics and Programme Implementation, out of 866 projects, each costing Rs. 20-crore or more, 297 projects spread over 13 Ministries are running deficiently and are much behind the schedule. To complete them, more than Rs. 24,000-crore is required. This amount is sufficient to wipe off poverty and alleviate the sufferings of the farmers, or complete water supply projects in a large number of villages. According to the same report, the total estimated cost of 866 projects was over Rs. 3,24,473-crore. Now, it has gone up to about Rs. 3,75,888-crore.

The delay up to over 16 years has been observed in some acute cases. Some of the Ministries disclosing large number of delayed projects are road transport (93), telecommunication (36), power (27), petroleum and coal (25 each), and shipping (22). Civil aviation has 12 delayed projects, while steel and urban development have 11 such projects each.

The Government of India has spent more than Rs. 2,000-crore per year on sick and loss-making PSUs since 1996. If restructuring package of loss-making but non-sick PSUs is included, the amount will reach well over Rs. 17,000-crore. The loss-making companies have repeatedly faltered despite all efforts to revive them.

There are a large number of money-guzzling projects, which are continuing at the cost of the taxpayers' money. According to the I&B Ministry, Prasar Bharati receives a grant of Rs. 1,000-crore from the Ministry against a revenue of Rs. 600-crore every year. Another estimate says the Government TV company has been losing over Rs. 1000 annually.

Out of 243 Union Government-owned companies, only 143 are making profit. Of these too, a majority made only marginal profits. In fact, PSUs made a loss of Rs. 9,000-crore during 2004-05. Worse, 73 PSUs are chronically loss-making units.

Another report shows that in the past three years, food grain worth Rs. 31,500-crore has been siphoned from the public distribution system, making it a state-sponsored munificence for black marketers, corrupt babus, ration shop owners and others.

As for the North-East, of the eight States there, not a single grain of wheat supplied to Sikkim, Meghalaya, Manipur, Mizoram, Nagaland and Assam reaches the targeted poor. Arunachal Pradesh can claim to be a little less corrupt as 96.2 per cent of its PDS wheat gets diverted. Manipur takes the cake as 97.7 per cent of its rice allocation is siphoned, with Nagaland following close behind at 88.6

per cent of rice being diverted. Similarly, in 2006-07, Rs. 3,289.71-crore worth of rice and wheat was stolen in Uttar Pradesh. The corresponding figure in West Bengal and Madhya Pradesh was Rs. 1,913.76-crore and Rs. 1,038.69-crore.

The acknowledgment of failure or weakness of any system or project is the first step toward rectifying the same. But the real problem arises when the Government tries to cover up and says all is well.

In the era of coalition Governments, even the Prime Minister is not able to take a stand and say enough is enough. It is not that the delay in these projects is due to inefficiency. A substantial part of delay is due to rampant corruption. The main corruption breeders are red-tapism and lack of transparency and accountability.

Another factor is gross delay in finalising the cases of corruption during trial. As on January 1, 2006, 6,414 CBI cases were pending in several courts in the country. Over 2,300 were over eight-year-old and 198 were more than 20 years old. The nexus between dishonest politicians and corrupt bureaucrats enables the corrupt to retain their jobs. The result of their corrupt activities gets translated to ill-gotten wealth and properties. No wonder Transparency International, which ranked India at 72nd position among 180 corrupt nations in 2007, has said, "Maximum corruption takes place during Government procurements. For example, when the Government buys wheat or arms, or when PSUs procure material. It is also extremely difficult to quantify."

Arguing on a PIL filed in the Supreme Court in 2007, which seeks to alter the Representation of the People Act so as to strip MLAs and MPs of the right to remain members of legislatures during their judicial trials, the Centre told the apex court that the proposal was fraught with the risk of destabilising Governments in an era of coalitions. Discussing possible repercussions, the Centre observed: "The Government in power may be surviving on a razor-thin majority where each member counts significantly and disqualification of even one member may have a deleterious effect on functioning of the Government."

The worst sufferers are the citizens of the country. Commenting on a case of corruption, the Supreme Court observed on March 7, 2007: "The only way to rid the country of corruption is to hang a few of you (that is the corrupt) on the lamp post. The law doesn't permit us to do it, otherwise we would prefer to hang people like you from the lamp post." It added, "Everywhere we have corruption. Nothing is free from corruption. Everyone wants to loot this country. The only solution for this menace is to hang some people in the public so that it acts as a deterrent for others."

Good governance does not come by rhetoric. As things stand today, good governance has become a chimera. There is no dearth of money to develop the country, if the Government shows its will that every single paisa would be used for the purpose for which it is earmarked. It is a paradox that we have hundreds of millionaires, but millions of poor. The situation will not change unless our leaders realise that they can do what they have to do.

1.4. Injustice: The Only Scenario

The assassination of Indira Gandhi on October 31, 1984, was both condemnable and regrettable, but the then Government winked at, if not exactly encouraged, the anti-Sikh riots, which led to the massacre of 2,733 Sikhs in Delhi alone and more than 3,000 all over the country.

It is both shocking and deplorable that the riots should have happened under the nose of the Central Government. Comparisons are odious, but the fact remains that the Central Government, after the assassination of Rajiv Gandhi in 1991, did take steps to ensure that no harm was done to Tamilians in Delhi and North India.

A top official told me that in order to prevent any backlash, the then Prime Minister Chandra Shekhar held a midnight meeting at his residence. He ensured that the Army and the police were out on the streets of Delhi by 5 am. Incidentally, the Gujarat riots stopped after the Government decided to give a free hand to a former Punjab Police chief to deal with the situation as he deemed fit. It was the same Gujarat Police which brought the situation under control in less than a fortnight in 2002.

If there is political will, there is neither any trouble nor riots. During the anti-Sikh riots the image of police was tarnished. It is easy to condemn the police. But having said so, it must be mentioned that it is an uphill task for the police to deal with Government-approved or sponsored agitations, riots, mass killing or even crimes.

It is not as if the problem is insurmountable but the fact remains that in our country it is action and not inaction that is penalised.

In 1984 riots were so pervasive, that no Sikh, regardless of his position, felt safe. In fact, a top Sikh Communist leader whose credentials cannot be doubted had to face the wrath of a mob when he went to condole the death of Mrs Gandhi. It will not be fair to name him except to say that he was a deputy to the chief of the Communist party for a number of years.

Commissions after Commissions have been set, but the victims have remained unredressed. The Nanavati Commission Report and the Action Taken Report had to be revised under pressure from the Left. The Prime Minister has assured that action would be taken against all those mentioned in the report.

One junior Central minister who was mentioned in the report had to go unsung and unremembered. In an infantile attempt at defence, the Congress spokesman of whom no notice was taken by the media reportedly said that it was the Congress which gave the country its first Sikh Prime Minister and first Sikh Chief of the Army Staff. I cannot fathom whether he implied that it was the Congress's way of expiating for its sins in the 1984 riots.

The best way to wash one's hand of any problem is to set up a Committee or a Commission. The members sit on the reports for years on the pretext of examining them. This is all that has been happening for the last 21 years. It is not the victims but members of Commission who have derived the maximum benefit and mileage from the appointment of these commissions. Most such bodies are headed by retired officials. None of them has the authority of a court of law or power the power to punish anybody. Their recommendations and observations are not binding either in a law court or on the Government.

A newspaper had reported in 1984 that SHO, Karol Bagh, was roughed up in his office by a Congress leader. The ugly incident followed a heated argument between the leader and the police over the arrest of a large number of suspects, who had allegedly looted property. In a drive, the police raided several areas around Karol Bagh and seized looted articles worth several lakhs of rupees. The then MP had said, "Let them take away the recovered property but there is no need to arrest. These people are not criminals."

The Nanavati Commission has noted that there is "credible material" against some people in Government, Parliament as well as a former Minister and his supporters. This report is almost on the same lines as the reports of the previous commissions. None of them fixed responsibility for the massacre, treating the riots as the handiwork of a few stray individuals.

The fundamental questions, what should be done and who should be held ultimately responsible for these riots, have been carefully avoided in the present report. Thus, justice still remains a chimera for the victims of the holocaust of 1984. However, tribute must be paid to the media for not allowing the issue of anti-Sikh riots to be put swept under the carpet. It is the media which has kept the hope for justice still flickering among the riot victims.

1.5. Impersonation: The Other Man

Recently, a duo posed as a Minister of State for Home and his private secretary and allegedly spoke to a gangster in a jail in Uttar Pradesh. The news was the story of the day, which, if true, exposed the nexus between criminals and politicians. The man posing as the Minister vehemently denied having spoken to any criminal. Ultimately, CBI investigation and laboratory tests proved that the voice was not that of the Minister. The same duo had reportedly tried to enlist the help of a district police chief, which was declined as the area fell beyond the jurisdiction of that police officer. They are now cooling their heels in the jail.

Impersonation is not uncommon for obtaining pecuniary and other benefits. A good actor can pose as somebody important, impersonating voice of someone else to get a favour done or to take some other advantage. The first big case of such fraud after Independence was when a man mimicked the voice of then Prime Minister and asked the chief cashier of a nationalised bank to deliver an amount of Rs. 60 lakh to a specified person. The cashier, without verification or cross-examination, delivered the amount to one Nagarwala. The police traced the recipient of the money who mysteriously died in police custody and the chief cashier was dismissed subsequently.

Once I received a phone call as an Inspector General of Police, CRPF, on the eve of recruitment, purportedly coming from late

Rajesh Pilot, the then Minister in the Home Ministry. I was told to take down the names and details of persons whom the so-called Minister wanted to be recruited. Again the person on the other end asked me to repeat the names and make sure that all the 10 persons were recruited as constables. Later, I promptly rang up the Minister's house and wanted to speak to him. His staff told me that the Minister was on the visit to the North-East and was expected to return after two days. Then I told them that I had received a call from him, asking for some persons to be recruited. I told them that the recruitment would be done strictly on merit. I was told that even his office could not contact him and were sending only wireless messages to keep him apprised of whatever was going on and so his speaking to me was not possible.

Impostors have sprung up in every walk of life, whether it is for getting a driving licence, a mark sheet or even a medical certificate. One of the biggest problems that the Government is facing is the large number of so-called freedom fighters, who are getting pension for having taken part in the 1942 Quit India movement. The Centre is currently providing pension to 1,69,961 people, including 22,479 from West Bengal. Other States that figure prominently in the list are Andhra Pradesh (14,572), Maharashtra (17,581), Bihar and Jharkhand (24,870), Uttar Pradesh and Uttaranchal (17,990) and Karnataka (10,082).

The Central Government has received nearly 36,000 complaints from across the country. Some of the complaints, incidentally, show that pension has been granted to some 'freedom fighters' who were infants at the time of Independence in 1947. Incidentally, the number of freedom fighters is much more than the official figure recorded by the British. With the passage of time, the number of such worthies should be getting reduced due to natural causes like death, but it shows no signs of abatement.

The Income Tax Department has also unearthed a huge scam running into crores of rupees of withdrawal of tax refunds by fake companies issuing fake Form 16. The cheats had floated bogus companies and had claimed refunds on the basis of tax deductible at source (TDS), supposedly deposited by the company. The Income Tax department's investigations have revealed that the name of owners and employees mentioned on the TDS certificates was bogus.

Such fraudulent companies that had paid no taxes and did not even exist, had succeeding in robbing the national exchequer of crores of rupees.

There have been cases in which, following the death of an MBBS father, his son, a homeopath, continues the business in his name. Sometime back, the Central Bureau of Investigation arrested a person who used to sell fake degrees like MBBS, BAMS, RMP. By the time he was arrested, he had reportedly sold over 5,000 fake degrees.

There are an estimated 30,000 quacks in Delhi alone, and their number in the country would easily cross a million. As against 30,000 quacks in Delhi, the number of registered doctors is about 26,000. Impersonation, for personal financial benefits, is emerging as a new type of crime, which has affected almost all sections of society. With fake doctors around, fake drugs cannot be far behind. According to the World Health Organisation, 35 per cent of fake drugs come from South-East Asia, which has a Rs. 4,000 crore spurious drug market.

These cases do not merely make a matter of deceit or impersonation. In certain areas like the counterfeiting of currency, they are capable of affecting adversely the economy of the country. In the last five years, fake currency worth Rs. 20 crore has been recovered, which is only the tip of the iceberg.

New technologies, like mobile phones and the Internet, accessible to common citizens, is also available to criminals and terrorists. Nowhere in the world has access to latest technologies been denied on the ground that crooks would misuse it. We are living in a world that has shrunk due to modern communication tools. In fact, the boundaries for impostors are irrelevant in the fast moving world. We can only take precautions so that we are not taken for a ride.

No preventive strategy is a guarantee against cheating. However, positive self-regulatory measures can minimise temptation. As the proverb goes, “Who will not be deceived must have as many eyes as hair on his head.” When faced with a problem one must use one’s head and not the heart. If it is not possible to do so, then one must remember what George Bernard Shaw once said, “A fool and his money are soon parted.”

1.6. Scams and Scandals: Standing Factors of Inflation

Benjamin Franklin once said, "There are three things that men are most likely to be cheated in: A horse, a wig, and a wife." One can easily substitute the word horse for wealth, as the former was considered a measure of a man's wealth at the time. The desire to become rich has been at the root of all scams recorded in history.

India is not new to scams — they have plagued us right from the time of independence. But the regularity with which they are taking place is truly shocking. Also, given that most of the scams involve the same old tricks of cheating such as underwriting or fudging company books, one will not be wrong in saying that history is repeating itself. The only thing that distinguishes one scam from another is that the companies and the principle actors are different. But the motive remains the same in each case.

The Rs. 7,000-crore scam that chairman of Satyam Computers Services Ramalinga Raju has admitted to has taken the wind out of corporate India. He has disclosed that the company's balance sheets were dressed-up over several years. It is a crime for which he and his brother as well as the chief financial officers of the company have been arrested.

There can be no doubt about the fact that this was a case of corporate fraud of epic proportions, which like other similar white-collar crimes will take centrestage in public memory for some time to come. In the aftermath of the fraud there has been a lot of talk about effective and transparent corporate governance and a system of institutionalised checks and balances.

The role of checks and balances is best illustrated in the thriller *Silver Blaze*, wherein Sherlock Holmes deals with the theft of an expensive racehorse on the eve of an important race. Asked whether there is any point to which Holmes wants to draw the Scotland Yard detective's attention, Holmes points to "the curious incident of the dog in the night-time." The detective replies, very aptly, that the dog did nothing, to which Holmes responds that the dog made no noise because it knew the thieves well. Perhaps, this is what happened to the internal and external auditors in Satyam's case. As it is, the laws in our country are so lax that a thief who has stolen a bottle of liquor gets almost the same quantum of punishment as that of a prince embezzler.

Much has been made of the role of independent directors in the Satyam saga. I asked an officer, who had retired from a top audit and accounts service, as to what he was doing these days. He said that he was an independent director in a large number of companies. Then I asked him as to how seriously he took his job, to which he replied that he was only interested in the sitting fees and perks, and that if he raised too many queries he would be eased out of the board.

The truth is that even Government companies and organisations do not function as models of probity and efficiency because of the continuous interference, not only in taking decisions but also in awarding contracts. Large amounts of funds are misused by those who exercise control over these companies from their seat of power.

When the infamous Harshad Mehta scam took place, Mr Manmohan Singh, who at the time was the Finance Minister, described the scam as a system failure and had subsequently declared that steps would be taken to rectify the situation. But promptly after that surfaced the Ketan Parekh scam.

Each scam that comes to light seems to be bigger than the previous one. And each of them is due to greed and the lack of any deterrence. The best of laws with the worst of men can be misused and the worst of laws with good men will never deter these corrupt practices. There is no coherent, integrated machinery in our country to deal with such fraud in the private corporate sector.

The responsibility of enforcing the law in the corporate sector is split between the Serious Fraud Investigation Office, Department of Company Affairs, SEBI, Banking Department and the State police. The police comes in the final picture and can take action only for offences of cheating, fraud and defalcation. A police case can mean a long-drawn affair, which may take even 10 years to be finalised.

Truly speaking, there is hardly any worthwhile punishment for the collaborators and the auditors in such cases of fraud. The Companies Act undoubtedly lays down the duties and powers of the auditor. But the penalty for non-performance is pathetic and puny. If an auditor fails in carrying out his duties properly, the maximum penalty is a fine of Rs. 10,000.

Incidentally, PricewaterhouseCooper, the firm which audited the books of Satyam, received a consolidated audit fee of Rs. 4.3

crore for the financial year 2007-08, almost twice as much as Satyam's peers like TCS, Infosys and Wipro pay to their auditors. Satyam promoters and others who have benefitted — some by insider trading — could not have carried out their scam with the fear of being found out by the auditors. According to one report, about Rs 800 crore was made by insider trading and sale of shares in this scam.

The truth is that there can be big or small money involved in auditing, depending upon the size of the company. No auditor, unless he wants to be out of the business, would be too harsh or expose any wrongdoings. There are many Ketan Parekh, Harshad Mehta and Satyam scams waiting to emerge if company auditors are willing to put their neck on the block and lose their business. But it is doubtful, if anybody would commit harakiri.

According to company law, for fudging of accounts there is a maximum fine of Rs. 5,000 and imprisonment of up to two years. No doubt the Companies Act does provide for special audit, investigation, reconstitution of the board of directors and even 'dawn raids'. But the penalties for non-compliance are as good as non-existent. Moreover, there is no mechanism even for test-checking a few corporate balance sheets and accounting statements certified by auditors.

Those who do not learn from history are condemned to repeat it. The investigation into the Enron fraud had also shown its auditors, Arthur Anderson, as guilty as Enron's CEO. No doubt that there are a number of very good companies with impeccable records, though the same cannot be said about every company. The Government must decide what it should do and then do it to end such occurrences. It would be prudent to remind it of what Mrs Indira Gandhi said: "My grandfather once told me that there are two kinds of people, those who work and those who take the credit. He told me to try to be in the first group. There was less competition there."

1.6.1. Plunder on Public Exchequer

For some people, money, irrespective of the way it is gotten, is the most important thing in life. For others, it represents health, strength, honour and beauty; its absence symbolises weakness, disgrace and ugliness. It is for this reason that people hoard and multiply it.

This is the age of sequels: One scam follows another. In March 2007, the media reported that the Enforcement Directorate and income tax authorities were looking into the unaccounted Rs. 35,000 crore worth property of a Pune-based punter Hassan Ali Khan who was not even an income tax-payee. They also indicated to the possible existence of terror and underworld links to the case and the likely involvement of a hawala racket. The figure, after a few days, has been reduced to one-fifth of the amount originally mentioned and the number of Swiss accounts held by him has gone down from 10 to five. The Government has not issued any official statement on the case.

Incidentally, many people don't know that there is immense scope for making fortunes in racecourses. I have been in the managing committee of one and a steward of the other. So I can say with some amount of authority that the allegations may be substantially true.

A Steward, in racecourse terminology, means a judge who, along with other half dozens fellow stewards, or judges, decides on the complaints of "race fixing". It could be done in a number of ways, including the deliberate withholding of the horse or causing obstruction to other horses or using excessive whipping.

Many a times, the game of race fixing is played in connivance with the horse owners, trainers and jockeys. I have been party to declaring a number of punishments awarded to stem the rot. This is one part of the story. The other is that horse-owners bet huge sums on horses that are sure to win. A deep analysis will show that some horses and owners are the favourites in races where the winner walks off with a small fortune.

Racecourses do not exist only in Mumbai, Delhi, Kolkata and Chennai, but also in many other cities like Bangalore, Mysore, Pune, Hyderabad, etc. The horses are transported from one racecourse to another and the dates of races are so arranged that they do not ordinarily conflict with the races elsewhere. In this game, licensed bookies play a big part in accepting private bets to avoid Government taxes. This helps them accept unaccounted money for betting.

A person with unaccounted money needs a place for its safekeeping. Here the hawala channels and tax heavens come handy. The same money is later used either in buying high pedigreed horses, which cost a king's treasures abroad, or for living luxuriously abroad in villas and palaces. However, as a precaution, a token amount is sanctioned from Government agencies and sent through the formal legal channels for the purchase of horses and therein hangs a tale. Governments get entertainment taxes running into hundreds of crores, whereas the figure could be much more if all the taxes were paid.

For every law, there is a loophole. It is exploited to the hilt. No human ingenuity can conceive laws, rules and regulations that could meet all possible situations.

Hassan Ali Khan is only a symptom of the larger malaise in most fields - fake stamps, fake drugs, fake doctors, fake educational certificates, fake universities, fake police officials, fake currency and even fake judicial orders for getting bails! The Government's Employment Guarantee Act, which is said to have an ultimate outlay of Rs. 150,000 crore, to ensure that all citizens in rural areas are assured at least 100 days of work with a daily wage of Rs 60, is perceived as an opportunity for corrupt elements among bureaucrats and politicians to siphon off huge funds.

Regrettably, our country has become the land of rip-offs, con men and swindlers. There is hardly a field where one or the other major scam has not occurred. The Government, instead of being one step ahead to catch the corrupt and crooked, remains two steps behind in law, enforcement and other wherewithal.

Before the heat of one scam subsides, another takes over. In a reply in Parliament, Food and Agriculture Minister Sharad Pawar admitted on March 13: "Up to 100 per cent wheat in six of the eight North-Eastern States is being diverted from the Public Distribution System."

A planning Commission report said, "In 2003-2004, out of 14.07 million tonnes of foodgrains issued to below poverty line issue prices from the Central Pool only around 5.93 million was delivered to the poor families. Of the remaining 8.14 million tonnes, 5.12 million tonnes leaked out from the supply chain (FCI godown to retail outlets) because of corruption in the delivery system, while 3.02 million tonnes was delivered to unintended beneficiaries, that is Above Poverty Line." So practically, for every kilogram actually delivered to the poor, the Government had ended up releasing 2.4

kg, thus providing subsidy to those who were not needy or allowing unscrupulous people to pocket the gains. Almost all the wheat being made available to the malnutrition-ridden poor tribal people in the North-East, under the PDS, never reaches the intended recipients, as admitted by Mr Pawar in Parliament.

However, all is not lost. The degree of corruption and acceptance of scams depends on an individual sense of values, ethics cherished by society and the system of governance. These days, even self-confessed criminals and corrupt bureaucrats take refuge under the clause of "innocent till proven guilty". They take advantage of the delays in our judicial system, thus making the corruption a low-risk, high-profit affair.

Corruption starts at the level of bureaucracy. Simplification of rules and procedures, so that people do not have to come in contact with bureaucrats and visit public offices, will reduce the scope for corruption. Transparency and empowerment of citizens remain slogans despite the fact that the Right to Information Act has been enacted. Here the guilt lies with the Government which, in order to conceal some of its misdoings, is at odds with its declared policy. Protection given to the bureaucracy under Article 311 of the Constitution needs to be diluted. Finally, the criminal justice system should be strengthened so that all cases are decided quickly.

It is time the Government showed political will to curb the menace of corruption afflicting the nation as a whole.

1.6.2. No Check, 'Yes' from Public?

Whenever there is a deal in our country, wheelers-dealers are around to grease the required wheels so that it gets on without a hitch. Those who do not learn from history are condemned to repeat it. It is evident from the number of scams we have witnessed. The securities scam of 1992 involving Harshad Mehta, the 2001 Ketan Parekh case, interspersed with the telecom, fodder, urea, bitumen, and the Taj corridor scams. Then there have been shady defence deals involving the HDW submarines and Bofors field guns, as also the Airbus and the Oil-for-Food scandal - to name just a few. For every scam that is reported, there are many others that never get to see the light of day.

It is an age of sequels, where one scam follows another. Corruption and kickbacks have become a way of life and irrespective of the parties in power there are always allegations of bribery and kickbacks. The ratio of what surfaces, to what actually happens, is about five per cent. The Indian law courts presume every person to be innocent till proven guilty beyond a shadow of doubt. A person who is accused of accepting bribes can find enough loopholes to be acquitted. He has not much to do but cast a shadow of doubt on the evidence, deduced against him.

In the United Nation's Oil-for-Food programme for Iraq, apart from India, a number of other countries, too, figured in the Volcker list. Nations that were accused of being hand-in-glove in the conspiracy, made independent investigations into the matter. Australian Government's investigations revealed evidence suggesting that a commission of $2.5 million (Rs. 11.25 crore) was paid into a bank in Cayman Island in 1998 as part of an order for export of two million tonnes of wheat to India.

Surprisingly, in 2006, the Australian Wheat Board (AWB) again received an order, by the Government for imports of 500,000 tonnes of wheat, out of which 100,000 tonnes had already ar-rived in India. According to reports, an Australian commissioner obtained the documents, which show that AWB had paid $2.5 million as commission to India's United Front Government in February 1998 for export of two million tonnes of wheat. It is dubious as to why the money was paid into the bank in Cayman Islands or a contract that involved so much money (Rs. 1,200 crore) finalised during the last days of the IK Gujral Government.

The CBI, which probed the matter, was accused of delaying the investigation process. But one must understand that when investigations involve sources outside the country, a lot depends on cooperation from them as well. No investigating agency has the legal authority to conduct probes independently in another nation. In India, the procedure for clearance from the Central Government, the courts, other functionaries as well as sending letters rogatory, can take anything from a couple of months to even years. Subsequently, clearance may also be required from the Departments of Personnel, Law and External Affairs.

In the First Information Report, registered on September 11, 2001, the CBI had named the then Cabinet Secretary TSR Subramanian, the Food Secretary BK Taimni and former chairman of State Trading Corporation SM Dewan. It had alleged that wheat was procured at a price of $142.5 per ton and sold to Egypt at $135 per ton. The CBI contacted both the Australian Government and AWB, but no information was provided, forcing it to file a closure report on January 3, 2004.

After the recent hullabaloo regarding the oil for food programme, AWB made an exhaustive internal enquiry. It scrutinised correspondence and e-mails pertaining to the Indian contract of the pre-1998 period, when the company was still owned by the Australian Government. As the money was paid abroad, it is rather unrealistic to believe, that the Indian bribe receivers would ever confess to having received the kickbacks. In fact, even if they were caught red handed, they could make all kinds of excuses, such as that the money was loaned, that they were falsely implicated or that it was thrust into their hands against their will. Short of saying that they are all Yudhisthir incarnates, the accused in India will say anything.

The CBI, after sending the letter rogatory to Australia, got a cursory reply saying that two AWB officials had been contacted about India's request for information on the Rs 1,200-crore deal. While one official stated he was not involved in the contract, the other was unwilling to give any voluntary statement. The Indian High Commissioner in Australia said that the wheat imports had been handled in a clandestine manner. He said delegations met at the level of Deputy Prime Minister while he was kept out of it. The Supreme Court of India told the Central and State Governments, in August 2001, that it was their primary duty to ensure that the food grains (61 million tons, of wheat and rice at that time), under the control of the Food Corporation of India reached the starving people instead of being wasted.

The Attorney General admitted before the Supreme Court that there was something radically wrong with the system. He sought time from the Court to formulate a mechanism to provide food to the destitute. "Wastage", he said, "is not confined merely to the food sector but has spread to other sectors as well." Despite the right to information, the functioning of the Government and its deals with other countries remains shrouded in mystery. It is necessary that the citizens make a concerted effort to be informed or else the Government will remain apathetic, the outcome of which will be that all previous cases having outlived their sensational time span will be consigned to the dustbin of history and will remain a fleeting memory.

During PV Narasimha Rao's Government, when the Harshad Mehta scam broke out, a friend joked that the scam would feature in the newspaper until a cricket series came up, following which the attention of both the media as well as that of the Indian people would be diverted to a new 'tamasha'. The joke was not only prophetic but also laid bare a profound truth.

The record of contracts abroad is undoubtedly dismal, but not so much due to a lack of effort on the part of the investigating agencies, but rather as a result of the indifference shown by governments, whose officials and citizens are involved. It only reinforces what Edmund Burke once said: "All that is necessary for evil to succeed is that good men do nothing."

1.6.3. Merit Demoralized

The Mayawati Government in Uttar Pradesh has sacked more than 10,000 policemen in September 2007 on the ground that their recruitment and selection process was not fair. The State Government has also ordered an inquiry, headed by an Additional Director General of Police, to look into the alleged irregularities in the recruitment of 22,000 police and PAC constables through 55 selection boards during the previous Mulayam Singh Yadav regime.

The Uttar Pradesh Government says, "After the inquiry made startling revelations, about largescale corruption and gross nepotism in the selections, the Chief Minister felt it was appropriate to summarily sack the beneficiaries who would have only got down to misusing the uniform to retrieve whatever spent to get the jobs... Fake certificates, over-writing in the answer-sheets (of the selection exam), and even different handwriting in the same answer-sheets suggesting subsequent interpolations, besides largescale bungling in physical tests were detected during the course of the inquiry."

The Mayawati Government claims to have exposed one of the biggest recruitment scams in the State. The inquiry report has showed that in 10 selection boards, largescale irregularities were committed in the recruitment of constables. About 22,000 fresh recruitments were made during the three-and-half-year rule of the Samajwadi Party Government.

However, this is not the end of the story. A State official says, "So far we have only unearthed part of the racket; since the ongoing probe had so far scrutinised less than one-third of the recruitments, many more were bound to lose jobs." Together with constables, Ms Mayawati has also ordered the suspension of 12 senior officers belonging to the Indian Police Service, who headed the recruitment exercise. Of these officers, one was an Inspector-General, nine Deputy Inspectors-General and two Superintendents of Police. Besides, disciplinary proceedings have been initiated against 58 officers belonging to the lower Provincial Police Service. These include 18 officers of the additional SP rank and 40 Deputy Superintendents of Police.

Irregularities in the recruitment of police and personnel of other departments are not new in the country. There are a lot of money-making opportunities in Government jobs for those who wish to do so. It was revealed that one district police chief had paid as much as Rs 3.5 crore to the then Chairman, Ravi Sidhu, of the Punjab Public Service Commission to get his children selected in the State Public Service. Touts have confessed paying a whopping sum of Rs 16 crore to the former Punjab Public Service Commission Chairman. Randhir Singh Gill, alias Dhira, a tout, has revealed that the rate of recruitment varied between Rs. 15 lakh to Rs. 2.8 crore.

Punjab is not the only State to have a tainted Public Service Commission. A cash reward of Rs. 10,000 has been announced for giving information about former Chhattisgarh Public Service Commission member Amol Singh Salam. Salam has been on the run since he was booked along with former CGPSC Acting Chairman Khelan Ram Jangde for alleged corruption in the State civil services examination and recruitment process.

The arrest of former Maharashtra Public Service Commission Chairman SD Karnik, too, has raised serious questions about the manner of functioning of the State Public Service Commission and the alleged corruption therein.

A study conducted by 'The Centre for Media Studies' has revealed in its report that truck operators have to pay between Rs. 211 and Rs. 266 daily as bribe to officials of the Regional Transport Department and policemen all over the country for plying their vehicles smoothly. The report also reveals that each truck operator on an average pays Rs. 79,220 as bribe to officials annually. There are more than 36 lakh trucks in the country, operators of whom are paying a bribe of Rs. 22,200 crore yearly. Transport is a vital sector of our economy, and the money going into the pockets of transport officials and policemen could have been deposited with the exchequer, which the Government could use for improving the infrastructure.

It is no satisfaction for us that the malaise of scams and corruption is a common phenomenon across the world. Corruption is eating up the moral fabric of the country. If corruption, whether in recruitment or implementation of policies and programmes, is eliminated or even reduced by half, poverty and even rat race for Government jobs can be done away with. A Bench of the Supreme Court has observed: "The only solution to get rid of corruption is to hang corrupt elements. It added that today, everyone wants to loot the country. Corruption is rampant among us. Corruption has crept into all sections. If law grants us the permission, we would have announced death sentence to a few corrupt elements."

We had a spectacle of MPs being caught on camera for taking cash for asking question in Parliament. In another case, when some politicians were caught on camera taking kickbacks, all political parties in the State Assembly joined together in demanding a law to ban sting operations. Nobody said that it is good to expose the wrongdoings.

If the Uttar Pradesh Chief Minister, who has declared an income of Rs. 58 crore according to media reports, has taken this step to weed out corruption, it is welcome. If Ms Mayawati's Government is serious in ending corruption, it should implement police reforms and put in place a transparent system for recruitment to Government jobs.

The country's criminal justice system is on the verge of collapse, which has been admitted more than once by the powers-that-be. Yet, all reports for its reform, whether it is Mallimath Committee or several other commissions, remain in cold storage. Not controlling corruption is like plundering the nation for profit. The trouble in our country is that there are too many politicians who believe that they can fool all the people all the time.

The whole country suffers due to poor governance, as most citizens refuse to participate in politics. Things will improve only when all citizens start treating themselves as stakeholders in the governance of the country.

1.7. Highhandedness: An Unpardonable Sin

In 1996, the United Nations imposed trade sanctions on Iraq, effectively banning any nation's ability to trade with that country. However, five years later the UN allowed an exemption to the embargo and permitted Iraq to sell oil on the condition that its profits are used for the purchase of humanitarian goods meant to alleviate the misery and hardship placed on ordinary Iraqi people.

The need for an investigation into this programme arose as details of a scam emerged in the months after the US occupation of Iraq. After allegations of bribery against Mr Kofi Annan and Mr Benon Sevon, Administrator of the Oil-for-Food programme, the UN Secretary General appointed an independent committee to investigate the allegations. Mr Paul Volcker, the former chair of the US Federal Reserve, headed the committee. Its final report was released on September 28, 2005.

The independent inquiry committee led by Mr Volcker looked into the allegations that Saddam had diverted some $1.8 billion in kickbacks and surcharges. The report prepared after one-and-a-half year of investigation showed how Saddam's regime abused the humanitarian "Oil-for-Food" programme. In addition, the committee concluded that the regime awarded lucrative oil contracts to individuals and companies across 66 nations in order to create a diplomatic and political environment against the sanctions.

According to the report, since 1999, Iraqi officials have maintained a policy requiring 10 per cent kickbacks on humanitarian contracts. The following year, they began obliging surcharges of 10 to 30 cent per barrel of oil sold. "Many companies freely went along with Iraq's demands. Others made payments to third parties or agents while disregarding the likely purpose of these payments," the report said. Iraq sold oil worth $64.2 billion to 248 companies around the world and then spent $34.5 billion on food and medicine from more than 3,400 companies.

By 2000, the regime wanted flat 10 per cent "after-sales services fee" (ASSF) on all contracts to be paid to Iraqi embassies or Iraqi front-companies abroad. The amount was then routed to the regime. About $1.55 billion of kickbacks was received — $1.2 billion as ASSF and $530 million as inland transport fees. The price fixed for Iraqi oil became lower than market price, hence buyers were willing to pay kickbacks for buying contracts. This money - estimated at $229 million - didn't go into the UN-controlled account.

More than 4,500 companies have been involved in the UN Oil-for-Food programme. It is reported that more than half of them paid illegal surcharges and kickbacks to Saddam Hussein. The country with most companies involved in the programme was Russia, followed by France.

In an interview, Mr Paul Volcker said that while he knew the naming of companies and the exposure of international "machinations" would draw attention, he hoped it would not obscure his committee's purpose in keeping the focus of their work on the need for UN reform. He continued, "In my mind this part of our investigation, looking at the manipulation of the programme outside the UN, strongly reinforces the case that the UN itself carries a large part of this responsibility and needs reform."

The report also confirmed that as many as 119 Indian firms, including several pharma majors figure on the list of suppliers of humanitarian material to Iraq who either knowingly or unwittingly paid kickbacks to the Iraqi regime. The total amount paid by these Indian firms in the form of "after-sales service fees (ASSF)" and "inland transport fees (ITF)" - the two forms in which the kickback was collected - was $22.2 million.

Among the names that figure on the list are pharma companies like Cipla, Ranbaxy, Dr Reddy's, Wockhardt, Ajanta Pharma and Alembic, Tata International, Godrej & Boyce, Thermax and even the public sector Balmer Lawrie. However, the highest amounts shelled out by relatively lesser known entity of our country is by one Priyanka Overseas, which supplied a wide variety of items including tea, sugar and polypropylene bags. The company reportedly paid a total of $2.1 million as ASSF and ITE.

In the same Volcker Committee report, names of Mr. Natwar Singh, the Congress party and Bhim Singh figured as the non-contractual beneficiaries. Further, the report says that non-contractual beneficiaries were largely those seen as friends by the then Iraqi Government. Such a list comprised individuals and political parties from several countries across the world. Mr Bhim Singh has admitted that oil contracts were offered to him and other friends by Iraqi leaders. As per the Volcker report, Mr Bhim Singh is credited with having received the contracts for 7.3 million barrels as against four million barrels reportedly offered to Mr Natwar Singh.

According to Mr Bhim Singh, he returned the contracts with a note, "My love and friendship for Iraq cannot be bartered for material gains." It should not be forgotten that the Volcker Committee went by the records of Iraqi Government and other official records available to it. There is no reason to believe that the committee was prejudiced against the Indian leaders. It also needs to be realised that an inquiry committee is neither a court of law nor can it compel any individual to give any information, he or she does not want to give.

Prime Minister Manmohan Singh has said that there is insufficient evidence in Volcker Committee report but assured that his Government would look into the allegations made by it. About the conduct of politicians Mark Twain has rightly pointed it out: "Each of you, for himself, by himself and on his own responsibility, must speak. And it is a solemn and weighty responsibility, and not lightly to be flung aside at the bullying of pulpit, press, government, or the empty catchphrases of politicians.

Each must for himself alone decide what is right and what is wrong, and which course is patriotic and which isn't. You cannot shirk this and be a man. To decide against your convictions is to be an unqualified and inexcusable traitor, both to yourself and to your country, let man label you as they may. If you alone of all the nation shall decide one way, and that way be the right way according to your convictions of the right, you have done your duty by yourself and by your country hold up your head! You have nothing to be ashamed of."

The Volcker Committee's 500-page report has named the External Affairs Minister, Mr Natwar Singh, in two tables purportedly showing "non-contractual beneficiaries" of Iraqi oil sales. Under the head, "Sources of Evidence" in Tables 1 and 3 of the report for this section, there is an assertion that the information in the relevant tables is "broadly based on four sources", which are 1: "databases and records" maintained by the United Nations. 2: Records of the Government of Iraq, primarily from the Ministry of Oil and the State Oil Marketing Organisation (SOMO). 3: Records from various financial institutions involved in the oil financing transactions; and 4: Records provided by "certain entities involved in the purchase of oil from Iraq."

The allegations have been denied by Mr Natwar Singh and the Congress. Assuming that what he says is true, how has his name figured in documents of other countries is a question which needs to be answered. After all there can be no smoke without fire. It is a well-known ploy of politicians to rubbish anything which is inconvenient. Very few established institutions, governments and constitutions have ever been destroyed by their enemies, until they have been corrupted and weakened by their friends.

In this context, it is worth recalling Lord Acton's words, "I cannot accept your canon that we are to judge Pope and King unlike other men, with a favourable presumption that they do no wrong. If there is any presumption, it is the other way against holders of power. It is time that no reports of corruption even against the high and mighty are taken on their face value of denial. They should be brought to a conclusion either by indicting, or clearing them and no white washing the whole thing, as if nothing has happened."

1.8. Misappropriation: Thieves' Treasury

The term 'disaster' describes a happening which is not foretold, and which takes everyone by shock and surprise. It is also not necessary that the same disaster must get repeated again and again. If it was the Orissa cyclone in 1999, there was earthquake in Gujarat in 2002. The last in the list of natural catastrophes was the tsunami in December 2004. A massive undersea earthquake occurred off the coast of Indonesia on December 26, causing displacement of water in the Indian Ocean. The waves resulting from the jolt, called tsunami waves moved at the speed of 800 km per hour. These waves spread out in all directions and also hit eastern coast of India causing untold damage.

According to Government estimate, the total financial loss caused by the disaster is approximately Rs. 5,322.05 crore. Incidentally, the figure is only for the mainland and does not include the hardest-hit region, Andaman & Nicobar Islands. According to the Union Home Ministry, 376 fishing villages were affected in Tamil Nadu, 301 in Andhra Pradesh, 187 in Kerala and 33 in Pondicherry.

At least 1.25 lakh dwelling units were washed away by the tidal waves in Tamil Nadu, 17,381 in Kerala, 10,061 in Pondicherry and 1,557 in Andhra Pradesh. A total of 10,068 cattle head were lost: 9,367 in Tamil Nadu, 596 in Pondicherry and 195 in Andhra Pradesh. Agricultural losses were to the tune of the inundation of 2,669 hectares of cropped area in Tamil Nadu, 792 in Pondicherry and 790 in Andhra Pradesh.

According to preliminary estimates Tamil Nadu was the worst affected State not only in terms of loss of lives, but also in terms of economy of Rs. 2,730.70 crore. Kerala was next with loss of property estimated at Rs. 1,358.62 crore. The tsunami left Andhra Pradesh poorer by Rs. 720.73 crore and Pondicherry by Rs. 512 crore. One report from Port Blair, however, projects accumulated losses up to Rs. 2,500 crore.

Some of the glaring facts about the tsunami waves are worth recalling; (a) 90 per cent of over 10,000 fatalities, on India's south-eastern coast included fishermen and their families; (b) an estimated 35,000 boats were lost in Tamil Nadu depriving fishermen of their means to livelihood; (c) the energy released by the underwater earthquake was equivalent to 9,500 atom bombs that destroyed Hiroshima; (d) the tsunami waves have damaged 160 km of national highway and about 520 km of State roads; (e) the waves that swamped many towns threw back sewage, effluents and garbage into the sea; (f) the total world aid pledged for the victims of tsunami adds up to US $3 billion, with Germany alone contributing US $674 million.

Even as the Indian Government has said "no" to foreign aid, there was no bar on NGOs' extending support to relief efforts through other NGOs. However, the fact remains that the actual loss suffered by the victims is far more than what has been estimated. One solution is to conduct a census by using the 2001 figures. It will give a fair idea of people who have died or are missing. More than just a head count the census should also include the details of each house with a reasonable valuation. It must be borne in mind that it would be better to err on the side of generosity than underestimate the loss for the simple reason that it is the poorest of the poor who have been affected. Only a few among the rich or affluent were living by the seaside hence just a small number are reported to be affected. Thus the Hindi adage, Turant dan maha kalyan must be kept in mind to handle the relief measures that are continuing in the wake of the tragedy.

It is often said that one man's difficulty is another's opportunity. Rajiv Gandhi once said that out of one rupee spent by the Government for development, only 15 paisa reached the intended beneficiaries . This was true 17 years ago and there is little to suggest that things have changed now. Government funds theoretically belong to the public; therefore, nobody is held responsible if they are mismanaged. When a disaster of the magnitude of tsunami strikes, a number of organisations mushroom to collect funds for the 'needy'. However, the "needy" invariably are those who launch the scheme for collecting funds.

Recently, some students in a State capital decided to ask for contributions from people to help the tsunami victims. When questioned, they admitted that they would use the money for an outing and whatever was left of the collections would go as aid. Unfortunately, there is no legal regulatory mechanism that can check the possible misuse of money collected for aid. Ideally, the Government should earmark funds to NGOs like the Red Cross known for its transparency and fairness in dealings. These, in turn, should divert the donations for relief and rehabilitation efforts. In fact, the biggest problem faced by those desirous of contributing is to which agency they should donate so that the fund reaches the victims.

A number of newspapers and television channels have launched their own drives to ask for aid for the recent tragedy. Probably after two months the tsunami issue will be relegated to the background by the same media as it happened with other disasters like the Orissa cyclone or the Gujarat earthquake. Both these tragedies have already become hazy in the public's memory. What is the guarantee that crores of rupees collected to ameliorate the sufferings of tsunami victims would reach them and, if so, through what channel? Does anybody have figures of the funds collected for Latur and Gujarat earthquakes or even the Orissa cyclone by individuals or NGOs, and an account of how they were used?

There is as much corruption, politics and inefficiency prevailing among NGOs as there is in Government, public sector and private sector organisations. The public servants can at least be punished. However, there is no such apparatus that ensure accountability of the NGOs.

The NGO network in our country is mind boggling. In the Union Government 14 ministries have contracted 15,468 NGOs to implement their various projects. The Rural Development Ministry is the biggest contractor with 6,467 NGOs followed by the Ministry for Social Justice and Empowerment with 2,944, the HRD with 2074 and the Health and Family Welfare with 1038. A study conducted by the Johns Hopkins University shows that there are 12 lakh NGOs in the country and half of them unregistered. Most of them claim to be working in rural areas. It is estimated that these mobilised resources worth Rs 17,922 crore annually from Government and other sources.

From the point of view of Government contracting these NGO, it is indeed an important revelation that the total revenue spent on the NGOs is 7.7 per cent of the total Central Government expenditure (plan and non-plan) on social services. These figures are for 1999-2000 and would have appreciated since then. A Government of India communication to NGOs and State Governments says, "The headquarters of an NGO should be at the project location, so that the operations of the NGO reflect involvement with the community." It also says "absentee NGOs" are not to be assisted under the grant-in-aid scheme. Regrettably, none of the NGOs or individuals collecting funds for tsunami victims in either Mumbai, Delhi or North India have headquarters in the South.

Thus a framework for regulating the activities of these organisations already exists and only needs to be suitably extended and given a proper legal shape. The lessons learnt from malpractices during the Orissa cyclone that witnessed largescale bungling and misappropriation of funds by officials should not be forgotten.

Thus those who have launched tsunami-relief campaign in India must guard themselves against improprieties in financial dealings. Such should be the level of transparency that the public keeps track every rupee spent through websites. National disaster management authorities should be set up at the earliest both at the State and Central levels. Private individuals as well as Government officials should be wary of persons and organisations who have proclivity to raise alarm and launch a drive with the sole object of making a quick buck.

While all help should be extended to the victims of tsunami, no opportunity should be given to the dishonest and corrupt to thrive at their expense and line their pockets. It is time we reminded our leaders that "Corruption is like a ball of snow, once it's set rolling it must increase."

1. Demi-gods: Ugly Parasites

2.1. Demi-gods: Misguided Servants of Public

Sometimes in seminars, debates and discussions, a familiar question is asked: Who wants a clean system? Is it the politicians or the bureaucrats-or politicians and the bureaucrats? The perception of the common man is that most members of both classes are corrupt. The Central Bureau of Investigation raids on the residence and offices of the top brass of the DDA, on March 27, 2003, in New Delhi, led to the unearthing of a huge cache of cash. This recovery shows that public servants have reached an abyss so far as their integrity is concerned. Some of them are not even remorseful about the corruption they indulge in. A few actually justify it as a by-product of the system of democracy!

It does not suit the bureaucracy to end corruption. Its members need opportunities to make money which, if necessary, can be used to get their dependents plum jobs. This is what a Superintendent of Police in Punjab did some time ago, when he purchased jobs in the Punjab civil and police services from a former Chairman of the Public Service Commission.

There is also a political umbrella, and selective enforcement for the 'friendly' corrupt and dishonest. It is for this reason that scams are the order of the day. Ketan Parekh-mastermind behind the country's biggest share scam-is reported to have told Kolkata Police that, ever since he decided to manipulate the value of shares related to information technology and telecommunications, the Securities Exchange Board of India (SEBI) knew all the details, including who else was working with him. He ensured that SEBI officials looked the other way by paying some hundreds of crores to the officials as "cut money". These hefty payments ensured that SEBI did not seek any official explanation either from him or his associates, even though it was aware of their manipulations.

The State Bank of India in Uttar Pradesh published a notice in the newspapers on February 16, 2003, providing details of the oldest locker holders, who had neither been paying rent nor operating their lockers. There is nothing exciting about the notice. Except that, in some cases, when nationalised banks opened similar old lockers, they found them full of diamonds, gold, silver jewellery and cash worth crores. This is a case of easy come, easy go: Somebody, after stashing the lockers with valuables, had either died, forgotten his locker number or failed to inform his heir about it before his death.

Where does this kind of wealth take you? This is a question that has never bothered such worthies. Tax amnesty schemes in the past, which have hardly ever been successful, have only enabled the corrupt to convert their black money into white. The vicious circle of generating or even converting white money to black continues unabated in all sectors of life. Even honest purchasers of houses and flats are compelled to pay in black to acquire any property, as nobody wants to pay abnormally higher taxes or revenue duty.

Things only marginally improved between the 1950s to the 1980s, when the highest tax slab used to be 90 per cent and above. Still, a simplified tax structure will go a long way in improving tax compliance. The country's external debt has crossed one billion dollars and it stood at $ 101.3 billion (over five lakh crore rupees) as on March 31, 2002.

Without a shred of doubt, it is the right of every individual to spend his money in any way he or she chooses. But it is doubtful if the big partying that goes on in the country's metros is payrolled by money earned by the sweat of one's brows. India is a country of contradictions. Despite crores being spend on the health sector, the medical services available to ordinary Indians, especially rural India, are almost non-existent. Despite the talk of "health for all", a recent survey showed that the sector was the most corrupt of all in the country, leaving behind railways, police and many others.

When the Consumer Protection Act (COPRA) was promulgated in 1986, the medical and legal professions were left out. It was only after a lot of agitation that the medical profession was brought under the purview of COPRA. In countries like the UK and the US, the respective medical councils regulate medical services. But medical councils in India are so weak that, in their long existence exceeding half a century, they have shown themselves pretty incapable of taking the exemplary action of revoking the licences of defaulting doctors guilty of negligence or malpractices.

It is not surprising that, in their hurry to make millions, some doctors wield the scalpel purely for economic considerations, and not because it is essential or required. The fast-increasing number of black sheep in this profession is cause for worry. Only the fear of prompt and deterrent punishment by medical councils and courts can make such people fall in line. For the first time in India's annals, in fact, two Calcutta doctors were jailed for criminal negligence last May.

The Indian medical system, like many other systems including the methodology of governance, desperately needs proper, well-fanged and desperate remedies. A recent survey showed that the health care sector is the most dishonest in the country. Our road system is no better or safer. The estimated social cost of road accidents in India is Rs. 55,000 crore, according to the Planning Commission. That is just Rs. 5,000 crore short of what our country spends on defence. It is to be noted that 81,966 people were killed in road accidents in 1999, while the figure for 2000 was 78,911.

That is small wonder. A study by the Institute of Driver's Training and Research found that 28 per cent of the drivers of Government buses of the Delhi Transport Corporations were unfit. The institute also observed that many drivers had poor eyesight and most had slow responses. The latter is particularly dangerous, since timely response in impromptu situations is extremely crucial. It can make a life and death difference. But it would seem that, in the multitude of problems this country faces, somebody getting killed in a road accident does not evoke as much of a protest as someone being killed in a gang war.

The picture is not rosy on the defence front either. In the last three years, 31 Indian Air Force pilots have been killed and 68 planes lost in air crashes. This loss in terms of finances works out to be anything between Rs. 1,800 crore and Rs. 2,000 crore. And this is what has happened during peace time, not war!

Regrettably, our country has witnessed a down turn on the social, economic and governance fronts. A pro-reform and pro-people mindset is missing in the civil services, especially at the cutting edge levels. The education of the common man, for whom the entire system is supposed to exist, is the least of worries of those who operate the system.

A serving Union Cabinet Minister hit the nail on the head during the course of a lecture on February 20, 2003: "Be it the poor, the middle class or the educated upper class, all of them have looted the Capital of its environment and beauty. A major problem in governing the Capital is the presence of many agencies, working in different directions. As a result we all work a lot and a lot of noise is made, but the end result is nothing." He asked people not to get caught in the slogans of the day that are part of an official "propaganda machinery".

In most cases of rhetorical flourish, he added, "we miss out on the content. Those at the helm should be sure of the direction to be taken. If you think you can win the elections with these kind of concessions, then you are wrong. For, if people will vote you to power for allowing them to do certain things, then the same people will pull you down for bad health services that the city will face as a consequence. You can't build a nation with negative forces. We have to keep the core issues and problems in mind and try to solve them".

It is important to remember that is not right can be truly great. The answer to all our problems lies in right and good governance. There is still time for our leaders to make a U turn from the reckless path they have been pursuing.

2.2. Demi-gods: The Crops of Lawlessness

It is said that laws are like webs that catch small flies but let wasps and hornets break through. A section of our political class tries all sorts of tricks to escape the consequences of their misdeeds. In fact, a number of them are - or have been - on the centrestage of governance. Though law says all are equal, some politicians resent it despite paying lip service to this maxim.

In a historic decision on December 5, the Supreme Court has decisively intervened to stem corruption in the political system. It has said that public servants, including Chief Ministers, MPs and MLAs, can be prosecuted without any prior sanction. It has held that sanction under Section 197 of CrPC, which has been used to delay and shelve many prosecutions, is not necessary for prosecuting corrupt public servants. According to the apex court, taking bribe while in office clearly does not constitute discharging of official duty.

The court passed this order while dismissing a bunch of appeals filed by Railway Minister Lalu Prasad Yadav, his wife Rabri Devi, former Punjab Chief Minister Prakash Singh Badal, former Kerala Chief Minister K Karunakaran and several former Ministers. In its order, the court held, "It is available only when the alleged act done by the public servant is reasonably connected with the discharge of his official duty and not merely a cloak for doing the objectionable act... It is the quality of the act which is important, and protection of this section is available if the act falls within the scope and range of his official duty."

Section 197 of CrPC requires that a sanction of the competent authority should be there before a court can take cognisance of an offence committed by a public servant. This requirement was insisted upon even after a person ceased to hold any office and was no longer a public servant.

All political parties proclaim the need to fight corruption and criminalisation of politics. But in actual practice, these continue to flourish everywhere in the country. The Delhi High Court had given a ruling with far-reaching implications in November 2000, in which it had sought to help the electorate in securing information about the antecedents of candidates. The Election Commission was asked to supply relevant information about electoral candidates to enable the electorate to assess the capabilities of candidates who intend to become lawmakers. The court also said that if criminalisation of politics was to be prevented, the fundamental right to information must be enforced in letter and spirit. All candidates seeking election must submit relevant information about their background at the time of filing their nomination papers.

The High Court said, "Furnishing of false information will result in prosecution of the candidate. Persons with questionable background do not deserve to be occupying seats in Parliament and the Assemblies... Such persons need to be eliminated from the race... The irony is that those who live by breaking the law are turning into lawmakers and some of them had even found ministerial berths. It is a dangerous development, which does not augur well for the country and parliamentary democracy."

On an appeal filed by the Government, the Supreme Court not only upheld the High Court orders but also asked the Election Commission to take steps to comply with them. It is regrettable that instead of examining the guidelines, an all-party meeting rejected the Election Commission guidelines on July 8, 2002. Worse, Parliament passed a law literally invalidating the Supreme Court judgement. Later, the Supreme Court struck down this law after a PIL was filed against it.

Earlier, on December 17, 1997, the Supreme Court had ordered the setting up of a new anti-corruption organisation. It was taken up by the legislature in the form of the CVC Bill without any discussion in the Lok Sabha. The entire political class was united in its ambivalence on fighting corruption. The central theme of the new regime was the return of the infamous "single directive". This provision - Section 6A of the proposed CVC Bill - made it obligatory for the CBI to secure prior approval of the Union Government before conducting any investigation under the Prevention of Corruption Act, 1988, if the allegations related to an officer of the rank of Joint Secretary or above. The "single directive" had been thrown out by the Supreme Court in the Vineet Narain judgement on a fair argument, "Every person accused of committing the same offence is to be dealt with in the same manner in accordance with law, which is equal in its application to everyone." Thus, the protection enjoyed by the higher echelons of bureaucracy till December 1997 against investigation by the CBI was held illegal.

The above decision has been reiterated in the December 5 judgement of the Supreme Court.

The well-deserved judicial intervention comes in the backdrop of the refusal of the political class to break the mould of extraneous political influence and other considerations which had, in the past, enabled the corrupt and the crooked to escape punishment, thus making a mockery of the entire criminal justice system. The judgement has been welcomed by common people, as it puts some check on legislators who thought they could get away with anything. On the other hand, some MPs regarded it as judicial activism. It is disappointing that some people have wrongly interpreted the judgement. If the objective of all wings of Government - the legislature, the executive and the judiciary - is good governance, the apex court verdict should be appreciated.

It has been clarified that Parliament does not have the power to change the basic structure of the Constitution. The judiciary is the final interpreter of the Constitution. Nobody is above the law and unnecessary noise about judicial activism does no good to the country. In fact, it leads to further plummeting of the popularity of the elected class.

People are well aware that it is the self-preservation instinct of the political class that gives rise to this kind of clamour; it has nothing to do with national interest. But for the Supreme Court rulings, police reforms and equal turf for all political parties where Governors acted in a non-partisan manner would not have been possible. It is time the Supreme Court verdict was applied uniformly to the entire spectrum of public servants, whether elected or selected.

2. Mechanism of Combating Strategies

3.1. Whistle Blowing (not easy)

Satyendra Dubey, a young engineer working for the National Highways Authority of India, was murdered by the mafia on November 27, after he blew the whistle on corrupt practices in the Bihar stretch of the Golden Quadrilateral project. The public furore over his murder led the Prime Minister to declare that the guilty would not be spared "wherever they are." The killing also led to all political parties claiming that they would support a Bill guaranteeing the protection of whistle blowers.

Whistle blowing has various definitions. One, bringing an activity to a sharp conclusion as if by the blast of a whistle (Oxford English Dictionary). Two, raising concern about a malpractice within an organisation or through an independent structure associated with it (UK Committee on Standards in Public Life). Three, giving information (usually to the authorities) about illegal or underhand practices (Chambers Dictionary). Four, exposing to the press a malpractice or cover-up in a business or government office (Brewers Dictionary, US).

Whistle blowing has a bearing on the general public and all institutions, not merely those indulging in corruption or other criminal activities. The reason is that every business, whether government or private, is exposed to the risk of things going wrong or of being looted by the corrupt. In fact, people who first sniff out some wrongdoing are those who work in or with an establishment. These are the people who are best placed to sound the warning, send the distress signal or blow the whistle.

Often, these individuals have to live with the fear of being harmed, physically or by the loss of their jobs. Unless a government or an organisation has the laws as well as the culture and practice that signify that corruption or any other illegal activity can be safely exposed, people are bound to choose victimisation over the prospect of destroying their careers. At the same time, many individuals and companies in the private sector pay bribes to public servants for fear of losing contracts. They do not blow the whistle, since their present and future economic interests can be damaged and their staff harassed. Let alone shielding those who expose corruption-consider the Dubey case-there is no security even for witnesses or criminals-turned-approvers who want to testify in proceedings against their former colleagues or accomplices. Far from being rewarded, a person is not even ensured that his life is safe after having provided the necessary evidence that may help the police and the government to secure convictions in sensational cases.

Effectively, anyone who informs the authorities about corruption is left to fend for himself. At present, there is no institutional help for those who blow the whistle about bribery and other criminal activities. It goes without saying that, unless people are facilitated and assisted to speak out when a bribe is offered to or solicited from them, the fight against corruption cannot succeed. It is doubtful that business concerns would voluntarily provide information about demands for bribes. The result is that the authorities have to depend on gaining evidence either from the bribe-giver or the recipient.

More, the legal position as it prevails discourages the majority of the people from raising issues related to serious malpractices. The reason is that they do not want to get involved in lengthy legal wrangles. This is not surprising since even criminals may file defamation suits against whistle blowers! Mediapersons exposing corruption and crime too have no special protection. We do not have a constitutional provision like the one in America which specifically prohibits the US Congress from making laws that curtail press freedom.

Needless to say, any legislation related to whistle-blowing needs to be publicly debated before it is passed. For, care needs to be taken on one count: Such a law must not provide a handle to unscrupulous persons to use sensitive information for their personal gain, or for blackmailing people, innocent or otherwise. Malicious workers and aggrieved competitors can make damaging disclosures without serving the public interest. We need to create a safety mechanism, and have a widely acceptable procedure for whistle blowing.

It is generally believed that, if someone is seriously concerned about exposing corruption or any other wrongdoing, the only option available to him is to tell his bosses or the person responsible for putting matters right within the organisation to which he belongs. Or he may blow the whistle before the highest authorities-as the NHAI engineer did-or the media. Then there is the vast category of people who want to do the right thing, but are forced to keep quiet.

Which is not surprising. There simply is no guarantee the whistle blower's interests will be safeguarded. Unless there is a legal or departmental assurance, he will face reprisals in the form of harassment, suspension or dismissal, as has happened recently with the former Director-General of Bihar Police, who spoke out against the political patronage extended to criminal elements in that State.

Whistle blowers, at least in India, have reasons, right or wrong, to suspect that corruption or the protection of criminals implicates and incriminates the powers-that-be. He has reasons to believe that such a nexus is condoned by the highest authorities and, hence, that the matter will be covered up. This leads to a situation wherein unscrupulous competitors, managers or political leaders come to believe that anything goes because it is blinked at.

In this state of affairs, there seems to be no respect for the confidentiality of a complainant's disclosures, and no sense of the need to protect his identity-the Dubey murder case makes this pretty evident. Time and again, similar disturbing disclosures are made in official inquiries conducted by Commissions or Committees set up to look into major scandals. They expose the fact people who worked in or with an organisation had been aware of irregularities but had either been too scared to sound the alarm, or had raised the matter in the wrong way or with the wrong person. Quite often, there is a tragic human cost.

Whenever there is a scandal or a major disaster that could have been averted, there is pressure for new laws or regulatory controls. The Committee of Independent Experts, while looking into a resignation matter related to the European Commission in March 1999, had remarked that the facts demonstrated "the value of officials whose conscience persuades them of the need to expose wrongdoings encountered in the course of their duties. They also show how the reaction of superiors failed to live up to legitimate expectations".

The primary aim of a legislation should be to use the whistle blower as a witness, not a complainant. His services cannot be made use of in the public interest without a strong and clear signal from the higher echelons of the Government and other organisations that they are dead against corruption and, hence, pledged to thwarting reprisals against the whistle blower. Such an approach should apply even when a whistle blower turns out to be mistaken, provided he has acted with honesty.

It is not a day too soon to adopt and pass protective legislation. It is doubtful that interest in passing a law will remain after the furore over the Dubey killing dies down and the press latches on to another equally juicy story. Many dishonest politicians, along with corrupt bureaucrats, are themselves involved in malfeasance and would be none too pleased with such an institutional antidote. The Prime Minister, however, has declared zero tolerance for corruption.

A good Whistle Blower's Act would be an effective way to cleanse the system.

An American legal expert, Thomas M Devine, has said : "Whistle blowers' protection is a policy that all government leaders support in public but few in power tolerate in private." I hope our Government proves him wrong.

3.2. Transparency (though a cry in wilderness)

Everybody who is a somebody on the Indian scene talks about ridding the country of poverty. No poverty reduction strategies can, however, produce results when corruption is rampant, and all or a substantial part of public money is siphoned off. The Census puts the urban population at 285 million as of March 2001. Today, it constitutes 27.8 per cent of a total population of 1,027 million, which contributes 60 per cent of GDP which, in turn, accounts for more than 90 per cent of Government revenue. The shortage of housing units is about 22.90 million. More than 90 per cent of the shortage is in housing meant for the economically weaker sections of society.

In 1992-1993, electricity boards' losses were Rs. 4,600 crore, and today the combined State Electricity Board losses stand at Rs 26,000 crore. We cannot achieve development objectives unless anti-corruption efforts are made an integral part of the scheme of things. We cannot have both corruption and good administration. One way of fighting corruption is to diminish the opportunities for it. An effective and practical legislative framework to prevent and combat corruption is an essential prerequisite.

More important, implementation capacity and funds are absolutely necessary, apart from cooperation and commitment at all levels of the Government as well as from NGOs. Public authorities, civil society and the private sector have to complement and reinforce one another in making public resources flow in a more transparent manner. Governmental organisations need to be more transparent about their goals, results as well as their sources of income and expenditure.

The highest possible degree of transparency in all aspects of Government can only promote integrity in those who are charged with the full-time duty of public service. The Government, if it is serious about fighting corruption, should enforce legislation and procedures that provide the public and the media, in the best possible way, an optimum degree of access to information as contemplated in the Right to Information Act.

Corruption and bribery have moved to the forefront in discussions about the business environment. The President of the World Bank regularly identifies bribery as among the greatest threats to global economic development. Therefore, fighting corruption is crucial for attaining development objectives. Foreign investment and all-round development of our country is possible only in a congenial and corruption-free atmosphere.

One of the most regrettable features of the country is the durability and long innings of the corrupt. The corrupt- whether in politics or the bureaucracy-have more than the proverbial nine lives of a cat. In fact, some people openly accused of corruption and malfeasance have bounced back as kings or kingmakers. Why are the corrupt so durable? How does corruption function as a rule game? What does it say about morality? These are the questions we should ask ourselves and think of the best possible answers.

According to one report, at least 10,000 files relating to individual property transactions are missing from the Delhi Development Authority (DDA), and 10,000 files vanishing into thin air should be nothing short of a scandal. They are not mere files. They are 10,000 properties in which people are living or from which they are earning their livelihood, or are those which are necessary for getting free-hold conversions. The beauty of the system is that this will be considered mere negligence and the defaulters go unpunished.

It is doubtful if such files would go missing in a bona fide fashion. Most such crimes (since it is nothing short of a crime) take place with a view to extort money. So, theoretically, if a person were to claim ownership or not pay any dues to the DDA, there is no way the latter can legally prove its case in the court. Files go missing or are traced for a price. Negligence pure and simple has nothing to do with it.

The DDA has roughly 10 lakh files which pertain to flats, plots and industrial establishments. Tracing a 20 year or 30 year-old file or papers out of lakhs of applications for the conversion of property is simply out of the question, unless there is a proper method of maintaining records. So the result will be that thousands of applications for conversion cases of property into free hold would remain pending because of the missing files.

Misgovernance is the root of all evils. The dictionary meaning of the word 'govern' means to control or direct the affairs of a country (or city). The authorities in this country neither control nor direct. It is the easiest course to accuse citizens for failing in their duty. The result is that grievances go unredressed till matters come to a boiling point. That is when people smash police vehicles and block traffic, because no one bothers about corruption or negligence, or the simple matters of supplying drinking water, removing garbage regularly or lighting streets properly.

The first heavy rains every monsoon bring most cities to a halt. Power and water are not to be found every summer, and garbage dumps pile up throughout the year. Our Governments remains unmoved and unresponsive in the midst of disarray, because Government servants are generally apathetic. They are never punished for inaction. In other words, neither our Government nor public servants bother. It is important to understand that clerks, cops and touts are not only the backbone but also the bane of Indian administration. They forget they are meant to serve the people and not lord over them.

Some people mistakenly believe that corruption facilitates faster and better service. There are no paper formalities in corruption since no receipt is given for money taken or entries made in the records. Our Constitution and laws are fine and say the right things about the executive, legislature and judiciary. But the fact remains that the rules, regulations and procedures, based on archaic laws enacted more than 100 years ago, are the main cause of corruption today. Political parties talk only about big corruption and not about the all-around small-time corruption which is everywhere and which affects the common man at every step. No political party has taken up the cases of the worst sufferers of this harassment. Not even the communists-who claim to take up cudgels on behalf of the masses-are interested.

The Government can be guilty of inaction. But we as citizens are also to some degree responsible. Roads can lie broken for years, power failures can be surer than sunrise. Criminals could plot their next strike in the shade of colony trees, within the view of the policemen. But none of us thinks of forming a pressure group and petitioning the relevant authorities. It is a fact that Government agencies are forced to act once citizens mount collective pressure. It is exactly like arriving at a sweeter taste in proportion to the sugar we add. If people start acting by themselves, they can make a lot of difference.

Corruption should no longer be seen by a common citizen as an accepted cost of doing business with the Government or wresting services that public servants are duty bound to perform. Corruption should no longer be tolerated as an unavoidable aspect of Government. Every body recognises that the consequences of corruption are devastating not only to the economy of the individual, but also the economy of the country. Worse, they are absolutely devastating to the poor, the legitimacy and stability of the Government and the moral fabric of society.

Our dejection over the state of the country is partly an outcome of an attitude which shrieks that it is not our responsibility. It is easy to blame everyone else, including the Government, for mismanagement and then do nothing further. The real test of citizenship is not only to fight against and be intolerant of corruption, it is also to discharge one's duties as a citizen. There are not shortcuts in this fight.

3.3. Sting Operations (though no justice behind)

As Larry Gelbert says, "I think one of the by-products of the communication explosion is a sort of 'corruption fatigue'. We have lost our ability to be shocked or enraged by the machinations of politicians. We have been battered with such frequency that we have become indifferent. We are punch drunk with scandals."

The objective of a sting operation is to catch the corrupt and spy on those involved in illicit or anti-national activities. The miniature audio-video technologies including pin-hole cameras makes it easy for any one to clandestinely make a recording of a conversation or some dubious action. There are several ways in which a camera can be concealed-inside briefcases, pagers, cigarette lighters, cellphones, fountain pens, smoke detectors, or even spectacle frames.

Using a briefcase makes it easier to hide the recording equipment, the transmission cord and the battery. In some cases, a few components for secret recording are attached to the body of the user. If a connecting cord is used, it is possible for an observant person to detect something unusual in the actions of the person who is recording and might put the former on alert. Most of these gadgets either possess a self-activation mechanism or one that has to be activated manually. The briefcase cameras get activated when the briefcase is kept in a particular position.

There are no laws or guidelines for conducting sting operations in India. Officially, the anti-corruption agencies of the Government conduct sting operations to catch the corrupt. In such cases, numbered and chemically treated currency notes are given to officials demanding bribe. This money does not come from the Government but from the complainant and is the investigating agency's property till the final verdict has been delivered on the case. Thus, the use of Government money for the conduct of such sting operations is generally frowned upon because it means encouraging corruption.

In the US, the FBI conducts nearly 170 sting operations annually in order to investigate complaints of bribery, extortions, narcotics, smuggling, sale of cigarettes to minors, child sex, etc. In fact, the US has laid down rules for such sting operations, which have emerged over the years from various departmental instructions and rulings of the judiciary. These measures include the following:

* Sting operations could be mounted only on those and/or against whom some evidence of criminal activity already exists and in cases where such an operation is considered necessary for procuring conclusive evidence.

* Permission for sting operations must be obtained from appropriate courts or the Attorney General. This safeguard has been included to prevent those conducting the operation from committing offences like impersonation. Moreover, the identity of the complainant is not revealed unless he has himself made the details of his complaint public or disclosed his credentials to any other office or authority.

* After concealing the identity of the complainant, the designated agency shall in the first instance make discreet inquiries

to ascertain if there is any basis for proceeding further with the complaint. For this purpose, the designated agency shall build an appropriate machinery.

* Either as a result of discreet inquiry or on the basis of the complaint itself (without any inquiry), if the designated agency is of the opinion that the matter requires further investigation, it shall officially seek explanation from the Head of the Department of the organisation concerned. While doing so, the designated agency shall not disclose the identity of the informant and also request the head of the organisation to keep his identity secret in case it is revealed to him.

* After obtaining response from the organisation concerned, if the designated agency is of the opinion that investigation reveals either misuse of office or it substantiates the allegation of corruption, it shall recommend appropriate action to the government department or organisation. These shall, inter alia, include the following: (a) Appropriate proceedings to be initiated against the accused Government servant. (b) Appropriate administrative steps for compensating the loss incurred by the Government as a result of corruption or misuse of office, as the case may be.

* Those conducting the sting operation are required to maintain a concurrent written record of the various stages of the operation. While the transcript of the recordings may be edited, the films and the tapes themselves should not be. Where there is evidence of editing, it is automatically presumed that the recording is not authentic.

In India, the Central Vigilance Commission is the designated agency that addresses corruption. This Government body receives written complaints or disclosures of allegations of corruption by an employee of the Central Government or of any corporation established by or under a Central Act, Government companies, societies or local authorities owned or controlled by the Central Government. The disclosure or complaint is supposed to contain full particulars of the case and should be accompanied by supporting documents or other material. The designated agency may, if it deems fit, demand further information from those who have made the disclosure. If the complainant is anonymous, the designated agency shall not take any action on the matter.

The question is, how does one define a "whistle-blower"? He should be a person who has the knowledge of unlawful acts committed at the highest echelons of administration, which should be checked in the larger interests of the public. This definition excludes those who leak information for personal aggrandisement.

Nobody wants to pay bribe if that could be helped. Currently, only the elite in our society have an easy access to goods and services. This is because they enjoy both power and pelf; and they can use their influence and money. It is only the needy-from the poor or the middle classes-who are forced to divert a large proportion of their income to pay bribes. At the same time, besides putting the culprits behind the bars it is equally important to protect the innocent.

Some of the Government departments, where corruption reigns supreme and affects the common man are:

* Ration shops selling kerosene. Shopkeepers sell kerosene in open markets while a commission paid to officials makes sure that they look the other way.
* Fake ration cards are readily available. Many food and civil supplies officials selling forged cards were arrested recently.
* Driving licences too can be faked as touts easily help people in getting them made without the mandatory driving tests.
* Corruption is rampant in DDA too. Converting a leasehold flat to a freehold one would mean shelling out at least Rs 35,000 extra for an MIG flat. Why does the DDA not charge a one-time enhanced amount to avoid avoidable harassment to the public?
* In police department too, one has to pay in order to speed up action on the report filed.

In all the above cases, sting operations would go a long way in stemming the rot in these departments.

The current dispensation under the leadership of Dr Manmohan Singh-a man of impeccable integrity keen on ameliorating the lot of the common man-has earmarked huge funds for development. This is the most opportune moment for dealing with the corrupt who are parasites feeding on the prevailing structure. If only the Government decides to take this fight to the streets and encourages the print and electronic media to expose the guilty, there would be a sea change in the quality of service rendered to the public. Today, a vast majority of public servants are neither dedicated nor interested in ameliorating the lot of their fellow countrymen.

As long as money is inextricably linked with the political and executive processes, we would not see the end of corruption. As Mr Alberto Fujimori, the ex-President of Peru had said, "Fighting terrorism is dangerous, but fighting corruption is far more dangerous. The 'big powers' are very strong." The country's leadership should introduce a new culture of transparency and accountability that will lead to the reduction, if not elimination, of corruption. For this, legalised sting operations aimed at exposing the guilty will prove more effective than any other measure tried so far.

3.3.1. Discussion Continued

Corruption is like garbage that collects. Unless removed daily, it makes our habitat unliveable. We are seeing garbage pile up in India, acting as the single-largest obstacle to development. A TV sting operation on March 9, showed what is known to those who have dealt with any government department. It showed 82 employees accepting bribes from businessmen and traders. The TV channel enlisted the businessmen to expose the dirt prevailing in the New Delhi Sales Tax Office.

The officials, including some women, were seen demanding and accepting bribes to issue certificates and licences. The Delhi Government must have been shocked to realise that the major chunk of revenues collected from traders was pocketed by officials. Once the scandal broke, it suspended 30 officials perhaps out of compulsion. Some noises were made about "strictest action" against "employees caught on tape". The nature of the action was not clarified.

This is neither the first nor the last sting. Tehelka had started the trend-use of technology to expose scandals-in India. Recently, even a reel villain felt the impact, turned as he was into a real life villain in a sting operation. Conversations between leading film stars and underworld dons have also been recorded.

The advent of miniaturised audio and video technology, especially pin-hole cameras, enables clandestine recording. Such equipment costs anything between \$500 and \$5,000 plus depending on quality, and generally has four components: A miniaturised camera, a miniature video recording device, a cord to transmit signals and a battery cell. The use of the cord can be avoided through wireless transmissions. There are various ways of hiding a camera-inside a briefcase, a pager, a cigarette lighter, a cellular telephone, a fountain pen, a smoke detector or even in the nose frame of spectacles!

Most gadgets have a self-activation or a manually operated mechanism. The briefcase camera gets activated when the briefcase is kept in a particular position.

Sting operations may be carried out by the media, NGOs, politicians, scientists, or international investigative agencies. Nowadays, sting operations worldwide are being conducted with official sanction. What purpose do they serve? If they are directed against people involved in criminal activities, it will expose them. The threat of exposure could deter a potential criminal and thus avert a criminal act. The aim is to expose anything from corruption, the drug trade, espionage, adultery, to terrorism and anti-national activity.

No laws or guidelines exist for sting operations in India. The Government's anti-corruption agencies conduct stings to nab the corrupt. Numbered, chemically treated currency notes are given to officials demanding bribes. This money is not the Government's, but the complainant's. It becomes case property during judicial processes against the accused. Providing money on Government account for stings is generally frowned upon as a means of encouraging corruption.

In the US, the FBI conducts nearly 170 operations a year, to investigate complaints of bribery, extortion, narcotics smuggling, sale of cigarettes to minors, child abuse, etc. Ground rules have been laid down over the years by departmental instructions and judicial rulings. One is that sting operations can be mounted only against persons against whom some evidence of criminality exists, and such an exercise is considered necessary for getting conclusive evidence.

Permission for stings must be obtained from appropriate courts or the Attorney-General. This safeguard has been put in place since those who organise stings may themselves commit offences of impersonation or criminal trespass under false pretexts so as to catch criminals red-handed. The complainant's identity is not revealed unless he himself makes the details of his complaint public or discloses his identity to any other office or authority.

After concealing the complainant's identity, the designated agency makes discreet inquiries to ascertain whether any basis exists for proceeding further with the complaint. For this purpose, it has to devise an appropriate machinery.

If the designated agency is of the view-either as a result of the inquiry, or on the basis of the complaint itself-that the matter requires to further probing, it has to officially seek comments/ explanations from the head of the department of the concerned organisation or office. While doing so, it cannot disclose informant's identity. It must also request the concerned head of the organisation to keep this a secret if, for any reason, the latter comes to know the identity.

After obtaining the concerned organisation's response, the designated agency may feel that investigations either reveal misuse of office or substantiate allegations of corruption, it has to recommend appropriate action to the concerned government department or organisation. It could ask for appropriate proceedings to be initiated against the concerned government servant. Or it may demand appropriate administrative steps for redressing the loss caused to the government as a result of the corrupt act or misuse of office, as the case may be.

Concurrent records in writing of the various stages of a sting operation must be maintained. While transcripts of recordings can be edited, films and the tapes cannot. If there is evidence of editing, there is the automatic presumption that the recording is not authentic.

The Central Vigilance Commission, for instance, is authorised, as the designated agency, to receive written complaints or disclosures on allegations of corruption or misuse of office by any employee of the Central Government or of any corporation established by or under any Central Act, Government companies, societies or local authorities owned or controlled by the government. The disclosure or complaint must contain full particulars, accompanied by supporting documents or other materials. The designated agency may call for further information or particulars from persons making the disclosure. If the complaint is anonymous, it should not take any action in the matter.

A "whistle-blower" is a person who has knowledge of wrongdoing in high places, and alerts the authorities with the express intention of having it checked in the larger public interest. Such a definition would necessarily exclude those who leak information for the benefit of an interest group or for personal aggrandisement.

Nobody wants to bribe anybody if he or she can help it. Only the elite manage to get the services they need through influence or money. The needy-the poor or the middle classes-pay a larger proportion of their income as bribes. Hence, apart from putting bad guys in jail, it is equally important to protect victims.

Corruption reigns in departments for kerosene and rations. Shopkeepers sell controlled price items in the open market. A cut ensures that officials look the other way fake ration cards are easily available. Many food and civil supplies officials were nabbed recently selling cards. Touts can also easily get you a driving licence without a test. Rates vary. DDA procedures have also come under a cloud. Converting leasehold flat to freehold could mean shelling out at least Rs. 35,000 extra for an MIG flat to touts. Why can't the DDA charge a one-time enhanced amount to curb harassment to the public? Police are also suspect. You have to pay for getting action on your complaints. Sting operations would do a lot of good to all these areas.

The Government run by a man of impeccable integrity, Mr Manmohan Singh, would naturally want to ameliorate the lot of the common man by earmarking huge funds for development. This is the time to deal with the corrupt who fleece honest tax payers. Once the Government decides to take this fight to the streets and encourages the media to participate, we may witness a sea change in the quality of services rendered to people by public servants.

Taking on political and electoral corruption-by which governments with wafer-thin majorities are formed-must also be part of the struggle. Our leadership needs to introduce a new culture of transparency and accountability. Using legalised sting operations will prove more effective than any other measure tried so far.

3.4. Vigilance: Fettered Watchdog

The Madras High Court, in its ruling on January 5, 2005, said: "Any advice or opinion to besought from the CVC can be only on procedural matters, and if any advice is given in the matter of appreciation of evidence, proof of charges, or the quantum of punishment, such shall be ignored and not be binding on the disciplinary authority (of the concerned Government office). Any regulation to the contrary will be wholly without jurisdiction and inoperative." This has naturally ruffled a few feathers in the Central Vigilance Commission (CVC).

How can it be so! In the scheme of things, as they stand at present as well as in the past, the CVC, though created by law in 2003, is only an advisory body. In fact, the original resolution of 1963 made it clear that the role of the CVC was only advisory, though each department was expected to pay utmost consideration to its recommendations. Even after the direction of the Supreme Court to give the CVC a statutory shape on December 18, 1997, the Central Government has only transferred the superintendence of the anti-corruption work being done by the CBI to the CVC.

The CVC has been authorised to review the working of the CBI. Nonetheless, the Act clearly provides that the CVC would have no authority to instruct the CBI, to investigate any case in a particular manner. In other words, the final decision regarding the fate of a case would rest with the departmental hierarchy in the CBI. However, the CVC can monitor the progress of investigation. Apart from the above statutory framework, the CVC can refer cases to CBI for investigation/inquiry.

Whatever be an individual's or an organisation's feeling about any judgement or scheme of things, the underlying issue is that it is finally the privilege of the appointing authority to take any action against the people appointed by it. Similar is the case in real life as well, as even in the private sector. It has always been so for Government employees since the British times. Actually, no action can be taken against any Government employee without the sanction of the appointing authority. Even the courts do not take any legal cognisance of any case or chargesheet for any lapse against any public servant without the sanction of the Government.

As the Government's work has increased manifold, various institutions have been created to give their inputs so that proper and just decisions can be taken by the Government. In fact, for taking action against the employees appointed on the recommendation of the Union Public Service Commission, whether they belong to the IAS, IPS or any other service of a specified level, the advice of the UPSC is mandatory for taking any action, involving both the departmental lapse or corruption-related case. Though the UPSC is a statutory body, it is, however, not obligatory for the Government to accept its recommendations.

Nonetheless, if the Government were to differ from its views then it has to lay a statement on the table of Parliament enumerating its reasons for the same. After all, the UPSC has been an historic institution created in the early 20th century. In the long span of its existence, it has proved its integrity, competence and efficiency. Unfortunately, the same cannot be said of the Vigilance Commission, whose functioning has largely depended upon the personality of the person heading the department.

Some CVCs have been in the forefront of the fight against corruption, while others have taken it as a sinecure and post-retirement reward. The institution is still to evolve into its true colours. One former Central Vigilance Commissioner had decided to put the names of corrupt officials on its official website. But with the change of guard and an outcry against the CVC, the proposal was aborted.

It is perhaps unfair to find fault with the Central Vigilance Commission, as the Government itself is not clear as to what it expects from it. Institutions are built over a period of time and not in five or six years. They also evolve and develop in response to the needs of society and the kind of rulers a country has. It is clear that most politicians, with few honourable exceptions, are full-time professionals.

In other words, their means of livelihood is politics. So is their source of known and unknown rewards, which go with the occupation of a political office. In reality, getting into legislatures, whether at State or Central level, means an unwritten immunity, from any state action for any present or past wrong-doings. Incomes Tax cases, law violations, or graft cases are either put on the slow track or back-burner or altogether dropped, depending upon the position of a legislature vis-a-vis the ruling party and his usefulness to it.

In the Assembly elections to Jharkhand, Bihar and Haryana in February 2005, corruption has not been considered an issue at all. It was so during the 2004 Lok Sabha elections. Now the fight between politicians of various hues boils down to: "You or your party has made enough. Now it is our turn and we will leave no ploy or ruse unused to throw you out." Similarly, periodic raids by the CBI are revealing, wherein the UDC or LDC or, for that matter, even class four employees have become millionaires within decades. There is an interesting story of an official whose wife earned Rs. 5 crore in just 57 days in diamond trade along with a willing partner for the money laundering of ill-gotten gains of her husband. It is one record I have not been able to comprehend, where a person's earning rate exceeds Rs. 8.75 lakh a day or more than Rs. 1 lakh every hour, on an eight-hour a day working schedule. Mind you, the officer was a young entrant through the UPSC, with less than 10 years of service-appointed in one of the revenue departments.

The CVC should not bother about the fact whether its advice is heeded or not, or even whether it is constitutionally binding. It needs to reintrospect whether any of its efforts have helped the common man and whether, with its efforts or fear, there is one rascal less in the governance machinery of the country. In the fight for turf, the main objectives are getting lost and side-tracked. A former Central Vigilance Commissioner once said, "India's economy today is a standing monument to corruption and inefficiency of four specific departments, namely the Customs, Central Excise, Income Tax and Enforcement Directorate. It is the evasion of taxes and the failure of these departments to check illegal activities that has crystallised into the large percentage of black money in the economy. The quantum of black money has been estimated between Rs. 40,000 crore to Rs. 100,000 crore. Industries today depend on black money. The film industry, a substantial part of the construction industry and a large number of small industries too run on the basis of black money."

People have little patience. They are not bothered about the niceties or any fine distinction between the technical role of various institutions to bring about transparency and honesty in governance. They want the fear of God instilled in the corrupt and dishonest. Based on this acid test of governance, the Government in general and the CVC in particular has not performed superbly. It has been found wanting not only by Indians, but also by the world community. Transparency International has already classified India as the 83rd most corrupt country in the world, with a score of 28 out of 100 on the corruption perception index. The most important characteristic of any individual or nation is its integrity during day-to-day course of action. Even 58 years after Independence, the country has only been sliding down in certain crucial areas. It is time to reminded our rulers the sagacious observation of Rudyard Kipling: "We have 40 million reasons for failure, but not a single excuse."

3.4.1. CVC: Barking Dogs Seldom Bite

At least in our democracy, corruption has become a part of the system. The justification trotted out is that political parties need funds, which are collected in cash. 'Donation' in cash, as opposed to payment by cheque, is generally unaccounted money. Black money is generated only by black transactions. Black transactions and corruption sustain each other. This is generally done by doing favours for a price, for bending or twisting laws or giving sanctions with the help of obliging civil servants at decision-making levels.

The Central Vigilance Commission Bill 2003, passed by the Lok Sabha, was carried by voice vote in the Rajya Sabha on August 7, 2003. Under this Bill, a three-member commission, each member with a fixed tenure of four years, will be appointed on the recommendation of a high-level committee, for overseeing the working of the CBI. Lest it be forgotten, a CVC has been in existence since the 1960s, as a result of the recommendation of a committee headed by K Santhanam, which went into the whole gamut of circumstances leading to corruption, and the steps required to curb it.

The Santhanam Committee recognised the malady of corruption and observed in 1962: "The tendency to subvert integrity in the public services, instead of being isolated and aberrative, is growing into a well-organised, well-planned racket." It also observed, 40 years ago, that corruption had increased, to such an extent that people had started losing faith in the integrity of public administration. Corruption in certain areas had spread even to that level of administrative hierarchy from which it was conspicuously absent in the past.

In its judgement of December 18, 1997, the Supreme Court in the Vineet Narain case, popularly known as the Jain hawala case, looked into the entire issue of purifying public life and controlling corruption. It also looked into the question of the validity of several executive directions, including the so-called Single Directive which required the CBI to take the prior permission of the Government to start any inquiry, or look into any malfeasance on the part of officers of the Joint Secretary level and above. Mind you, this permission is separate from sanction for prosecution, which in any case is required in matters pertaining to all public servants from peon to Cabinet Secretary, should it be decided to prosecute them.

The Supreme Court held: "Obviously, where the accusation of corruption is based on direct evidence and it does not require any inference to be drawn, dependent on the decision-making process, there is no rational basis to classify them differently. In other words, if the accusation be of bribery, which is supported by direct evidence, of acceptance of illegal gratification by them, including trap cases, it is obvious that no other factor is relevant and the level of status of the offender is irrelevant." It is for this reason it was conceded that such cases-of bribery, including trap cases-are outside the scope of the Single Directive.

It also said: "No serious attempt was made by the learned Attorney General to support inclusion within the Single Directive of cases in which the offender is alleged to be in possession of disproportionate assets. It is clear that the accusation of possession of disproportionate assets by a person is also based on direct evidence and no factor pertaining to the expertise of decision-making is involved therein. We have, therefore, no doubt, that the Single Directive cannot include within its ambit cases of possession of disproportionate assets by the offender. The question now is only with regard to cases other than those of bribery, including trap cases, and of possession of disproportionate assets being covered by the Single Directive."

Thus, the protection enjoyed by the higher echelons of the bureaucracy till December 1997 against CBI investigations was held as illegal, as the Government's power of superintendence did not include the power to interfere with the CBI's power to investigate; and the classification of offenders on the basis of their rank was not rational, hence opposed to the right to equality guaranteed under the Constitution.

In the present CVC Bill, the field of choice of appointment is restricted only to retired bureaucrats and retired officers of public sector undertakings. It would have been better if the field of selection could have included eminent public figures and jurists or judges of the Supreme Court. Else, CVC appointment would mean an extension of service by four years, like the UPSC or the Election Commission. It is not as if talent is available only in retired bureaucrats.

The CVC, under the Bill, will exercise superintendence over the functioning of the CBI in so far as it relates to investigation of offences under the Prevention of Corruption Act, or an offence with which a public servant can be charged.

What the apex court had declared as illegal has been smuggled back, and the position is almost the same as it was before the CVC Bill was passed. In fact the court in its judgement had laid down certain guidelines for the functioning of the public office holders. One, holders of public office would have to be as open as possible about decisions and actions, giving reasons for the same and restricting information only when wider public interest so demanded.

Two, accountability and honesty. Public office holders would have to be accountable for their decisions and actions to the public and submit themselves to whatever scrutiny was appropriate to their office. The court also held that "it is trite that the holders of public offices are entrusted with certain powers to be exercised in the public interest alone and, therefore, the office is held by them, in trust for the people. Any deviation from the path of rectitude by any of them amounts to a breach of trust and must be severely dealt with, instead of being pushed under the carpet. If the conduct amounts to an offence, it must be promptly investigated and the offender, against whom a prima facie case is made out, should be prosecuted expeditiously so that the majesty of law is upheld and the rule of law vindicated. It is the duty of law, therefore, to guard against erosion of the rule of law. The adverse impact of lack of probity in public life leading to a high degree of corruption is manifold. It also has adverse effect on foreign investment and funding from the International Monetary Fund and the World Bank who have warned that future aid to underdeveloped countries may be subject to the requisite steps being taken to eradicate corruption, which prevents international aid from reaching those for whom it is meant. Increasing corruption has led to investigative journalism, which is of value to a free society. The need to highlight corruption in public life through the medium of public interest litigation invoking judicial review may be frequent in India but is not unknown in other countries".

Sometime ago, the Government, am-ending Section 33(B) of the Representation of the People Act, declared that "no candidate shall be liable to disclose or furnish any such information in respect of his election, which is not required to be disclosed or furnished under this Act or the rules made thereunder".

This provision was to be effective irrespective of any judgement or directive of the EC to the contrary. The court struck it down on March 13 this year on the ground the new law violated the fundamental rights of citizens guaranteed under Article 19(1) as interpreted by the court. Interpretation of the Constitution is the judiciary's domain. There is no doubt a law creating two classes of public servants, one Joint Secretary-level and above and lesser mortals below, will meet the same fate as the amendment to the Repre-sentation of the People Act. The Single Directive was held as violative of the fundamental right to equality in 1997. It cannot become legal in 2003 (Section 6 of the CVC Bill) when big fish like the Vice-Chairman of the DDA and Chairman and other senior officers of the income tax, customs and other services have been caught indulging in blatant corruption.

Must the Government face judicial flak, and yet continue to pass laws that are discriminatory in nature, to protect a few?

3

Indian Politics and Democratic Fallout

1. People, Politics and Dilemma

In the general election beginning from April 20, Indians between the ages 18 and 35 years-approximately constituting of 59 per cent of the 67.4 crore voters-would be exercising their franchise for the first time.

According to one survey, only 14 per cent of this segment is interested in elections or electoral politics, while 53 per cent are interested onlookers. What is healthy is that some of them feel that not participating in election is almost a crime. A few of them feel that politics is rather dirty. A handful of them, according to the survey, were not sure whether Atal Bihari Vajpayee heads a BJP or a Congress Government. They can be forgiven, because the total readership of all papers in magazines is not even 100 million out of a population over one billion.

It is not so only among students, but in other segments of society as well. Once I was heading an examination for promotion of sub-inspectors to inspectors in the Central Reserve Police (CRPF), which fell one day after Mahatma Gandhi's birth anniversary. I asked a potential promotee as to what was the role of the Mahatma Gandhi vis-a-vis the CRPF. He replied that Gandhi had done a lot for the welfare and promotion of Central Reserve Police Force, while the reality is he had nothing to do with it.

The involvement of some politicians in scams and scandals has painted the entire political class in black colours. Actually, in the perception of the people, honesty and politics are poles apart. Some of the youth feel that the media surveys and the projections by spin doctors, give some politicians an undeserved, larger than life image. Charisma and achievements are centred around one individual, thanks to debates and media management, leaving no scope for a younger, suave leader to emerge in the election. General election in our country revolves around a spectacle of mass contact, either through rath yatras or roadshows, fiery speeches and slogans. Occasionally, there are ritualistic references to poverty, corruption, unemployment etc. Film stars, small screen artists, jaded actors and actresses of yester years, one-time celebrity cricketers, retired bureaucrats, singers, party hopping politicians, are all jostling for a place on the supposedly winning side. They are lined up before the media in the hope that they will be a draw to pull voters to the respective parties. The target of political parties ,no doubt, is the young voter, who, they feel, would be lured into casting votes for them simply because they boast of a galaxy of celebrities and filmstars.

Unfortunately, there is no focus on real issues, like corruption, pending projects, or simplifying rules and procedures so that the common man is saved from the harassment of bureaucratic delays and red tapism that getting one's work done from the babudom generally entails. Politics has been reduced to the theatre of the absurd, wherein voters, especially the young ones, are lured by all kind of gimmicks.

Defectors switch parties, ostensibly for reasons of moral indignation and rage, but actually for more unprincipled and unethical reasons. A supposed communalist transforms himself into a secularist, and vice versa in one day. One political party has promised creation of one crore jobs in its manifesto. Incidentally, the present strength of the Central Government employees is just 3.2 million. The financial burden of sustaining the bureaucracy is eating up a substantial chunk of the Central revenue. Pray, how does the political party, which has proposed to create one crore job, propose to pay them?

Obviously, political parties are economical with the truth. Promises, counter-pledges and assurances, in the game of one-upmanship and announcement of populist measures, has been the hallmark of all elections. Election 2004 would therefore be no different, except that this time the polls would also be fought in television studios, with politicians of different parties throwing mud on each other, and providing side entertainment to the voters.

There would be a lot of heat without any focus on the real problems of the common man. The grand spectacle of democracy has become a comedy in party offices and television studios. Today, if one looks carefully, one would find that all parties stand for the same thing or nothing. For some politicians, election means merely securing a job for the next five years.

Even the elected representatives are not willing to talk about good governance during the period they are in office, or generate fresh ideas on how to get their policies implemented. They care only about their reelection. However, voters are not as ignorant as politicians may think. Young voters want quality life.

According to another survey, 30 per cent of the people are concerned with reducing the menace of corruption, whereas 24 per cent want prices to be controlled. Twenty-two per cent want poverty to be reduced. Seventeen per cent are asking for more jobs. Surprisingly, only three per cent are interested in reducing Hindu-Muslim tension. Only one per cent of those surveyed showed interest in the construction of temple at Ayodhya, and again only one per cent were concerned with better India-Pakistan relations.

Ninety two per cent of the youth surveyed expressed their intention to vote, or that they are likely to vote, and only two per cent said that they would not vote. Out of the two per cent, 70 per cent said this was because they distrust politicians and are disinterest ed in politics. Ten per cent of the last category of two per cent said that they would not vote, as there was no difference between the candidates of different political parties.

The same survey showed that 37 per cent of the youth wanted good education, 33 per cent wanted good jobs, 27 per cent wanted to have quality life, as against three per cent who wanted fun or enjoy life. Eighty seven per cent considered the forthcoming polls as very important or somewhat important. Only 10 per cent did not consider the elections important, whereas three per cent were undecided. However, 30 per cent considered unemployment a major issue, whereas the prices of goods concerned 13 per cent.

Ten per cent considered the polls unimportant and three per cent had no opinion. Sixty four per cent of the youth said that the election will affect their lives and 36 per cent denied any role of elections in their life. Continuing in the same vein, 86 per cent felt that election will improve their lives to either some extent or to a large extent. Only 11 per cent felt that voting and elections did not matter. However, one unique feature of election 2004 is that, apart from the role of candidates, the media is dictating and analysing the pace of campaign and what parties should have done or what they have not done.

The alertness of the print and television media has led to political parties using the latest technology in disseminating information about their claims or counterclaims or other activities. The use of the latest technology and electronic voting machines has sounded the death knell of booth capturing. Of course, it does not mean that there cannot be malpractices. Conniving officials can cooperate with unscrupulous persons in enabling them to press more than one voting button on the electronic voting machines. During the last elections, where a voting machine was used, a candidate told me that he had managed to compromise the official's money or intimidation. The result was that without even participation of the actual voters, their votes were cast.

Despite all its shortcomings, Indian democracy has been among the most participatory and vibrant in the world. In 1999, 60 per cent of Indians voted, as against 40 per cent of the Canadian, 41 per cent of the British and Germans, and 48 per cent of Americans. In California, the voter turnout was only 30 per cent. It is for this reason that 85 per cent of the people surveyed in India feel that their votes matter. So election to bring in the governing elite who will determine the country's future is serious business. And it is time again to remind citizens to be critical and select the best while voting.

It would be apt here to quote Robert F. Kennedy, "It is from numberless diverse acts of courage and belief that human history is shaped. Each time, a man stands up for an ideal, or acts to improve the lot of others, or strikes out against injustice, he sends a tiny ripple of hope, and crossing each other from a million different centres of energy and daring those ripples build a current which can sweep down the mightiest walls of oppression and resistance."

1.1. Issueless Elections at Bid of Caste

Caste will play a dominant role in the 2004 elections. Though most political parties do not admit it, caste plays a major role in electoral battles. During my visit to various parts of the country, I have found that caste is the mainstay of all calculations; it determines who wins or loses.

The last time castes were enumerated in a census was in 1931. Now only the castes listed in the schedule and linked to Articles 341 and 342 of the Constitution are enumerated in any census. The proposal to include caste in the census of 2001 was not agreed to.

Any calculations based on caste alone is, however, likely to go haywire due to migration, shifts in caste status and differential rates of population growth. For the elections to dissolved 13th Lok Sabha, the total voters turnout was 60 per cent, against 42 per cent in the third general elections. Also, come elections, fulltime politicians get ready to change parties to ensure being returned or their continued presence on the political scene. Politicians are normally power hungry and opportunistic. Asked why he left his party which did not give him the seat he wanted, a deserter countered: Who is not power hungry?

In this fight for power the conditions of the poor is the least of priorities. According to a nation-wide survey by the National Sample Survey Organisation, as many as 80 lakh families live in about 52,000 slums in the country. They constitute 14 per cent of the total urban population.

The survey showed that 50 per cent of non-notified slum dwellers had no access to public toilets. These are the Government's own figures. Obviously, India is not "shining" for them. The worst affected areas are in West Bengal, Andhra Pradesh and Maharashtra. The growth of slums is due to urbanisation and lack of adequate facilities for employment or health or education. Urban-centric policies take after the Mughals who left the rural areas to their own fate. A large number of migrants, struggling to meet both ends in the city, build shelters, wherever they find vacant space, leading to encroachments on public and private land and unplanned growth. Corrupt bureaucrats wink at these for a price.

Unscrupulous politicians extend them patronage to use them as votebanks. In fact, frequent elections-held every year or once in every two years in the States because of dissolution of Assemblies before the completion of their terms-are not only a great drag on the exchequer, but also a cause of populist governance against good governance, which all political parties claim that they will provide. Both Vice-President Bhairon Singh Shekhawat and Deputy Prime Minister LK Advani, have been pleading for a constitutional amendment making for simultaneous elections to the State Assemblies and Parliament. This, however, does not suit corrupt and unscrupulous politicians.

Remarkably, politicians have performed repeated volte faces on reforms, supporting or opposing them as is convenient. It is a fact that reforms were launched when the Congress was in power. It was, however, Chattisgarh's Congress Government that opposed disinvestment. But in the April-May 2004 elections Congress is owning the policy up. Laying the foundation stone of the Ayodhya temple was Rajiv Gandhi's brainchild. When the BJP successfully hijacked its agenda and left it behind, the Congress cried foul and said it was a communal approach. The party seems to believe that what it does is the best, but someone else who does it is a crook. It is not something peculiar to India, but is found in politicians worldwide.

In the 2004 parliamentary elections, all kinds of methods including colourful posters, buntings, pamphlets and ear-splitting propaganda on loud speakers across cities, towns and villages, will be used for campaigning. This is apart from approaching the voters through telephones, emails, and SMS. Nearly 35 million Indians own mobile phones and 10 millions have access to the Internet. Mass scale use of technology is going to cost undisclosed millions of rupees.

Terrorists and other disgruntled groups would doubtless view elections as an opportunity to make their presence felt sabotage, assaults and assassinations like that of the husband of the State Tribal Minister of Andhra Pradesh on March 18, 2004 near his home at Paderu village in Visakhapatnam District. On the same day, terrorists killed the Vice-President of Youth Janta Dal in Qamarwari area of Srinagar at point blank range. Incidentally the 2002 Assembly election saw the killings of a number of political activists apart from two candidates. The terrorists, whether called Naxalites or Hizbul Mujaheedin claim that their struggle is for the people when they are actually waging war against the people of India.

We have first-rate election laws in the country giving full tax exemption to donors to political parties. The disclosure of contributions is mandatory and free broadcasting time is provided to recognised parties. With the entry of nearly 47 private news channels, politicians do get limited time to debate and air their view. That is the only interesting part of the elections. Otherwise the political speeches are drab, marked by claims and counter-claims and charges are hurled at one another at random. Elections are a great leveller. Some who strut like monarch of all they survey now, could be on the road after the elections.

Poll predictions are risky and are often wide of the mark. The following figures tell a story of their own. In 1998, India Today-ORG predicted 234-249 seats for the BJP and its allies, 150-165 for the Congress and 120-130 for the United Front. The Frontline-CMS poll predicted 225-235 for the BJP, 145-155 for the Congress and 120-135 for the UF. The CSDS put the BJP and others at 249. The Outlook-AC Nielsen survey predicted 155 for the Congress and its allies, 102 for the UF, 231 for the BJP and its allies. The result? The BJP and its allies got 254, the Congress and its allies got 147, and the United Front got 96.

In 1999, India Today-ORG gave the National Demcratic Alliance 322-336 seats, the Congress and its allies 132-146 and others 70-80. The Outlook-SMS survey gave the NDA 319-329 seats, the Congress and its allies 122 and others 135-145. The Pioneer-RDI survey gave the NDA 313-318 seats, Congress and allies 140-150 and the others 84-86.

The result? NDA 297 and the Congress and its allies 134.An old saying has it that a drowning will catch at a straw. Political parties are out to cultivate film stars, of old and new vintage. I have my reservations about the matter as I would vote for a party just before some actress or actor of yesteryear has joined a political party. A survey has confirmed that it really does not make any difference either to the fortune of a candidate or a political party.

Indeed, a newspaper reported that a film star joined a political party for a price. Even if this is not true, all, including film stars, join a political party for rewards in kind if not cash. The former can a political office or a membership cf Rajya Sabha. Some film stars have become Ministers and Chief Ministers. So having outlived their acting careers, stars are seeking a post retirement job.

Of course, all political reward bureaucrats who serve their Governments loyally. So why blame retired or semi-retired film stars for trying their luck? Their fates and those of others will be finally determined by the Indian voters whose innate common sense is well known and who are unlikely to be swayed by gimmicks, propaganda or road shows or slogans. Ultimately, governance alone will matter.

1.2. The Riots

The communal problem in India has existed for long. Recent instances of violence in Gorakhpur, Mangalore, Bangalore and Indore bring back the country's attention on this festering problem. The ongoing unrest in Gorakhpur is neither the first nor the last of its kind. Such occurrences at some places have not only been prolonged, but have also resulted in loss of many innocent lives.

The police is often blamed for not handling the situation well. The National Police Commission (1977-81) in its report on communal riots observed: "In many cases of troubled cities, the police and the magistracy just withdrew when anti-social groups indulged in violent crimes. The deployment of Magistrates on such occasions appears to have reduced to almost a farce... There is a tendency amongst the officers to avoid taking responsibility in dealing with the situation. They either avoid going to the trouble spot, or when they happen to be present there, they try not to order, the use of force, when the situation so demands, or better still, slip away from the scene leaving the force leaderless."

The report further added, "We have reasons to believe that this reaction of the officers was more a calculated decision on their part rather than a reflex action out of cowardice. They consider it prudent, to avoid getting involved in ordering the use of force. It is unfortunate, that after such riots, it is only those officers who had taken some action in dealing with the situation, who are accused of all sorts of misdoings and they have to face harassment and humiliation in the inquiries that follow... To deal with the situations as they arise, it is essential that officers act on their own in their best judgement, and not seek instructions from higher quarters where none are necessary."

State Governments are generally seen tackling communal riots in an ad hoc manner. Regrettably, as every vote counts in a democracy, all political parties look for such incidents to bolster their electoral prospects.

A number of commissions have analysed the genesis of communal violence and stressed the need for controlling rumours effectively, which aggravate the situation. During a riot, the least that any Government can do is institute thorough investigation and follow it up with successful prosecution. This prevents further crimes and discourages potential mischief-makers. Stringent punishment awarded to a rioter acts as a deterrent and makes the criminal-minded realise that "crime does not pay". The problem of riots cannot be isolated from general law enforcement in any State. Strict and impartial law enforcement on a day-to-day basis is the only way to control communal violence.

There is no straightjacketed solution to fit all situations in dealing with communal riots. The National Integration Council suggested that the District Magistrate and Superintendent of Police be made responsible for communal disturbances.

While dealing with communal violence, the police can at best undertake fire-fighting operations, as long-term measures are vested in the political leadership. The police, however, should ensure that all laws are enforced without prejudice.

The following are the causes for failures in controlling communal riots. Often the administration fails in intelligence gathering and forging communication links in time, as well as in making a correct appraisal and evaluation on intelligence reports. Even when intelligence of likely trouble is available, there is reluctance to make preventive arrests of anti-social elements, thanks to political interference.

These days with the means of faster communication available, the police cannot take any step without the knowledge of some local politician. Politicians also try to pose as friends of victims and never forget to visit the riot-hit areas with an eye on votes. A Union Minister was recently denied entry into Gorakhpur because it was felt that his visit could affect the ruling party's minority vote-bank.

The police department has been politicised to such an extent that the hierarchical control and command of the department has almost been done away with. State politicians in power communicate directly with the officers in charge of police stations to give directions as to what and how any action should be taken and who should be arrested and who should not be touched. It is for this reason that the State Governments do not want to let go their control over the police by fixing tenures of officers, despite the orders of the Supreme Court to that effect.

Interference with the police system by extraneous elements, especially politicians, encourages the law-enforcers to believe that their respective careers do not depend on their performance, but by currying favour with politicians. No wonder decisions taken at powerful political headquarters are implemented without question at the operational level. The frequent bypassing of the normal chain of commands results in the atrophy of the supervisory structure. It, therefore, fails to operate effectively even in matters that do not attract extraneous interference.

The role of police during the 1992-93 Mumbai riots came under severe criticism from several quarters, especially the Srikrishna Commission, which implicated 32 officers for anti-minority bias. The same feelings were expressed by the People's Union of Civil Liberties about the 1984 anti-Sikh riots.

Though the problem of communalism can only be solved through political sagacity, a lot can be done by police officials at the ground level by taking adequate preventive measures. In communally sensitive areas, peace committees should be organised before, during and after the riots. In riot-prone places, action should be taken to direct persons in possession of firearms to surrender them as a precautionary measure.

Nothing is impossible; there are ways to handle every problem. What is required is political will to deal with even the worst of situations. Bertrand Russell once observed: "We have, in fact, two kinds of morality side-by-side, one which we preach but do not practice, and another which we practice but seldom preach."

1.3. Dynastical Menace

With elections to the 14th Lok Sabha around the corner after the dissolution of the 13th Lok Sabha on February 6, 2004, focus has shifted to dynastic rule. Democracy has no scope for dynasties, though certain kinds of dynasties have been thrown to the top both at the State and Centre in our country. Thomas Paine had said: "One of the strongest natural proofs of the folly of hereditary right of Kings is that nature disapproves it; otherwise she would not, so frequently, turn it into ridicule by giving the mankind an ass in place of a lion."

The fact remains that elections are about seizing power in a democracy. The power won by popular consent is reportedly for the good of the people. In democracies, political parties tend to zero in on anything which will fetch them votes. Democracies have also not lagged behind in creating myths around some families, projecting them as dynasties ordained to rule. The Bush regime is reportedly spawning such a huge forest of spouses, sons, daughters, siblings, etc., in positions of power that some columnists in that country call US as a "Nepotocracy". In Sri Lanka, after the assassination of Bandranaike, his wife Sirimavo succeeded and now their daughter is the democratically elected President. Similarly, widows and daughters of the former rulers of Bangladesh have been taking turns to rule that country, as did Ms Benazir Bhutto, daughter of Zulfikar Ali Bhutto, who became the Prime Minister of Pakistan. In India, Jawaharlal Nehru made his daughter Indira Gandhi the Congress president and later she succeeded him as the Prime Minister after the demise of Lal Bhadur Shastri. A Congress president DK Baruah had proclaimed at the height of sycophancy: "Indira is India and India is Indira."

The trouble with full blown sycophancy is that its object comes to believe what his or her underlings say. Indira Gandhi was grooming her younger son Sanjay to take over the reigns of the country, when he was killed in a plane crash. Left with no other alternative, she brought her elder son Rajiv, who was reportedly an excellent pilot with the national airlines into the mainstream of politics. He ultimately succeeded her after her unfortunate assassination by her bodyguards. There was a small interregnum when, after the assassination of Rajiv Gandhi, his wife Sonia Gandhi remained behind the scenes. It was only a question of time before she dethroned Sitaram Kesri and took over the reigns of the Congress party. Now in the family tradition, her son and daughter have made entry into politics as primary members of the Congress party. It is only a question of time before they are given an active role to be groomed for possible occupation of the ultimate and the highest office, which Indian democracy can offer.

It will be unfair to single out only the Nehru dynasty as ambitious and power centric. Kashmir has had three generations of the Abdullahs, starting with Sheikh Abdullah, Mr Farooq Abdullah and now Omar Abdullah. Haryana has had Devi Lal as Chief Minister and now his son Om Prakash Chautala is the Chief Minister. The latter's one son is an MLA and another a Member of Parliament. Similarly, former Chief Minister of Punjab Partap Singh Kairon's sons were MLAs and later ministers. Former Punjab Chief Minister Parkash Singh Badal's son is also a Member of Parliament. Similarly, the son of present Chief Minister of UP, Mr Mulayam Singh Yadav, is also a Member of Parliament. Ms Rabri Devi succeeded her husband Laloo Prasad Yadav as the Chief Minister of Bihar after he had to demit office following his arrest in the fodder scam case.

Many former chief ministers of Madhya Pradesh and Maharasthra, Gujarat, Orissa, Andhra Pradesh, Karnataka, Kerala, Tamil Nadu and a number of other states have ensured the presence of their closest kith and kin or their caste men, either in the States or Central legislature-NTR Ram Rao, Biju Patnaik, Karunakaran. In fact, the effort is to pass on the mantle to the son, daughter or wife. Academically, there is nothing wrong in a doctor's son becoming a doctor or an IAS or an IPS officer's son following in the footsteps of his father or mother by joining their service. There have been cases where almost all members of a family have either become civil servants or doctors or even teachers. But academics apart, the sons and daughters of the members of the political elite start with the advantage that their proximity, to established leaders gives them. Powerful families have traditionally passed their mantle down from one generation to another in India, China, and Japan. Of course, in democracies, dynasties are not like the Mughal or Gupta dynasties. They are subject to the will of the people. People can reject them at the hustings. There is no such thing as automatic succession in free democracies. In fact, there is no such thing as dynasty in 21st century India. However, some self-serving sycophants and hangers-on, for their personal benefit, create dynasties of rulers. Maybe, such people feel that in a democracy people can be fooled into accepting even political non-entities whose sole qualification is that they happen to be born into a particular family.

Any aspirant to future leadership has to base his or her claim not on promises or on belonging to any family, but to past records and credentials. There is no need to be obsessively preoccupied with any dynasty. We need not raise any new dynasty to beat any other dynasty. Of course, Nehru and his progeny are called Gandhis, though they are no relations of Mahatma Gandhi, and have ruled the country with the electorate's consent for over 37 years in independent India. Winning elections is like selling movie tickets, declared Governor of California Arnold Schwarzenneger in his first address, pledging to carry California out of its imminent bankruptcy. For him, running a state is like selling movie tickets. "If I can sell tickets for my movies like Red Sonja or Last Action Hero, I can sell just about anything. California is the easiest sell I've ever had," I beg to differ, Governor Schwarzenneger. Politics is not all about showmanship, though good looks and good speeches matter. There may be a few who are lured by the tag of dynasty or the polish of a public school education. These go a long way in creating charisma.

Like a corporate bigwig has the advantage of putting the members of his family on a footing almost near the top, members of a political dynasty generally do not have to start their career at the grassroots level. They, by and large, start either as members of the state or the national Legislatures, or in a prominent position in the party. Besides, after elections, if they get elected, they claim that it is their merit or nation-building activities which has got them elected and not dynastic connections. Nevertheless, the dynasty factor does not disappear with elections. They are conscious of their status and never fail to remind others of it either. For instance, Punjab Chief Minister Captain Amarinder Singh, is still referred to as "Maharaja".

For want of icons or role models in the country, people will make heroes out of zeroes. We have witnessed filmstars being catapulted into the role of top political leaders. Quite often, reel life merges with real life and the culture of sycophancy helps. Be that as it may, the time for such gimmicks is over. People now prefer to measure people by the yardstick of good governance and performance rather than pedigree and lineage. 21st century India expects much more with more than 50 per cent of the lectorate under 35 years of age. Beware political parties, you can fool some of the people some of the time, all of the people some time, but not all of the people all of the times.

1.4. Regional Outburst

Under our Constitution every citizen has the fundamental right to live anywhere in the country and carry on his profession or trade. Being a 61-year-old democracy, every Indian should know this as well as the fact that nobody is above the law. But vote-bank politics means that if your action is going to benefit the party it is all fair game, even if it is against the law. For starting any political party or for becoming a politician no qualification is required, except that you have to be a rabble-rouser, indulge in hooliganism and be an expert in damaging public property— in short, things which can attract public and media attention.

These days Mumbai is in the news because of a local politician's violent efforts to carve out a niche for himself in Maharashtra politics. Mr Raj Thackeray and his Maharashtra Navnirman Sena want to capitalise on the 'sons of the soil' ideology, much like the Shiv Sena did in the 1960s. Both the Sena and the MNS believe that Maharashtra is only for Maharashtrians, and that they alone should get preference in trade, business, jobs, etc. Also, both these parties believe in violence and brutality to make their point. Expressing aversion towards non-Maharashtrians one of their leaders had said, "*Ek Bihari sou bimari*" (One person from Bihar is equal to a hundred diseases). However, this is nothing new and Mumbaikars are no strangers to such parochial politics.

The State of Maharashtra was formed on May 1, 1960, by splitting Bombay State into Marathi-speaking Maharashtra and Gujarati-speaking Gujarat. Similarly, NT Ram Rao had come to power in 1982 solely on the 'Telugu pride' plank. The demand of a Punjabi Suba led to the trifurcation of old Punjab into Punjab, Harayana and Himachal Pradesh, while Chandigarh was retained as a Union Territory.

Thus, the brand of parochial politics that Mr Raj Thackeray is today pushing is nothing original. While dismissing a PIL seeking action against Mr Thackeray and de-recognition of his party, a Supreme Court bench comprising Chief Justice KG Balakrishnan and Justices RV Raveendran and Markandey Katju on February 23, 2008, expressed their dismay at the 'sons of the soil theory' saying that its divisive nature conflicted with the constitutional guarantee to every Indian citizen to work and settle in any part of the country. The bench elaborated, "We know what is happening. The sons of the soil theory is not acceptable. We will not permit balkanisation of the country."

What the Supreme Court said is unexceptionable and absolutely correct. Nonetheless, it is also true that many conflicts, both in India and abroad, including in Kenya, Uganda, Fiji and many other countries, have their roots in the 'sons of the soil theory'.

Basically what this theory espouses is that the original residents or the natives of a particular place should get preference over those who are not. It blames outsiders for eating into limited resources and thereby making lives miserable for the natives by taking away jobs and other benefits. Surprisingly, while the Constitution lays down the principle of equality, most States overtly or covertly want all available resources and opportunities to go to the locals first. They want to be fair to their own people, which in turn means being unfair to non-natives who come and settle in their States.

What this does is degrade the rule of law. Such parochial politicians are confident that the local administration and the police will not touch them. These hoodlums masquerade as foot soldiers of a populist cause that they know will have some sympathisers. These are usually frustrated, unemployed local youth who have nothing better to do.

Mr Raj Thackeray and his MNS *goondas* were solely responsible for the reprehensible attacks on north Indian students who had come to Mumbai to appear for the Railway Recruitment Board examination. The MNS activists went on a rampage, assaulting the students mercilessly on the day of the examination. These hooligans were also responsible for destroying public property and burning buses after their so-called leader was arrested. And that only happened after the media built up pressure and exposed how the country was being held hostage by this man and how the State Government was simply turning a blind eye to his politics of hate and violence.

The question now arises as to what are the police doing? This has been answered by Prof David H Bailey who says, "In India today, a dual system of criminal justice has grown up, the one of the law and the other of politics. With respect at least to the police, decisions made by police officials about the application of law are frequently subject to partisan review or direction by the elected representatives. The autonomy of the police officials in specific and routine application of law has been severally curtailed. This is not only true of law and order situations. People accused of crimes have got into the habit of appealing to political figures for remission from the law. Police officials, throughout India, have grown accustomed to calculating the likely political effect of any enforcement action they contemplate... Altogether, then the rule of law in modern India, the frame upon which justice hinges, has been undermined by the rules of politics".

The Government of the day, by pampering hooligans and holding back the police from performing their duty, is ruining this nation.

They say every action has an equal and opposite reaction. As per several reports about 35,000 migrants, mostly from Uttar Pradesh and Bihar, have left Maharashtra, out of fear of being beaten up or otherwise physically harmed. If what is being practised by a few in Maharashtra is followed by other States, then nearly millions of Marathis can be equally affected. What is ominous is that the backlash has already begun in Bihar and UP with angry protesters setting trains on fire. Railway stations have been ransacked and in a Marathi School in Kanpur has been damaged.

There is no denying that Mr. Raj Thackeray has taken things too far. The state can no longer afford to sit back. The monster must be tamed before it is too late.

1.5. Defiance to Law and Justice

Goa Education Minister's son Rohit Monserratte was recently arrested in connection with the alleged rape of a German teenager.

The Minister's son, an MBA student, was accused by a German woman of raping her minor daughter in October. It took more than a month for the police to arrest him. As it normally happens, the Minister claimed that the case was politically motivated to tarnish him personally. Finally, the German woman had to withdraw her complaint, claiming that she did so under extreme pressure from some very 'powerful' people.

This is neither the only high profile case involving a Minister and nor will it be the last. A grandson of a former Chief Minister of Punjab was also allegedly guilty of raping a foreign tourist. Another son of a former Chief Minister who is now a Governor of a State had the mortification of being arrested on charges of raping the domestic help. The son of a Director-General of Police from Orissa was not only arrested but also convicted and sentenced for rape. He jumped bail and his father, who had stood surety for him, was suspended from service.

Such is the severity of the problem that high profile people misusing their posts and offices does not surprise anyone anymore. Recently, a Union Minister of State beat up the airport manager of an airline at Patna airport after he was not allowed to board a flight. The only 'fault' of the airline employee was that he did not delay the flight's departure to suit the Minister's late arrival at the airport.

The Union Civil Aviation Minister says that no one has the right to break the law. But the accused Minister in question has claimed that this was all 'mischief' on part of the airline and has subsequently denied assaulting the official. Earlier this year, another politician brazenly abused his power in similar circumstances. A Rajya Sabha MP from Kerala, Mr. PV Abdul Wahab, was accused of entering the cockpit and abusing the pilot. But the MP defended himself, alleging rude behaviour by the latter.

These are just a few instances of arrogance of power tempting the high and mighty to bend rules and resort to high-handedness. Misuse of one's official position to defend oneself in sex scandals and other incidents does not happen only in India. There was the infamous case of former US President Bill Clinton having an affair with a 22-year-old White House intern, Ms Monica Lewinsky. The news of this extra-marital affair and the resulting investigation eventually led to the impeachment of Mr Clinton in 1998 by the US

House of Representatives. But he was subsequently acquitted on all charges (of perjury and obstruction of justice) in a 21-day Senate trial.

Mr. Clinton admitted in the taped grand jury testimony on August 17, 1998, that he had had an "improper physical relationship" with Ms. Lewinsky. The same day he gave a nationally televised statement admitting his relationship with Ms. Lewinsky was "not appropriate".

As per the notes of the former head of French Police Intelligence, Mr. Yves Bertrand, the present French President, Mr. Nicolas Sarkozy, had an affair with the wife of one of his present Cabinet members about four years ago, when he was serving as the Interior Minister. This alleged episode is one of a multitude of damaging secrets reported from the private notebooks of Mr Yves Bertrand.

IMF chief and former French Finance Minister Dominique Strauss-Kahn had been investigated over alleged abuse of power involving a subordinate. He was caught red-handed after the woman's husband discovered an e-mail sent in January, 2008. Mr. Strauss-Kahn owned up to the episode and later stressed that his transgressions had ended. He issued an apology to the woman, the IMF staff and his French TV-personality wife Anne Sinclair for what he called "my error in initiating this relationship". He was let off on the ground that his effectiveness was not affected.

Earlier, Mr. Paul Wolfowitz was forced to resign from his job as President of the World Bank in May 2007 after it was established that he had intervened to secure unmerited promotions and severance payments for his female companion, who was working for the organisation.

As far as our country is concerned, even if somebody is caught with his pants down, the standard excuse is that it is either vendetta or that he was involved due to some extraneous considerations. There has not been a single case where a politician or a public servant-cum-criminal has admitted his offence or felony. Though it is widely claimed that you cannot legislate morality, yet in actual practice little else is done.

The country's law and order system is in a shambles, as has been observed by more than one Chief Justice of India. As per the figures released by the Supreme Court of India, in June 2008, there were over 2.92 crore cases pending in about 12,000 plus subordinate courts, 21 High Courts and the Supreme Court. The figures do not include the cases pending in various tribunals and quasi-judicial bodies such as the Central Administrative Tribunal, Income Tax Tribunal and Debt Recovery Tribunal. If these cases were also to be accounted for, then the arrears would be far beyond the alarming figure of three crore.

Out of the total 2.92 crore cases, over 2.54 crore cases are pending in subordinate courts while 37.43 lakh cases are pending in various High Courts. The Supreme Court's share of pending cases is 45,887.

Uttar Pradesh tops the list of States with the maximum backlog of cases with 48.74 lakh, followed by Maharashtra and Gujarat with 40.45 lakh and 34.20 lakh cases respectively. West Bengal (including Andaman and Nicobar Islands) and Bihar occupy fourth and fifth places with 21.94 lakh and 13.73 lakh cases respectively.

Among the High Courts, Allahabad tops the list with 8.19 lakh pending cases, followed by Madras with 4.28 lakh cases. Bombay, Calcutta and the Punjab and Haryana High Courts have 3.69 lakh, 2.83 lakh and 2.57 lakh cases respectively, all awaiting disposal. The Sikkim High Court has just 80 pending cases. Uttarakhand has 20,984, Himachal Pradesh has 27,690, Jammu & Kashmir has 46,640 and Jharkhand has 49,970 pending cases.

The best disposal has been from the Supreme Court, where disposal was more than filing during January-March 2008. Against a total of 21,429 cases filed, the Supreme Court disposed of 22,68 cases. Unfortunately, the biggest litigant is the Government as 70 per cent of the cases filed involve the state. If the Government redresses the grievances of the people at the initial stage itself, people will not be forced to go to court and the Government will not have to appeal against the decisions of it own quasi-judicial bodies or tribunals or commissions. It is not enough for the Government to simply ensure justice. It should also ensure that justice is promptly administered.

1.6. Power, Corruption and Law

Notwithstanding the laws against corruption, the country has witnessed a steep rise in corrupt practices. Both the volume of money and people involved have reached an all-time high. A Hindi newspaper published from Ranchi recently reported it had an audio CD to prove a Minister of the Jharkhand Government guilty of corruption. The latter had allegedly accepted a bribe of Rs 50 lakh for propping up a candidate in the Rajya Sabha polls held in June 2004. However, the Minister concerned, who was subsequently dismissed, has denied the allegations saying it was a conspiracy to ruin his political career. This is the standard excuse trotted by all who are caught in the net.

The more laws we have, the more loopholes we create to enable the corrupt to escape. Scamsters either go unpunished or are dealt with perfunctorily. The investigation into the Taj corridor project by the CBI led to the registration of a number of cases against officials and politicians in 2003.

But none of the accused was considered pariah either in political or official circles. In fact, all political parties show a keenness to embrace anybody who can add to their kitty. The biggest swindle going on right under the nose of the Central Government is the rampant encroachment on Government or public lands in Delhi. When complaints are made, the standard reply is it is not possible to determine when the land was encroached upon. The Government proposes to videograph all large tracts of unoccupied Government land, ostensibly to fix responsibility as to in which official's time was it encroached.

However, the real problem lies in encouraging slums for vote bank purpose by politicians themselves. Occupation of Government property thus cannot be tackled by the officials. The problem, therefore, has to be addressed by the political class. Unfortunately, however, no politician of any hue is willing to discard populism in favour of hard options and good governance.

There is a saying in Hindi, "When the fence itself starts eating the crop in the field, who will save the field?" This is happening in all aspects of the working of the Government almost every day. The Delhi Police did an excellent job of detecting the leak of CBSE and AIPMT paper leak in April 2004. The CBI arrested two Delhi policemen, including the investigating officer of the case, for allegedly accepting bribe of Rs 2 lakh from the father of prime accused. The accused were caught red-handed while accepting the money.

It was the first installment of the money being handed over to them. It is very disturbing that the law enforcement officials have themselves become partners with law breakers. Earlier, the former Commissioner of Mumbai Police as well as an Inspector General of Maharashtra Police and some other officials, were arrested. This month, a Deputy Inspector General in Tamil Nadu and a Deputy Superintendent of Police were arrested for colluding with the accused in the infamous Telgi stamp scam.

More often than not, the people have arrived at the firm conviction that there is no escape from corruption. Even in bureaucracy, it is a well-known fact that there are plenty of "cold storage" postings for those who would like to go by the book. Political masters deem it wiser to keep such "strange creatures" at a safe distance, away from the administrative mainstream, where they can cool their heels while manning inconsequential departments or posts, irrespective of their professional qualifications and competence. In fact, quite often, competence and skill have nothing or little to do with most postings. There are no laurels for doing any job well or doing it according to the book.

No topdog, whether of the political or bureaucratic class, wants the rule book shown to him every time the laws or rules are bent to accommodate his or her wishes. If somebody does so, it is interpreted as displaying qualities not conducive to "smooth" functioning of the Government or the administration. In reality, such a boss is also unwanted by the corrupt subordinates, as he is inflexible and would come in the way of making money. Sometimes even the colleagues of an upright person are unwilling to associate themselves with him lest it spoils their chances of a "wet" posting.

As for journalists, former Prime Minister Atal Bihari Vajpayee once said, "Journalism started as a mission, turned into a profession, now it's but mere sensation." Notwithstanding what politicians may say about the media, it is largely the press which keeps the Government and public servants on their toes. If it was not for the media, many scams now hitting the front-pages, would not have been exposed.

The public generally admires kindness and generosity, openness, honesty, understanding, and the courage to stand up to what is right. These are qualities which should normally be part of governance. But what they get is discourtesy, greed, acquisitiveness, meanness, egotism and self-interest from the rulers. There is an almost total lack of accountability and transparency. These are the main reasons behind the growth of corruption. In truth, bureaucracy is accountable to its own hierarchy, and politicians to Parliament, and on neither of these does the public have any control.

Even replies to questions raised in Parliament are prepared by the bureaucracy and ministers have to go along with them. Once, when the present Prime Minister was the Finance Minister of the country, I happened to be present at his briefing for the replies to Parliament questions. As Director General of Narcotics Bureau (which in 1993-94 was part of the Finance Ministry), I had gone to see Dr. Singh in connection with my part of the work relating to Parliament. Another section of the Ministry, which had considerable public interface, had prepared replies to a question which amounted to saying that it (Finance Ministry and the banks) had done tremendous public service.

Dr. Singh said that it was all lies. How could he be expected to say that the service provided by the nationalised banks was the best and there was no corruption or bribery? He said he would not lie. But the bureaucrats pleaded with him that as Minister incharge, he must defend his department. He said the Government must focus on improving services rather than finding alibis.

Unfortunately, acquisition of power for personal gains, with a few honourable exceptions, has become the hallmark of our polity. Coalition politics has come to mean a backseat for good governance. When survival in office becomes paramount, it leads to the confirmation of what has been public knowledge for long: That people enter politics to enrich themselves rather than serve the nation. Politics, instead of being public service, has become a vehicle for self-service. Caste politics has further divided the polity. The poor remain where they were while their caste leaders have built palaces and fattened their bank balances. Even our best and tallest leaders avoid talking about caste divisions.

With a view to garner votes, a commission was set up to identify the economically backward sections amongst the higher castes. In reality, there are no benchmarks of political or bureaucratic morality left. These have been lowered to a point of no return. The main issue before us is controlling corruption and ousting the criminal elements from the polity.

Unfortunately, only noises are made to end these problems without anybody tackling them seriously. Nothing that is not proper, upright and honourable can be truly great. Colton said: "In life, we shall find many men that are great, and some men that are good, but very few men that are both great and good." It is for our present leaders to prove they are both great and good.

1.7. The Nexus with Crime

In India, like in any other democracy, voting is a process through which people elect their rulers. The choice of candidates, however, does not rest withthe voters, but on the party leaders. The overriding considerations of the latter are loyalty, winnability and pliability. A candidate's ability or specialisation in any field which can come in handy for the country's development, or for that matter can give the party a positive image, is secondary. This is in contrast to Singapore where political parties woo talent keeping their future prospect in mind. Unfortunately, this does not happen in India. If an official gets a plum post-retirement job, or is given a ticket for contesting elections, it is usually a reward for services rendered to the party in question.

Once in a while, a few independent candidates manage to get into the legislatures, but again they are exceptions rather than the rule. Such candidates are often hampered by the cost of contesting elections which is prohibitive, and, which can range from Rs one crore to Rs 15 crore for a Parliament seat. I know of one case in the last parliamentary election in which the expenses incurred by a political heavyweight who lost reportedly touched Rs. 32 crore! A substantial portion of that amount was spent on purchasing votes and voters, and on bribing other candidates to withdraw, or spoil the chances of some other candidate on caste, religious grounds. Elections have thus become an industry in itself, with tickets changing hands at high prices. Politics has become a profitable business, a commercial enterprise, with low personal investment but astonishing returns.

In the election to the 14th Lok Sabha, about Rs 3,000 crores is expected to be spent by the political parties and individual candidates. A contestant who lost the last election said he was not unhappy as his collections exceeded his expenses by Rs one crore! It goes without saying that he pocketed the excess as labour charges. It is unlikely that there will be any raids or seizure by the Income Tax Department during the election period. This has never happened in the past and there is no reason why it will be any different this year.

Congress president D Sanjiviya had said way back in 1962 that his partymen who were paupers, had become multimillionaires in a short time. The chairman of Ludhiana City Improvement Board Trust said on March 14, 2004, "I got a call from a senior AICC leader that funds to the tune of Rs100 crores are required by the AICC for elections, following which I suspended a Rs 250-crore project. He, however, refused to divulge the name of the caller. He also said, "I am not able to control corruption in the trust and it seems I am a failure and wasting my time by not getting anything done. One person cannot fight the system and that is why I decided to resign. It seems that corruption is institutionalised."

Of course, the Congress has denied the allegations. The fact remains, that elections are an expensive proposition and, as far as possible, no candidate would like to spend his own money. The election laws framed by our legislators are full of loopholes, allowing enough space for money power. Donors to political parties get full tax exemption, but the disclosures of contributions is mandatory and free broadcasting time is provided to recognised parties. With the entry of multiple private news channels, politicians get limited time to debate and air their views. That is the only interesting part of the elections. Otherwise, the political speeches are the same with charges flying thick and fast. Also, notwithstanding their claims and protestations against fielding people with criminal or unsavoury backgrounds, most political parties tend to bend the rules, since winnability is what counts in the battle.

One reason why the desire in candidates to contest and win elections is so strong, is that it confers on them a kind of immunity against any executive action. And if he happens to belong to the ruling party, he can bend the administration. The other reason is that many MPs and MLAs have no other ostensible means of livelihood, except what they reportedly earn from the Government as legislators or as former legislators. Every party is willing to patronise and enrol aya rams and gaya rams as long as they can deliver from either caste or religious vote banks. The unabashed use of caste and religion is encouraging casteism, regionalism and religious fundamentalism, and almost all politicians are party to this.

In recent times, the desperation to win has prompted political parties to rope in film stars, put up roadshows or go on elaborate yatras to trumpet their achievements. Elections have been reduced to a carnival of loudspeakers, public meetings, surrogate advertising, dramas, and plays. Once I told a Union Minister representing a hill constituency, that perhaps he did not have to bribe voters as the hill people are reportedly simple, honest and truthful. He replied that this was the 21st century and that I should wake up to the realities. It was not necessarily in cash that voters expected to be paid. They prefer blankets, heaters or liquor. I asked another candidate how he would foot his election bill. He replied that people give donations as a kind of advance investment, to use his good offices, in case he was elected.

Mounting election expenditure is a matter of concern . Elections at the local, municipal and state assembly levels have become a regular feature of our democracy what with State assemblies often getting dissolved before their terms are over. This is not only a drag on the exchequer, but also encourages populism as against good governance which all political parties claim that they provide. Both Vice-President Bhairon Singh Shekhawat and Deputy Prime Minister LK Advani have been pleading for an amendment in favour of simultaneous elections to State assemblies and Parliament.

The forthcoming elections are seeing some new trends. These polls, unlike in the past, will be fought on issues of economic performance and governance. The BJP has unleashed a flurry of sops for what has come to be known as the "feel-good factor" Concessions range from cheaper airline tickets to computers and cellphones. Cynics have dismissed this largesse as election gimmick. However, in the course of 2004, in which eight per cent growth has been registered over and above a five per cent growth over a decade, this is not quite so. After years of confused politics with frequent changes in governments, the trend is towards a choice between two coalitions. The Congress and its allies and the NDA are competing on promises of better governance and faster economic reforms. The movement towards a two-party coalition system is one of the more positive developments in our politics. The question is whether a two-party coalition system will eventually evolve into a two-party system? And, finally, veterans are giving way to their younger successors cutting across party lines.

Notwithstanding the flaws in the Indian electoral system, the fact is that there is no better alternative than democracy to elect representatives to Parliament. Electoral malpractices abound but the collective decision of voters is most politically correct. As past trends show, people threw out Indira Gandhi with a vengeance in 1975 for imposing Emergency, and then brought her back when a conglomerate of parties which comprised the Janata government failed to provide a feasible alternative. As far this election is concerned, the surveys and polls show the NDA has an edge.The present coalition has been good for the country, and helped it in moving forward in many areas-economy, telecom, external relations, and induction of private players in areas like insurance. However, it would be best to keep our fingers crossed and wait for the "Ides of May" by which time all the parliamentary results will be out.

1.7.1. The Nexus with Treason

The world we live in is not ideal. The rulers are not ideal nor are the people who send criminals to the portals of power as their representatives. The following information about our legislators in 2000 is an eye opener: Twenty-nine had been accused of spousal abuse, 19 had been accused of passing bad cheques, 117 had bankrupted on at least two businesses, three had been arrested for assault, 71 could not get loans dues to bad credit histories, 114 had been arrested on drug related charges, eight had been arrested for shop-lifting, 21 are current defendants on various lawsuits, 84 were stopped for drunk driving in 1998 alone.

At least 100 MPs faced criminal charges ranging from minor misdemeanours like disturbing peace, rioting murder, rape and dacoity. Nearly 33 per cent were found to be involved in heinous crimes. About 12 are charged with murder, 10 with attempted murder and 11 are acknowledged dons.

Even before the present Government secured a vote of confidence from the 14th Lok Sabha, the Manmohan Singh Government faced embarrassment over the induction of Mohammed Taslimuddin into the Council of Ministers because of his criminal antecedents. In fact, it was the Rashtriya Janata Dal president La..ı Prasad Yadav who secured him a berth in the Cabinet when seven cases had been filed against him during the former's tenure as the Chief Minister of Bihar.

There was no stopping or lessening of the cases against him even after the wife of the RJD leader, Mr Rabri Devi, succeeded him as the Chief Minister. There are 11 cases filed against the MP from Kishanganj alone, which are of heinous crimes including attempt to murder, extortion and violation of the Arms Act and cheating. The Minister, like his RJD boss, himself a Union Minister, is on bail, which can be revoked by any competent court. In all fairness to the tainted ministers, it would be safe to assume, that some cases could be the result of personal vendetta or rivalry by their rivals or disappointed opponents. In all fairness to the criminals in positions of power, there is little in their hands, to help the fellow criminals if they go too much out of their way. With a vigilant press and an effective judiciary, the criminals have little chance of escaping if the evidence against them is marshalled and it stands in the court of law

Taslimuddin was earlier included in the HD Deve Gowda-led United Front Government in 1996 as Minister of State for Home, on the insistence of the Bihar unit of the Janata Dal. Following an uproar over his criminal antecedents, he was forced to quit office. With a friendly Government in power, which prefers to overlook the criminal activities of their political supporters, the charge-sheeted politicians continue to roam about though technically they are in jail or hospitals, or in police or judicial custody. The Supreme Court on July 20, this year ruled that Bihar's tainted politician Rajesh Ranjan alias Pappu Yadav be "immediately" shifted from the Patna Medical-College Hospital to the Beur jail. In a related development, the same High Court ordered the dismissal of a fast track court judge in Siwan for granting bail to RJD MP Mohammad Shahabuddin and allowing him to attend Parliament in violation of an earlier HC order. The apex court too has ordered JD (U) MP Prabhunath Singh to surrender in a court in Bhagalpur in a case related to the murder of four persons. Prabhunath had been evading arrest for several years.

Thanks to a spirited judiciary, committed to upholding the highest values and an equally alert and watchful press, the going is to be tough for the criminals masquerading as successful politicians. Criminalisation of politics is not something which happened only in 2004. In the last elections to the 13th Lok Sabha and State assemblies, as many as 700 legislators including 40 MPs with criminal background won. In the 1996 elections, 1,500 out of 13,950 candidates had criminal cases against them. In 2002, as many as 15 MPs and 635 MLAs had cases pending against them. It may appear outrageous that 21 major national and regional political parties of dissimilar and separate ideologies and bitter foes of each other, joined hands to reject the Election Commission's directive in pursuance of the Supreme Court order seeking information on a candidate's possible involvement in any criminal case. They went a step further and passed a law, which was declared void by the Supreme Court. The truth is that all lamentation on the criminalisation of politics by the politicians both inside and outside the legislatures, whether at the State or the national level, is seasonal and opportunistic. Nearly all political parties, except perhaps the Left, believe in power at any cost, even if it means embracing the devil and giving him a share of the cake. They are not bothered about the past of their associates, but what their association can fetch them now and in the future. Even in the present Parliament, as per the affidavits filed, at the time of contesting elections, the following number of elected MP's from the States mentioned against them, had cases pending against them. The list below is out of the eventual winners, and their number comes to exactly 100 out of 543 Members of the Lok Sabha. In other words, it means that almost every fifth member of the Lok Sabha has had, or will have, a brush with the law, with cases pending against them.

Andhra Pradesh: Two; Chhattisgarh: Two; Uttar Pradesh: 21; Bihar: 12; Punjab: Five; Rajasthan: Three; West Bengal: Four; Maharashtra: 12; Kerala: Five; Madhya Pradesh: Seven; Gujarat:

Five; Jharkhand: Six; Karnataka: Six; Haryana: Two; Goa: One; Orissa: Three; Tamil Nadu: Three; Delhi: One. It s true that most cases are old and minor in the perception of the accused. But they no longer take away the odium out of them. The world's largest democracy has nearly one-fifth of its law-makers who, at one time or the other, broke the law which they had sworn to uphold. Compliance with the law is done as per convenience and not as a sacred duty. Earlier, there used to be censure, disapproval and denunciation about anybody involved in court cases being given a party ticket for election to Parliament or assemblies. Now the Lakshman rekha has been crossed by several political parties. While there can be no objection to a criminal becoming a legislator, there is a serious impairment of values if such a person is made a minister. This is because all political parties have such worthies in their ranks in the State as well as the Centre. There is an Urdu saying: Iss hamam mein sab nange hein (in this bath, all are naked). The only job left out of the purview of criminalisation is that of the Prime Minister. (It happened once that a Prime Minister was also charge-sheeted in the infamous JMM bribery case.)

This too may come to pass, if we let things go on as they are. Even today, an accused in a number of serious cases, who is a Union Minister, has declared that one day he would like to occupy the prime ministerial office. One present Union Minister is absconding to evade the execution of an arrest warrant, so that he can get the whole matter stayed from a higher court in appeal. His house had to be searched by the police to trace him. It beats everything. William Shakespeare once said: "If to do were as easy, as to know, what were good to do, Chapels would be Churches and poor men's cottages prince's palaces. It is a good divine that follows his own instructions; I can easier teach twenty, what were good to be done, than be of the twenty to follow mine own teaching."

It is a journey down the hill partly because of the atmosphere of casteism, money and muscles power prevailing in the country, and partly due to the indifference of the good citizens who choose not to vote to keep criminal elements out. It is time a concerted drive was launched by the enlightened citizens and the media to expose the menace, to which our country is falling prey. We have been independent for the last 57 years and, as a democracy, we are responsible for the state of the nation. Opportunity has hair in front; behind she is bald; if you seize her by the forelock, you may hold her. If you let her escape, there is no way you can catch it again. Shall we let this opportunity slip? If we don't, what is there to prevent Abu Salem or Chotta Rajan or Dawood to get a berth in the Rajya Sabha or even Lok Sabha? Some dacoits, earlier, were after all elected with money power. Let not the wake up call be too late.

The author of Mitrokhin Archives (Mitrokhin defected to the UK in 1992 carrying with him classified material which, according to the FBI, was the most complete and extensive intelligence ever received from any source) Vasili Mitrokhin collaborated with Christopher M Andrew, a historian at Corpus Christi College, Cambridge. Prof Andrew is considered an authority on espionage.

The archives devote two chapters to India. It says, "By 1973, the KGB had 10 Indian newspapers as well as a press agency on its pay roll. The newspapers and the agency have not been identified due to legal reasons and apprehension of defamation. During 1972, the KGB claimed to have planted 3,789 articles in Indian newspapers. The figure became 4,486 in 1974 and 5,510 in 1975."

Page 322 of the memoir says, "On at least one occasion, a secret gift of 2 million rupees from the politburo to the Congress was personally delivered after midnight, by the head of PR, Leonid Shebarshin in New Delhi. Another million of rupees was given to a newspaper, which supported Mrs Gandhi." The archives goes on to say on pages 328-329 that a total of 10.6 million roubles was spent in India, to strengthen support for Mrs Gandhi and undermine her political opponents. Money was paid to the Congress through conduits like LN Misra. After his assassination, the KGB gave his widow Rs. 70,000.

The book goes on to say that according to Oleg Kalugin, who became the head of the Soviet Foreign Counter Intelligence in 1973, on one occasion KGB turned down an offer from an Indian minister to provide information in return for $50,000 because it was already well supplied with material from defence and foreign ministries. He is reported to have remarked: "It seemed like the entire country was for sale; the KGB and CIA had penetrated the Indian Government; neither side entrusted sensitive information to Indians, realising their enemies would know all about it the next day."

Expectedly, both the CPI and the Congress have rejected the insinuations made in the archives. However, it is hardly expected of any political party to accept that it had received money from foreign countries in exchange for intelligence information. But does the track record of politicians in our country inspire us to accept whatever they say as unadulterated truth? It is a fact that the Indian Communist parties always looked towards China or Russia for guidance and inspiration. Some former intelligence officials have jumped into the fray calling the allegations as 'concocted'. On the other hand, it is hardly surprising on the part of the US or the erstwhile Soviet Union to increase their sphere of influence either by spreading ideology or giving aid to those in power in other countries.

The KGB disclosures took another curious turn when senior CPI(M) leader Jyoti Basu said on September 19, that he had no knowledge if the Soviet intelligence agency provided funds to the Congress and the CPI. However, he added that the Americans definitely gave funds to the then Prime Minister Mrs Gandhi to curb the spread of Communism in the country. "The former US Ambassador to India Daniel Patrick Moynihan had stated this in his book. Had he not written the book, we would not have known about this," he added.

The revelations should stimulate the Government to reconsider whether FDI should be allowed in print and visual media, which can manipulate public opinion in favour of any country or any issue. It also highlights the need to tighten the process of receipts of foreign funds in India, either through Hawala or otherwise. It is also essential that political parties should realise the need to look at the source of funding more closely because, according to the Archives, the money received from the USSR was used to subsidise the elections campaign of at least nine Congress candidates. The present tendency to overlook the source of money as long as it is received, needs introspection. After all, election is the hallmark of Indian democracy.

Election to Parliament can cost anything between Rs. 5 to Rs. 15 crore and to Assembly at least Rs. 2 crore. Let us not fool ourselves into believing that the archives are full of lies. Call it spying or information gathering, the fact is that such activities are quite common and done without a pang of guilt the world over.

Some time back a "top secret" memorandum written by an official of the US National Security Agency was published in The Observer, London. It reported that in an attempt to further the war resolution, American spies were "mounting a surge" of surveillance targeting countries in the Security Council - especially "against" six undecided countries.

The spy activities intercepted diplomatic communications on home and office telephones and e-mails in search of "the whole gamut of information that could give US policymakers an edge in obtaining results favourable to the US goals." The NSA memorandum requested the help of British intelligence in the surveillance. Daniel Ellsberg, who in 1971 leaked the Pentagon Papers exposing decades of US deception in Vietnam, wrote, "Katharine Gun's revelation of a classified document urging British intelligence to help the US bug the phones of all the members of the UN Security Council to manipulate their votes on the war may have been critical in denying the invasion a false cloak of legitimacy."

As the world teetered on the edge of war in early March 2003 with the United States and Britain pressuring the UN Security Council to give up on weapons inspections and authorise a war against Iraq, a news story broke that made headlines in most parts of the world. The story made UN war resolution lose its momentum. Of course, 29-year-old British woman, Katharine Gun, a translator at the British intelligence agency GCHQ, is facing two-year imprisonment for acting on her conscience and helping to bring to light the spy memorandum.

A former State Department official says, "This is standard procedure. There's nothing atypical about monitoring the comings and goings of foreign diplomats in order to assess their likely behaviour in diplomatic form." And, "Everybody spies on everybody at the United Nations." Another former State Department official reiterated under condition of anonymity. "You can call it spying or you can call it vote getting, but when you're conducting a get-out-the-vote drive - which is what this is - you try to get information any way you can."

It is time we put our own house in order, so that not only our country but our politicians earn a good reputation for themselves. All should know that our leaders cannot be bribed easily. Had it been the case, they would not have been on Government's pay roll. If we cannot totally eliminate the activities of foreigners on our soil, then let us at least be alert and have agencies which do what is expected of them.

1.8. Flippant Creatures: Politicians

Politicians are flippant creatures. They speak what will catch public attention and keep them in the limelight. Once I was talking to a politician from Punjab, who later became its Chief Minister and was even elected to the highest office of the country, about the assets, needs and liabilities of a politician. He said that the biggest asset of a politician is to be in the limelight. Otherwise, he is forgotten. Then, I asked, what should a politician do when there is nothing to write about him in the media? "He should get some news published, howsoever good or bad that may be, even if he has to pay for it," he observed.

Former Union Home Minister Mufti Mohammed Sayeed has called for allowing dual currency in Jammu & Kashmir. He said, "Like Europe, which has one currency, we want the currencies of both the countries (India and Pakistan) in Kashmir on both sides of the Line of Control... As in Europe, where people can travel to nearly 40 countries on a single passport and without any visa, we want people to travel on both sides of Kashmir without any restrictions. We want Jammu & Kashmir to become a model for SAARC nations which will have one economic zone."

In a paper presented about two months ago in Pakistan, Mr Sayeed's daughter, Ms Mehbooba Mufti, in order to please the terrorists, suggested dual power-sharing arrangement between India and Pakistan for 'undivided Kashmir' as an amicable settlement of the contentious issue.

The Mufti's statement shows either his ignorance of the ground realities both in Europe and Jammu & Kashmir, or it is a deliberate attempt to pander to the terrorists. None of the 40 European countries faces the problem of terrorism. As it is, Jammu & Kashmir has been given special privileges which none of the other 27 States and seven Union Territories enjoys. In the Kashmir Valley, which is a Muslim majority area, there has been almost total ethnic cleansing of the minorities.

The result of the terrorist activities, funded and supported from Pakistan-occupied Kashmir and Pakistan, has been that nearly 3.7 lakh Hindus and Sikhs were forced to migrate from the Valley. The continuing terrorist attacks are a part of an orchestrated campaign designed to cleanse Jammu & Kashmir of its indigenous Hindu and Sikh population and bring the area under Muslim control - either through merger with Pakistan, or as an independent, Islamic state. The Talibanisation of the Valley is almost complete.

Indian law prohibits migration of Indians from other States into Jammu & Kashmir, though Kashmiris can go and settle anywhere in the country. IAS and IPS officers of the Jammu & Kashmir cadre, even after serving 40 years in that State, cannot buy property there. A proposal to allot them land in the Valley was termed in the State Assembly as the "return of the East India Company".

On one occasion in the past, land for a Government office was not registered in the name of the President of India as he was not a 'Kashmiri'. Unwittingly, the harping on special status for Jammu & Kashmir has led to the preservation of pro-Pakistani and fundamentalist Muslim character of the Valley.

Liberalism has disappeared and women are forced to wear the Islamic veil and dress in accordance with the code prescribed by the *ulema*. Music, too, has been proscribed. Sometime back, a local Urdu-language newspaper in Srinagar published a Press release issued by Hizb-ul Mujahideen demanding the Kashmiri Pandits leave the State so that it can join Pakistan.

Kashmiri Pandits, instead of being called the victims of terrorism, are euphemistically described as 'migrants'. They languish in refugee camps in squalor and disease on dole from the Government. From time to time, the Chief Minister of Jammu & Kashmir gives a call to them to return. But each time such announcements are made, there is a terrorist attack against the remaining Hindu populace in the State, sending a clear message to the Pandits.

When Mr Sayeed quotes "people of 40 countries" travelling without let or hindrance, can he quote one instance where people from one European country have been forced to quit their hearth and home on the ground of religion or race? Can he cite from any of the 40 countries the extent of terror manifested in Jammu & Kashmir, as shown by a police souvenir of Jammu & Kashmir Police?

It said that there were 56,041 incidents of violence, including 10,093 explosions, 29,931 firing incidents, 5,561 cases of arson, 763 rocket attacks, 4,597 abductions, 229 cases of hanging to death, 275 arms snatching cases and 4,592 other acts of violence between January 1990 and December 2002. It further added that more than 30,000 civilians were killed during the 14-year-long militancy, while 60,000 terrorists died during the same period. The security forces seized 24,785 AK-type rifles, 9,387 pistols and revolvers, 58 carbines, 1,003 RPGs, 91 light machine guns and self-loading rifles, 742 rocket launchers and 2,270 rocket boosters during the same period. Besides, 6,865 kg of RDX, 47,219 grenades, 5,228 anti-personnel mines and 4,176 rockets were captured. Worse, Jammu & Kashmir is related to, in one way or the other, most terrorist attacks taking place in the country.

What India has been doing for the people of Jammu & Kashmir is much more than it has done for those belonging to other States. Since 1990, the State has managed to get more than Rs. 35,571.3 crore in grants and assistance. In 2001-02, for instance, it got, Rs. 4, 577 crore from the Centre, or over 70 per cent of the total assistance to the 27 remaining States and eight Union Territories. It has got more money and financial assistance than any other State every year since 1995. Add to this, projects in the State worth Rs. 25,000 crore being funded by the Centre.

A Kashmiri gets eight-times more money from the Centre than citizens belonging to other States. While per capita Central assistance to other States increased from Rs. 576.24 in 1992-93 to Rs. 1,137 in 2000-01, that for Jammu & Kashmir spiralled from Rs. 3,197 to Rs. 8,092. To get a perspective, translate the numbers: If this cash were to be dispatched by money order, each Kashmiri family (with five members on an average) will get Rs. 40,460 every year.

For all that tall talk of autonomy or independence, the fact is that Jammu & Kashmir cannot sustain itself without the Centre's support. In 2001-02, the State spent Rs. 7,516.6 crore, of which Rs. 4,577 crore - or 60 paise of every rupee spent - came from the Centre. The State's non-development expenditure was Rs. 2,829 crore, including a salary bill of Rs. 1,193 crore, while its revenue was barely Rs. 1,095 crore.

Mercifully, Mr. Sayeed's idea of using Pakistani currency in Jammu & Kashmir and allowing safe passage to terrorists has no takers in the country.

1.8.1. Flippancy

Politicians are predisposed not to see spending Other People's Money as a problem, because spending Other People's Money is what politicians do for a living. If politicians thought there were something wrong with it, they would be in a different line of work.

- Michael F Cannon

The UPA Government has decided to provide a relief package to dependents of terrorists — those men who fought against the integrity of India and were killed by the security forces in encounters in Jammu & Kashmir. They did nothing for the country except attempting to destabilise it and kill innocent civilians. They tried their best to demoralise and assassinate those who were standing against them and for our nation.

The extent of damage done by the terrorists, whose families are to be rewarded, can be gauged from the souvenir of Jammu & Kashmir Police released in 2003. It says that there were 56,041 incidents of violence, including 10,093 explosions, 29,931 firing incidents, 5,561 cases of arson, 763 rocket attacks, 4,597 abductions, 229 cases of hanging to death, 275 arms snatching cases and 4,592 other acts of violence from January 1990 to December 2002.

More than 30,000 civilians were killed during the 14-year-long militancy. The security forces seized 24,785 AK-type rifles, 9,387 pistols and revolvers, 58 carbines, 1,003 RPGs, 91 light machine guns and self-loading rifles, 742 rocket launchers and 2,270 rocket boosters during the same period. Besides, 6,865 kg of RDX, 47,219 grenades, 5,228 anti-personnel mines and 4,176 rockets were seized. Due to terrorism, 3.70 lakh Hindus and Sikhs were forced to leave the Valley and there has been almost total ethnic cleansing of the minorities from there.

The Government decision is, hence, shocking. The policy is the first of its kind in the whole world. It will cover hundreds of families whose men took to guns and led the Pakistan-backed separatist movement, killing and maiming thousands of innocent civilians and men of security forces. Imagine if the US were to follow such policy, it would give compensation and pension to the families of all those who were responsible for the 9/11 attack or killers of President Kennedy, or Sri Lanka would extend similar treatment to the kin of those who killed its two Presidents or Bangladesh would compensate the killers of Sheikh Mujibur Rahman!

If implemented, the policy will make India look foolish in the eyes of the world, especially since our rulers are crying hoarse over terrorism. Incidentally, India is still bound by the UN resolution that demands strict action against terrorists. That the Government has also decided to come out with an aid package for the Kashmiri Pandits, rendered refugees in their own country, must have been an afterthought. Now, if the Government decision applies to the killers in Jammu & Kashmir, there is no reason not to extend it to other terrorists - Maoists and rebels in the North-East. The following chart will give an idea of the terrorists and killers in the other parts of the country.

Forty-five per cent of the country's geographical area, covering 220 districts, is in the grip of insurgency. In the last 20 years, 64,000 people have been killed in terrorist violence. In October 2003, 55 districts in nine States were affected by Maoist violence. In October 2004 it spread to 156 districts in 13 States. Since 1989, 13,000 civilians and 5,500 security personnel have been killed in Naxalite violence. Since that is so, the Government should ask itself why peace-loving taxpayers should foot the bill to compensate terrorists' kin just because it may help the Congress grab some extra votes when Jammu & Kashmir holds its next Assembly election.

The compensation money is added to the following bonanza that only one State, Jammu & Kashmir, is fortunate to receive from the Union. On November 17, 2004, Prime Minister Manmohan Singh had announced an "economic revival plan" of Rs. 24,000 crore for Jammu & Kashmir in Srinagar. That was a grant of an additional Rs. 5,712 per capita. In the period 2000-2003, the State got Rs. 13,188 crore, which is more than three times what a much poorer State, Bihar, got - Rs. 4,047 crore. When you consider the Rs. 14,085 crore net resource transfer by the Centre, with Rs. 13,188 crore as a grant, you will get an idea of the magnitude of dole that Jammu &

Kashmir gets. A similar "economic revival plan" for Bihar would amount to Rs. 47,458 crore.

The Jammu & Kashmir Government employs 3.5 lakh people, making it a ratio of 34.5 Government employees to every thousand persons. To get a better idea of the enormity of the State's assistance in employment, note that the Rajasthan Government employs less than double the number of people despite being about five and a half times bigger than Jammu & Kashmir in terms of population.

Why such largesse for Jammu & Kashmir when the State does quite well in terms of socio-economic development? Its literacy level is at the national level (65.4 per cent). Its sex ratio (923:1000) too is almost at par with the national average (933:1000). Its birth rate (19.9:1000) is lower than the national average (25.8), its death rate (5.4:1000) lower than the national average (8.5/1000) too. With infant mortality rate at 45:1000, per capita income at Rs. 12,399, 10th Five Year Plan per capita allocation of Rs. 14,399, it has no reason to complain about the Centre's doles.

It is nobody's case that Jammu & Kashmir does not get enough. In 2002-2003, the State raised a mere Rs. 936 crore by way of taxes when its total non-tax revenue was Rs. 4,745. Bihar collected Rs. 2814 crore by way of taxes and had a total non-tax revenue of just Rs. 2062 crores. In the last 10 years its poverty level has dropped from 25.17 per cent to a mere 3.48 per cent. The poverty level in India is around 26 per cent. Quite clearly, therefore, the nation's generosity and bounty is lavished upon Jammu & Kashmir very unfairly even as the State Government's accounts have not been audited for over a decade. No one really knows what was spent where and who got what.

The Indian Government's decision amounts to the Government rewarding the terrorists for killing our brave soldiers. It may be no surprise, if the Government comes out with a package to offer a similar scheme to the perpetrators of the 1993 Mumbai blasts, 2006 trains bombings, the Sarojini Nagar and Govindpuri blasts and perhaps even the next of kin of the terrorists who attacked the Parliament House as well as those who attacked the Jammu & Kashmir Assembly. The media has already hinted that all this is being done, in view of the forthcoming general election. If that's true, it proves what Joseph Sobran said about the US, which is also applicable to our country: "The difference between a politician and a pickpocket is that a pickpocket doesn't always get indignant when you tell him to keep his hands to himself."

1.9. Hold the Drink

RSS sarsanghchalak KS Sudarshan, in an interview to a TV channel in the second week of April, said that former Prime Minister Atal Bihari Vajpayee and BJP president LK Advani should retire and make way for the younger generation. The two concerned may not agree with his argument, but it will be better if the country does not ignore it altogether.

Mr Sudarshan reminded, "Atalji has been saying again and again that he's tired and getting old. So we asked them to step aside and bring new faces." Asked as to who should be the replacements, the sarsanghchalak said that it was for the BJP to figure that out. He further observed, "When he (Vajpayee) became the Prime Minister, we told him that as he was getting old and needed someone to look after him, it would be good if his son-in-law could take care of him. But I asked him to ensure that he did not interfere in the Government or party affairs. Mr Vajpayee said my suggestions were good, but it was a bit difficult for him to follow them."

In a forthright assessment, the RSS sarsanghchalak rated Mr Vajpayee as an inferior Prime Minister. He placed him not only behind Jawaharlal Nehru and Mrs. Indira Gandhi, but also below PV Narasimha Rao. In a frank assessment of Mr. Vajpayee's private secretary, for whom the then Prime Minister had once threatened to resign, the RSS chief observed, "He was aligned with both Ms Sonia Gandhi and us." Later the private secretary refuted the charges levelled against him.

As expected, the BJP, a political arm of the RSS, dismissed Mr. Sudarshan's observations. It is surprising given the fact that the post of a sarsanghchalak is sacrosanct for both the BJP and RSS. Mr. Sudarshan was only expressing the need of grooming the younger generation. Nobody lasts forever, and not often do we see a politician retiring gracefully. One should realise that RSS is both the ideological and spiritual guide of the BJP. Moreover, Mr. Sudarshan was stating a truth when he said that Mr. Vajpayee and Mr. Advani (both aged 80 and 77 respectively) should make room for generation-next.

At the BJP's silver jubilee celebrations, the former Prime Minister regretted that he had been unable to function as efficiently as before, and wished success to the party with Mr Advani at the helm. The issue of leadership is an internal affair for any political party. But one should remember that India is a country with a youthful workforce making its mark abroad. In contrast, its leaders normally flourish politically between the ages of 70 and 80. Western countries with ageing population prefer to elect young politicians. No wonder, their decision-making is quick and more effective.

John Kennedy was elected the President of the US at the age of 43. The point is simple: If 43 is old enough to be a leader of the most powerful country, then 70 and above is too old. Indian politics, in contrast, is dominated by grandfathers who are well past their active life. Some of them alternate between hospitals and offices, and sleep through their official meetings. Some politicians of the CPI (M) have been honest enough to seek retirement on the ground of age. Government departments headed by the old leadership is less likely to show any dynamism in touching new horizons. Our politicians have crossed all limits of retirement age. Supreme Court judges retire at the age of 65 and Government officials at 60, but a politician can carry on till he dies. Besides, there is a minimum criteria of education and age for clerical jobs. But no such obligation has been made for politicians.

In fact, the country's leadership is quite touchy not only about age, but also physical fitness. A few years back, the Time magazine introduced then Prime Minister Vajpayee as a person "who drank heavily in his prime and still enjoys a nightly whiskey or two at 74" It added that Mr Vajpayee "takes painkillers for his replaced knees and has trouble with his bladder, liver and one remaining kidney" It further wrote, "A taste for fried food and fatty sweets plays havo with his cholesterol. He takes a three-hour snooze every afternoo on doctor's orders and is given to interminable silences indecipherable ramblings and, not infrequently, falling asleep i meetings." The article went on to say that Mr Vajpayee would be a unusual candidate to control a nuclear arsenal. The Time repor quoted a Russian correspondent who claimed that Mr Vajpayee di not appear to be very attentive during his meeting with Russia President Vladimir Putin. The report regarded Mr Vajpayee' stewardship as "less and less comforting". It said that the frail bachelor "seems shaky and lost, less an aging sage than an ordinary old man". Quoting a diplomat, the article wrote that Mr Vajpayee appeared "half-dead" during his meeting with a Western Foreign Minister.

In India, special rights of the Press and the Government control most of the people's life. Not surprisingly, the criticism of those in power is mostly avoided here. So the first reaction of the then Government, as well as the media, was to conceal the Time report. Not a word was said about it until an independent newspaper decided to break the silence. Then, as usual, there was a mad rush to brand the report as a part of a conspiracy by forces inimical to India. Others sought an apology from the magazine, and called the report baseless and mischievous. Still others accused "forces within the country (of having) aligned with the outside forces to malign the country's leadership". Indian media is generally reluctant to talk about the political leaders' private life, including his age and health, especially when he is in power.

If the two-year-old Time report and observations of the RSS sarsanghchalak can make the BJP and other parties realise the need to infuse new blood in the decision-making, this would do a great service to the nation. There is nothing wrong in getting old. Everybody goes through this process. But one should realise that the energy level differs from age to age. When the Government retires executives at the age of 60, then there is no reason why our leaders on the verge of 'expiry' should carry on indefinitely.

Incidentally, the age of retirement for the Government servant in 1963 was 55. It was subsequently raised to 58 and it now stands at 60. There is an unhealthy tradition in India to glorify the politician in power. Nobody talks of their lapses. Most politicians place their personal and petty factional interests above the interests of the country and the party they actually represent. They are motivated more by the lust for power, position and perk. Anyone raising any issue not to their liking or need, is considered a "political enemy". Politicians seek immortality through politics, both in India and abroad. The list includes many of the great and the notorious alike - Ataturk, Stalin, Suharto, Henry Parkes. No wonder, Marshal Tito of erstwhile Yugoslavia once observed, "Political death is the most horrible death of all."

Politicians in power, with exceptions like Prime Minister Manmohan Singh, consider themselves eternal and immortal. They should learn to retire gracefully, though it is a difficult and tough job. Nobody can stop an idea whose time has come. The idea of politicians retiring at some age is bound to bear fruit. Truth goes through three steps: First, it is ridiculed; second, it is violently opposed; finally, it is accepted as self-evident.

1.9. Favouritism

The purpose of elected representatives at the Centre or in the States, as well as of Government employees either with the Central or State Governments, is to administer and govern in the best interest of the citizens of the country.

According to one NGO, the aggregate cost of governance by 800 politicians at the Centre, the 6000 in 30 States, and the 18.7 million employees of the Central and State Governments, cost the country about Rs. 1800 crore per day or Rs. 650,000 crore a year. About 1.87 per cent of the population governs 1020 million Indians. This works out to about $138 billion or nearly 30 per cent of India's GDP!

The basis of governance in our country is the Constitution. All institutions are formulated, regulated and run as per the rules laid down by the Constitution, including the fundamental rights and the appointment of constitutional authorities. The constitutional institutions include all judicial appointments of the High Court and the Supreme Court, appointment of the Election Commission and the appointment of the governors. Article 153 of the Constitution says there shall be a Governor for each State.

The Governor shall be appointed by the President by warrant under his hand and seal. The former will hold office during the pleasure of the President. He shall hold office for a term of five years from the date on which he is appointed.

However, the Inter-State Council, which consists of all the chief executives of the State governments (that is, the chief ministers, or the governors, where the State is under the President's rule), as well as the Central Government, and is headed by the Prime Minister, has accepted the Sarkaria Commission recommendation about gubernatorial appointments.

It has accepted a code for the appointment of governors in the future, under which they would be barred from entering active political life-that is, after they end their tenure. They, however, can be appointed for a second term. Another of the commission's recommendations, which has been accepted by the Inter-State Council, is that the appointment of Governor would be in consultation with the respective State Government.

The Governor's office has long been looked at as some kind of central interference in the governance of a State. Technically, all holders of constitutional posts hold their offices during the pleasure of the President, which in reality means the Government of the day.

But in actual practices, some of these constitutional posts, especially of governors, have become sinecures to reward the faithful or all those who have toed the party or done a government's bidding all their lives. Such appointments have now become political in nature. They are done either to get rid of the inconvenient members or shut the mouth of a politically inconvenient colleague or other party men.

In this era of coalitions, it is not uncommon for ruling partners to demand a share of the pie of gubernatorial appointments. The Raj Bhavans have also been reduced to a refuge of the dead wood of political parties. It would not be wrong to say that there is no criterion or minimum qualification for the appointment of governors. The closer such a worthy is to the grave, the better are his chances of appointment.

It is, therefore, nothing unusual to see a few governors demitting their office horizontally despite the best of medical facilities. Left to the bureaucracy, had they had their way, they would have "encadred", even the Raj Bhavan in their jobs. But perhaps I have jumped the gun. The fact is, without even "encadring", a number of Raj Bhavan jobs are held by retired bureaucrats, police officers, judges and Army officials. This is a kind of an informal quota and temptation held to various segments so that each one of their members can hope to adorn the Raj Bhavan some day.

The rest are headed by the appointees, who at one time or the other, belonged to the ruling party or parties or were its sympathisers or supporters. Regardless of whether a person has affiliations to any political party, the fact is that all such appointments are political gifts or rewards or a parking slot, and are indeed politically sponsored.

The absence of any criterion makes it easy to make such appointments, which requires lobbying, political pressure and canvassing. Once a Joint Secretary, who was my batch-mate since we joined service the same day and in the same year, told me that for two posts of joint secretaries in the Commerce Ministry, 153 recommendatory letters had been received from a couple of chief ministers, Union ministers and MPs.

It is easy to conceive the number of recommendations, which might be received by the Prime Minister of the day, for such appointments. After the election in 1977, the first shot in this direction was fired by the Janata Party Government, which asked all governors to resign. In fact, it went a step further and asked all State governments to quit and ordered fresh elections to the State assemblies.

This exercise was repeated when Indira Gandhi returned to power in 1980. It has become a well established norm that when a change of Government takes place at the Centre, all the former appointees call are told to quit. They see the writing on the wall and seem to think that voluntarily leaving their jobs is a more honourable option, than to be dismissed.

The drill in the Home Ministry for withdrawing the Presidential Pleasure is almost set. A senior Home Ministry official rings up the governor to be removed and requests him to send in his resignation. Rarely has there been a case in which a governor facing the sack on the change of the Government has not complied with the request. A political party, in the former NDA Government has urged the present Government to not remove the governors appointed by it, and has expressed the hope that it would not be done. But the new regime at the Centre has sacked four governors.

Perhaps it would have been better not to make such a suggestion. In America, all presidential appointees sink or swim with the incumbent. Though we do not have a presidential form of government, in actual practice, most governors are political appointees.

It would raise the standard of public life if all political appointees resigned on their own with the change of Government, as the Lieutenant Governor of Delhi did, whose term, in any case was about to get over. It would save them the embarrassment of being asked to leave post-haste, and sometimes unceremoniously. When one's innings is over, it is time to clear the field and say a graceful good-bye. But, as they say, hope springs eternal in human breast.

It is time to remind what Lord Krishna said in the Gita: "It is the wonder of wonders that people should see others dying, but somehow feel that death would not touch them or forget them." It is also time the practice of alternating between active politics and gubernatorial appointment was done away once for all. It would be a good idea to have a law-instead of a code which has no authority or legal sanction-that once a person has held the office of the Governor, he be debarred from participating in active politics and from holding any other office in the Government, as it has been done in the case of appointments of the Central Vigilance Commissioners.

1.10. Striking at Work Ethos

Strikes seem to have become the flavour of season. The Government is the largest employer in the country with a total of 18.7 million employees of the State and Central Governments.

The Finance Commission had this to say about the Central Government's employees salary bill of 2002 including pensions, "More than 98 per cent of staff strength lies in Group C and D employees or what the Fifth Pay Commission calls supporting and auxiliary staff who account for about 95 per cent of the wage bill currently at Rs. 30,230 crore (including allowances, but excluding pensions of another Rs. 15,000 crore. The total bill now has crossed Rs. 70,000 crore in case of the Central Government. "

According to a Hyderabad based NGO the cost of governance of India with 800 politicians at the Centre and 6000 in the States, and 18.7 million employees of the Central and State Governments is about Rs. 1800 crore. This comes to about US$138 billion or nearly 30 per cent of India's GDP. Still each successive regime at the Centre and the States promises more Government jobs. But more jobs do not necessarily mean more productivity. Fragile governments with a tenuous majority conveniently indulge in populist measures which are not necessarily in public interest. The orders and observations of the judiciary are overlooked for fear of annoying the allies with whose support the Government survives.

In fact, the executive not only expects but conveys implicitly and explicitly the enforcement agencies to deal with all agitations and strikes with kid gloves. Take for instance the ongoing strike against the modernisation of airports. The airport employees struck work against Government's proposal to entrusting the work to private agencies.

Private operators would have expected their employees to earn their salary by putting in their best. However, the work ethics in Government are underscored by the lackadaisical approach of the various departments. Indeed, the reason behind the strike by the airport employees from February 1 to 5 was to safeguard their jobs. The strike involved not only work stoppage but also was calculatively announced to disrupt normal life. It also grossly violated the guidelines laid down by the Supreme Court.

The apex court has repeatedly ruled that nobody has a fundamental right to strike. It also held in 1998, while dismissing the CPI(M)'s appeal against a Kerala High Court judgment banning strikes that "No political party or organisation can claim that it is entitled to paralyse industry and commerce in the entire State or nation and is entitled to prevent the citizens not in sympathy with its viewpoints, from exercising their fundamental rights or from performing their duties for their own benefit or for the benefit of the State or the nation." In the same case (CPI(M) vs Bharat Kumar), the apex court had said, "There cannot be any doubt that the fundamental rights of the people as a whole cannot be subservient to the claim of fundamental right of an individual or only a section of the people."

In the 1962, Kameshwar Prasad vs State of Bihar case, the Supreme Court upheld the rule prohibiting strikes. It said the rule "cannot be struck down, as there is no fundamental right to resort to a strike." At the same time, it knocked down another rule forbidding employees to hold even demonstrations. It said, "A ban on demonstrations violated the fundamental right to freedom of speech and expression as well as to assemble peaceably."

Again in 2002, the Supreme Court ruled on the law on strike while upholding Ms Jayalalithaa Government's tough action against 1.70 lakh employees who had struck work for three weeks despite the invocation of ESMA. The court said (a) there is no fundamental right to go on strike (b) there is no legal/statutory right to go on strike (c) there is no moral or equitable justification to go on strike. It added that "strike as a weapon is mostly misused".

The Delhi High Court's observation on a petition filed by AAI on February 2, 2006, was, "Agitators can't hold dharnas/ demonstrations within 500m from the main gates of the airports all over the country. The right to strike must be balanced with larger public interest. The striking employees cannot cause loss to public property, inconvenience to the public at large." It also issued a direction, against "continuing the strike in any manner and creating any obstruction in the functioning of the domestic and international airports".

Despite the High Court orders passengers flying in and out of airports faced severe inconveniences. The terminals remained dirty and toilets were virtually unusable. Besides, the employees had laid siege on the roads in front of the airports to prevent passengers from reaching the terminals in order to fulfill their objective of shutting down the airports. Apprehending that the strike could turn violent, the security forces had to be on high alert. The agitators' foremost intention was to bring about a break down of law and order and compel the authorities to use force.

In another case in order to sabotage the opening of another fast track court in the Capital lawyers of the Delhi Bar Association demonstrated violently in January 2006. Hundreds of lawyers marched towards the mediation cell on the third floor of the Tis Hazari Courts building breaking through police barricades shouting slogans against the Chief Justices of India and the Delhi High Court. Their demands included the closure of mediation cell opened to resolve long-standing disputes pending between litigants. They are even now protesting against the newly opened Rohini court complex.

Unfortunately, even the elite do not respect the highest judiciary if a ruling does not suit them. However, it must also be admitted that it is only protests which move powers that are otherwise unresponsive. Obviously, Mahatma Gandhi's methods are being applied in the wrong way. It is a problem with Indians that they put self above society's interests.

It is hard to explain how the opening of a new court can clash with lawyers' interests if the common objective of both is to provide prompt justice. Strikes obstructing the working of courts directly affect the life and liberty of persons who are on trial or in jail. 26 million cases are pending in the courts, some for over 20 years. Litigants routinely become old and some even die waiting for the final judgment. This prolonged delay in the disposal of the cases further worsens the situation.

Democracy cannot function effectively without an expeditious judicial system. In other words justice delayed is democracy denied. The problem is unless one becomes a nuisance for others, one is not heard. What we are witnessing is a strife of interests masquerading as a contest of principles. This is the reason behind most strikes. It eventually boils down to the fact that there is only one power that really counts.

The power of political pressure and the knowledge of its application. What we need is forward-looking leadership which can tackle the problems facing the nation so that the country can progress peacefully. There is a difference between a politician and leader. While a politician focuses only on the next election a statesman thinks of the next generation. The choice is left to the leaders - whether they desire to be statesmen or self-serving petty politicians content to live by the day.

2. Maoism

On July 25, the Chattishgarh Assembly held a secret sitting for the first time. No visitors or journalists were allowed inside the House. The secret session was called to discuss the Maoist menace, described by Prime Minister Manmohan Singh as the "biggest internal security challenge ever faced by our country".

Chief Minister Raman Singh said that in-camera sessions were to allow members to discuss the issue "openly and freely". There, legislators avoid speaking out either about the Maoists or measures to be taken. They fear they may be targeted, even killed. So MLAs had been briefed not to speak about the secret session. Even minutes of the discussion have been kept under a veil of secrecy.

This underscores the fact that the menace of Maoists is no less than a war. People have not forgotten the attack on Parliament on December 13, 2001, or the October 30, 2001, attack on Jammu & Kashmir Assembly. Then, should legislators have gone into hiding there too - as a sign of surrender? As per the Union Home Ministry, Maoism and other Left-wing extremism-related incidents are outnumbering the strikes by terrorists in Jammu & Kashmir.

As many as 550 attacks by Left-wing extremists were recorded in the affected States, as compared to 466 terrorist attacks between January 1 and April 30, 2006. In the same period, 281 persons, including security personnel, were killed in Maoist attacks till April 30, 2006, while the fatal casualties in terrorist acts in Jammu & Kashmir totalled 141. While 516 civilians were killed in 2005 in 1,594 incidents of Maoist violence, 219 civilians were killed in 550 incidents during the first four months of 2006.

Moreover, 153 security personnel were killed in 2005 in Maoist-hit States where 62 more were murdered till April 30, 2006. On the other hand, 223 Maoists were killed in 2005 and 93 till April 30, 2006.

The Maoists have grown from 156 districts in 13 States in September 2004 to 170 districts in 15 States by February 2005. Their aim is to paralyse the administration of the country. They have warned that Maoist guerrillas, numbering more than 20,000, could target industries and the Railways in a bid to bring mining activity in Orissa, Chhattisgarh, Bihar and Jharkhand to a standstill.

Many experiments have been tried with a number of terrorist groups to draw the Maoists back to the mainstream. These include the repeal of strict laws like POTA and TADA, the unilateral ceasefire by the Government in Jammu & Kashmir, talks held with the separatist Hurriyat Conference in that State, talks with Maoists in Andhra Pradesh, ULFA in Assam and the Naga militants. In the North-East, the Prime Minister's efforts to rope in ULFA for talks have been rebuffed, despite two rounds of talks with the People's Consultative Group. The Army was directed to abandon anti-ULFA operations midway to create a 'conducive atmosphere' for dialogue. It only helped the terrorists to regroup and reorganise, rejecting all Government initiatives.

Populism, just before the 2006 Assam election ensured that the Foreigners Act and other stringent rules were amended to make it compulsory for all illegal immigrants to be tried by a tribunal. In the confusion, not a single deportation has taken place since, on July 12, 2005, the Supreme Court struck down the controversial IMDT Act. The same story has been repeated in the negotiations with Naga militants too.

In Andhra Pradesh, the Maoists used the 2004 ceasefire to regroup and work out new strategies of attacking the state. The result is there for all to see: After regrouping, the Maoists carried out 1,533 attacks in 2004 and 1,594 in 2005. The more than a decade long terrorism in Punjab was dealt with a crushing blow without interlocutors, who come in plenty. If any interlocutor can solve the problem of terrorism, what for do the Prime Minister, the Home Minister and their bloated Ministries with officers - who even looking after the cleanliness of bathrooms of their offices - exist?

Whenever terrorists attack, predictable rhetoric of condemnation and calling the episode a cowardly act follows. Our politicians, while dealing with any problem, resort to doublespeak. On the one hand, they say that terrorism will be eliminated; on the other, they talk of "peace process".

Double talk has an adverse effect on those fighting murderers and assassins. Security forces, bearing the brunt of guns, armaments and firepower of terrorists, get the impression that their lives are expendable, as the leaders flip-flop between pursuit and peace alternately. When force is necessary, it must be applied boldly, decisively and completely. It must also be backed by strong legislations that protect those on the forefront of the battle.

As the laws stand now, the standard of proof required to convict a terrorist is impossible to get. You need a proof and a witness who might not have just seen the crime, but also could identify the criminals and further be foolhardy enough to depose against them in an open court. He/ she must also be willing to go again and again to the court, as it is not uncommon for lawyers to demand adjournments till the witnesses get fed up. Again, the witness must be willing not to expect any magnanimity or charity from those against whom he deposes - without any protection from the state, as there is no witness protection programme in our country.

Over 6,000 persons have been killed in different parts of India in Maoist-related violence in just over a decade. Landmines, improvised explosive devices, targeted attacks on the police and civilian personnel are employed extensively. Intelligence agencies have evidence of large-scale extortion by Maoist groups from targeted individuals and organisations. Documents recovered in 2005 from the coastal regions of Andhra Pradesh by the police contained accounts of money extorted: From a Telugu Desam Party member, it was Rs. 500,000; from bidi leaf contractors Rs. 60,000, from lorry owners Rs. 20,000, and from an administrative block officer Rs. 5,000. This is only the tip of the iceberg.

The Maoists who seized power in Nepal have only emboldened their ideological companions to have similar ambitions in India. Already, the Indian terrorists have made no secret of this desire.

The Government needs to adopt a two-pronged strategy of talking peace and suppressing violence firmly at the same time. It is the duty more of the Centre than the States to ensure that citizens are not harassed and are well protected.

3. Public can Cure Political Cancer

The Chief Election Commissioner, Mr JM Lyngdoh, in a television interview in December 2003 said that politicians are like cancer to society. He is not the only one to have expressed such views. Abraham Lincoln once said: "If ever this free people, if this Government is ever utterly demoralised, it will be, from this incessant human wriggle and struggle for office, which is but a way to live without work."

To be a doctor, you need to study medicine, to be an engineer, you need to study engineering, to be a lawyer, you need to study law, but to be a successful and a triumphant politician, you only need to be an expert in the art of winning elections. It is a paradox, but too true, that two kinds of men best succeed in politics. The first category is of people with no principles, but of great talent. The second is of no talent, but of one principle, that is implicit obedience to their political party bosses. An amiable but correct or right politician is no match for a loud mouthed politician, who might be tenaciously and persistently wrong.

William Shakespeare said: "A politician is one,that would circumvent God. There are no rules or conditions either fixed variable, or the requirement of a degree, to become a politicians."

The only thing that bars a person from becoming a politician is imbecility or insanity. The Chief Election Commissioner has been damned for saying what is public knowledge. But where he has erred is in tarnishing all politicians with the same brush. There are more honest and dedicated politicians than those whom the CEC had probably in mind. Bashing of the electoral processes and politicians is normal in any democracy, as they are the most visible part of the governance. Compared to what Americans think of their politician, what the CEC has said about Indian politicians is just short of a tribute to them or calling them angels.

William Anderson once wrote: "Political elections do not choose leaders of society. Rather, they are an exercise in which groups of people choose individuals who will assist them in looting other groups of individuals, those folks who were unfortunate enough not to be able to elect their own political strongman." The process can be downright blatant, as is the case in African and Asian countries, or it can be relatively subtle, as it is in the United States, where the trappings of "constitutionality" and "rule of law" hide many of the more nefarious goings on".

It is a fact that corruption is far more widespread and universal in the political class than previously conceived. Evidence of it is available everywhere including in developing and even highly industrialised countries like Japan, Korea or Indonesia, Pakistan, Bangladesh and, of course, our own country, wherein prominent politicians, including presidents and prime ministers and ministers, have faced charges of corruption. This represents a method or an approach of privatisation or disinvestment of the state in which its power is not shifted to the market as privatisation is normally understood, but to politicians, government officials and bureaucrats in position of authority. A doorkeeper of American Congress said of the politicians there: "Eighty per cent were hypocrites, 80 per cent liars, 80 per cent serious sinners except on Sundays. There is always boozing and floozing...I don't have enough time to tell you everybody's name."

Political leaders and parties cutting across the party lines have condemned either openly or subtly the Chief Election Commissioner's critical remarks against politicians. Some of them said that such observations by a constitutional authority would weaken democracy. They also felt it will diminish the sanctity of the high constitutional post and called his remarks "improper" and advised him to "observe restraint". The Prime Minister himself described his remarks as improper. There is no doubt that it is the voters who decide who to vote for and it is the job of the Election Commission to conduct free and fair elections. It is a fact that there is a great deal of corruption and nepotism in our political life. It exists in a larger measure in the bureaucracy.

The war of words on any issue is unending. Sometimes truth is more bitter than any other pill. The remarks of the Election Commissioner, though not to the liking of the political class, should lead to their doing some introspection. Our critics should be seen as our best friends, who tell what we should be doing differently.

Any sweeping condemnation of politicians or any other group of society, however justified or well deserved in the view of the sayer, is not sustainable or endorseable. As the political class is the most visible on the print and visual media, they are the first to be faulted, though it is a fact that the bureaucracy hiding behind the facade of files and rules is often the more guilty.

A survey conducted by a weekly magazine, in which people were asked about their view of politicians, 76 per cent felt they are corrupt; 36 per cent felt they are above the law. When asked whether politicians with criminal charges against them should be banned from public life, an overwhelming 86 per cent said "yes". Conversely, only 35 per cent felt that politicians contribute to economic growth, while 79 per cent thought they are excessively concerned about their personal safety. Naturally, 82 per cent felt we spend too much money on their protection. Then, 55 per cent felt women politicians are better than men and 79 per cent felt there should be reservations for women in legislatures. Eighty-seven per cent demanded accountability from the political class as a whole and 90 per cent felt there should be minimum qualification for politicians. Interestingly, 76 per cent felt that the media devotes too much time and space to politicians with 85 per cent contending that they are publicity hungry.

While politicians are 14th in terms of liking or approval of public, the bureaucrats share honour with them on the next rung. Obviously, people feel cruelly short-changed by the rulers, be they bureaucrats or politicians.

Another significant cause for people's abhorrence of the political class is the entry of law-breakers as law-makers into the portals of our legislatures both at the State and the Central levels. In the elections held in December 2003 to the four State assemblies, all parties put up candidates with criminals cases pending against them. In Madhya Pradesh, 153 candidates with criminal antecedents contested elections and 43 of them won. The matching figures for Rajasthan were 104 and 23; for Chhattisgarh 73 and 11; and, for Delhi 70 and 25. I asked a senior politician as to why his party gave tickets to people with criminal background. He explained that in the last elections his party had religiously declined to sponsor any such candidate.

On being rebuffed, such candidates were sponsored by another party and they won. After all, politics is about being in power and not about morality. So all parties decide on the candidates on the basis of their "winnability" - hence they are reluctant to say no to the "winnable" candidates. With the passing of the amendment to the Anti-Defection law, the party bosses should definitely be in position to resist any arm-twisting by tainted legislators. What is morally wrong cannot be politically right. There are greater expectations from our leaders to rid the country of poverty and misery and be a role model. While we cannot have angels as our politicians and rulers, let us as citizens and voters play our role to keep the "cancer" out of the portals of power. It will force the political parties to put their house in order.

4

Crime: The Challenges Overgrown

1. Crime Beyond Statistics: A Present Scenario

Recently, the Supreme Court ordered the imposition of death penalty on four people in two separate cases. In one case, the convicts - a husband and wife - had killed eight members of a family, including four children, for property. The accused had escaped gallows for nearly seven years.

It is not that in every case of murder, death sentence is awarded. In 1980, the Supreme Court for the first time laid down the guidelines for classifying cases under the "rarest of rare" category for awarding death penalty in the Bachan Singh vs State of Punjab case.

Considering the extent of crime in India, which runs into over 32,000 murders committed annually, the imposition and execution of death sentence does not happen even in one per cent of all the cases.

Capital punishment, or the death penalty, is the execution of a convicted criminal by the state as a punishment for his crimes. Historically, the execution of criminals and political opponents has been in practice everywhere to punish crime. It has also prevailed in order to suppress political dissent by following a duly laid down procedure or law.

Contrary to popular belief, the country witnesses a large number of criminal activities for which a few culprits get the punishment they deserve. In 2004, 18,32,015 cognisable cases were registered, on which police action has been taken. Out of these, 33,608 were cases of murder and 27,880 related to attempt to murder. In 2005, 18,22,602 cognisable cases were registered by the police. Out of this, there were 32,719 were of murder, while 28,031 were for attempt to murder. Since 1988, the figure for murder and attempt to murder has been 28,771 and 20,687 respectively. The highest figure of murder in the country was in 1992 when 40,105 persons were killed and 31,202 faced attempt to murder.

Patna High Court chief justice JN Bhatt observed in 2006: "The conviction rate of criminal cases in India was only 6.5 per cent. It was telling on the deliverance of justice particularly with regard to women who need to be compensated adequately along with emotional support to overcome the trauma of being victims of heinous crimes, including rape."

Terrorists have been committing mass murders and except for a microscopic minority, they have been getting away with it. Terrorism is a low intensity war. In the four high intensity wars our country fought, we lost a 5,468 people. In the low intensity war over the past 15 years, on the other hand, we have already lost 61,013 civilians and 8,706 security personnel. This figure does not include murders committed and the terrorists killed in encounters.

Almost six lakh people in India have become homeless because of terrorism. Terrorism has also been bleeding the country. Rough estimates suggest that more than Rs 75,000 crore are annually spent on our armed forces, including paramilitary forces and police, to fight insurgency and cross-border terrorism in the country.

Just look at another data: Explosives confiscated by our security agencies weigh over 58,000 kg. Had they not been confiscated, they would have probably been enough to take care of every inch of Indian soil. Whether one calls it insurgency or terrorism, the plain truth is that two of our Prime Ministers have been assassinated. Besides, the temple of our democracy, Parliament, witnessed jihadi assault a few years back, along with Raghunath temple in Jammu & Kashmir and Akarshdham in Gujarat, as also Sankat Mochan in Varanasi and Ram temple in Ayodhya. The financial capital of India, Mumbai, witnessed the dans macabre of terrorism in the form of Mumbai blasts in 1993 and July 2006. Delhi, too, saw the brutal face of terrorism in 2005, just before Diwali, which left scores of people dead and many more injured.

Terrorism weakens democratic values and enfeebles the economy. Doing away with the death penalty, which is definitely a deterrent, will only encourage criminals. The problem is that in our country, far too few actually get punished.

In Pakistan, says Amnesty International, at least 150 were sentenced to death and 13 executed in 2001. In 2003, the numbers were 140 and eight. By 2004, they had climbed to 278 and eight, raising the number of those under the death sentence to 5,700. In 2005, 394 criminals were sentenced and 15 executed. In Bangladesh, 357 were given the death sentence since 2001 and at least 10 got hanged.

According to the Home Ministry, only 55 people were executed in India since Independence. But the People's Union for Democratic Rights, a leading Indian civil rights group, says that 1,422 executions were carried out between 1953 and 1963. The PUDR bases itself on Government records, particularly the Law Commission's 35th report (1965) on 16 States. Tamil Nadu, now known for its Information Technology achievements, topped the list with 485 executions. Currently, about 1,700 prisoners in different jails await execution, according to one report.

This figure, even if it is assumed that it is wholly true, is nowhere near 1,51,122 murders committed in the same period. This figure is based on the statistics provided by the National Crime Records Bureau for the same period. Incidentally, 12,17,324 murders have been registered with the police between 1953 and 2005.

Thus, it may be seen that not even 10 per cent criminals accused of murder get the punishment they deserve. We have a system of almost endless appeals where legal processes drag on for years, giving an opportunity to the culprits to escape the punishment-more on technical rather than substantial grounds. Even if appeals fail, there is a final petition to the Governor or the President, where influence and recommendations work to commute the death sentence into life imprisonment.

Life imprisonment does not mean imprisonment for life but incarceration for about 14 years, which further gets reduced to about 10 years with parole thrown in for good behaviour.

The Indian criminal justice system has several checks and balances before allowing a death sentence to be carried out. In fact, our justice system is attuned to show more sympathy to criminals than victims.

The imperative principle of justice is that punishment should be based on the gravity of crime. There is no doubt that prison sentence is an effective deterrence. But with some hardened criminals, death sentence alone is the effective solution, if the law and order is to be maintained properly.

2. Challenges: Iron Balls to Chew

1.1. Kidnapping, a Thriving Industry

Long before the terms 'terrorism' or 'guerrilla warfare' were coined, Robin Hood in his tales played the original guerrilla. In India, there have been many versions of this fictional character like Daku Mohar Singh, Man Singh and Malkan Singh of the Chambal, the late Phoolan Devi, as also the forest brigand Veerappan. However, unlike Robin Hood, they were not necessarily pro-poor. Robin Hood, according to legend, was cheated out of his land during the Norman conquest which makes his escapades excusable. But the same cannot be said of the present-day alleged criminals, dacoits, kidnappers and murderers. The recent spate of abductions that have hogged media attention have occurred for one single reason: Lawlessness.

Any news of kidnapping invariably generates public interest because of the human angle involved. The films of yesteryears are a fantastic mix of celluloid myth and reality in which the hero, an oppressed peasant often sought revenge from the landlord by eloping with his daughter. Of course, such stories are far from reality but abductions, goondaism and other crimes are very much the order of the day in Bihar. Why Bihar, this is true of other States as well. But the recent spurt in abductions as well as the allegations that the Government is providing protection to criminals involved in kidnapping has definitely tarnished the image of Bihar.

Politicians who were at the helm in Bihar considered these abductions a ploy to discredit their Government. Bihar has led the country in many of its struggles. The Biharis were in the forefront of the freedom struggle. However, things have changed drastically today. There is nothing worse than kidnapping children to extort money. According to a politician in Bihar, the State is the world's crime capital where abduction for ransom functions as an industry. He also added that "cases of kidnapping, looting, extortion and murder have spiralled compelling more than 10,000 businessmen to flee the State".

The root of the problem lies in the fact that official statistics do not show the real extent of crime. When a crime is committed, the immediate response of the police is to play down its impact. There is delay in registration of cases with the police doing so only when it is pressured. The reason behind this procrastination is simple. The performance of any police officer is evaluated on the basis of the criminal cases registered in his area. The only way to find the incidence of the crime is to examine the police records. However, that too depends upon the wishes of the officers in charge of the police station. During 2002, there were a total 21,850 cases of kidnapping and abduction in the country.

Kidnapping for ransom is Bihar's biggest industry. Between 1992 and 2001 the State police recorded 24,338 cases of kidnapping. According to unofficial estimates, the real figure may be 10 times higher. Kidnappers invariably threaten victims with dire consequences if they go to the police. The authorities in Bihar say that more than 100 kidnapping gangs operate in the State. They prey on one and all. In case the victim is not from a well off family, the relatives are given an option to pay in instalments. In case they do not comply, the victim faces death.

What adds to the sense of insecurity is the feeling that even some powerful politicians are involved in the racket. An SP who busted a number of kidnapping rings said that in her three years on the job, she had arrested suspected kidnappers who were hiding in the homes of local politicians. Her inquiry into a doctor's abduction led her to arrest one MLA who was charged with "15 to 20 cases of arms smuggling, kidnapping and murder". The official was summoned twice by the State Assembly to explain why she had targeted the politician "unfairly". It must be remembered that no police officer derives pleasure from targeting innocent politicians.

They usually are on the look out for gang bosses, most of whom are used by politicians as musclemen during elections.

Some of them have become power centres unto themselves and even members of the Legislative Assembly. One MLA of a State estimated that about 40 of his colleagues in the last Assembly ran kidnapping syndicates. The police did not contradict this. In fact, according to unofficial sources the figure is understated.

Though Bihar is the third largest State of the country, nobody seems willing to invest there. What is more, no professional feels secure in Bihar and this is evident by the exodus of doctors from the State. As a nation, we cannot allow this state of affairs to continue. This not only tarnishes the image of the country, but also keeps criminal infested States from getting involved in the development process.

The nation's Capital holds the dubious distinction of a spiralling crime rate. As per the latest national crime survey, Crime in India, 2002, Delhi has beaten Bihar in cases of kidnapping and crime against women, particularly rape. 37.1 per cent (130 out of 350) kidnappings and abductions of children up to the age of 10 years that were reported in the country took place in the Capital. It also reported 391 cases of kidnapping and abduction, almost half of the total 777 cases reported all over the country. Interestingly, Bihar reported only 26 cases of kidnapping and abduction during the same period. This also is a reflection on the laxity of the police in registering cases.

The Capital continues to remain unsafe for women with 24 per cent (320 of 1,312) of the total rape cases registered in 35 Indian cities. Delhi also registered 34 per cent (759 out of 2,251) cases of abduction in 35 cities. Even molestation and dowry deaths at 356 and 108 respectively remain the highest in Delhi, which also tops in heinous crimes like murder and attempt to murder. The figures for these are 438 and 373 respectively. The Capital is followed by Mumbai with 252 murders. Delhi being the nation's Capital, it is difficult for the police to conceal the cases. This is also due to the presence of an active electronic and print media that is eager to bring to light all such cases. However, in other far flung corners, such accessibility of the media is unheard of.

In recent days, we have come across a number of reports of kidnapping of minors. By and large most abductions take place with the intention of pocketing large sums of ransom money. Today, kidnapping has turned into a highly profitable industry with any one who is well off running the danger of falling a victim. Needless to say, this is true of areas where this business is rife. These are mainly regions in which there is utter lawlessness.

The best that the citizens can do is to take preventive measures. All kidnappings and abductions are preceded by unspectacular preparations though the kidnapper expects a spectacular impact. In order to deal with them, it is important to remember that an abductor or attacker is always on the look out for an easy victim. If a person is perceived as an easy target, he or she is more likely to be abducted. This may sound simplistic, but is in fact true.

Law and order is a state subject and there is little that the Central Government can do except issue advisories. Incidentally, this power has never been used by any Government at the Centre. Ideally, the Centre should organise special training programmes for officers belonging to law enforcement agencies. Such personnel should be deputed in areas prone to kidnapping in order to deal effectively with the threat. In fact, when it allocates funds for the modernisation of the police forces, it should also make it a point to link up the same with the occurrence of crime. In the periodic conferences where all State police chiefs congregate, the Prime Minister should raise the issue of abductions. When the highest authorities show their concern for this growing menace, the law enforcing agencies are bound to act expeditiously to find a solution to this problem.

1.2. Web of Drugs

The recent involvement of a high profile deceased politician's son in a case of drug abuse has focussed attention on the problem and sale of narcotics in the country. The criminalisation of drug use and trade is covered under the Narcotic Drugs and Psychotropic Substances Act. From the law enforcement agencies' point of view, crime involving narcotics forms a small portion - 0.7 per cent - of the total cognisable IPC crime in the country.

In spite of a punitive and rehabilitative approach, the issue of drug demand and control still remains elusive. For long India was producing opium to satisfy the medicinal requirement of the world. It was only in 1985 that the Narcotics Drugs and Psychotropic Substances Act was passed. Both cannabis and opium have been traditionally consumed for social and cultural purposes in many parts of the country. The religious use of cannabis continues to exist especially among followers of Lord Shiva. bhang (a drink made with tender leaves of cannabis) is used by common people to celebrate Shivaratri and Holi. But the Shaivite sadhus (religious priests who live ascetic, celibate lives, often in isolation) consume hashish and or marijuana. This is to help them concentrate and meditate under harsh climatic conditions. Some sadhus consume cannabis products daily in large quantity. For them, offering a pipe of cannabis is similar to offering a cup of tea or coffee to visitors.

Though such religious use has existed for centuries, there has been no provisions made other than to state that the use of bhang is legal, and yet cannabis leaves - the source for making bhang - is illegal. There are no measures for legally cultivating cannabis and collecting tender leaves. In States like Rajasthan and Gujarat, the use of opium drink was a part of culture, where guests are greeted with few drops of this drink. Prior to the amendment of the NDPS Act in 2002, one could be arrested for trading drugs if one was held in possession of 250mg or quarter of a gram.

In the drug trade, a loose network of disposable actors have always ensured that not even a dent is caused to those in this field. Today it is considered more a social evil than a crime. Therefore, not many are willing to furnish information about it though there are general rumours and media reports about its use in big parties. Drug consumption was carried out openly, legitimised by cultural norms and restricted by traditional demand. It was also free of underground dealings. Instead of reducing drug supply, the imposition of laws has resulted in the replacement of culturally sanctioned use by traditional suppliers with criminal networks.

The natural psycho-active plants commonly found in India include cannabis, poppy, khat and dhatura. Cannabis and opium are part of the cultural and religious elements in the country, which was used and kept under control for thousands of years. The international community, however, views these two drugs as particularly troublesome. Lessons learnt during the last two decades indicate that targeting traffickers and traders has fewer negative effects. It does not require providing alternative means of livelihoods, to those who are affected by strict enforcement of laws and illegal trade in narcotics. So much so, nobody shall launch an andolan or an agitation of Narmada Bacho andolan-kind for them. The illicit drug trade is a low-risk but a high profit activity. In order to eliminate it, the situation needs to be reversed: The illicit drug trade must be made a high-risk activity.

The present drug control strategy of India can be traced back to the Single Convention on Narcotics Drugs of 1961. The NDPS Act is designed to conform to the Single Convention of 1961, which the Indian Government had signed in 1964. India was committed to the international goal of eradicating all cultural uses of cannabis within a 25-year period - till 1989.

India is one of the world's top producers of licit opium, and is the sole producer of opium gum. To meet India's share of anticipated world demand for licit opium in 2000 and rebuild domestic stockpiles toward an International Narcotics Control Board, the recommended level was about 750 metric tons. The Government set a harvest target of 1,200 metric tons, of which 870 metric tons was meant for export, 130 metric tons for domestic use and 200 metric tons for buffer stocks. To meet this goal, the Government continued to license a historically larger number of farmers and an increased area for poppy cultivation.

However, in 2001, the total licensed area has been reduced from 35,271 hectares to 25,375 hectares in 2001. Those cultivators who had failed to achieve qualifying yields at least 45 kilograms per hectare in States like Madhya Pradesh and Rajasthan were de-licensed. On the other hand, criminal elements produce heroin from both diverted legal opium and illegally grown opium, no reliable data are available on the extent of production.

Nevertheless, the NCB sources are of the opinion that farmers often hide the exact quantity of their yield and sell off some in the black market. The Government periodically raises the official price paid to farmers to increase incentives to licit cultivators. This graduated scale of payment to licensed farmers is designed to encourage greater productivity and prevent diversion to the black market, where opium can fetch prices as much as 25 times higher than the base price of Rs. 630 per kilogram.

For one kilogram the Government pays a farmer Rs. 250, which is not only meagre but also a fraction of the drug's value on the black market. In 2001, there was a decrease in the floor purchase price of opium from Rs. 280 to Rs. 270 per kilo. This led to induce the farmers to divert sales to drug traffickers instead, who paid a much higher price.

Preventing substance abuse, or coping with it when it happens, are matters of concern for society and Government. Drug prevention is a shared responsibility. The reasons for drug use are varied. The world is filled with opportunities to use drugs. It is for parents, teachers and society to prepare the youth to make positive choices. High self-esteem will enable them to resist peer pressure to use drugs, but not always. The Government should accept that the law enforcement hypothesis would never work alone. It should also focus on treating drug abuse as a health problem with social and economic implications.

During my spell as Director General of Narcotics Control Bureau of India, I was exposed to the world of drugs, narcotics and psychotropic substances - through the NDPS Act as it was called. This stringent law provided a minimum of ten years punishment upon conviction. In fact under the then Act, there was no judicial discretion to impose a lesser sentence if the case was proved.

This is one organisation that is charged with the responsibility of enforcing the Act and rehabilitating the drug abuser, a process that falls under its charge along with the Ministry of Social Welfare. Frankly speaking, not many police officers are concerned with drugs. Even if some are interested, to most drug enforcement is one of the marginal duties unrelated to their mainstream work of preventing and detecting crime.

In fact, no police officer gets credit for busting the rings of drug peddlers or consumers of drugs like heroine, cocaine and other psychotropic substances. A few years back in Vienna, the Secretary General of the United Nations Drug Control Programme, Mr Jacomalli, told me that the drug abuse problem will become more acute in the future than what the world conceives. He said that drug companies are into making unheard of and inconceivable drugs.

He asserts that there is research going on in the world that says if you want to feel and behave like a lion you just have to pop a pill and lo, you can brave the world. Similarly, if you want to be in an amorous or happy mood, you just have to pop a different pill. The problem is underestimated until some celebrity, or a regular of Page 3, is caught in the net of narcotics. It has happened recently in Mumbai, Delhi and Dubai, where so-called paper celebrities were caught with their pants down and immersed in drugs.

The NDPS Act of 1985 sets the statutory framework for drug law enforcement in India. The main elements mandated are to control the cultivation, production, manufacture, possession, sale, purchase, transportation, warehousing, consumption, inter-State movement, trans-shipment and import/export of narcotics, drugs and psychotropic substances. The NDPS Act is, in effect, a comprehensive code not only for the control and regulation of Narcotics Drugs and Psychotropic Substances, but also for the control of select chemicals like heroin and other psychotropic substances that are commonly known as precursors - substances which can be used in the illicit production of narcotic drugs.

India is the world's largest producer of licit opium. The entire produce is required to be purchased by the Government through a Narcotics Commissioner. Due to the heavy price difference between Government and black market rates, a portion of the licit opium poppy crop is diverted to the illicit market. Opium obtained both through diversion and from illicit poppy cultivation is processed into heroin in India. Heroin is most often found in the form of a crudely refined heroin base called "brown sugar," although white heroin hydrochloride (HCl) is also produced.

India's large population includes a significant number of drug abusers, although precise estimates are not available. Heroin, hashish, and pharmaceutical drugs are readily available and widely abused. Brown sugar heroin is primarily produced for domestic heroin users since there is little market for this type of heroin outside of India. Incidentally, one kg of heroin costing about Rs 1 lakh after processing is sold for nearly $1 million (Rs 4.5 crore) on the streets of New York.

India produced 726 metric ton of opium from 19,393 hectare planted with opium poppy for the world's pharmaceutical industry.

This amount fell short of the targeted 900 metric ton, reportedly due to severe drought conditions. In 2000, India produced 1,302 metric ton of opium gum, which was an increase from the 970 metric tons produced in 1999. India is the only country that permits the legal extraction of opium gum. All pain killers and pain relievers, like morphine are byproducts of opium.

The illegal diversion of opium leads to the production of drug abuse substances. Opium is processed into heroin in illicit laboratories all over India. These laboratories generally produce a low-quality brown heroin base (referred to as brown sugar). Many countries in the world are reconciled to the use of soft drugs. For example possession or consumption of hashish or marijuana, or what we call bhang is no offence in the Netherlands, though it is so in our own country. Cannabis cultivation is illegal yet widespread in India.

No estimates as to the size of this illicit cultivation are available. Both marijuana and hashish are processed in India. The Kullu Valley in Himachal Pradesh is known to produce marijuana, thus attracting a lot of foreign hashish buyers. However, although a percentage is sold in the international market, local people use the majority of marijuana/hashish.

India is also the world's largest producer of illicit methaqualone. Methaqualone is one of three categories of depressants, and is usually marketed under the brand name Mandrax. Large seizures of Mandrax are not uncommon. For example, in September 2000, over two metric tons of Mandrax powder was seized near Hyderabad. In February 2001, 1.4 metric tons of Mandrax tablets were seized in Bombay. A serious Mandrax abuse problem exists in South Africa and, although methaqualone laboratories and tableting operations have been seized in South Africa, India remains the source for a substantial amount of the Mandrax abused in South Africa.

Furthermore, a wide range of pharmaceutical drugs legally produced in India is illicitly used. Phensidyl (a cough medicine containing codeine), buprenorphine (a narcotic), and diazepam (a sedative) are all widely abused throughout India. The official drug seizures present a gloomy picture. In 2001 alone, 813 kg of heroine, 23 kg of morphine, 2,321 kg of opium, 5,164 kg of hashish and 75,943 kg of marijuana were seized by law enforcement.

The capital's rich, bold and beautiful drug abusers have highlighted the problem once again. These are people who do not take drugs to overcome their miseries or troubles: They take drugs to get kicks. The incarceration of the high and mighty is the best way to send the message that however beautiful or rich you may be, there is no way you can be allowed to trifle with the drug laws. An official of the Narcotics Control Bureau (NCB) jokingly said about the accused that 'sare darzi (all fashion designers) aur nai (and hairstylists)' were involved in substance abuse'. One member of their fraternity, a fellow fashion expert, said that a majority of Page 3 regulars are addicted to drugs.

"You have to understand that a majority of Page 3 people are drug users. I can assure you of that. Then why just attack fashion designers and hairstylists? It is in very bad taste and can have adverse effects," says Habib, the hairstylist. Yet, it is a cheekiness of the highest order, that people violate the law, justify their actions and then ask why they are being singled out. If this logic is accepted, then every criminal will say, why single out only thieves when dacoits and scamsters are ruling the roost?

Combating drug abuse is multifaceted and complex. Governments and NGOs can provide rehabilitative care to drug abusers and their families and guidance to the medical profession to ensure that drug rehabilitation care finds a secure place in medical and nursing schools.

Trade and Industry can develop substantive abuse programmes to help their affected employees overcome drug abuse and become more effective employees. Government and lawmakers can pass effective legislation that supports increasing budgets for drug law enforcement agencies, controlling diversion of legal, but often abused, opiate and psychotropic drugs and ensuring that drug rehabilitation programmes are sufficiently funded. More than anything else, it is time the Government took serious measures to combat this disease, before the virus infects the entire Nation. Drug use is in no way a healthy way to alleviate emotional and personal problems: It just won't work.

2.2.1. Drugs: Dilution of the Poison

Worldwide, annually, June 26 is set aside as a day to focus on the scourge of drug abuse. It is an opportunity to appraise past activities and strategies, as well as assess present legislation and practices relating to drug control. Besides, it is a platform to embark upon novel and more effective approaches to curb the problem of drug abuse in the country.

Today, more youngsters use illegal drugs than before. During my posting as Director General of Narcotics Control Bureau of India, before moving to the CBI, I was exposed to the world of drugs. Our country is governed by the Narcotics, Drugs and Psychotropic Substances Act. It is administered by the Narcotics Control Bureau. Its enforcement is also the responsibility of the police, CBI and Customs.

Despite the lip service paid on the need to exterminate this evil, the fact remains that the consumption of narcotics is on the rise across the world. Enforcement agencies do not treat the cases relating to narcotics as a big deal, as it consists of just 0.7 per cent of the registered crime in India.

In fact, not many police officers know about drugs. Even if some are interested, it is one of the totally marginal duties that has nothing to do with their mainstream work - of preventing and detecting crime. And, no police officer gets credit for bursting drug peddlers.

India is the world's largest producer of licit opium. Due to the major price difference between what is being paid by the Government and that provided in black market, a portion of the licit opium poppy crop, which is grown in Madhya Pradesh, Uttar Pradesh and Rajasthan, is diverted to the illicit market.

Opium, obtained through both diversion and illicit poppy cultivation, is processed into heroin in India. Heroin is often found in the form of a crudely refined heroin base called "brown sugar". Heroin, hashish, and pharmaceutical drugs are readily available. Incidentally, one kilogram of heroin, costing about Rs. 10,000 after processing, is sold for nearly one million dollar (Rs. 4.5 crore) on the streets of New York. Pain killers like morphine are the by-product of opium.

It is the illegal diversion of opium that leads to the production of drugs. Many countries in the world are reconciled to the use of soft drugs. For example, possession or consumption of hashish or marijuana, or what we call bhang, is no offence in Netherlands, though it is so in India. Cannabis cultivation is illegal, yet widespread, in India.

No estimates as to the size of this illicit cultivation are available. The Kullu valley in Himachal Pradesh is known to produce marijuana that attracts a lot of foreign hashish buyers. However, the majority of marijuana/ hashish is used by the locals, although a percentage is sold in the international market.

India is the world's largest producer of illicit methaqualone, which is one of three categories of depressants and is marketed under the brand name of Mandrax. Our country remains the source for a substantial amount of the Mandrax abused in South Africa.

A wide range of pharmaceutical drugs, including phensedyl (a cough medicine containing codeine), buprenorphine (a narcotic), and diazepam (a sedative) are legally produced in India. At the same time, these are widely used in India. The official drug seizure, which apart from domestic source also include Pakistan, Afghanistan and Mynamar, present a gloomy picture.

Combating drug abuse has many aspects and components. Parents, governments and NGOs can provide rehabilitative care to drug abusers and their families and guidance to the medical profession to ensure that drug rehabilitation care finds a secure place in medical and nursing schools. Trade and industry can develop substantive abuse programmes to help the affected employees overcome drug abuse.

Government can pass effective laws that support law enforcement agencies by increasing their budgets and controlling legal diversion. It should also ensure that programmes to rehabilitate drug abusers are adequately funded. It is time the Government took serious measure to combat the problem relating to drugs before it infects the entire nation. Use of drugs is not the right way to alleviate emotional and personal problems. They don't really work.

2.2.2. The Practice of Quacks

Our country is full of quacks, and fakes exist in all spheres of life, whether they pertain to purchase of textiles, electronic goods or medicines. Overabundant supply of spurious goods and services in the medical profession is particularly alarming. On every street, people with dangling stethoscopes and thermometers get away with posing as doctors. Only when somebody dies as a result of their quackery is there any hue and cry, calling for arrests of the mountebanks playing with public health.

The Supreme Court says, "A person who studies one system of medicine, but practices another is a quack." According to it, a practising allopathic doctor should register with the Medical Council. Ayurvedic doctors need to be registered with the Bharatiya Ayurvedic Chikitsa Parishad. Homoeopathic doctors, on their part, should do the same with the homoeopathic board. The Government's 'anti-quackery' drive is years-old, but there are no tangible results yet, despite the orders in place for compulsory registration.

It is doubtful if quacks would take the risk of registering themselves with medical councils. If people parading as doctors do not, there seems to be no mechanism to ensure they do. A few inspectors are only too willing to be compromised for a price. In fact, most homeopathic doctors freely prescribe allopathic medication, as the police do not know the difference in the fine print or even the law, much less about Supreme Court judgements. Mandatory registration has, therefore, not made any difference.

There have been cases such as that of an MBBS degree holder who died and his son, a homoeopath, who continued the business in his name. Sometimes, both father-a homoeopath-and son-a qualified allopathic doctor-practise in different places in both streams. A few years ago, the Central Bureau of Investigation arrested a person who sold fake MBBS, BAMS or RMI degrees for a price. This person used to openly advertise in the name of the Delhi Degree College. By the time he was arrested, he had reportedly sold over 5,000 fake degrees. In one case, the quack who owned a clinic simply fled after a woman patient died. Her decomposed body was discovered later.

The menace of medical mountebanks persists, despite the Government's claim it is taking action. There are an estimated 30,000 dubious 'doctors' in the National Capital alone, and their number across the country would easily cross a million. As against 30,000 quacks in Delhi, the number of registered doctors is about 26,000.

With fake doctors all over the country, can fake drugs be far behind? According to the World Health Organisation, 35 per cent of fake medicines produced in the world come from India, which has a

Rs. 4,000 crore spurious drug market. About 20 per cent of medicines in the country are fake. Many drugs, including those commonly used for headaches and common cold, are either spurious or substandard. Of them, 60 per cent have no active ingredient, and 16 per cent have harmful ingredients.

Spurious drugs are a major threat to public health and well-being. They find a thriving market in South Africa, as well as in our neighbouring countries like Myanmar, Nepal and Bangladesh. Russia and Uzbekistan face the problem as well.

In India, the illegal trade spreads from Kashmir to the Kanyakumari. Bhagirath Palace in Delhi is reportedly the hub of these lethal products. Other places acting as breeding grounds include Lucknow, Ahmedabad and Indore where, as in other places, small-scale fake or substandard drug manufacturing units operate from garages, shanties and hovels. Most poor quality or fake medicines are churned out in slums, in the most unhygienic conditions. They are positively hazardous and can cause health complications leading to fatalities.

Spurious goods and drugs have been around probably as long as genuine ones have. Though the Government, consumer organisations and even physicians express anguish, the fact remains that the racket operates due to institutional laxity, casualness, neglect and even connivance. Some doctors are known to accept huge gifts, including cars, from dubious pharmaceuticals companies. In return, they regularly prescribe and promote the medicines these firms manufacture. Some smalltime doctors, including non-allopathic practitioners, also have links with and promote the racket.

Unofficial figures, as assessed by consumer organisations, estimate that more than 40 per cent of the medicines sold in the rural market are fake or substandard. That means three out of 10 fast-moving consumer goods (FMCG -a collective term for cosmetics, toiletries and processed food products) in the market could be fake. The rough estimate is 10 to 30 per cent of cosmetics, toiletries and packaged food are counterfeit. Of the soft drinks sold as major brands, 10 per cent is spurious.

It is believed that Rs. 4,000 crore worth of spurious drugs are sold every year; 61 per cent of computer software and 40 per cent of music goods are pirated. Revenue worth Rs 10,000 crore is lost to this criminal industry annually.

The AC Nielsen survey estimated that the annual loss to the FMCG industry stands at Rs. 2,600 crore and, to the Government in unpaid taxes, at Rs. 900 crore. An ORC survey of 12,500 retail stores completed in January 2002 found the counterfeit market to be five to 15 per cent of the total Rs. 60,000-crore annual sales for the industry. That would amount to between Rs. 3,000 crore and Rs. 9,000 crore a year.

Our drugs regulatory authorities have no teeth, few inspectors and even fewer experts. The laws are clearly inadequate, and the manufacture of fake drugs is not even a cognisable offence. This means that the police cannot register a case against such manufacturers. Fake medicines are covered by the Drugs and Cosmetics Act, 1940 or the Copyright Act. An accused can be punished for only two or three years. Cases drag on. Often, he is let off with a mere fine of a few thousands rupees.

The identification of fake or substandard medicines is not an easy task. The following suggestions can help in discovering or ascertaining spurious drugs. It is a mandatory requirement that the key ingredients, date of manufacture, and batch number of a product are mentioned on the label of the container. A fake may not possibly have it on the pack. Its printing, packaging in terms of design and colour will be inferior. Any printed lettering may come off. Pay close attention to advertisements regarding packaging. Chances are that, in the case of lookalike products, the manufacturer's address will be missing. But in most cases, spurious products carry full details and are a close replica of the originals. It is wiser to beware of huge discounts offered by retailers that are not backed by the manufacturer. This is mostly to lure unsuspecting buyers. However, there is no guarantee, that a fake may not pass off as original despite vigilance on the part of the consumer.

The Mashelkar Committee, set up in 2002, has recommended an amendment of the Act and the setting up of a national drug agency with some teeth. Till that happens, we have to live with the present situation. For the perplexed and baffled consumer, there is no choice but to be well-informed and vigilant, and to safeguard his interest by carefully examining the goods or medicines he buys. His health, well-being and life may depend on it.

The Government's offensive has to be stronger than what it has been or is at present. Manufacturing companies with huge investments can never win the war against counterfeiting on their own. At best, they can hire some private detectives who may keep an eye on fake manufacturers for some time. To ensure that the rising tide of spurious products subsides, disincentives of hefty fines and imprisonment are necessary. These punitive measures need to be accompanied by a Government and industry-sponsored campaign to raise public awareness in the interest of the consumer.

1.3. Woman and Crime

Sex has caught the imagination of kings and commoners alike since time immemorial. Thrones have been lost and kingdoms bartered or sacrificed for women. Both in politics and crime, women have always been active. Whether it is the legendary Helen of Troy or Ms Simpson, an American divorcee for whom Edward VIII gave up the British throne; from an illiterate girl to a lecturer, using sex for pelf or power is the common story.

Somehow we in India have been rather hypocritical about our interest in sex. All love triangles and quadrangles centre around sex. Our leaders, at least some of them, have been discreet in their affairs. One ex-Chief Minister never concealed his interest in beautiful women. He also openly confessed that he liked wine and the company of beautiful women.

A Deputy Chief Minister of an important State was too drunk to realise that he should not have made a pass on an airhostess. He did not stop there and asked the airhostess to sit on his lap. The result was that he lost his job. People in power, both in politics or bureaucracy, have the advantage of their position. Their prominence and high position ensures them immunity.

There are countries like Australia, Holland, Sweden and a few States in the US where prostitution is legal. This situation has several advantages. For example, in the American State of Nevada, clients have to use condoms; refusal can mean a jail term. To get a licence, a sex worker goes through the Sheriff's office, the Health Department and the State Prostitution Department. She is given a crash course in AIDS before she gets a licence. Health checks are carried out once a week, and if someone tests positive for HIV the licence is revoked permanently. The out-of-work prostitute, however, is entitled to a monthly dole from social security. Prostitution is a fact of life, and trying to curb it provides loopholes for corruption. The law in Bangladesh requires a woman to simply file an application before a first class magistrate to obtain a licence for prostitution.

Even late President John F Kennedy had a fling with Hollywood actor Marilyn Monroe. John Profumo lost his job for using the services of a prostitute, Christine Keeler, who was suspected to have Russian links. Thailand, jokingly called "Land of Thighs", has the largest number of women sex workers. In 1985, when the US decided to cut its Army's presence by more than a half, there were murmurs of protests, as to what would happen to the women employed in the profession of providing 'comfort' entertainment. In a survey conducted in 2005, India ranked second only behind Brazil in terms of people's preoccupation with sex. Not for nothing has India been known as the land of Kamasutra!

In a recent case, partners of lecturer Kavita Chowdhary killed her over the distribution of black money. A prime accused, who has been arrested, has revealed that that she used to make films of her sexual acts with Ministers and senior officers for blackmail. They had another partner with whom she fell out over sharing Rs 35 lakh allegedly extracted from former UP Minister Meerajuddin of the Rashtriya Lok Dal. This was the price the former Minister reportedly paid for getting back a CD of his "obscene act".

The arrested accused also claimed that the murdered lecturer had possessed similar CDs of former Meerut University vice-chancellor RP Singh and then Fine Arts Minister Brijendra Pratap Singh. He also implied that she might have had a CD of then UP Minister Babulal. Otherwise, he queried, "Why would the two exchange 57 phone calls in a week or so?" He has categorically cleared Samajwadi Party Minister Kiranpal of having any hand in the murder or the sleaze. Minister Babu Lal, too, has reportedly resigned on 'moral grounds'.

According to the police, Kavita, a lecturer in Meerut's Chaudhury Charan Singh University, had been at her parental home in Bulandshahr for a few days, until the afternoon of October 23, when her brother dropped her at the Hapur Chowk to catch a bus for her hostel room in Meerut. But from there, Ravinder Pradhan and Yogesh, the third partner took her to Ghaziabad, where they spent the night. Next morning, they drove her towards Bulandshahr. After sedating her with two tablets of Alprax they strangled her to death and dumped the body tied down by stones in her own bag in the Ganga canal. And then they burnt her belongings.

It is alleged that Ravinder Pradhan and his associate Yogesh strangled Kavita after she demanded more money. No good results ever come out of any crime. Greed leads to more greed. Kavita, the lady in question and the main bait, had reportedly used blackmail on prominent persons. Her murder has all the trappings of a Bollywood potboiler. This is reminiscent of the Madhumita Shukla case, which had hit national headlines three years ago.

It is a new trend where even educated women indulge in prostitution for quick money. In Jammu & Kashmir, two Ministers, Additional Advocate-General and one senior IAS officer were chargesheeted by the CBI for their involvement in sex scandal in July 2006. Similarly, one Inspector General of Jharkhand Police is facing a criminal case for his role in sexual exploits. Incidentally, prostitution is legal in Jammu & Kashmir. The Srinagar sex scandal has led the Government to think of repealing an old law, which legalises prostitution in the State.

In 1997, the case of Anjana Mishra came up. She alleged that Orissa's Advocate-General, Indrajit Ray, tried to molest her when she had gone to meet him at his house to discuss the case against her husband, Subhash Mishra, an officer of the Indian Forest Service. People in high positions have no defence against any allegation being made against them. There is nothing private about people in public life. One of the drawbacks of being prominent is that each action of the person, whom he meets, on what social terms, is all subject public exposure.

It is a fact that in a free and open society, people have the right to know what their 'rulers' do. Pen is definitely mightier than the sword. Investigative journalism has come to stay. Sex sells like nothing else and it makes good copy. Let the people in power take note of it and stay above board. It is not only Caesar, but Caesar's wife, too, who must always remain above suspicion.

1.4. Trade of Organs

The lure of money leads to strange situations. A new type of commerce is flourishing. It is the replacement of organs for leading a healthy life. Voltaire said, "The fate of a nation has often depended on the good or bad digestion of a Prime Minister." Police in the national capital has arrested three members of a gang who were charging between Rs. 80,000 to 1.5 lakh for a kidney.

The gangs used to go to blood banks, contact professional blood donors who are generally poor, and persuade them to sell their kidneys. Another hunting ground was Government hospitals, including the well known ones, where poor people would come from all over the country for treatment. Criminals also collect information about the prospective recipients through networking with ward boys and technicians of super speciality hospitals. An agent contacts the recipient and then introduces the donor to him. Before striking a deal, the donor is asked to pose as a relative of the recipient. To avoid detection, the donor is asked to change his name. Gangs do the appropriate briefing of prospective donors.

Trade in kidney sales has its ramifications all over the country. One Delhi gang has reportedly sold over 50 kidneys all over the country. In Delhi alone, apart from Indian Army's Research and Referral Hospital, three more hospitals including one in Gurgaon are reportedly involved in the racket. Sometime back a similar scam was reported in Punjab, where some doctors were arrested on the complaint of a Bihari migrant. Such offences have not only occurred in Delhi, but have been replicated in many other states including Punjab, Karnataka, Kerala, etc.

The Karnataka experience, with change of names in all the states, has been replicated all over the country. It is rather distressing. The Transplantation of Human Organs Act, 1994, is the existing law to "provide for the regulation of removal, storage and transplantation of human organs, for therapeutic purposes and for the prevention of commercial dealing in human organs". It makes trade in kidneys illegal and any kidney-for-cash transaction a criminal offence. It is punishable with a term of imprisonment ranging from two to seven years and a fine of Rs. 10,000 to Rs. 20,000. The Act defines persons who can donate kidneys as "near relatives", specifically spouses, mothers, fathers, sisters, and brothers. It also recognises the concept of brain-stem death and makes provisions for the development of a cadaver-based organ transplantation programme.

The aim of the Act, however, has been defeated by two built-in drawbacks. First, trade in kidneys or other human organs, or any other violation of the Act, is a non-cognisable offence. It means that neither the CBI nor the police can start any investigation on its own into such violations. Under Section 22 of the Act, a court can take cognisance of offences committed under the Act only on a complaint made by the appropriate authority or an officer authorised by it, or by an individual who has given prior notice of not less than 60 days to an authority.

Despite this, suspiciously large number of kidney transplants by unrelated persons have taken place. Some 19 suspected brokers and middle men were picked up from the premises of several prominent hospitals in Bangalore in 2002. Another grave flaw lies, in Section 9(3), which permits unrelated donors, to give their organs for reasons of "affection and attachment towards the recipient or for any other special reasons". This means, that they can donate their kidneys to patients, provided they can convince the State Authorisation Committee, that they are "donating" and not selling their organs. If the committee is convinced, that money has not changed hands, it can allow the kidney donation. The willingness of the committee, to be convinced, that the unrelated live kidney donations, are being made on account of "affection and attachment" or for some other "special reasons" is a key factor working in favour of the kidney trade. Neither donating kidneys, without money changing hands, nor highly questionable or unreliable factors such as recipients and donors, living away from each other, or any suspiciously doubtful connections, have stood in the way of the transplants. The Authorisation Committee interrogates the donor and recipient separately and asks them a standard set of questions about their relationship-how long they have known each other, a description of the area the other lives in, and so on. Agents, tutor, donors and recipients to endure what has become, a standard and predictable format of interrogation. The donor must submit a ration card, a residence certificate from the police, an affidavit stating the donor's willingness to donate the kidney, and hospital documents.

The Mandya District Police, in Karnataka, found that up to 80 per cent of the verification documents could be forged. In that district alone, nine persons arrested for working as agents in the kidney transplant racket unearthed in January 2002. A member of the Karnataka Authorisation Committee says, "It is difficult to tell when a financial transaction takes place. Often the donor will say that he has worked for the patient for many years, that the patient has helped his family, and he's deeply attached to the patient."

An analysis of the reported cases highlights the following features of the commercial racket in kidneys. "Vested interests are promoting unrelated (live) transplants. Large sums of money are shared by doctors and hospitals that perform such transplants," according to a doctor. A fourth of 274 cases of unrelated live donors, which went before the Authorisation Committee in Bangalore, were shown to be of dependant relationships, to the recipients or their families-as housemaids, watchmen, factory workers and

Karnataka Authorisation Committee, a body set up under the Transplantation of Human Organs Act, 1994, gave clearance to 1,012 patients in Karnataka, who, between January 1996 and March 2002, were officially cleared to receive kidneys from unrelated live "donors". The approval for all these donations was given to ensure that no buying and selling of human organs takes place. The availability of kidneys is most difficult. About one lakh people are being diagnosed with end stage kidney diseases every year. Less than 10 per cent of them can afford transplantation. In cases of a biological mismatch, the recipient may have to spend years waiting for a donor. The solution lies in cadaver donations, like the eyes donation. "Live donation is great, if it is altruistic, but only cadaver donation can put an end to org sale," says a Doctor heading transplant surgery. Globally, 90 per cent of all transplants are from brain-dead donors. The flagrant violation of the law is due to more demand and less supply. The Act, by allowing unrelated donors to "donate" their kidneys after obtaining the sanction, provides legal cover to the buying and selling of kidneys. Unfortunately, in the kidney trade, the prevailing approach is that the poor can be bought.

What can be done to improve the situation? One, hospitals conducting transplants must have an ethics committee. Two, they must maintain detailed clinical documents and indications for the transplant. Three, keep the details of blood groups and cross-match reports of all relatives of the patients. Four, ensure that all recipients of kidneys are residents of the same State and known for at least three to five years. Five, notify the authority if a transplanted organ is rejected or if a patient dies. If emotional attachment is claimed with the recipient by the donor, it should also be verified by an appropriate authority. Such trade is not possible unless there is a doctor-broker nexus. Finally, it being a technical matter, it will be best if investigations into such offences are conducted by a specialist body like the State or Central Medical Council instead of the police who have no expertise in the matter.

3. The Other Lapses

1.1. Media and Crime

Bollywood personalities have long been known to patronise musclemen. For two reasons. One, they need black money, without which it seems no film can be made. Two, the lifespan of film actors and actresses is limited. Whatever they earn in their heydays is an income for life. When I once raised these questions with the prominent film-maker, Mahesh Bhatt, in a TV programme, he gave me the impression he thought I, guilty of blasphemy, was talking through my hat-or should I say turban? He vehemently denied there were any black money dealings in the film industry, though he did admit extortion and black mail threats were possible.

The latest to join the bandwagon of those alleged to have sought the help of gangsters is actress Shilpa Shetty's father Surendra Shetty, recently granted bail by a Surat court. He had been interrogated in police custody after being denied anticipatory bail. This had to do with an extortion case registered by Surat Police, on the complaint of one Mr Pankaj Agarwal, owner of Praful Sarees. The latter claimed Mr Shetty had sent a gangster, Dinesh Shetty, of the Mumbai-based Fazlur Rehman gang to extort money from him. Shilpa had apparently done some modelling for Praful Sarees. It is said the company owed her nearly Rs 25 lakh for the assignments. Mr Agarwal claimed the gangster asked him to cough up the money. A case was registered at the Umra police station in Surat. Dinesh Shetty was arrested and, later, he alleged he had been hired by Shilpa's father.

Mr Shetty's counsel claimed Mr Agarwal was trying to implicate his client since the businessman did not want to pay the money he owed the actress. According to him, Mr Agarwal had signed a one-year contract with Shilpa in 1998, a starlet at the time. The company continued to use Shilpa's image even after the contract had lapsed. It has been said Mr Agarwal owes Shilpa close to Rs. 80 lakh for using the advertisements over the past four years.

Shilpa, on the contrary, says: "The media is creating unnecessary hype ... The information of my parents' involvement in the matter is completely wrong and is affecting my reputation." The police have interrogated her since.

Whatever the truth of the case, the fact is that organised gangs are a parallel financing industry. This industry has its own hierarchical structure with a strong, ruthless leadership, and its own code of conduct for members. Its aim is profit or political clout. The gangs serve their objectives with the help of sharp-shooters, telecom experts, casino operators, computer wizards, corrupt policemen, politicians and anyone else coming in handy.

Contrary to popular belief, organised crime as a phenomenon has long existed in one form or the other in our country. Big landlords or moneyed people have always maintained private armies or musclemen armed with swords, lathis or illegal weapons. In 1669 in Bombay, Governor Aungier formed a militia of local Bhandari youth to deal with organised street gangs that robbed sailors. Thugee flourished in central India till the 19th century, with armed thugs masquerading as pilgrims or wayfarers, who won the confidence of unsuspecting travellers and looted and murdered them. A British India police officer, William Sleeman, virtually crushed Thugee through his campaign between 1831 and 1837.

Thanks to the introduction of prohibition after Independence, bootlegging became a thriving business. Illicit trade in liquor attracted the covetous attention of hitherto loosely mobilised street gangs. Thus, the seeds of organised criminal activity were sown in India's commercial capital. The first of the recognised gangsters in Bombay was Vardharaj Mudaliar, popularly known as Vardha Bhai. He ruled the roast for over a decade by organising bootlegging in a systematic manner, and spreading a protective umbrella over several lesser gangs dealing in illicit liquor. He soon diversified his activities: Gold smuggling, matka gambling, extortion and supari killings.

Mudaliar had to flee Bombay under relentless police pressure. His near contemporaries were the gangs of Haji Mastan, Yusuf Patel and Karim Lala. Mastan and Patel made their millions in gold smuggling, and Lala, a Pathan, dealt in drugs. They were followed by Dawood Ibrahim and company. Bitter internecine gang warfare and the liquidating of all his rivals led to Dawood's emergence.

Mumbai's underworld dons seem to have become role models for other mafias in the country. The Bombay serial blasts in March 1993-which left 257 dead, 713 maimed and property worth hundreds of crores damaged-forced the nation to look at the menace seriously. For the first time, the country realised the immense potential of organised criminal groups to jeopardise internal security, courtesy their use by Pakistan's ISI.

More recently, the media shook up the nation by highlighting excerpts from film actor Sanjay Dutt's conversation on November 14, 2001, with an alleged gangster named Chhota Shakeel. These tapes were played by the prosecution before a special court trying film financier Bharat Shah and three others in the underworld-Bollywood nexus case. The tapes showed Shakeel calling the shots from Pakistan and certain film personalities both cowering before and more than willing to oblige the ganglord.

At the time, the Maharashtra Control of Organised Crime Act (MCOCA) court had rightly advised the media to observe self-restraint while reporting the case. This was in view of the fact certain parameters, like continuous recording and non-editing, meant to provide a true picture had to be observed for admissibility of tape-recording evidence. Those tapes, and perhaps the current case involving Shilpa Shetty's father as well, show how the underworld continues to exert a big influence on the film industry. The mafia will not let go of any chance to extract or extort as much as possible from cash-rich Bollywood personalities. During the past few months, at least 60 extortion calls have reportedly been made to film industry people. The callers have used the names of gangsters like Dawood, Chhota Shakeel or Chhota Rajan. The Shakeel-Dawood gang, the Abu Salem gang and the Chhota Rajan splinter groups are those that reportedly intimidate Bollywood.

Among Bollywood personalities facing threats are filmmaker Rajeev Rai, Manmohan Shetty and Rakesh Roshan, and stars like

Aamir Khan and Manisha Koirala. Yet nobody from the film industry or outside seems willing to go public with his or her problems. The affected parties seem to have more faith in the words of gangsters than in state protection. This menace will grow if everybody remains concerned only with solving his or her own problems or buying peace by acquiescing to extortion. There is no witness protection act in our country, whereby people deposing in sensitive cases can be enabled to change their identities and settle far away from the place where they testified, with the help of the state.

The existing legal system is too weak to deal with gangsterism. The law needs to be changed, so that the onus of proving that a person has no links with gangsters or crimes like kidnapping for ransom, and has not sought mafia help, should lie on the accused. Victims and witnesses in most cases involving mafia dons turn hostile on their first appearance in court. This will continue to happen so long as the present legal system is in place. The ultimate decision in any case lies with the judiciary. Any police officer deviating from the path of duty or getting mixed up with the criminals should be summarily dismissed.

Last but not the least, the state should not become a party to the emboldening of dacoits and gangsters. Two years ago, forest brigand Veerappan had made extortion almost legal, with the two mutually hostile Governments of Karnataka and Tamil Nadu vying with each other to yield more ground to the criminal. Reportedly, Veerappan extorted over Rs 30 crore from the authorities for releasing film actor Raj Kumar. It was the Supreme Court's intervention which made the States realise they had a greater duty to upholding the law than to an individual.

1.2. Mafia: An Every Household Face

Who says, that crimes can be buried with the passage of time? Nemesis has habit of catching up at the most unexpected moment. Italian police arrested Bernardo Provenzano, boss of all bosses of the Sicilian Mafia, on April 12, 2005 after 43 years. It was the biggest news for Italy. It overtook the media coverage of the photo-finish Italian elections, which were being held at the same time. Provenzano, who was arrested in a farmhouse not far from Corleone- the hilltop Sicilian town - which has been made famous by Mario Puzo's, Godfather novels.

Even in reality, Corleone has raised, a vicious mafia family that dominated organised crime on the island for decades. Mafia left a trail of blood in murder of prosecutors, reporters and investigators. Till his arrest, Provenzano was the uncrowned king of Italian mafia and head of the Corleone family. He has already been sentenced to life imprisonment for half a dozen times, as member of the so-called Mafia Cupola.

The police had been keeping tabs on Provenzano's wife and two sons, who returned to Sicily in 1993. On April 12, the police investigators spotted a bundle of laundry being sent from her house to a remote farmhouse. As investigators elucidated by saying that they saw a hand come out from a door to take the package, and they decided to act.

Provenzano did not put up a struggle when the police special forces burst into the farmhouse. When the mafia boss was led to a Palermo police station, bystanders called out insults. The persistence of Italian Police must be appreciated in arresting Provenzano. The police, had few photographs of him and latest one was a 1959 snapshot. The police artificially aged the image on a computer, and picked up his trail, after he reportedly, underwent surgery in a clinic in Marseille, France, in 2003. Around a year ago, the circle began to "progressively close in around Provenzano and his accomplices," according to Giuseppe Pisanu, the Italian Interior Minister. It was also revealed that cameras had been planted in fields surrounding Corleone, where, according to Pietrò Grasso, Italy's top anti-mafia prosecutor, the ailing mobster had come "to take refuge" near those "he most trusted".

Provenzano's capacity to outsmart the police for 43 years was considered am emblem of the state's inability to eradicate the mafia. Many historians view the mafia as a product of Sicily's tumultuous history. For example, the mafia's code of behaviour can be traced back to centuries of corrupt and brutal government by foreign conquerors of Sicily, which taught most Sicilians to regard government with suspicion and hostility. Because of loyalty agreements, the Italian mafia remained both secretive and extremely powerful.

In the early years of the 20th century, only the very rich could vote in Italy. The mafia used this selectivity to garner votes through various strong-armed means. In this way, the criminal organisation was able to control many political offices.

It was determined the mafia leadership would support the Christian Democratic Party, and that they were accepted into the political organisation without any further discussion. The British and American, after the World War II, were pleased with what was happening and tacitly gave their blessings.

Mafia in India, however, is state-based rather than country-based. For instance, the criminals in Bihar and UP have their own pockets of influence, from where they contest elections. The police dare not take action, as the Indian mafia leaders including dacoits and criminals had powerful supporters, in high position in the Government.

In 1950's, many said that the mafia was responsible for more arrests in Italy than the police. These hoodlums won high praise for their actions from the media, police and the people. In 1955, a member of Italy's highest court, Giuseppe Guido Lo Schiavo wrote an outright defence of the Mafia: "People say the mafia does not respect the police and the judiciary. It's untrue. The mafia has always respected the judiciary and justice, has bowed before its sentences, and has not interfered with the judge's work." However, the position changed when drugs appeared on the scene in a big way. When police tried to shatter the heroin trafficking, by the mafia, during the 1980's, the mafia killed chief prosecutors, police officials and major politicians.

Nevertheless, over a period of time the they have expanded and also became more sophisticated. It entered into the business of moving nuclear and other radioactive materials from countries like Russia to the non-nuclear wannabes as Libya, Iran and Iraq.

Another mafia operation, which bears close resemblance to the education racket in our country - leakage of examination papers and sales of degrees - is that of Sicily mafia, which actually took over the University of Messina. In the police raid that followed, 76 people were arrested, including politicians and prosecutors. For a price, you could get a degree, pass your subjects or have your grades increased. In our country, to a limited degree, the mafia groups do join hands in getting tenders for the Government work. But there is no all-India network, perhaps due to the sheer size, of the country.

Mafias are same all over the world. But compared to the Italian mafia, Indian mafia is place, industry or work specific. The Indian mafia, which is more visible in Mumbai, Bihar, and UP, was earlier involved in the smuggling of gold, later on silver, electronic items, mobile phones, extortion and taking over properties and settling disputes. Unlike Italian mafia, some of the criminals, including terrorists have made it to Indian Parliament. Another important feature of Indian mafia, is that some of them have reportedly become the agents of the Inter-Services Agency of Pakistan and were instrumental in the biggest mayhem of India, that is the Bombay blasts of 1993, which left 267 dead and over 1000 injured.

There are hardly any inter-mafia war in Italy, unlike India, where inter-gang warfare claimed 52 lives in 1996, and the figure has continued to rise since then. Times are changing and the new generation of mafioso are not going to be contented with extortion, shakedowns or murder. The globe has join together to a degree that the moving and laundering of money has become one of the easiest things, thanks to the mobile phones and internet. Mafia knows it very well.

Mafia's interest remains the omnipresent money. The higher the lure of the money, the easier it is to pick up recruits, whether for drug trafficking or human trafficking. Governments, especially in democracies, move slowly in meeting challenges. It is time to remind our Government to be proactive, to deal with the menace. Albert Einstein said, "The world is a dangerous place, not because of those who do evil, but because of those who look on and do nothing."

2. Cure: Unity of the Right

As a nation, we only occasionally discuss criminalisation of politics. The is galling considering it runs through the country and cuts across all political parties. It is, therefore, unfair to accuse only Bihar of electing tainted politicians to the portals of powers. Almost all the political parties, with the exception of the Left, have given tickets to charge-sheeted persons when it has suited them. This is neither morally acceptable nor desirable. We need to take a look at Christian values, which allow only such persons to hurl stones at sinners, who have themselves been guilty of not committing any sin.

Criminalisation will not end with a few convictions; on the other hand there are instances of tainted politicians like Ms Jayalalitha, Mr PV Narasimha Rao and Mr Buta Singh getting acquitted on technical grounds. Even the conviction of Mr Sukh Ram in a lower court was allowed to remain in abeyance till a decision was taken in a higher court, on his appeal. Politicians talk about rooting out corruption or ending criminalisation but are themselves, most of the time, party to it either by connivance or by convenience. Run-of-the-mill politicians have no passion for promoting probity and fairplay amongst their colleagues, who happen to be in power at any point of time.

There is no smoke without fire. The very allegations, leave aside indictment, only reveal the culture of abusing political power for staying or surviving in office. Corruption or criminalisation is not a monopoly of any political party. No political party can say it has not patronised the corrupt and the criminals and given them a certain degree of respectability. They denounce it publicly, but accept the same privately. The induction of charge-sheeted ministers in the new Government, headed by one of the cleanest politicians in India, only confirms what has been public knowledge for several decades.

Politicians owe an explanation to the public as to how, in the course of their so-called public service, they have moved from rags to riches, beating even the royalty of yore. No party ever disowns a criminal or a corrupt person if he has even a remote chance of winning an election. In the last 57 years, none in the country has ever thought it fit to put in place laws for dealing with political corruption or criminalisation, to say nothing of making an example of the corrupt.

In fact, a new culture has developed, wherein no political party wants to condemn others because an enemy today might become an ally tomorrow. So nobody really celebrates the discomfiture of anybody, whether it is of Ms Mayawati or Ms Jayalalithaa or Mr Badal or Mr Chautala or Mr Yadav, and the Taslimuddins and Shahabuddins of Bihar. When there were discussions over the Supreme Court order on Representation of People's Act, almost all parties were opposed to any change. They felt that mere charge-sheeting of a person was not proof of guilt, whether for murder, dacoity, extortion or simple political rioting and agitation.

When the Delhi High Court told the Election Commission that the antecedents of poll contestants be disclosed, the Government promptly filed an appeal. The matter went to the Supreme Court, which held the amendment to the election statute bad in law and struck it down. Political parties go for winners, irrespective of their backgrounds. There are serious gaps in the law to prevent criminals from getting into State and Central legislatures. Their entry to such august houses amounts to treating the law-breakers as law-makers.

A committee headed by Justice HR Khanna, Nani Palkhivala and Justice Lentin had proposed that a person convicted of a criminal offence as well as one against whom a charge has been framed in a criminal court, should not be eligible for election in any legislature. But their recommendations are gathering dust. Political parties have not shown the necessary seriousness in the matter, for the obvious reasons. These days, politics is largely a matter of having enough muscle and money power.

Money politics, sustained on black market, naturally strengthens the politicians' nexus with smugglers, black-marketeers, bootleggers and the underworld dons. It leads to the perversion of the system. In the Telgi stamp scandal, names of only some politicians surfaced, with many more to come. One police officer indicated the involvement and association of the then Home Minister of a State who ultimately resigned from office.

Unfortunately, no democracy is free from tainted politicians, or the deviants, which are but different tinges of criminalisation. An American had this to say about his country, "I have, in my life time of 79 years to date, lived through and with:

- Two presidents who had mistresses unknown to their legitimate wives.
- One President, whose mother did not know who was the father was of her child.
- One President, who shouted from the rooftops about drugs, but was on them himself.
- One President who accumulated illegal cash in his White House safe deposit box.
- One President who lied under oath to a grand jury.

- Two presidents who had sex in the White House with women other than their wives.
- One President who had orgies nearly every day in the White House with White House personnel.
- A Vice-President who was found guilty of tax evasion.
- A Secretary of Defence who lied to the Congress and was charged with improper conduct and got off only because a President pardoned him! What else can you expect from a generation of Americans who have lost their way? Our culture sponsors them, generates them and teaches them to be thieves, liars, cheats and crooks."

Our politicians lie through their teeth day in and day out. American novelist Henry Miller (1891-1980) said: "One has to be a lowbrow, a bit of a murderer, to be a politician, ready and willing to see people sacrificed, slaughtered for the sake of an idea, whether a good one or a bad one."

The position is that political tribes and their antics are totally discredited in the perception of the common man in our country. For one politician standing exposed and disgraced temporarily, there are countless others whose hands are perhaps dirtier but have escaped public scrutiny. Those caught are perceived as thieves. But those undetected are considered saints. Indeed, there has been a tremendous fall in the standards of public life everywhere and no society and institution has been spared. According to one political party, another major political party sponsored 78 persons with criminal cases pending this year.

A committee headed by a former home secretary with Director, CBI, and others as members, confirmed that criminalisation of the political and administrative apparatus had become all-pervasive. This was back in 1992-93. Linkages between the underworld, politicians and the police were illustrated by the exposure of network in the Bombay blasts cases in 1993.

The committee report revealed that a network of mafia gangs has been running a parallel system making the official machinery irrelevant in critical areas of public life. Unfortunately, these danger signals have not been taken seriously and continue to be ignored. In the present scheme of things, with a few exceptions like the Prime Minister Manmohan Singh, and a minuscule of others, there is no premium on honesty and integrity or probity in public life.

There has been total erosion of faith in the viability and vitality of the present governing system. The situation could become explosive if corrective measures are not initiated urgently. A balance between integrity, exercise of power and accountability needs to be worked out.

It is for us to ensure that no criminal is deified. Ultimately, it is the people who need to agitate collectively. If criminals get elected with the polling percentage being extremely low, a great degree of fault lies with the people who choose not to exercise their franchise. Every citizens needs to stand for his right.

5

Terrorism: Extended Cult of Corruption

1. Terrorism: The Challenges Intact

Terrorism is defined, in the dictionary, as "the unlawful use or threatened use of force or violence by a person or an organised group against people or property with the intention of intimidating or coercing societies or governments, often for ideological or political reasons". Terrorism is also used by small, organised gangs, as in Kashmir, to wage war against established nations. A terrorist war is dissimilar to conventional war between two countries. A conventional war with battle lines, battlefields and military-trained professional combatants is extreme and rigorous. It also has a commencement, a middle and a conclusion. A terrorist war- terrorist acts, to be precise-consists of random acts of violence against the 'enemy', including civilians where they live and work.

The purpose of terrorism can range from coercing a group of people, or even a government, into yielding some or a variety of demands, or for extracting revenge for a perceived wrong. It can also be to harass a government. These days, terrorists have an incredible armoury at their disposal, literally and figuratively. Not only can they commandeer an enormous number of weapons of annihilation and devastation, they are also well versed in the use of technological and communications systems and normal air, road and rail networks.

Communications gadgets, including mobile phones, are both relatively inexpensive and easy to acquire. This enables terrorist groups to organise, plan and augment their strength through recruits. Several terrorist groups, both in Jammu & Kashmir and in Pakistan, have used the Internet. The Indian defence establishment was against the use of cellphones in J&K, where terrorists would use them to plan major strikes by tying up loose ends at the last minute or even changing their programme, depending upon the threat perception.

Bombs made of common fertiliser and gasoline loaded on to a truck can be driven to the door of a targeted structure to cause massive damage. Terrorism over the last 20 years has leaned on attacks resulting in as many fatalities as possible. Consider the massive number of victims in the bombing of two US Embassies in Kenya and Tanzania in 1998.

In horrific bomb blasts in the world's largest Muslim country, Indonesia, 187 persons were killed and 230 injured or missing on October 12, 2002. The strike in the tourist paradise of Bali was the handiwork of terrorists aided and abetted by the Al Qaeda, which also executed the 9/11 strikes in the US. This outfit has already threatened more attacks on American economic interests. The surge of terrorist incidents the world over clearly shows that the Al Qaeda is alive and kicking. Despite the global coalition against terror, there is no knowing what will be the next target, or where. Freelance Islamic terrorists want to have a free run in their pursuit of world domination.

Despite international action on containing the Al-Qaeda, this network has a worldwide presence. It is poised to "strike again at its leisure"-this warning comes from a UN expert panel group which, in a report released in New York in October last year, says: "Members (of the Al-Qaeda) and their associates are deployed in many countries ... and, given the opportunity, they will have no compunction in killing as many people as they can (in) those nations that do not conform to their religions and ideological beliefs."

It is essential for India not to overlook what is happening on the ground elsewhere just because such incidents occur at a distance. In neighbouring Pakistan, there is no difference between the Pakistani Army and so-called jihadi terrorists where their objectives are concerned. The Pakistani Army uses terrorists masquerading as holy warriors to further its aim of destabilising India.

There is no doubt that, despite being a lackey of the US, Pakistan continues to harbour Al Qaeda terrorists. The capture of Al Qaeda's number three man, Khaled Sheikh Mohammad, in the first week of March 2003 confirms what was always known: That Pakistan is playing a double game. It is only a pious and futile hope that intelligence and evidence gleaned from documents, laptop computers and mobile phones taken from the house where Mohammed was apprehended may lead to the discovery of Osama bin Laden.

A prominent Yemeni cleric apprehended in Germany-on charges of financing terrorism-used a mosque in Brooklyn New York, to help funnel millions of dollars to Al Qaeda operatives. US federal officials said in March that he had boasted of personally delivering $ 20 million to bin Laden. In New York, Police Commissioner Raymond W Kelly said that Al Qaeda operatives "did their fund raising right here in our own backyard in Brooklyn."

Three well-coordinated suicide bombings on May 12 in Riyadh, the Saudi Arabian Capital, once again turned the spotlight on the Al Qaeda. They had all the hallmarks of an Al Qaeda strike. Thirty-four people, including at least 12 US nationals, were killed in attacks on three residential compounds, housing mainly foreigners. Two hundred people were reportedly wounded. Nine terrorists involved in the mission were also killed. The blasts took place a few hours before US Secretary of State Colin Powell was to reach Riyadh on an official visit.

The US State Department had issued a warning on May 1 that terrorists "may be in the final phases of planning attacks" on US targets in Saudi Arabia. The strikes came soon after 19 suspected militants had escaped arrest by the Saudi security authorities, who had raided their hideouts. The suspects, 17 of whom are said to be Saudi nationals, had fought in Afghanistan and Chechnya. The Saudi Government claimed the attacks were masterminded by no less than bin Laden himself, who had given the green signal to target foreigners and members of the royal family.

On May 16-17, five bomb attacks tore through the coastal Moroccan city of Casablanca, killing dozens and damaging a Jewish community centre and two Western targets. The official death toll was at least 40, with nearly 60 injured. The attacks were near-simultaneous. The Al Qaeda's involvement was thought likely, as it maintains a presence in Morocco.

The Al Qaeda's new military chief, the Egyptian Saif Al-Adel, is a sharp terrorist mastermind. He carries a reward of $ 25 million on his head. He has so far succeeded in keeping bin Laden safe from detection despite the worldwide manhunt. Leadership changes were reportedly necessitated by the capture of Khaled Sheikh Mohammad, who is supposed to have planned the strike on the 9/11 World Trade Centre twin towers in New York.

Bin Laden and other important Al Qaeda members are believed to be hiding in the Pakistan-Afghanistan border region. There are reports of the Al-Qaeda regrouping in Pakistan and Chechnya, besides Kenya and Sudan. The organisation is said to be aiming at new targets within the US. It is not surprising that a senior American Embassy official in Pakistan described that country as the epicentre of terrorism in the first week of June. India may take heart in the fact that it is not alone in harbouring this spot-on perception of Pakistan.

Despite the US-led coalition against terror, Islamic terrorism is no less a threat to India now than before. In fact, no country is safe. Certainly not Russia, where 17 air force men were killed and 12 injured on June 5 in Mozdok at the Chechen border, when a woman suicide bomber walked up to their bus and detonated the explosives strapped to her body. It is not for nothing India has been warning the world about the dangers of the tentacular expansion of terrorists and the Talibanisation of societies in many parts of the world. The global community must realise that one cannot allow state terror sponsors disguised as friends to get away with insisting they oppose terrorism even as they hunt with the hound and run with the hare. Sooner or later, the world, particularly the US, will have to deal with Pakistan the way it has dealt with Iraq.

1.1. Terrorism: Growing Stronger Every Day

Whenever terrorists strike in India, one gets to hear some readymade names of the perpetrators, or their organisations, or the country/ countries that are giving them sanctuary. Our

Governments, both at the Centre and the States, give standard response, calling the terrorists cowards, murderers of innocents and back stabbers. The leaders render hollow rhetoric that terrorism will be dealt with severely.

All this big talk ends with a visit to the scene of the crime. People have started ignoring all such vacuous proclamations. Some of them do not even go through the statements by politicians in the newspapers following any terrorist attack.

Two explosions, one at an amusement park and another at a popular eatery, killed at least 42 people and wounded 75 in Hyderabad on August 25. The usual fall guy according to the State and Central Governments were terrorists "from across the border". However, Pakistan has denied India's accusations of Islamabad's hands in the recent bombings in Hyderabad. It says, "These are terrorist attacks and we condemn them. We are ourselves victim of terrorism and remain committed to fight terrorism. It is always better to investigate rather than speculate."

But the truth of the matter is that it was Pakistan that first gave not only training but also shelter to the Taliban and other jihadis. Now it's not able to control the monsters of its own creation, which are running amok in its own territory.

Terrorism is the most critical issue facing our country. To strengthen and augment our Government's anti-terrorism efforts, we urgently need a more fundamental approach that neutralises the very base of terrorism.

But first of all, the Government should be clear whether it wants to beg for talks before the terrorists who have spurned all offers in Andhra Pradesh, Assam and Jammu & Kashmir. For some strange reason, constant rebuffs by the terrorist organisations do not deter either the Prime Minister or the Chief Ministers from repeating the plea endlessly. People will go all out to assist the Government if it is consistent and does not give the impression of bending before the terrorists.

The Government says that there are ISI modules all over the country. Why does it not instruct the intelligence agencies to go all out to liquidate them? When a foreign-trained terrorist comes to India, he needs logistic support in the form of a place to live, transport and a mobile phone. He has to study potential targets which when bombed would produce the maximum effect. Obviously, he has a local host. Therefore, the intelligence agencies must focus on the terrorists' local supporters.

If a policy like this exists, there are at least no signs of its execution on the ground. Otherwise, how could the terrorists strike Hyderabad twice in less than three months? The Government fixes the tenure of the Home Secretary, Defence Secretary, Director, Intelligence Bureau, and Director, R&AW in a way that there is continuity in dealing with security. Except for giving extension to such officers, there has been no change in the ground situation, as the following chronology of the major terrorist attacks in the country shows.

In August, bombs rip through crowded public areas in Hyderabad; police fear at least 42 are killed after a bomb at the city's Mecca Masjid kills 11 people in May.

In September 2006, at least 30 people are killed and 100 injured in twin blasts at a mosque in Malegaon. In July 2006, seven bombs on Mumbai's commuter trains kill at least 187 people and injure more than 700. In March 2006, twin bombings at a railway station and a temple in Varanasi kill 20 people.

In October 2005, three bombs placed in markets in Delhi, one day before Diwali, killed 62 people and injured 300.

In August 2003, two taxis packed with explosives blew up, one outside a Mumbai tourist spot and the other in a busy market, killing 52 and wounding more than 100.

On December, 13, 2001, terrorists attacked Parliament. On March 1993, a series of bombings in the Mumbai stock exchange and in trains, hotels and gas stations in the city, killed 257 people and injured more than 1,100.

The biggest challenge now is how to defend our country against terrorist organisations that have no compunction about killing or fear of dying for their causes, however ill founded they are. Conventional strategies of defence, such as large standing armies, nuclear bombs and even Star War-style defence, as the US has anti-missile shields, are increasingly irrelevant and have little or no deterrence value in countering hit-and-run terrorists.

Between 2000 and 2003, terrorist attacks in India accounted for 75 per cent of all such incidents in the world. It is fair to assume that groups based in Pakistan carried out a number of those attacks. The report shows 203 international terrorist attacks in India and none in China. There is a problem with the idea that democracy will create new thoughts and action, which should reduce anybody's desire to engage in terrorism. Terrorists usually represent fringe groups with little support from the mainstream population. They know that they enjoy little public support, but generally think that they are right anyway, perhaps believing that their cause is authorised by god.

Since they know that they already have little public support, why would they take the chance of contesting elections? If they are attacking a dictator who does not give in to their demands, why would they hesitate to do the same against a democracy that does not yield before them?

Indeed, many current terrorist leaders haven't had anything good to say about democracy. Osama bin Laden openly opposes it, preferring instead to establish a new 'caliphate'. Other members of Al Qaeda see democracy as a Western imposition of secularism, godlessness and apostasy.

India is our country and it is the duty of each one of us to contribute to its defence. Most terrorist bombings happen because nobody reports having seen anything out of place or someone suspicious before the incident. A simple approach would be: If you see something, say something. On its part, the Government should not harass the person reporting the whereabouts of suspicious characters. Such a report may help deter or prevent an act of terrorism. Every citizen should become the eyes and ears of law enforcement agencies in the fight against terrorism.

1.2. International Instances of Terror Dilapidation

War is a cruel reality. It brings devastation and misery after the dust has settled. The war on terrorists disguised as the 'Taliban' (students) in Afghanistan would have been a distant dream but for the September 11, 2001 attack on the World Trade Centre twin towers in New York. It was the most daring terrorist strike in history. And it was meant to send a signal to the US: Though America saw itself the world's sole superpower after the Soviet Union's demise, there were people who could find chinks in its armour and use its own armoury against it.

Naturally, the US looked upon 9/11 as a rude slap in its face. The needle of suspicion pointed to Osama bin Laden, a Saudi whom the CIA had reared through Pakistan and funded with millions of dollars in Afghanistan, to throw out the Russians. The exact figure poured into the Afghan war is not known, but with weapons and money spent on buying loyalties, the figure would have crossed three billion dollars.

"It is pretty inexpensive," Steven Kosiak, an expert on military spending from the Centre for Strategic and Budgetary Assessments, has said, noting that the Gulf War cost more than $ 60 billion while the Kosovo operation against Serbia-which included 78 days of bombing raids-cost around three billion dollars. One of the biggest outlays in Afghanistan-$ 634 million-was for the deployment of extra ships and some 400 planes in the neighbouring region.

The cost of ammunition and bombs, used against Taliban targets and Al Qaeda hideouts, was around $ 185 million in October 2002 alone. The price of bombs varies greatly. A conventional one tonne bomb costs $ 2,500 and a CBU-89 cluster bomb $ 50,000. A Cruise missile fired from ships or planes can cost anything between one to two million dollars. Keeping planes in the air is also expensive, ranging between $ 5,000 dollars an hour for an F-18 fighter and $ 13,700 for the B-2 stealth bomber which had flown from mainland America to drop bombs on Afghanistan.

The US feels that the Afghanistan operation was modest in many ways, certainly when compared to the Gulf War. US warplanes launched some 90,000 sorties against Iraq, compared to just 2,000 in Afghanistan during the operation's first month. But, in any conflict, there are a lot of hidden costs, so the above figures may not be taken as definitive, to the last cent.

The US did succeed in vanquishing and dethroning its erstwhile cronies, the Taliban, with its own might and the active assistance of the perennial turncoat called Pakistan. The Americans have literally made a quiet exit from Afghanistan, leaving only a token presence in the form of a peace keeping force, to take on new commitments as the world's global police.

It has left a battered, bruised, distressed and shattered Afghanistan in the hands of the Afghans faithful to it. On June 1[illegible] this year, the Senate Committee hearing saw Senators and othe[illegible] witnesses make several observations. One was that "the reconstruction efforts have quite a way to go" before the goal of a peaceful Afghanistan was realised. Another was that "concerns about persistent insecurity and a slow political and economic reconstruction process are prevalent throughout Afghanistan". Still others said that, despite the military success in Afghanistan, "peace remains elusive".

One Senator voiced concern that the US was not adequately focusing on nation-building: "Al Qaeda and Taliban remnants appear to be reconstituting themselves, mounting a concerted effort to destabilise the Government, impede reconstruction, and terrorise the population in the hope of making Afghanistan ungovernable until the US gets tired and departs." Another observation was that democracy would be possible only when "warlords realise that their continued relevance lies not with their armies but with the new emerging democratic system".

It was also felt that Afghanistan's new administration under Mr Hamid Karzai had "lost the initiative. The policy drift in US Afghan policy must first be resolved in Washington". A new reconstruction push to increase security was thought essential "for blending security and development". The current constitutional drafting process was said to be "secretive" and apparently strongly influenced by Islamist hardliners. "There was little or no public input", and there were reports about intimidation of the advocates of democracy and political reformers.

The US committed itself to spending over $ 2,000 million in assistance to the people of Afghanistan since 2001. In March this year, the European Commission announced a 400 million package (in euros) of reconstruction aid for Afghanistan for 2003-2004, concentrating on rural development and food security, economic infrastructure, public sector reform and healthcare.

The US-with assistance from France and others-is trying to train and equip a new Afghan National Army. This is a tall order, as local warlords are fiercely independent and barely recognise the Government in Kabul. India has already pledged aid of $ 100 million and gifted aircraft and buses to that country. A few achievements in specific fields of reconstruction barely touch the fringe of the problem. The Rabia Balkhi Women's Hospital in Kabul has been reopened.

Vaccination of 4.3 million children has been done against measles and 700,000 cases of malaria have been treated. Other urgent requirements are revitalisation of the polio eradication programme surveillance system; completing the rebuilding of 72 hospitals, clinics and women's healthcare centres; and building or repairing 550 heathcare centres.

In the field of education 1,000 schools need to be rebuilt or repaired, as well as 30,000 teachers trained to man them. Printing of 15 million textbooks for 2.9 million students, 30 percent of whom are girls, is required. Since the fall of the Taliban, more than 2.2 million Afghan refugees and 600,000 internally displaced persons have returned home. A lot of funds and vast infrastructure are required to rehabilitate them.

Battered and forgotten Afghanistan, with next to nothing in economic and military power, is in a Catch-22 situation. It must surely be a strange world in which one nation attacks another, destroys it and, then, as a kind of reparation or to salve its conscience, helps 'reconstruct' the country it flattened in the first place. At present, of course, the world's interest in Afghanistan has been overtaken by that in Iraq. The stakes of the US-whose defence budget for the year 2003-2004 is $ 369 billion-have certainly shifted to Iraq, where it reportedly spent $ 20 billion on the war this year. A friendly Iraq can be a reliable source of oil needed by the West. Money realised by sale of oil can offset reconstruction costs. Also, contracts to companies back home are a given, leading to employment generation and development of the American economy. In other words, Iraqis will pay for reconstruction via oil sales.

Afghanistan has no such attraction and has ceased to be relevant to the US. More, there is no Soviet Union around. After some time, aid to Afghanistan, pouring in torrents a year ago, will become a trickle and then dry up. It will be a repetition of the raids of Ahmed Shah Abdali on India, who invaded the country 15 times only when he needed its wealth!

Modern-day Abdalis camouflage their designs in high sounding moralistic rhetoric, to argue that what they did by attacking others was a favour, and that the affected countries should be grateful. There no longer seems to be any defence against the world's mighty save the generosity of the 'victor' towards its victim or victims.

Whatever the rich nations or the not-so-rich neighbours of Afghanistan may do, that country has to ultimately rouse itself to work its own renewal. But first, it must be united in its resolve to place Afghanistan above all other considerations. The Afghan story is a lesson for us: Only by being united and peaceful can a nation progress.

2. Terrorism: Features and Tactics

2.1. Suicide Terrorism

Suicide terrorism is the flavour of season, whether in India, Sri Lanka, West Asia or Pakistan. Suicide terror attack is invariably politically motivated. It is aggressive, brutal and generally executed by an individual or a group of individuals. The latest high profile victim of suicide terrorism is Lieutenant-General Sarath Fonseka, Sri Lanka's Army chief. His convoy was targeted inside the high security zone of Colombo's main military base.

According to reports, a woman posing to be pregnant entered the hospital compound; normally, relatives of soldiers being treated at army hospitals are allowed within the high security compound for lunchtime visits. The bomber, who slipped in with others, jumped in front of the commander's convoy as it moved past the hospital, and blew herself up.

In response, Sri Lanka launched air strikes on LTTE bases in the eastern part of the country on April 25. It is the aim of suicide terrorists to cause death through blowing themselves up along with a predetermined target. Over the past two decades, instances of suicide terrorism have increased. Such attempts are not restricted to any area or place. There are a number of organisations that use this method. Fifteen such outfits have been identified, which resort to the use of suicide tactics against their enemies.

These are the Liberation Tigers of Tamil Eelam (LTTE) in Sri Lanka and in India (168 suicide bombings); Hizbullah and pro-Syrian groups in Lebanon, Kuwait and Argentina (52); Hamas in Israel (22); Kurdistan Worker's Party (PKK) in Turkey (15); Palestinian Islamic Jihad in Israel (8); Al Qaeda in East Africa (2); Egyptian Islamic Jihad (EIJ) in Croatia (1); Islamic Group in Pakistan (1); Babbar Khalsa International in India (1); Armed Islamic Group (GIA) in Algeria (1).

By February 2000, about 275 suicide terror incidents had occurred all over the world. India has been a target of suicide terrorism since LTTE killed former Prime Minister Rajiv Gandhi in 1991. Islamist terrorists targetted Parliament - apart from numerous and almost daily such attacks in Jammu & Kashmir. The following figures of terrorist violence, including suicide killing, tell their story. Between the 1988 and 2001, there were 47,235 incidents in J&K, in which 15,246 terrorists, 11,377 civilians and 4,102 security personnel were killed, adding up to a total of 30,725 lives.

The objective of terrorism, irrespective of the brand or the audacity involved, is to compel the government of the day towards a particular course of action. It is true from Lebanon to Israel and from Sri Lanka to Kashmir and Chechnya. Take, for instance, Al Qaeda: It fits this pattern. Its avowed objective has been to force the United States to leave the "holy land" of Saudi Arabia. 9/11 was the most audacious instance of suicide bombing, along with the one on Indian Parliament on December 13 in which all the terrorist who stormed it were killed.

Almost all suicide terrorist attacks are part of a coherent strategy. They are never isolated or random incidents. Democracies are uniquely susceptible to such attacks for the simple reason that they have to follow the law and meet all legal requirements before any action can be taken against a terrorist. The US, UK, France, India, Israel, Indonesia, Egypt, Russia, Sri Lanka and Turkey have all been targets of suicide attacks in the past two decades. Interestingly, each of these countries is a democracy.

The worldwide annual total of terrorist incidents has fallen almost to half: There were 348 attacks in 2001 as opposed to 666 incidents in 1987. Yet, the number of attacks in which the terrorists intend to kill themselves along with their victims has grown from an average of three per year in the 1980s, to 10 per year in the 1990s, to more than 25 in both 2000 and 2001.

We have to face the reality that suicide terrorism has come to stay. The question is how should democracies, including our country, respond to this problem? Experience has shown that reacting with heavy military and retaliatory offensives only leads to more attacks in which innocent bystanders are often harmed. This leads to public sympathy for the terrorists, without hampering their networks.

In their frustration some countries facing terrorism change their tactics and go in for making concessions to political causes supported by terrorists. India did this in announcing unilateral ceasefire against the J&K terrorist in 2001-2002. But the policy had to be abandoned in favour of a proactive approach in dealing with terror. Suicide terrorists were reportedly the reason why the US and French military forces were forced to abandon Lebanon in 1983. The Israeli forces left most of Lebanon in 1985 as well as the Gaza Strip and the West Bank in 1994 and 1995, due to suicide terrorism.

Making concessions does not always work, especially since the terrorists have learned that suicide terrorism strategy usually pays. Occupying a country with the use of force to eliminate terrorism is no solution, as we have seen in Afghanistan and Iraq under the US leadership. It is time to urge that in the rush to treat terrorists as "our children gone astray", we need to remember what George Washington had said: "Government is not reason, nor eloquence. It is force. And like fire, it is a dangerous servant and a fearsome master."

Unfortunately, discussing or granting of concession or favouring them in the ways desired by them too is not a solution. The exchange of terrorists for the former Home Minister of India's daughter, or bartering terrorists for the hijacked Indian Airlines flight from Kathmandu to Kandahar, has only emboldened the terrorists. It follows a common pattern. Concessions given have never satisfied the desires and purposes of suicide terrorists. In fact they send a wrong message to terrorist leaders, that the party they are dealing with is powerless and susceptible to intimidation and bullying.

There are no cut and dry solutions to this problem of suicide terrorism. The best approach for the Government would be to focus on domestic security while doing what can be done to neutralise the terrorists by effective governance. The Government, while willing to talk to the terrorists, should never give the impression that it is weak or unwilling to use force to defend the integrity of the country. It was Mao who had said that power flows from the barrel of the gun. Terrorists have to be given the message that though they may have gun, actual power flows from the guns of the Government.

2.2. Politico-insurgency

Bhutan has been a reluctant host to terrorist groups in the Northeastern states of India. These militants had first infiltrated and then imposed themselves on that country. On May 17, 2003, Bhutanese Foreign Minister Thinley had announced in Dhaka that his Government had warned ULFA rebels with use of force if they refused to withdraw from the Himalayan Kingdom peacefully. Mr Thinley also said the Bhutan Government had held two meetings with senior ULFA leaders and asked them to fix a date for another meeting, probably the last, to fix a deadline for withdrawal. India, of course, had been requesting Bhutan to take action against them, so that they do not use that country as a base for terrorist activities against India.

Bhutan served notices on three militant groups, ULFA, NDFB and KLO, on the December 13, 2003, through the national newspaper, Kuensel, saying it was left with no option but to entrust Royal Bhutan Army with the duty of removing the militants from its soil in accordance with the decision of the 81st session of National Assembly. After a lapse of 48 hours, from the time of the issue of notice, the Royal Bhutan Army (RBA) started operations on December 15, 2003. The crackdown was on three insurgent groups: The United Liberation Front of Assam (ULFA), the National Democratic Front of Bodoland, (NDFB) and the Kamtapur Liberation Organisation (KLO). These groups were using Bhutan for their subversive activities in India's Northeast for the last 12 years.

There were at least 30 to 40 well fortified camps sheltering over 3,000 heavily-armed militants of the three outfits along the entire stretch of southern Bhutan bordering the states of West Bengal, Assam and Arunachal Pradesh. Of these camps 13 of ULFA, 12 of NDFB, and five of KLO have been destroyed. Some terrorist leaders have been arrested. It is reported the RBA has arrested some terrorists and more than 160 of them have been killed in the flush-out operations. Of the dead, 100 belong to the NDFB, 38 to ULFA and 12 to the KLO. The Royal Bhutanese Army also suffered losses. About 34 personnel have been killed and many injured since

December 15. Bhutanese operation has lead to the recovery of 500 AK-47 rifles, over 100 pistols and other sophisticated weapons like anti-aircraft guns, 60 mm mortars, Self Loading Rifles besides 150,000 rounds of ammunition and 80,000 rounds of ammunition for AK rifles.

Bhutan has also taken action against its own citizens who were collaborating with the terrorists. Top ULFA leaders as well as the KLO chief have surrendered following the operations. Such was the pressure from the Bhutanese Army, that its top brass have appealed to the King to call off the operations. It is also a fact that ULFA cadres, some of which are based in Bangladesh, have been asked by Pakistan's ISI to retaliate and strike at targets in India for the operations in Bhutan. The ULFA has already given a call to the Bhutanese living in Northeast to leave. It called for bandh as protest against the Bhutanese military action. The bandh flopped. It is also a matter of concern that Northeastern terrorists managed to enter Bhutan from Indian states. Obviously there was failure in checking and preventing the entry of the Northeastern terrorists into Bhutan.

West Bengal's Jalpaiguri district has a 150 km border with Bhutan. The flushing out of the terrorists from their hide-outs will go a long way towards controlling terrorists activities in the Northeastern states in India. As a result of Bhutanese operations, an estimated 3,000 to 4,000 terrorists from the Northeast in Bhutan would try to sneak into Indian Territory. An octogenarian ULFA leader and one of the founder-members of the outfit, Bhimakanta Buragohain, popularly called Mama, who ULFA had said was killed, was presented before mediapersons along with three others by the corps commander on December 27. An ULFA ideologue, Burahagohain was first said to have been killed in the continuing operation by Bhutan, and later handed over to the Indian Army on December 26.

Buragohain has now made an appeal from Army custody to the rank and file of the outfit to lay down arms and hold discussions with the Government for a peaceful solution to the Assam problem. So far, 76 persons, including 45 women and 31 children, have been handed over to the State Government. Of these, 37 women owed allegiance to the ULFA and the rest to the National Democratic Force of Bodoland (NDFB). The Assam Chief Minister, Mr Tarun

Gogoi, has said the State Government would provide amnesty only to those militants who surrender by January 31, 2004.

As a result of the pressure of the Royal Bhutanese Army and the Indian Army, terrorists have run away from Bhutan. Meanwhile, over 20 new camps of ULFA and NDFB have come up in Bangladesh, especially in the Chittagong, Sylhet, Habibganj and Sherpur areas. The issue of Bangladesh's support for these terrorist will be taken up when Prime Minister Vajpayee meets his Bangladesh counterpart during the ongoing SAARC summit in Islamabad. While Bangladesh Foreign Minister Morshed Khan has denied the existence of these camps, Indian agencies have irrefutable evidence in this regard. It is the responsibility of Indian security forces to deal with them.

In spite of this, our neighbours, Bangladesh and Pakistan, have not learnt any lesson- they continue to harbour terrorists. Action by Bhutan is a small contribution to India's fight against terrorism. Bhutan has population of just seven lakh and an army of only 12,000. India is morally bound to come to its rescue, should the remnants of terrorists in Bhutan try to create trouble for it. It will, of course, depend upon the request of Government of Bhutan, which undertook a military operation after 138 years in its history. It is not the end of terrorism. The following groups are still operating in North East:

The Kuki National Army: The Kukis have settled in Myanmar, Manipur, and Nagaland. In Myanmar, they are known as the Kuki Chin. In 1987, the Kuki National Organisation (KNO) demanded an autonomous state within Myanmar. These were Kukis from Myanmar. A similar group, the Kuki National Front (KNF), demanded "Kukiland" comprising parts of Myanmar and Manipur, India. They are operating in Manipur and Nagaland.

National Socialist Council of Nagaland (NSCN): It was founded by Angami Zapu Phizo, who began his secessionist movement for an independent homeland for the Nagas. NSCN is still active and the Government has been talking to it to bring peace to Nagaland. The NSCN based in Nagaland (Muivah faction) demanded Greater Nagaland, a cross-border entity which would comprise parts of Myanmar, Nagaland, and Manipur.

All Tripura Tiger Force (ATTF): This insurgent group is the most dreaded in Tripura. The ATTF has carried out ambushe against the Tripura State Rifles. It has links with the NSCN and the ULFA. Recent reports suggest the ULFA has provided arms to the National Liberation Front of Tripura and the ATTF.

United Liberation Front of Assam (ULFA): It was founded in April 1979. In 1986, it established contacts with Kachins in Myanmar to receive arms and arms-training. Subsequently, the ULFA cadre were trained by both factions of the NSCN. Since 1990, they have been in touch with Pakistan. Some of its cadres have undergone intensive training with the Mujahideen under the supervision of ISI.

Bodo Security Force: This group, which has looted the armouries of central paramilitary forces, including the CRPF and the BSF, demands separate Bodoland.

The Bhutanese operation must not lull us into complacency of any kind; it does not mean the end of terrorism in the Northeast. In fact, it should spur us to persuade our neighbours,Bangladesh, Pakistan and Myanmar, to emulate the example set by Bhutan, and expel terrorists from their territories. Each country is guided by its national interest and it is for us to sell this idea to our neighbours. Nowhere in the world has victory over terrorism been achieved through lectures and making the terrorists see reason. To buy peace, successive governments have given one concession after another to terrorism-affected states. It will be wise to break the back of terrorism and then talk to its perpetrators.Talking from a position of strength will leave no option for the terrorists except to sign on the dotted line.

2.3. Red-Insurgency

Andhra Pradesh Chief Minister N Chandrababu Naidu escaped a bid on his life on October 1. The attack was the handiwork of naxalites-specifically, the People's War Group (PWG)-who set off a series of powerful landmine blasts at the foothills of the famous Venkateswara Temple. Four others, including a State Minister and an MLA, were injured in the remote-controlled blasts on the road to the temple. This was the second time the PWG tried to kill Mr Naidu. The first was made in 1998 in Karimnagar district, where he had gone for an election campaign. At the time, the police had found Claymore mines hidden in a bullock cart minutes before his arrival. Claymore mines were devised during the Korean War and used by the US Army in Vietnam. It explodes in a particular direction and sprays its lethal contents in a 60 degree arc.

This attack on the Andhra Pradesh Chief Minister raises very important issues about the security threat to VVIPs. The State Administration obviously did not realise the gravity of challenge posed by this extremist grouping. Nor were they mindful of the fact naxalites should be treated as terrorists-vigilance in their case is equally imperative, since they too thrive on creating a climate of terror. Around 600 policemen and civilians have been killed by PWG. Almost same number of PWG terrorists have been killed in encounters during the last four years. Reportedly, eight State Cabinet Ministers, are on the naxalite hit list. Another 72 of 182 TDP legislators are also targeted. Besides, 31 Congress MLAs out of the total of 91 and four of 12 BJP legislators have been marked for a similar treatment by the PWG. Twenty-six IAS and IPS officers are also under threat.

In May, 1991, LTTE terrorists succeeded in killing Rajiv Gandhi, a former Prime Minister on the campaign trail. Other terror victims were Punjab's Chief Minister Beant Singh, who was killed by Sikh terrorists right in the porch of the State Secretariat at Chandigarh.

Terrorist strikes against public figures are successful due to serious lapses on the part of those involved in the security of the protected person. On occasion, the latter is also responsible for his own tragic fate. In their desire to remain in close touch with the public, VVIPs do not like to submit themselves to irritating security restrictions. VIP killings may also occur due to involvement of corrupt officials in assassination attempts -such as in Jammu & Kashmir, where policemen were were said to collude in the killing of a J&K Minister.

If a terrorist group does not have sophisticated means at its disposal, it usually follows the simplest method: It keeps its eyes open to see if the strict security cordon and procedures concerning the target are lax enough to make an effective and fatal strike possible. The usual routine followed by the Government to mitigate the unpleasant fallout of a successful or an aborted terrorist attack is to order what it proclaims is a thorough inquiry by an outside agency. Or it sets up a commission to identify security loopholes and recommend ways to plug them. Three such Commissions- the Thakkar Commi-ssion, the Verma Commission and the Jain Commission- were set up in connection with the assassination of Rajiv Gandhi.

Since such attacks continue to take place, it seems official complacency is only shaken when an incident occurs. Rarely are lessons learnt from the past. At the most, some police and security personnel heads roll. It was expected that the mother of all terrorist depredations-the attack on Parliament on December 13, 2001-would serve as a wake-up call for those meant to safeguard national interest to tighten up VIP security by plugging loopholes. The hope seems to have been belied.

One reason for laxity is the politicisation and polarisation of the police force. The Parliamentary Standing Committee on Home Affairs has said that the country's police machinery is "politicised and politically polarised". Making this observation in its 88th report submitted to both Houses of Parliament in 2002, the Committee, headed by Rajya Sabha member Pranab Mukherjee, asked the Home Ministry to "make earnest efforts to depoliticise the institution of police before it becomes too late to retrieve it from the morass of degeneration".

The Committee described the police force as a "pawn in the hands of its (political) masters". All its members were unanimous in the view that the country's intelligence-gathering machinery and performance would improve greatly if a "proper system of accountability" were evolved. They asserted that policemen sought political "patronage essential for their survival and ... personnel are found to be divided in camps having distinct political leanings".

The Committee also observed that "this connivance of the police with the powers-that-be is giving rise to cynicism among the people". It called this "very dangerous" for "the continuance and survival of democracy". Recommending the preparation of a blueprint for a "model police force" to be followed by all States, it asked the Home Ministry to ensure modernisation and accountability by following a "definite plan of action" that would establish "unity of command and direction".

A related and major problem is that States are averse to any Central initiative that touches their rights vis-a-vis the State police.

Strengthening or toning up of the latter and improving the security system depend on individual Chief Ministers, some of whom do not treat the problem with the same gravity as others.

Indeed, terrorism looks less threatening when viewed from the air-conditioned confines where seminars are held, or cosy offices, or simply from a distance. Its true nature becomes an ugly reality only in the affected place. While one wing of the Government talks of dealing with it with a firm hand, other sections of the polity that are least knowledgeable about the grave situation hedge their bets with ifs and buts. Nobody talks about the rights of the victims. Yet many want a militaristic approach to ensuring that the 'human rights' of terrorists are protected!

These are the sections that must realise that terrorists are waging a war against the state and Government established by law. Naxalites, on their part, openly proclaim their lack of faith in the present system of democratic governance and their decision to overthrow it by force. There is no doubt that such groups or organisations should be treated on par with foreigners invaders. They do not deserve the protection provided by the very Constitution they want to undermine in the very country they want to destabilise. Terrorists do not respect anybody's rights, whether of families or individuals. They should be paid back in the same coin.

True, there is always the risk of misuse of power and misapplication of stringent laws. But armchair criticism of the security forces is unacceptable. The practical difficulties the security and law enforcement agencies face and the grave risks taken by those on the field, who dirty their hands so that others are safe, also need to be appreciated. Maintaining a balance between security and 'human rights' is the perennial dilemma, a difficult problem, at the operational level when it comes to tackling terrorism. We should consider, first of all, that there are no eager witnesses of terrorist strikes who happily depose in the courts. Assume that somebody is present at the scene of a terrorist killing. It is still doubtful he will enthusiastically testify in the absence of a witness protection programme. Who will not be intimidated by the threat to life faced from terrorist elements?

How many times must we allow enemies of humanity to get the better of the nation before we educate ourselves about the real nature and dimensions of the anti-terror combat? You do not allow weeds in your garden. Similarly, you cannot adopt a mild approach to terrorism in your nation. You have to hate mindless carnage enough to crush its perpetrators. Terrorism and weeds are not things you handle gently-you destroy them.

3. Sponsorship and Other Elements

3.1. Pakistan the Thriving Bed of Terrorism

Religion is a sensitive issue. Battles have been fought over issues that may prima facie appear trivial. In a country like ours with a multi-ethnic population, incidents of religious fracas have been quite common. And terrorists fish in the troubled waters to incite violence as their alternative means to disrupt normalcy in this country.

On March 30, 2002, in the attack on Raghunath Temple, Jammu, seven persons were killed. On September 24, the same year, two terrorists attacked Akshardham temple in Ahmedabad, killing 35 people. In 2005, bomb blasts rocked Varanasi; 21 were killed and over 62 injured when terrorists targeted Sankat Mochan temple and the city's railway station. Then there were bombings in Malegaon in Maharashtra in 2006 and Mecca Masjid in Hyderabad in May this year, claiming many innocent lives.

The terrorist attacks at Raghunath temple in Jammu and Akshardham temple in Ahmedabad were attempts to provoke the majority community to retaliate and thus cause civil strife. The foul ploy did not work. The terrorist strategy failed in Delhi too in 2005, as law-abiding citizens' desire to live in peace mercifully prevented communal riots, though the blasts occurred on the eve of Eid and Diwali, on October 28 that year. The Delhi bombings killed more than 50 persons and seriously injured more than 100.

After failing to provoke Hindus to attack Muslims, the terrorists triggered more blasts on April 14, 2006 during the Friday prayers in the Delhi Jama Masjid badly injuring a dozen. After that, three compartments of the Lahore-bound Samjhauta Express were burnt to ashes to cause both communal disharmony and spoil the peace initiatives taken by India and Pakistan.

Thereafter, a mosque and a graveyard respectively in Nanded and Malegaon in Maharashtra were bombed on the occasion of Shabe-Baaraat at a time when the devout were offering prayers, killing 13 persons injuring over 27.

Mecca Masjid is known as one of the historical mosques in southern India, It was built in the 17th century and the bricks used in its construction were reportedly brought from Mecca, the holy city after which the mosque was named. A bomb placed in a tiffin box near this mosque's wuzukhana (water storage for ablution before offering namaaz) was exploded through a remote control device, probably a mobile phone. The terrorist attack claimed 16 lives and wounded 67 people.

There was mass outrage at the terrorist attack and the police had to open fire to control the furious public. Though the attack was intended to fuel communal riots, the nefarious objective failed.

The needle of suspicion in every such case invariably points to the terrorist groups thriving in Pakistan. It's ironical that the proclaimed Islamic republic supports elements that offend Islam through terrorism. Poetic justice may be seen in the April 28 incident when Pakistan's Interior Minister Aftab Khan Sherpao and his son Sikander, also a Member of Parliament, were injured when a suicide bomber blew himself up at a public rally, killing 30 people and wounding 50 in the NWFP.

"For years, terrorist camps (in Pakistan) have been only half a secret, as everybody knows they are there, but no one would officially admit it," said a Pakistani official under the condition of anonymity, adding, "They are hidden; no ordinary people can go there." The camps are used by terrorist groups such as Jaish-e-Mohammed (Army of Mohammed) and Lashkar-e-Tayyeba (Army of the Pure). For more than a decade, the Inter-Services Intelligence Directorate has been sponsoring such groups to attack India to keep Pakistan's dispute with us over Jammu & Kashmir alive, just as it nurtures the Taliban to pursue Pakistani interests in Afghanistan, Western intelligence sources have noted.

Pakistan's name is increasingly being mentioned worldwide in the context of terrorism. When police in Britain foiled a major terrorist attack targeted at trans-Atlantic flights, for example, the investigation trail led them to Pakistan. Be it Al Qaeda or Lashkar-e-Tayyeba (LeT), they cannot survive for a day without active support from rogue states. All terrorist groups are interlinked. They plan attacks on religious places of both the majority and minority communities in India with covert directions from our recalcitrant neighbour. In fact, Sikh terrorism of the 1980s could not have continued for long but for its support.

It is important to reiterate a warning issued by the UN expert panel group whose report on terrorism says, "Members of Al Qaeda and their associates are deployed in many countries across the world and, given the opportunity, they will have no compunction in killing as many people as they can from those nations that do not conform to their religions and ideological beliefs and which they perceive as their enemies."

There is a long history of sponsored terrorism. And there have been many rogue states besides Pakistan - Libya, South Yemen, Syria, Iran, Cuba and North Korea - that would go to any extent to create problems for the countries they do not like. Throughout history, terrorism has been used by those who could not prevail upon others either by persuasion or example. But the mischief has inevitably failed eventually every time, either because people - terrorists may or may not realise - cannot be frightened to submission.

Yet, the menace of terrorism cannot be left to die its own natural death. A Jammu & Kashmir Police publication in 2003 said that there were 56,041 incidents of violence, including 10,093 explosions, 29,931 firing incidents, 5,561 arson, 763 rocket attacks, 4,597 abductions, 229 cases of hanging to death, 275 arms snatching cases and 4,592 other acts of violence between January 1990 and December 2002. More than 30,000 civilians were killed during the 14th year of terrorism in the State during the same period. The security forces seized 24,785 AK-type rifles, 9,387 pistols and revolvers, 58 carbines, 1,003 RPGs, 91 light machine guns and self-loading rifles, 742 rocket launchers and 2,270 rocket boosters during the same period. Besides, 6,865 kg of RDX, 47,219 grenades, 5,228 anti-personnel mines and 4,176 rockets were also seized.

Let us not underestimate terrorists. Any target for them is easy enough to strike as long as they can show to the world that they are mightier than established Governments. Most of them are brainwashed to believe that for their dastardly acts, their seats in heaven are booked. Let the terrorists' delusion remain. In fact,

Governments can make terrorists meet their god without further delay.

3.2. Pakistan: The Eatalist

Whenever there is a terrorist attack the finger of suspicion rightly points towards Pakistan, a country that has sheltered, trained and protected terrorists over the last three decades. Whatever Government there may be in Islamabad, Pakistan has always tried to bleed India with a thousand cuts. Irrespective of the fact whether it is under Army or civilian rule, our western neighbour has been following a consistent anti-India policy. By now it has a small section of people embedded within the Indian population who act as sleeper cells and provide logistical support to terrorists engaged in *jihad* against India.

Even if Pakistan's current rulers want to end this menace of terrorism, for terrorism has equally devastated Pakistani society in recent years, they would have to step on the toes of the Pakistani Army that supports terrorist organisations like the Lashkar-e-Tayyeba through the rogue ISI. The Army has even described these terrorists as freedom fighters. It sees these *jihadis* as acting on their behalf and in their own interest and therefore, supports them fully.

Pakistan President Asif Ali Zardari has vowed to crack down on anti-India terrorists and recently even made a show of 'arresting' some suspects in connection with the Mumbai terror attacks. All civilian leaders in Islamabad at least claim that it is in Pakistan's interest to ensure that the country does not become a refuge for terrorists. But given the persuasions of the powerful Army they have but little choice in the matter.

The recent terror attacks on Mumbai, which claimed 164 lives and injured over 300 civilians, have re-opened the wounds of thousands of people in different parts of India who in recent years have been helpless witnesses to the horrors of terrorism. The following is a list of terror strikes in India over the last 12 months:

May 13, 2008 (Jaipur): 63 people killed in serial bombings.

July 25, 2008 (Bangalore): One person killed in a low-intensity bomb explosion.

July 26, 2008 (Ahmedabad): 56 people killed after 16 synchronised bombs went off.

September 13, 2008 (New Delhi): 20 people killed in six bombings across the city.

September 27, 2008 (New Delhi): Three people killed after a crude bomb exploded in a busy market.

September 29 2008 (Modasa, Gujarat): One killed and several injured after a low-intensity bomb went off near a mosque.

September 29, 2008 (Malegaon, Maharashtra): Five people died after a bomb went off in a crowded market.

October 01, 2008 (Agartala, Tripura): Two people killed and 100 injured in serial bombings in crowded market places in Agartala.

October 14, 2008 (Kanpur): Eight people injured after bomb planted on a rented bicycle went off in the Colonelganj market.

October 21, 2008 (Imphal, Manipur): 17 killed in a powerful bomb explosion near Manipur Police Commando complex.

October 30, 2008 (Assam): At least 76 killed in serial bombings across Assam.

November 26, 2008 (Mumbai): 164 killed and over 300 injured in *fidayeen* attacks on the Taj Mahal Palace, Chabad House, Oberoi-Trident Hotel and CST. There were attacks in other parts of Mumbai as well, and the hostage situation at the two hotels and Chabad House lasted for more than 60 hours. Nine terrorists were gunned down, while one was caught alive. As many as 20 policemen and two NSG commandos were killed, while 26 foreign nationals were among the dead.

More than 600 people have been killed and hundreds maimed and devastated in terror strikes in India in the last six years. Now, the question is what options do we have to deal with this menace? Whenever there is a major terrorist attack one solution which is always touted is undertaking military strikes to destroy the terrorist camps in Pakistan. However, terrorists are difficult to isolate and pinpoint and a military strike on Pakistan, even if targeted at terror camps, will lead to a full-scale war between the two countries. There are no rules in war, and therefore, there cannot be an agreement between the two warring parties that only conventional weapons will be used.

We are often told that tough anti-terror laws are prone to abuse. Hence, the new laws that have been passed by Parliament, while plugging many loopholes, are perceived as not sufficient to deal with terrorism. Assuming that the anti-terror will be misused, does it mean that we should not have stringent laws against terrorism? It seems that some of our leaders are more bothered about the human rights of terrorists than the human rights of hundreds of innocent civilians who are being butchered by *jihadis*. Human rights are for human beings and not *fidayeen* squads.

Tough circumstances require tough responses. The Government should give clear orders to the forces at the border to shoot down all intruders. It should also display boards at the border that anybody entering India illegally will be shot dead. Let there also be periodical loudspeaker announcements at the border to that effect, so that nobody can say that he was taken unawares. It is true that people across the border sometimes unwittingly stray into Indian territory. These people should be treated humanely and deported back to their homeland. Instead of waging war, it will be prudent for India to fence the entire border and strengthen border patrolling.

One thing is clear: Most Pakistani rulers, whether Army or civilian, survive only on hate-India-sentiments. They talk of peace when they are out of power. Even Benazir Bhutto as Prime Minister indulged in war rhetoric, not unlike her father Zulfiqar Ali Bhutto, who had publicly pledged to wage a 1000-year war against India. This was later repeated by Benazir Bhutto; then Prime Minister VP Singh had responded by saying that Pakistan would not last even a thousand hours if it embarked on a misadventure.

War rhetoric apart, the only way we can deal with terrorism effectively is to make it cost-prohibitive. It will be best to deal with it on our own territory and on our own terms than on the territory of Pakistan. Thus, we must focus on clamping down on terrorists and their supporters at home first.

3.3. A Thorn between Two Flowers: A Review of Indo-Pak Relationship

While addressing a massive public rally on April 18 in Srinagar, Prime Minister Atal Bihari Vajpayee said: “We once again extend our hand of friendship to Pakistan, but the desire ought to be on both sides.” He once again launched a fresh peace initiative, with the condition of reciprocation. It was the first rally to be addressed in Jammu & Kashmir by a Prime Minister in the 15 years. In continuation of Mr Vajpayee's offer, India and Pakistan broke the political ice on April 28, and moved closer towards a resumption of the long-stalled bilateral dialogue when the Prime Ministers of the two countries had a telephonic conversation.

This was the first direct bilateral political contact at the highest level in more than a year. Pakistani Premier Mir Zafarullah Khan Jamali was the one to telephone Mr Vajpayee, and extend to him an invitation to visit Pakistan. It is obvious that Pakistan was under pressure from the international community to respond positively to Mr Vajpayee's initiative. Hence, there was a radical change in the tone and tenor of its response. India has been sending the signal that Mr Vajpayee would be willing to travel to Pakistan to attend a postponed SAARC summit if the leaders could sign concrete economic agreements, rather than discuss Kashmir in a forum clearly not meant for thrashing out bilateral issues.

Mr Vajpayee reportedly emphasised the importance of economic cooperation, cultural exchanges and people-to-people contacts between the two countries, as well as the importance of reviving civil aviation links. A visit to Pakistan by Mr Vajpayee in the next few months would be a small price to pay, if Pakistan does agree to end its opposition to normal trade and people-to-people interaction. The two Prime Ministers were said to have agreed to consider these measures as the first step towards a restoration and normalisation of ties. Mr Jamali is also believed to have affirmed Pakistani opposition to terrorism.

Pakistani Foreign Minister Khurshid Mahmood Kasuri, on his part, has said: "Pakistan is neither sponsoring nor encouraging anyone into venturing into the Indian side of Kashmir. It does concede the possibility of some making it despite vigil". Twice bitten and twice shy, it is natural that the Indian side would insist on seeing the Pakistani Prime Minister's assertions translate into action on the ground. A similar commitment by Pakistani President Pervez Musharraf on January 12, 2002, was honoured more in its breach.

At the time, under Anglo-American pressure, Pakistan gave strong verbal commitments to end terrorism. This had the effect of defusing the tensions between the two countries, at a time their armies were locked in an eyeball-to-eyeball confrontation. On the issue of infiltration, the Pakistani Foreign Minister recently said that Pakistan was ready to accept foreign observers, including UN representatives, to monitor the situation. He has named seven countries for India to consider with regard to "joint monitoring" of the Line of Control. The countries identified are France, Russia, the United Kingdom, the United States, China, Saudi Arabia and Iran.

This proposal is not new. But it is the first time Pakistan has actually gone ahead and named the countries the representatives of which could form part of the proposed joint panel. India has rejected as "self- serving and impractical" Pakistan's proposal for international verification and monitoring of cross-border infiltration. This is a charge Islamabad has consistently denied.

India, on its part, has been proposing joint patrol of the LoC by Indian and Pakistani forces. The offer was repeated by Prime Minister Vajpayee at the Almaty Summit in Russia in June 2002. At the time, Pakistan had rejected the proposal on the plea that it was not feasible. It felt it was unworkable on account of the mistrust between India and Pakistan. That is where matters stand now.

The annual report of the Union Ministry of Home Affairs for the year 2002-2003 shows that the chief areas of concern for this nation remain concentrated on terrorism in J&K, particularly the "incremental use of suicide bombers". There were 10 suicide attacks in 2002. It was also said that 60 to 70 per cent of terrorists operating in the State are from outside, "under the direct control of Pak ISI," with local people "playing the role of porters and guides".

During his interaction with an Indian representative in March this year, General Musharraf absolved his country of sponsorship of terrorism in J&K, by describing those crossing over as "freelance jihadis". He added that the decade-long war in Afghanistan in the 1980s had given birth to so many of them that it was beyond the control of any state to keep a check on them. He also said that it was worth pondering whether it was correct to expect the relatively smaller Pakistani force to seal the porous border, when the larger Indian contingent could not do so.

It is not as yet clear whether the Pakistani President wanted the menace of 'freelance jihadis' to be collectively dealt with by India and Pakistan, or whether his statement was a ploy to win international sympathy. India, however, feels Pakistan is playing a game.

All over the world, mischief makers within discontented groups-with or without the support of rogue regimes - seek the attainment of their causes through the barrel of the gun. In January, 1998 on Republic day, terrorists killed 23 Kashmir Pandits in Wandhama village near Ganderbal. They repeated this carnage by taking the lives of almost a similar number of people in Nadimarg in March this year.

We should, in fact, take General Musharraf at his word and make the price of terrorism in India so prohibitive that anybody would think twice before engaging in brutality. So far, the chief reason for India not having won spectacular victories against terrorism is that the Government's right hand does not know what its left is or should be doing. The system of Government functioning is too bureaucratic. For instance, if you send a proposal requiring the sanctioning of any equipment, you could go on answering queries for years together.

Recall the case of the army wanting to buy scooter mobiles, which could be used to traverse through snow. The numerous questions that were asked were both bolts from the blue as well as absurd. The proposal was sanctioned only after the Defence Minister ordered bureaucrats to go and see things for themselves and spend a few weeks with the troops.

Uniformed services, whether the army, the BSF or the CRPF, are too disciplined to take their grievances to the press. The result is that bureaucrats sit tight on proposals for ages, which-given the absence of equipment-has an adverse impact on the fight against terrorism. Take the case of the attack on Parliament on December 13, 2001. My information is that a'l the gadgetry required for the security of Parliament was not in position till last month. Yet the only way we can get the better of terrorism is to give the best of equipment to our forces, so that they can finish the problem at the entry point itself. This is something that needs to be monitored at the Prime Minister's and Home Minister's level.

Having proposed talks with Pakistan, Mr Vajpayee will face stiff opposition from the hawks in the country. But all over the world, it only dialogue that has led to solutions to seemingly intractable problems. Talks will be more fruitful if they are backed by heavy casualties suffered by the foreign mercenaries operating in our country. Talks under international pressure, massive elimination of terrorists and the visit of US Deputy Secretary of State Richard Armitage may persuade Pakistan to see reason. For all one knows, it may fall in line to actually fight terrorism alongside India, instead of exporting it to this country. There are hopeful signs so far that, this time, Mr Vajpayee might succeed in ending five decades of hostility.

1. Terrorism with High Morals

4.1. The Backbones of the 'ism'

The terrorists struck in a big way in Delhi on September 13, killing more than a score of innocent people and injuring many others in a series of coordinated bombings. The bombs, the first of which exploded at 6.15pm, all went off within 45 minutes of each other, targeting three posh and highly crowded market.

All the bombs were of low intensity, consisting of a cocktail of ammonium nitrate, gunpowder, ball bearings and nails, with timer devices. They were same as the bpmbs used in Jaipur, Bangalore and Ahmedabad. All of them were triggered using electronic timers.

Apart from one, all the bombs were strategically kept in dustbins to avoid detection. The responsibility for the attacks has been claimed by the Indian Mujahideen; a homegrown terrorist group with links to Pakistani terrorists that first came to prominence in May following the Jaipur serial bombings. The group followed that up with bombings in Bangalore and Ahmedabad in July.

The Gujarat Government says that the terrorists arrested by its police had confessed that their next target would be Delhi. It also claims that it had accordingly informed the Union Government. In the e-mail sent before the Ahmedabad blasts, the Indian Mujahideen had said; "In the light of injustice and wrongs on the Muslims of Gujarat, we advance our *jihad* and call our brethern under it, to unite and answer these irresolute Kaffireens of India. We call you, O Muslims of Gujarat, to elevate yourselves from the fears of these wretched Hindus, to unify all your courage and bravery that you have in your hearts."

Jihadis invoke religious sanction or quote religious texts to justify their acts of terrorism. They do not shy away from admitting the religious nature of their ultimate goal, that is the Islamisation of society. Literature found with the activists of the Students Islamic Movement of India talks of this goal. Since the *Jihadis* use the cloak of religion, they easily draw support from some sections of their co-religionists.

Jihadis are active in India not because India is the Number One enemy of Islam, but because it is considered to be a soft target. India is widely seen as the country 'most affected by terrorism' after Iraq. Our counter-terrorism responses have been rather muted and quite often non-existent.

Regrettably, when terrorist attacks take place in our country, the intelligence and security agencies are in deep slumber. The have no clue as to where these attacks could take place and vague, unspecific communications are passed off as intelligence input. Intelligence failure has repeatedly been the rule rather than the exception.

For targeting terrorism, we need a citizens' network to serve as an information gathering mechanism. We need to involve village panchayats, area committees, residents welfare associations, housing societies, etc. These organisations have, in the course of their normal activities, access to information that can help in monitoring suspicious activities.

Yet, this wealth of information is not tapped by the various intelligence agencies. The present political establishment is of no help at all. What we get as assurances are the same old repeated standard statements that terrorism will be dealt with strongly. But when and how are questions no one seems to have answers to. When will the Government learn that this is not a low-intensity conflict? This is a war, and innocent citizens are increasingly getting caught in the firing line.

The sooner the Government realises this, the better it will be. You cannot give excuses and not fight this war. There are no rules in killing an enemy who is out to kill you. The Union Government should rise above vote-bank politics and enact strict anti-terrorism laws of its own if it does not want to approve the laws passed by State Governments. There is some element of truth in the grievances of the States that when a terrorist attack takes place, the blame is squarely laid on the State Government for its failure to tackle terrorism. At the same time the States are not allowed to use tougher laws to tackle terrorism. As a result, anti-terrorist laws passed by the Rajasthan and Gujarat Governments are gathering dust in the portals of power in New Delhi.

Vote-bank politics and minorityism are among the factors that inhibit significant action against *Jihadis*. There is already a feeling in some sections of the country that the majority is being taken for granted.

Inadequate policing is a major constraint in tackling terrorism. It has been known for long that India's law enforcement machinery is severely under-staffed. The country's police to population ratio, already very low compared to many other countries, is getting worse. Data released by the Union Home Ministry shows that the ratio has declined from 143 police per 100,000 citizens at the end of 2005, to 126 per 100,000 citizens at the end of 2006. There is need to rectify this aspect immediately.

On the other hand, the criminal justice system is no better. There is no real fear of the law. The UK had introduced a special system for protecting the identities of certain witnesses in special cases by letting them tender evidence in anonymity. The Law Lords recently declared this provision illegal. However, Justice Secretary Jack Straw has said the Government would introduce legislation on a priority basis to enshrine the use of anonymous witnesses where intimidation is a risk. India needs to consider a similar amendment to the Evidence Act.

Apart from this, we must employ the latest technology to assist our security forces in the war on terror. In this respect market associations installing CCTV cameras will go a long way. It is worthwhile to spend a small portion of your earnings in improving your own security. The Government, on its part, should stop making hollow statements that are not backed up by deeds.

The UPA needs to realise that if the Government cannot assure security to the people, it should forget about development, industrialisation and higher economic growth. There can be no dialogue or understanding with terrorist groups. Either we can defeat terrorists or be defeated by them. The choice is ours.

4.2. Failure: The Reasons Behind

We are entering a new era in which the entire concept of security has changed drastically. The new concept also embraces security of people and not just of territories or nations. In terrorism, violence is intentional and used as a means to achieve political ends.

Government and terrorists are constantly engaged in a predictable conflict in which each side tries to influence or control the activities of the other. Terrorism is nothing but a violent method of coercion, a process of wrangling based on power to hurt and intimidate the other party.

The objective of terrorism is to bring change in a government's political position vis-à-vis the demands of terrorists. If opportunity permits, the terrorists would also aim at the destruction of military establishment.

Terrorists bank on the element of surprise and select an appropriate time. It is usually when the defenders are least expecting an attack and have least knowledge of terrorists' intentions and capabilities. Therefore, the government can ill afford to let its guard down.

The terrorists generally select urban locations to strike, which makes for a spectacular impact. Hence London, New York, Parliament House in Delhi or attack on Ram temple at Ayodhya. These days most terrorist attempts are suicide attacks. Today terrorists are not only educated but also technology savvy. Terrorism, in different guises, is raising its head in Punjab, the Northeast and States like Jharkhand, Bihar and Chhattisgarh.

Moreover, what might be a matter of life and death for India many not necessarily be so for other countries. In October 2003 British Prime Minister Tony Blair had said to the then Indian Prime Minister that Kashmir (a terrorist-infested area) was not a priority in the US-led war against global terror.

Of course, he sugar-coated the blunt message with the usual verbal assurances about how India was a "vital member in the international coalition against terrorism and how cross-border terrorism would be taken up later on." He used the right phrases and platitudes about India's "political maturity" and its "statesman-like stature".

Post-London explosions, one can only hope that he has learnt his lessons, and that Great Britain is equally susceptible to the horrors that India has been exposed to for decades.

Actually, so many terrorist attacks have taken place that a kind of ennui has set in among people. The other major problem is the lack of specific and sharp intelligence. As it was evident in Kargil, the country's intelligence was unaware of Pakistani-sponsored terrorists infiltrating into Indian territory for months together.

A plethora of intelligence agencies exist such as the Army's Defence Intelligence Agency and other civilian wings like the Intelligence Bureau, R&AW, State CID and Intelligence. Paramilitary forces like the Border Security Force, Central Reserve Police, and others have their own intelligence wings. Rarely, do senior officers go to field to collect intelligence information. These agencies have a norm that intelligence would be gathered by officers only up till the level of DSP.

The other major reason for failure in dealing with terrorism is the lack of consistent government policy. Each time the security forces succeed in strengthening their positions through sustained anti-terrorism drive, somebody pipes up to say, "Let us be charitable." The Government of India has twice in the past announced unilateral ceasefire in Kashmir

It proclaimed that no action would be taken against terrorists if they surrendered. With such an approach, all efforts made by the security forces came to naught these were sacrificed at the altar of ill-conceived political initiatives. However, it must be borne in mind that at no time had the terrorists asked for the ceasefire or that the security forces should stop action against them.

Let us not be misled about the intentions of the terrorists. In J&K they resorted to ethnic cleansing which resulted in the exodus of Hindus and Sikhs from the Valley. They were forced to migrate to Jammu, Delhi and other parts of India. The Sikh terrorists, before they were eliminated, had a similar aim.

The terrorists have a regular system of training as the following extract from a manual of a terrorist organisation reveals, "When arrested, the volunteer will... feel that he has failed, resulting in a deep sense of disappointment. The police are aware of this disappointment and act upon this weakness by insults... " Further:

"The most important thing to bear in mind when arrested is that you are a volunteer of a revolutionary organisation, that you have been captured by an enemy force, that your cause is a just one, that you are right and that the enemy is wrong and that as a soldier you have taken the chance expected of a soldier and that there is nothing to be ashamed of in capture.

"You must bear in mind that the treatment meted out to you is designed to break you and bleed you of all the information you may have with regard to the organisation to which you belong.

"They will attempt to intimidate you by sheer force of numbers and by brutality. Volunteers who may feel disappointed are entering the first dangerous threshold because the police will act on this disappointment...

"The purpose of an interrogation is to get a confession; if the interrogators knew what they were searching for there would be no need for questioning; therefore, interrogation is necessary only when the police is unaware of information which would lead to conviction. The best way to ward it off is to 'say nothing'...

All police forces start from a strong suspicion or a clue, therefore when a volunteer is arrested, they strive to build on that clue and the only way that can be done is by obtaining information from their victim."

These are some of the points emphasised in the terrorist camps in Pakistan. There are 29 which operate in PoK, 15 in North West Frontier Provinces, three in Northern Areas and seven in Pakistan's Punjab. They are the largest suppliers of terrorists all over the world - whether London or elsewhere.

Managing internal security of the country and dealing with terrorist groups in its different parts requires a high degree of preparedness. There is no limit to the kind of weapons and tricks which the terrorists might use.

Apart from conventional weapons like rifles and grenades, there is no knowing as to when they may use nuclear, biological and chemical weapons. The problem is that governments everywhere traditionally respond slowly. Many a time, they have responded well after the disasters have struck.

What is the use of having a Government or laws if they cannot prevent the terrorists from having an influence over any area in the country? The latest incidents in Srinagar and Doda indicate that it is not the Government but writ of the terrorist outfits which runs there. At present there are no specific laws to deal with terrorists as POTA has been struck off the statute book.

One cannot expect people to watch the activities of the terrorists in silence in terror-prone areas. At the same time, it is unlikely that they would be keen to expose themselves to the wrath of terrorists or even the legal delays in bringing the culprit to book.

What is meant is that the war against terror cannot succeed unless the security forces have the support of the local people in terrorist infested areas. Punjab militancy is a good example. Unless there is greater cooperation from the people living in such regions, success will be limited. At present it is difficult to guess how many more acts of terror will force the government out of its slumber.

6

Terrorism: Instances and Measures

1. Terrorism: Instances

1.1. Fake Notes in Circulation

Delhi Police claims to have busted a major ISI network on June 25, which was reportedly being used to push fake currency into our country. Three arrested men - Nayeem, Wasim and Mohammed - have revealed that Thar Express, the 'friendship train', running between Munnabao in Pakistan and Jodhpur in Rajasthan, is being used to smuggle fake currency into India. Initial investigations have revealed that the three men arranged for the fake currency in Dubai. Counterfeit currency amounting Rs. 33 lakh was seized from them.

Their interrogation has also revealed that the ongoing rate of exchange is Rs. 40,000 to R.s 65,000 for one lakh of fake currency, depending upon the quality of notes. Earlier in April, two persons, who allegedly smuggled over Rs. 50 lakh worth of fake currency from Pakistan into India, were arrested. The quality of Rs. 500 and Rs. 1,000 notes was so good that only an expert could tell they were fake.

The department of revenue intelligence has reportedly seized consignments of counterfeit currency worth over Rs. 1 crore from Mumbai, Chennai and Kozhikode Airports between March and May. Possibly, a huge quantity of made-in-Pakistan notes may have already been pumped into the Indian market before transiting through Dubai and Colombo, the distribution and storage centres. It is from these two places that seasoned smugglers bring the fake currency to India. Customs officials often miss the currency bundles during checks at airports as X-ray machines fail to detect them.

Early May, the Directorate of Revenue Intelligence arrested a man carrying Rs. 20 lakh worth of fake currency, all printed in Pakistan, at Kozhikode Airport. In February, three persons were arrested from Chennai Airport with over Rs. 30 lakh in Indian fake currency. It might appear bizarre that a 77-year-old woman, Laiquan, a resident of Delhi's Trilokpuri area, was arrested for trying to smuggle in fake Indian currency of more than Rs. 10 lakh in February at the Indira Gandhi International Airport in Delhi while returning from Lahore.

It is also believed that Pakistan's ISI is using Dawood Ibrahim's network across Thailand, Nepal, Bangladesh, Dubai and India for financing terrorist activities and destabilising the Indian economy through the circulation of fake Indian currency notes (FICNs). Till 2000, the number of FICNs in circulation was 61,000 million pieces (of different denominations) worth Rs. 1,69,000 crore, according to unofficial estimates. The actual seizures were merely worth Rs. 5.57 crore in 2002, Rs. 5.29 crore in 2003, Rs. 6.81 crore in 2004 and Rs. 1.12 crore in 2005 (till March).

There is no way counterfeiting currency can be stopped. The dubious business is probably as old as the era when money was conceptualised. Before the introduction of paper money, the two main ways of doing it were, one, mixing base metals in what was supposed to be pure gold or silver and, two, 'shaving' the edges of a coin so that it weighed less than it was supposed to.

An English couple, Thomas Rogers and Anne Rogers, was convicted on 15 October 1690 for "clipping 40 pieces of silver". Thomas Rogers was hanged and his wife Anne Rogers was burnt alive. In America, counterfeiting invited death penalty. Paper currency printed by Benjamin Franklin bore the phrase "to counterfeit is death".

Several countries have used counterfeiting as a means of warfare. The idea is to overflow the enemy's economy with fake notes so that the real value of its currency plummets. In 1776,

Great Britain did this during the Revolutionary War in the US to reduce the value of the "continental dollar". This tactic was also employed by the US during the American civil war. During WW II, the Nazis, through Operation Bernhard, took Jewish artists in the Sachsenhausen concentration camp and forced them to forge British pounds and American dollars

Today, the finest counterfeit banknotes are US dollar bills produced in North Korea. The fake North Korean copies are called "super-dollars" because of their high quality. Bulgaria and Colombia are also significant sources of counterfeit currency. In the UK, police recovered £2.2 millions worth of fake notes in 2004.

In the US, one out of every three homes had an ink-jet or other high-quality printer in 2002. In 2002, 39 per cent of the fake currency in circulation in the US was made using a computer, up from eight per cent in 1992.

When fake money is circulated, it leads to the reduction in the value of real money. It also results in an increase in prices, also called inflation, caused due to more money getting circulated in the economy. The word-of-mouth of fake currency diminishes the acceptability, confidence and credibility of a country in the comity of nations. Industry and business does not run in counterfeits, which in turn leads to the increase in the prices.

Our Government is shackled with a bureaucratic mindset that is loath to change. At least 20 countries in the world including Australia, New Zealand and Romania, with variants in Bangladesh, Brazil, China, Mexico, Singapore and Sri Lanka, are using plastic notes, which are supposed to be more durable because they are made of non-porous polymer with a special protective coating that prevents absorption of moisture. Such notes are said to be more counterfeit-proof. Some countries like Mexico that have used polymer technology have clear stamp-sized plastic windows - difficult to forge. Once they wear away, the notes can be recycled.

The Reserve Bank of Australia first experimented with polymer currency notes in 1988 to mark the Australian bicentenary. It switched to plastic money completely by 1996. New Zealand and Romania have done the same. It is worth trying this experiment at least with lower denomination notes in our country.

Government should encourage fair and fearless reporting of fake currency. So far, any person reporting the existence of fake notes in the market has become the primary suspect.

As for the citizens, the following tips can be useful. Have a close look at the cash you receive. Compare a suspect note with a genuine note of the same denomination and series. Pay attention to the quality of printing and paper characteristics. Look for differences not similarities. The genuine note has a lifelike facial portrait of Mahatma Gandhi. It stands out distinctly from the background. The counterfeit portrait is usually lifeless and flat. Details merge into the background, which is often too dark or marked or dappled. Note the person and remember the place from where you received a fake note and promptly inform the law enforcement agency about it. It is our duty to protect our currency.

1.2. Sleeping over Sleeper Cells

Terror has struck India once again. On November 23, three cities of Uttar Pradesh — Lucknow, Varanasi and Faizabad — witnessed well-coordinated bombings in a span of 15 minutes, which left at least 15 people dead and more than 70 injured. The first blast took place in a court complex in Varanasi at 1.05 pm. The second one occurred two minutes later in the same city. At 1.15 pm, another blast took place at the Lucknow court complex.

An e-mail, which warned of an attack on lawyers minutes before the bombs went off in the three cities, was sent from a cyber cafe in east Delhi. The mail, in pidgin English, received by television news channels read: "Now the Islamic raids is going to take place against lawyers within minutes. Insha-allah." It further said, "We are neither any foreign mujahideen nor even we have any attachment with neighbouring countries' agency like ISI, LeT, HuJI, etc. We are purely Indians." The mail listed incidents from Partition to the Babri Masjid demolition and the post-Godhra Gujarat violence as the causes of Muslim restlessness.

Another e-mail received by a television channel on November 24 said that KK Nagar in Chennai would be targeted on November 30, Ghaziabad on December 10, Delhi on December 25 and Kolkata on December 28. Such threats are generally intended to harass and mislead the authorities. Yet, the Government can't afford to take such messages lightly. It's better to take all steps to wipe out terrorists from the country.

Uttar Pradesh has witnessed a number of dastardly terrorist strikes since 2005. At Dashashwamedh Ghat, Varanasi, a blast took place on February 23, 2005, claiming seven lives, besides injuring nine others. This was followed by a jihadi assault in Ayodhya on July 5, 2005, in which all the six terrorists were gunned down. Then, 23 days later, occurred the Shramjeevi Express bombing, which claimed 12 lives, besides injuring 50 others. On March 7, 2006, in Varanasi, serial blasts at Cantonment railway station and Sankat Mochan temple claimed 21 lives. This was followed by the Gorakhpur serial bombings on May 22, 2007, injuring at least six persons.

Uttar Pradesh's legal fraternity feels that the well-coordinated blasts in the court premises were in retaliation of a virtual ban imposed by the lawyers on taking up the cases of terrorists. Incidentally, all the three courts targeted have been holding the trials of major terror strikes in the State over the past two years.

This belief is based on facts. Five accused — Asif Iqbal, Irfan Khan, Mohammed Nasir, Shakil and Aziz — arrested from Jammu and Delhi and charged with hatching a conspiracy for the attack on the Ramjanmabhoomi complex on July 5, 2005, are currently being tried at the Faizabad district court. The lawyers, however, refused to defend the accused. Finally, the State Government had to appoint amicus curiae for their defence in the courtroom. The same is true of the accused involved in the Sankat Mochan case. Likewise, in Lucknow, lawyers thrashed three Jaish-e-Mohammed terrorists who had planned to abduct Mr Rahul Gandhi.

It is worthwhile to recall major serial bombings in the country to emphasise the gravity of the situation. The 1993 serial Mumbai blasts killed at least 257 people and injured 1,400 others. On February 14, 1998, the Coimbatore bombings killed at least 46 people and injured 200 others. On August 25, 2003, at least 50 people were killed in a terrorist strike in Mumbai. Thereafter, on October 29, 2005, Delhi witnessed three blasts, killing at least 62 people and injuring more than 155. The Varanasi blasts of March 7, 2006, led to the death of 28 people.

Mumbai was again under jihadi assault when at least 187 people were killed due to serial bombings in local trains on July 11, 2006. Then, on September 8, 2006, came the Malegaon bombings, which killed at least 38 people. The Mecca blasts, Hyderabad, of May 2007 killed 11 people. In August 2007, the city was again under turmoil as bombs ripped through crowded areas, killing at least 42 people.

The Government has a dismal record in tackling terrorism. Our intelligence agencies have been far from successful in anticipating or intercepting the details of the activities of the terrorists. They only become wiser after the event has taken place and give a detailed description as to how the terror was perpetrated. There is no oversight mechanism or parliamentary committee to oversee their working and hold them accountable.

Even in the US, a Committee of Legislators calls the CIA and the FBI to account. The standard of intelligence collection, for preventive action is dismal. The Islamist jihad is aimed fulfilling the vision of Ayatollah Khomeini, who first presented his vision to a group of 120 Pakistani Army officers on a visit to Iran in 1993. He told them: "We are at war against infidels. Take this message with you - I ask all Islamic armies nations, all. Muslims, all Islamic and all heads of Islamic states to join the holy war. There are many enemies to be killed or destroyed. jihad must triumph."

The most effective form of counter-terrorism tackles not the terrorists, but the very idea that motivates them. This strategy involves two main steps: First, defeat the jihadi movement just as the fascist and Communist movements were defeated. This task falls mainly on the Government, which must establish its credibility that it can protect the citizens of the country and pay the terrorists in their own coin. The Government should support and encourage liberal Muslims, who can interpret Islam as the Muslim United Coalition, did by placing advertisements in British newspapers regarding the emergency services as "courageous" and praising the British Government for its "calm and proportionate" reaction to the crisis. The advertisements quoted the Quran: "Whoever kills an innocent soul, it is as if he killed the whole of mankind. And whoever saves one, it is as if he saved mankind."

Whatever Pakistan may say, there is no doubt that it has a vital role in most terrorist attacks on India. Lt Gen (retd) Hamid

Gul, who was the Director-General of the ISI in the late 1980s, used to say that keeping the Indian security forces bleeding with the help of the jihadis was equivalent to the Pakistan Army having an extra division at no cost to the Pakistani exchequer. Pakistan's President Pervez Musharraf, too, shares this belief.

We are facing a war right inside our country, supported by some local elements. It is time to strike them hard and not indulge in rhetoric.

1.3. Temples and Mosques

In a daring attempt to destroy the makeshift Ram temple, six suspected Lashkar-e-Toiba terrorists struck at the disputed Ram Janmabhoomi complex in Ayodhya on July 5. Two of them were reportedly human bombs. The terrorists were in the age group of 25 to 35 years. The security forces at the site performed incredibly well by killing all the attackers.

The aim of this dastardly terror strike was obviously to heighten communal tension, spread chaos, widen the chasm between Hindus and Muslims, disrupt the Indo-Pakistan peace process, undermine the efforts of General Musharraf towards improving relations as well as derail the country's economic progress. There would have been a perception that the Pakistani General and his corps commanders had a role to play in the attack since they may have made no sincere effort towards dismantling the terrorists training camps inside POK and Pakistan.

The modus operandi of the terrorists in the Ayodhya attack was exactly the same as the one that took place in Akshardham temple in Gujarat in November 2003. This is the third major attack on a temple site. The terror strike at the Raghunath Temple in Jammu in 2002 too is a case in point. The jihadi attack on the heavily fortified Ram Janmabhoomi temple complex in Ayodhya raises the question whether our intelligence agencies failed yet again to apprehend such attacks. I admit that no intelligence report can be hundred per cent accurate. Collection of intelligence is based on inputs provided by the field staff who move in public and to whom people are able to talk with freedom.

Even in case of 9/11 the intelligence agencies had no inkling that a terror attack of such magnitude would occur in the heart of

New York. The same was true of bomb blasts in London. The general intelligence reports and circulars issued from time to time by probe agencies are useless. Such agencies invariably try to shrug off their responsibility by saying that they had issued the warnings. So many vague pieces of information are received that the poor official in charge of receiving them does not know which to consider and which to ignore. Ultimately, it is left to the police constables to trace and deal with the invisible enemy who can spring a surprise any time and undertake any terror operation with ease.

The fanatical jihadi attempt at Ayodhya is a grim reminder of the fact that the war against terror is likely to be a long drawn one. Moreover, it will not be won by half-hearted measures by those who subscribe to vote-bank politics. Terrorists intend to start strife and panic among different sections of society as well as derive mileage and publicity by targeting holy places of the majority community. The Government should realise that despite its claims that terrorism is under control, the terrorists have not lost their ability to strike at will at high profile and sensitive targets. By their actions, the jihadis have reiterated time and again that they would not be shy of using the most violent means to attack places of their choice.

While it is historically true that when Muslim invaders expanded into non-Muslim domains, the desecration of temples was inevitable. The reason for this was that in kingdoms belonging to Hindu rulers, the king was personified as the deity. At times temples were converted into mosques to indicate the arrival of a new Muslim king who had ousted his Hindu counterpart.

However, when India became independent the leaders sensibly chose the ideal of secularism. This meant that India had no state religion. Thus neither could we raise another Somnath temple, nor did we have the license to damage any structure belonging to a minority community - whether Muslim, Sikh or Christian. Terrorism cannot be eliminated by adopting a soft approach. There will naturally be a quibble on legal grounds and attempts to ward off responsibility by saying that law and order is a State subject. However, the fact remains that national integrity, sovereignty and security of the country is the responsibility of the Central Government.

The Government and security agencies need to change their strategies in dealing with terrorism. This is because terror attacks involving suicide bombers have replaced hit and run terrorism. The most prominent example of this was the 9/11 attacks in the US.

The question is, what is the modus operandi of these jihadi terror groups? The first thing they do is choose a prominent public place as their target which may include pilgrim centres, railway platforms, bus stands, airports, shopping centres in important metropolitan cities like Mumbai, Kolkata, Chennai, Bangalore, and Delhi. This is exactly what happened in London on July 7. Whatever excuse may the Government may give, the most common of them being that the size of security forces is too small to be deployed in all public places scattered across the country, security personnel cannot shirk their responsibility to protect citizens from such unexpected attacks.

Obviously, it is easy for terrorists to penetrate thickly populated areas which attract tourists on account of their religious importance or scenic beauty. Instead of direct attacks terrorists use toys, briefcases, transistors, lunch boxes, school bags and other commonly used items to plant explosives. An attack, like the one in Ayodhya, or for that matter in London or New York, requires months of preparation, precision and planning. Also, such attacks cannot succeed without the support of a segment of the local population.

Nobody, including the intelligence agencies, can predict which place or person will be next target of the terrorists. Thus we must learn a few lessons from all the terrorist strikes in the past. The most noteworthy of these observations are: One, the need to sensitise citizens and seek their active cooperation in getting information about any unusual happening in their neighbourhood or strangers they may have come across in areas which could be potential targets.

Two, it is necessary to have a "national citizen's register" so that at any given time the whereabouts of a person could be verified. The biggest problem is that we do not have a national card identity or even voter's I cards, which would help us in identifying aliens among us. Three, it is essential to achieve better coordination among intelligence agencies. It is only when they would together that they would be able to gather information more easily.

Four, terrorism needs to be a viewed as a national problem and not something which is the responsibility of the ruling party alone. We must be fully prepared to tackle future jihadi attacks. Five, we must be better equipped to apprise the international community of any impending terror strike. It is time all nations unanimously agreed that the terrorist pose a global threat. Also the world should know the dangers inherent in dealing with terrorism and the nations must whole heartedly support one another in curbing the menace.

Finally, despite the support promised by other countries to fight terrorism in India, as a nation we should learn to be self reliant. We must realise that eventually it is only Indians who can address the issue and crush the phenomenon. Therefore, seeking help of other countries would be futile. The fight against terrorism should get the topmost priority. The issue should not be swept under the carpet in favour of non-issues as often happens in our country. The Government should realise that it has already received a number of wake-up calls and it is time authority swung into action.

1.4. The height: Nip the Bud

India's financial capital, Mumbai, came under *jihadi*attack from November 26 till November 30. It was the most terrible and daring terror attack this country has seen till date. The terrorists used AK-47s, grenades, bombs and other explosives to carry out a devastating *fidayeen* strike on some of the most posh areas and hotels of Mumbai. The encounter with the terrorists lasted for 60 hours. By Saturday evening, the bodycount had risen to 195, among them 20 personnel of security forces. More than 300 people have been injured. In the coming days, the death toll could increase.

All this is the work of a group of terrorists. They came via sea to Mumbai, despite the substantial presence of the Navy and the Coast Guard in the region. If the Mumbai sea border cannot be considered to be secure, I shudder to think of the condition of our maritime defence along other coastal areas.

It makes no difference how you label terrorists. Whether you call them, *fidayeen* or Indian Mujahideen or anything else, a terrorist is a terrorist. In this instance an outfit calling itself the 'Deccan Mujahideen' has claimed responsibility. It even dared to call the Indian Army and the Maharashtra ATS weak outfits.

Terrorist attacks have literally not left a single part of India untouched. From Kashmir to Kanyakumari, over the last decade or so, terrorists have killed thousands. Most often these mass murderers get away scot-free. This is because there are plenty of politicians who are more than willing to defend them to safeguard their respective vote-banks. Also, there is no dearth of human right activists who believe that only terrorists have rights and not their victims.

Following is a chronology of some of the major attacks in India in the past five years:

March 13, 2003 — A bomb attack on a commuter train in Mumbai kills 11 people.

August 25, 2003 — Two car bombs kill about 60 in Mumbai.

August 15, 2004 — A bomb explodes in Assam, killing 16 people, mostly schoolchildren, and wounding dozens.

October 29, 2005 — 66 people are killed when three blasts rip through markets in New Delhi.

March 7, 2006 —At least 15 people are killed and 60 wounded in three blasts in the Hindu pilgrimage city of Varanasi.

July 11, 2006 — More than 200 people are killed in seven bomb explosions at railway stations and on commuter trains in Mumbai.

September 8, 2006 —At least 32 people are killed in a series of explosions, including one near a mosque, at Malegaon town in Maharashtra.

February 19, 2007 — Two bombs explode aboard the Samjhauta Express, in Haryana. At least 66 passengers, most of them Pakistanis, are burnt to death.

May 18, 2007 — A bomb explodes at Mecca Masjid in Hyderabad, killing 11 people.

August 25, 2007 — Three coordinated explosions at an amusement park and a street stall in Hyderabad kill at least 40 people.

May 13, 2008 — Seven bombs rip through the crowded streets of Jaipur, killing at least 63 people in markets and outside temples.

July 25, 2008 — Eight bombs explode in Bangalore, killing at least one woman and wounding 15 others.

July 26, 2008 — 16 bombs explode in Ahmedabad killing 56 people and wounding 161. The 'Indian Mujahideen' claims responsibility for the attack and the May 13 attack in Jaipur.

September 13, 2008 — Five bombs explode in crowded markets and streets in the heart of New Delhi, killing at least 20 people and injuring scores more. The Indian Mujahideen again claims responsibility.

October 30, 2008 — 11 bombs rip through Guwahati and three other towns in Assam killing 76 people and wounding at least 320.

In the wake of the latest terror attack, Prime Minister Manmohan Singh has said that the Government will will bring the guilty to book. He has also said that the laws will be tightened to ensure that terrorists do not take advantage of legal loop holes, and that the security and safety of the people will not be compromised .

All this is easier said than done. With the passage of time, the gravity of these terror crimes will get reduced and with election around the corner, the UPA coalition partners would not like to be seen supporting any tough measures that could be perceived as anti-Muslim. More than anything, the laughable official stand of the Government has been that the existing laws are tough enough to combat terrorism. This is far from the truth and sends a wrong signal to the terrorists and their supporters.

The Prime Minster has more than once pointed out the gaps in our intelligence-gathering infrastructure. Instead of saying that there has been a complete failure of intelligence, he has used the word 'gaps'. There is no doubt that there has been a complete failure of intelligence, whether it was the July 2006 train bombings in Mumbai or the September, 2008 serial bombings in Delhi or the latest terror strike in Mumbai. The merchants of death have illustrated that they can strike at will, even in the supposedly safest areas of our country.

No matter how you look at it, it is the responsibility of the Union Government to maintain the integrity of the country against all aggression, foreign and domestic. The truth is that we do not have a clear anti- terrorism policy or strategy. What we offer are knee-jerk reactions to events as they happen. After that everything is forgotten till the next incident. We have now reached a stage where the media does not take notice of a terror strike unless at least a dozen people are killed!

The standard response, reactions and even the language of the leaders after each terrorist attack can be anticipated. Pre-rehearsed statements such as 'it was a cowardly attack', that 'innocents have been targeted', and 'strict action will be taken against the perpetrators' are dished out again and again.

To fight terrorism seriously what we need is technology like CCTV cameras, stricter border patrolling, maintaining a National Citizens' Register, and involving the Muslim community in the fight against terror. Most of all, what we need is the political will to defeat terrorism, without which everything else is entirely meaningless.

2. Terrorism: Tackling Measures

2.1. Wage Emending War on Terror

Terrorism is an invisible enemy which has plagued India since 1980s in one form or the other. Starting from Punjab and Jammu and Kashmir, terrorist violence has affected different States of the country at different times. The attacks on places which are important and at the same time vulnerable is not new. Indeed, each time terrorists choose a different spot with the twin objective of fanning communal tensions and sending home the message that they have the capability to strike at will.

The bomb blasts that rocked Varanasi on March 7 in which more than 30 persons were killed and 75 injured was the last major instance of terror attack. The targets in the holy city were the Sankat Mochan temple and the railway station. Immediately, a few political parties gave a call for bandh to protest against the unjustified killings. The bandh passed off peacefully. Sankat Mochan temple (built in the name of Hanuman who is considered as liberator from troubles by his devotees) has an idol which is said to have been installed by Tulsidas under a fig tree in the late 16th century. This temple is considered by many as one of Varanasi's three major shrines along with Kashi Vishwanath and Annapurna temples. Every Tuesday and Saturday devotees throng the Sankat Mochan Temple to make offerings. Another major attack on temple in India was on March 30, 2002, when Raghunath Temple in Jammu was targeted by terrorists.

On September 24, 2002, terrorists attacked Akshardham in Gujarat and killed 35 people. Targeting religious places is done with the aim of provoking Hindus to retaliate so that the communities to whom the suspected terrorists belong become the victims of their wrath. According to a report, Varanasi has become a store house of illegal weapons which are reported to have been smuggled from Nepal in connivance with some politicians of Uttar Pradesh and Bihar. So bold have the terrorists become that on the eve of Diwali, in an orchestrated attack on several markets in Delhi in October 2005, they killed 67 persons and injured over 260. Earlier, a group of terrorists had the audacity to attack Parliament on December 13, 2001, in which 12 persons were killed including six policemen and all the five terrorists.

Many are wondering what will be the next target - whether it will be Mathura. Lashkar operatives are being suspected of carrying out the recent attack as well as many others, though a little known outfit in Jammu & Kashmir has taken responsibility for this offensive. In fact, the name hardly matters as long as terrorist or a group of terrorists succeed in creating mayhem.

It really makes no difference whether we call terrorists Mujahideens or Lashkar operatives or criminals armed with Kalashnikovs and rocket-propelled grenades. Their deeds are the worst imaginable cruelty mankind has ever known. Bandhs, protests or strikes or condemnation by political leaders make no difference to them. In fact, right from Diwali in October, 2005 when bomb blasts rocked Delhi there has been a slow but sure increase in danger and insecurity and a defiant increase of frequency of jihadi attacks. Three Lashkar-e-Toiba terrorists including one believed to have been involved in blasts in

Varanasi, were killed in separate encounters in Delhi and Lucknow on March 8. The police claims that they were found in possession of some RDX and detonators. These terrorists are definitely not freedom fighters. They have spared no effort to kill whether it is by carrying out bomb blasts in Mumbai or hijacking an Indian Airlines plane to Kandahar or even attacking Jammu & Kashmir

Legislative Assembly and Parliament of India. Our neighbour Pakistan has systematically promoted the view often through dissemination of selective or false information that Kashmiri terrorists funded, supported and sheltered by them are good terrorists. The US has clearly said that "There cannot be good terrorists and bad terrorists." Obviously, our neighbour without whose shelter and protective umbrella no terrorist will be able to operate, thinks otherwise. For them they are good terrorists as they are furthering Pakistan's agenda.

The problem is that in a country of the size of India, where terror attacks keep occurring in different parts the State Governments do not respond adequately. It is because each political party, whether in power or out of it, wants to play the game of vote-bank politics. People, too, get used to terrorist incidents as they occur frequently. It is a feeling of ennui that has made people disinterested in terrorists who can choose soft targets of their choice and attack them as and when they feel confident about getting away after perpetrating a crime.

As terrorism is an invisible enemy, it cannot be fought with a large Army or a big police force. All the major terrorist attacks both in India and abroad have been masterminded and executed by a terrorist or a group of terrorists whose number does not exceed the single digit. Even after overthrowing the Taliban, launching a worldwide campaign against Al Qaeda and incarcerating Saddam Hussein, the US and the coalition against terror is nowhere near conquering it. Pouring more money into intelligence, police and the military does not mean that we have defeated or will defeat the forces of terror.

Conventional methods of fighting terrorism are to infiltrate terrorist cells, have enough spies as well as defences. But the problem is that nothing much is being done to defeat the hostile propaganda, beliefs and ideologies which give rise to terrorism. In our approach towards eliminating terrorists, which is based on the use of physical force whether by the State or any other agency, we seem to have come to a dead end. We need to go beyond these traditional approaches and build a long-term dual strategy of defeating terrorism through coercion as well as an ideological movement. Jihadi threat may not be uniform in all States but it is time we gave it the top most priority.

First, we need to look upon our response including various intelligence failures and review the events at least from the time of attack on Indian Parliament. The problems of terrorism are indeed tough. However, the fact remains that it is only the Government which can fight terrorism and not individual citizens. The Government should treat acts of terror as war against India and use all its military, political and economic might to vanquish the worst enemy plaguing mankind for the last three decades.

Terrorists thrive on people's insecurity and fears. Terrorism of any brand is uncondonable whether indulged in by Muslims or other minority or majority communities. But the problem is whether political parties both at the national or regional level have the requisite political will. It is necessary not only to be right, but also do what is required. This is what statesmanship is all about. It is for the Government to stop reacting in a knee jerk manner and act in a way that reassures the people that it means business.

2.2. Bullet for Bullet

Terrorists have struck again — this time in Bangalore, Ahmedabad, and Surat — sending a reminder that they can strike at will at any place at any time. They have used integrated circuits, timers and chips for the first time in their attacks, revealing that those behind the mayhem are highly educated and technology-savvy.

Another new factor is the use of gas cylinders placed with the bombs that killed 26 persons at the emergency ward of the Civil Hospital in Ahmedabad. A similar technique was used last year at Glasgow airport when Indian engineer Kafeel Ahmed, indoctrinated by Al Qaeda, and his accomplice rammed a jeep laden with explosives and gas cylinders into the terminal's wall. The use of integrated circuit chips and gas cylinders has confirmed the suspicion of intelligence agencies that the attacks, though planned and executed by local outfits, have been inspired by an organised, technically-oriented mastermind

The Union Government claims that State Governments were advised to take preventive measures about the likelihood of such terrorist attacks. Unfortunately, all such advisories are only general sermons which anybody without even being in the intelligence set-up can envisage. No specific or actionable intelligence has been provided.

The first salvo was fired by a non-Congress Cabinet Minister after the Union Cabinet Meeting that followed the blast. The Minister was so perturbed that he did not even care for conventional niceties.

Another Minister told mediapersons, "I think there is more information in newspapers than what the Home Minister told us (in the Cabinet meeting)."

The political response of the country determines its response to militancy. The only person to come out against terrorism and advocate a bullet-for-bullet policy, apart from Mr LK Advani, is Jammu & Kashmir Chief Minister Ghulam Nabi Azad. He has said, "How can you initiate talks with terrorists who after attaining training from across the border come to kill you? Either you have to kill them otherwise you will be killed... We may have talks with the neighbouring country, but as far as terrorism goes, there can be no tolerance towards terrorists and they should be dealt with a stern hand."

Unfortunately, whenever a terror incident happens, you can anticipate the standard response and even the language of the leaders. They use the same tone and tenor like "It is a cowardly act" and that "innocents have been targeted" and "very strict action will be taken against the perpetrators". But the ground reality is that such statements and announcements of compensation by the Government to salve its own conscience and to pay for its failure have become a routine affair till the next terrorist attack.

But the sufferer of all such terror attacks is the common man as the leaders are safe with their huge paraphernalia of security. Steps to improve the situation need to be taken — at legal, diplomatic and people's level.

At all the sensitive places close-circuit television cameras should be installed. New York has more than 50,000 such cameras. Incidentally, perpetrators of the London bombings in 2005 were nabbed with the help of CCTV recordings. These cameras, apart from keeping a record of suspicious activities of likely terrorists, can also help in detecting incidents of traffic violation, eve-teasing and other crimes like pick-pocketing, chain-snatching and rash driving.

The Union Government should set up world class forensic science laboratories in every State capital, of which there is a woeful dearth, apart from pulling up intelligence agencies for their failures. Tech-savvy terrorists need to be met on their own turf.

The Government is giving an impression of being soft on terrorists. All over the world, including in the oldest democracies, laws have been turned upside down to deal with terrorists. But in India, we still have laws framed by the British on the ground that the old laws are sufficient. It is time to bring in new laws on terrorism, thus putting the onus on suspected terrorists to prove their innocence. Every arrested terrorist must be subjected to narco-analysis test to find out his other colleagues and associates involved in the crime. Political parties naturally play politics in every thing they do. It is for this reason that a MCOCA-type law, which is in force in Maharashtra, has not been allowed in Gujarat, Rajasthan and Himachal Pradesh.

It is imperative that national security should be kept outside the ambit of politics and terrorism should be treated as a national threat and not an excuse for vote-bank politics. We have been hearing for a long time about the need to have a Federal Investigating Agency to investigate crimes like terrorism. The Centre-State conflict over the proposed agency seems specious: If the US can have the FBI despite a full-fledged federal system in which States have far greater autonomy than they do in India, why cannot we have a similar agency?

In fact, the top priority of the FBI is to "protect the US from any terrorist attack". There is simply no such agency in India mandated to take on terrorists at the national level. The CBI, which is primarily meant to deal with corruption, comes in if and when a State refers a case of terrorism to it.

The Union Government can issue an Ordinance creating a federal agency which will function in the States with their consent. In today's situation, there is hardly any State which will not give its consent. The Centre should strike while the iron is hot.

It must be clearly understood that in a country of our size and population it is almost impossible to reach consensus on any issue. But it is the job of the leaders to lead the country and show the will in the national interest.

2.3. FightTerror with Determination

Since 2000, there have been 1,120 deaths in 69 *jihadi* terrorist attacks in our country. In July 2008, 56 persons were killed in terrorist bombings on consecutive days in Bangalore and Ahmedabad. A day after the massive killings, 28 unexploded bombs were defused in Surat. In the last few years, there have been bomb attacks in Mumbai, Coimbatore, Srinagar, Ahmedabad, Delhi, Varanasi, Hyderabad, Bangalore and Jaipur. In some of these places there was more than one attack. The United States' National Institute of Counterterrorism says that between January 2004 and March 2007, the death toll in India from terrorist attacks was 3,674, second only to Iraq during the same period. In most of the major terrorist bombings, the name of one particular organisation, that is SIMI, has surfaced with definite consistency.

The Gujrat Police has claimed that SIMI was responsible for the 27 serial bombings that ripped through Ahmedabad in July. It has also been able to establish the trail of evidences to SIMI. Subsequently, a number of SIMI activists -including the suspected mastermind behind the bombings- have been arrested.

The Students Islamic Movement of India is a banned Muslim fundamentalist organisation that was founded in 1977. Ostensibly its purpose was to "to educate and enlighten Muslim youth in India". The SIMI, in its publications, lists the propagation of Islam and *jihad* for the cause of Islam as its main objectives. Activists of SIMI believe in a pan-Islamic state or a Muslim *ummah*. It says, in its literature and list of objectives, that it wants to convert India into an Islamic state.

A recent study by two scholars from Oxford University states that this is only part of a larger international trend. They have observed that over the years those with engineering degrees are over-represented in Islamic terror organisations. One of the 10 suspects arrested for his role in the Ahmedabad serial bombings holds a diploma in human rights from the MS University in Vadodra. A medical student was reportedly involved in the Jaipur terror strike in May this year. The mastermind of the Bangalore bombings in 2005 was also an engineer. The trend doesn't stop there. In the Ahmedabad terror strike the alleged mastermind is a teacher. Among the SIMI men arrested, Safdar Nagori is a mechanical engineer. Another person behind the Indian Mujahideen terror e-mail, Abdul Subhan Qureshi alias Taufique, is a computer whiz-kid. Whereas Iqbal Shaikh holds an ITI diploma in electrical engineering while Gyasuddin Ansari has an ITI diploma in radio technology.

The organisation reportedly gets extensive funds from West Asia. According to investigative agencies it has a core membership of at least 400 full-time cadre and two lakh members. It is also that the organisation has links with Islamic terror groups based in Pakistan and Bangladesh.

Let there be no doubt in the Government's mind that *jihadi* movements have been violent and coercive right from the very start. Today, the concept of *jihad* is being preached to re-conquer India through organisations such as SIMI. The emphasis in Islam is on conversion. During my recent visit to the US, my host who is a Hindu, told me that his daughter's Muslim classmates in high school were pressurising her to convert to Islam. Conversion of the so-called non-believers is an article of faith in Islam.

Nonetheless, what might come as a surprise is that many Muslims belonging to economically well-off families and having good educational backgrounds, choose a career in terrorism. Thus, the age-old perception that most terrorists come from poor economic and educational circumstances is not valid in all cases.

jihadis are working under the illusion that they can make India another Pakistan. They are taking advantage of India being a secular country. The Preamble of the Constitution is very clear about the rights of every Indian irrespective of his religion. It says:

We, The People of India, having solemnly resolved to constitute India into a

Sovereign Socialist Secular Democratic Republic and to secure to all its citizens:

Justice, social, economic and political;

Liberty of thought, expression, belief, faith and worship;

Equality of status and of opportunity; and to promote among them all Fraternity assuring the dignity of the individual and the unity and integrity of the Nation.

While every Indian citizen has been guaranteed the above freedom, they have to exercise it in consistency with the unity and integrity of the country. Given the spate of terrorist attcks in recent years, our law enforcement agencies are naturally under a lot to tacle terrorism. Terrorist organisations are extremely close-knit. They function only on need to know basis. On the other hand, we have antique laws that were framed in 1863 to deal with such organisations. For example, confessions made to the police under the law are not admissible in court. With thousands of cases still pending, our courts take an enormous amount of time to adjudicate and come out with a verdict. Today, there is no law against terrorism in the country in spite of the fact that it is perhaps the biggest threat to India.

Moreover, nobody wants to be a court witness and help the police prosecute terror suspects. The condition of witnesses in our country is best illustrated by the following extracts of a letter written by a Sessions Judge to the National Police Commission.

"The biggest single hurdle which inhibits the citizen from coming forward to help the police is the deplorable conditions prevailing in the courts of law. The lot of witnesses appearing on behalf of the State against a criminal is certainly pitiable."

In most cases the police faces an uphill task. In the absence of witnesses, acquittals are quite common. 99.9 per cent Muslims in India are peace loving and have nothing to do with terrorists and terrorism. But since nobody, irrespective of his community or religion, wants to get involved with the law, terrorists manage to get away because of the impossible standards of evidences required to prove any case.

It is essential to involve the Muslim community in the fight against terrorism. The community's presence should be increased in the intelligence and security agencies, as its members can more easily access and infiltrate *jihadi* terrorist groups and help the law enforcement agencies in exposing them. Laws in this country are framed by those who have no knowledge of the ground realities. Laws should be framed in consultation with judicial and law enforcement officers, rather than in air-conditioned rooms.

3. Terror and Police

Modern communications, including the fast-moving vehicles, air travel and Internet, have increased the frontiers of crime. Criminals do not respect state boundaries and they have the whole country as their turf. Indeed, the profile of the crime has totally changed since 1863, when the laws — the Indian Evidence Act, the Criminal Procedure Code, the Indian Penal Code and the Police Act — were enacted. New inventions and discoveries are as much available to the common man as to the criminals. Hitherto relatively unknown or less familiar crimes have proliferated, with the sole objective of getting rich quickly and making as much money as possible.

With the absence of boundary constraints, criminals commit crime in one State, live in another and run their business in some other. Jihadi assaults in Varanasi, Ayodhya, Lucknow and on religious institutions like Akshardham temple in Gandhinagar and Mecca Masjid in Hyderabad highlight this problem. One Abdul Karim Telgi, a resident of Karnataka, started his business of fake stamps in a small way. Quickly, he enlarged his 'business' to operate in as many as 13 States. So was the case with Harshad Mehta and Ketan Parekh, who shook the stock market in the 1990s.

Generally, no State Government gives up its control on the investigation of such cases, till the Supreme Court intervenes and orders that the same be investigated by the CBI. In the legal parlance, there is no such thing as the CBI, which was created by the Union Government, for which it continues to be the 'Special Police Establishment'. This Act confers concurrent and coextensive powers, duties, privileges and liabilities on the members of the Delhi Special Police Establishment (CBI) with police officers of the Union Territories. The Union Government can extend to any area the powers and jurisdiction of the CBI for investigations, with the consent of the concerned State Government.

However, there have been instances in which for political reasons — or to avoid investigation, by the CBI — some State Governments have withdrawn their consent, rendering the CBI toothless. Some States do not allow the CBI to investigate cases even against the Union Government employees on a case-to-case basis. It is believed by some that consents are given not on the case-to-case basis, but on the suitcase-to-suitcase basis. One needs to remember that the CBI generally investigates cases that are essentially against Union Government employees, or those concerning affairs of the Central Government. It also investigates the cases in which the financial interests of the Union Government are involved, or those referred to it by the State Government.

A Committee on Criminal Justice System under the chairmanship of Mr NR Madhava Menon, a former Director of the National Judicial Academy, has suggested the setting up of a separate authority at the national level to deal with serious crimes like terrorism, hijacking and drug peddling. This committee was set up in May 2006 to draft a national policy on criminal justice system. It has also reportedly recommended the acceptance of certain crimes as "National Crimes", besides giving the CBI the power to take suo motu cognisance of crimes impacting national security — terrorism and smuggling of arms, ammunition, etc.

All political parties have expressed dissatisfaction with the working of the police. The following committees and commissions have been set up since independence: The Kerala Police Reorganisation Committee (1959), the West Bengal Police Commission (1960-61), the Punjab Police Commission (1961-61), the Maharashtra Police Commission (1964-65), the Madhya Pradesh Police Commission (1965-66), the Delhi Police Commission (1967-68), the Assam Police Commission (1970-71), the Uttar Pradesh Police Commission (1960-61, 1970-71), the Tamil Nadu Police Commission (1971) and the Rajasthan Police Reorganisation Committee (1972-73). This was followed by the National Police Commission (1977-1981). Finally, the Justice Malimath Committee (2001-2003) was set up.

The list does not include other committees set up almost every year either by the Union or State Governments to suggest ways and means to improve the working of the police. Unfortunately, none of the police commissions, except the Madhavan Committee and the second Administrative Commission, have even applied their mind to set up of a Central Investigating Agency or treating some crimes — terrorism, mass killing or circulation of fake currency — on par with war against India.

In June 2006, the Second Administrative Reforms Commission, headed by Mr Veerappa Moily, recommended the setting up of a Crime Investigative Agency in every State and advocated a new law to empower the CBI to probe crimes like terrorism, sedition and human-trafficking at the State level. Even the Consultative Committee of the Union Home Ministry in its meeting held in December 2007 favoured this idea.

Among the States, Uttar Pradesh, which has been rocked by a series of bombings by terrorist outfits in recent years, along with West Bengal, Assam, Uttarakhand, Jammu & Kashmir, Jharkhand, Karnataka, Kerala, Goa and the Union Territory of Chandigarh, have written to the Home Ministry "disapproving" the idea. This despite the fact that most of these States are not in a position to carry out proper investigations independently. For example, one needs to take the classic case of the Samjhauta Express bombings, in which investigations are going on since February 2007 without any definite lead.

Replying to a debate in the Lok Sabha in November 2007, marked by sharp attacks on the Government, Union Home Minister Shivraj Patil came out in favour of a federal anti-terror agency. Even several police officials and security analysts feel that such an agency will ensure better coordination among different security and intelligence bodies.

Though the Union Government is seriously pursuing the idea of setting up a Central agency to investigate federal crimes in the country, it is faced with stiff opposition from 24 States that do not want the Centre to interfere. Great leaders do not wait to be called and give up their power when they are no longer needed. Selfish men and fools keep their power until someone throws them out. However, when some States oppose the proposal for a federal investigating agency, it does not mean that they are against the nation's Interests. It only means that they are for themselves.

4. An Appeal to the Eternal Court of People

In a unique effort of its kind, the first European "terrorism survival course" for the common man has been planned in the UK. It's a day-long course, which is not free. It will cost each participant £ 150, which is roughly equal to Rs 12,000. The course includes suicide-bombing scenarios, 9/11-style hijacking of aircraft and attacks with improvised explosive devices. The British no longer view terrorism as other people's problem. One recalls that a few years ago, when then British Prime Minister Tony Blair came to India, he made it clear that Jammu & Kashmir was not a priority in the US-led war against global terrorism, of which the UK is a part. The terror attacks in London and Glasgow have demonstrated that terrorists will not spare the British.

A report by the US Department of State has revealed that terrorist acts have increased by over 25 per cent and fatalities have increased by 40 per cent this year. Some 74,543 civilians were targeted and 20,498 killed in 2006. If there is one country that needs a training programme to involve the man in the street in the fight against terrorism, it is India. In this country, the Government and citizens must fight the battle against terrorism jointly.

According to the Government, two prominent Pakistani-based terrorist organisations, Lashkar-e-Tayyeba (LeT) and Jaish-e-Mohammad (JeM), have been responsible for several major attacks in major Indian cities. On July 11, 2006, terrorists set off seven blasts on packed commuter trains in Mumbai, killing at least 209 people and injuring more than 700. On March 7, 2006, terrorists bombed Varanasi, killing 21 and injuring 62 people. On September 9, 2006, terrorists set off a series of blasts outside a mosque in Malegon, killing 38 people and injuring more than 50.

On October 27, 2006, Karnataka Police arrested two suspected terrorists in Mysore, who allegedly belonged to the terrorist group Al-Badr. Police believed the suspects were employed as an advance team to establish a base in southern India from where they would facilitate terrorist attacks on 'high-value' targets, especially in nearby Bangalore, a high-tech hub.

Maoists, meanwhile, launched several attacks, expanding the profile of insurgency and expanding the rural territory under their control. On July 17, 2006, 35 people were killed, 80 injured, and approximately 250 people were missing following an attack by some 800 armed Naxalites in the Dantewada district of Chhattisgarh.

The United Liberation Front of Asom conducted multiple terrorist attacks against civilians and security forces in Assam, causing numerous deaths and injuries. In one of the more violent series of attacks attributed to ULFA, on November 5, 2006, several bombs exploded in a crowded market and at an oil refinery in Guwahati, killing 12 people and injuring a few dozen.

Our efforts are hampered by the outdated and overburdened law enforcement and legal systems. In fact, there is no law to combat terrorism and the Indian Penal Code, Indian Criminal Procedure Code and Indian Evidence Act passed in 1863 are still the laws ruling the roast. Democracies in the West, on whose pattern our governance and legal system are based, have jettisoned their old systems and have brought in new framework to deal with the changed circumstances and changed tactics of criminals.

This state of affairs highlights the need to involve ordinary citizens in the fight against terrorism and to change the laws. The only involvement of the Government in educating the citizens in the fight against terrorism so far has been the advertisements of certain dos and don'ts in English language newspapers by the police. But there is no specific attempt to train or educate citizens about their role in the fight against terrorism.

While terrorists carry unlicenced sophisticated weapons, it is nigh impossible for average citizens to get a license from the Government for possessing a non-prohibited bore weapon. A suitable training programme could be devised wherein all gun licensees are asked to participate in a training programme. A special obligation could be laid on them to come to the help of fellow citizens in need whenever terrorists strike. Apart from the licensees, interested citizens could be invited to join this training programme where right to private defence could be a subject.

The law in India recognises the right of a citizen to private defence. While defending one's life even causing death can be justifiable in some circumstances. Causing the death of a terrorist, who is out to get you, is fully justified. Other topics to be discussed in the workshop could include how citizens can help collect information on suspicious persons who might be trying to mix with the local population and whose mode of dressing, conversation and conduct may appear out of ordinary. Terrorists always use quicker means of transport and communication and stay in rented houses under false names.

Participants would also have to be sensitised to use of computers and mobile phones in terrorist activities. They have to be briefed on the necessary steps to take in case of a terrorist attack - like preserving the scene of crime till forensic experts arrive, cordoning the area, summoning medical aid and ambulances to transport the critically injured to the nearest medical centre. Familiarisation with the latest tactics of the terrorists of moving away from hurling grenades and indiscriminating firing to using mobile phones to trigger IEDs could also be a part of the course for the common man.

Mobile phones were used on May 18, 2007, to trigger the blasts in Mecca Masjid, Hyderabad, which led to the killing of 14 people and injuries to over 50. Also, two bombs connected to cell phones, kept in lunch boxes, were recovered. A similar modus operandi was adopted for the bombings on August 25, 2007 in Hyderabad's Lumbini Park and Gokul Chaat Bhandar.

Involving concerned citizens in the fight against terrorism is going to help the country. Some trained citizens could also be appointed as special police officers to help the law enforcement agencies. A provision to this effect does exist in our laws. The British course is being organised by a private organisation. It is time we encouraged voluntary organisations to come forward with such programmes to make citizens conscious and responsive to the problem of terrorism and supplement Government's efforts.

5. The Enemy Within and Without: Conclusion

Terrorism is generally defined as the unlawful or threatened use of force or actual violence by a person or an organised group against people or property. It is based on the intention of intimidating or coercing societies or governments, often for ideological or political reasons. However, it should be borne in mind that, despite debating the menace at length, the United Nations has not been able to come up with any universally acceptable definition of terrorism.

Today's terrorists are educated, technology-savvy and have at their disposal the most sophisticated weapons. They also have nuclear arms that have become much easier to procure and process. This explains why America woke up to a shock on September 11, 2001, when two of its own aircraft were used as missiles to demolish the twin towers of the World Trade Centre in New York. The scene was captured live by a TV cameraman who happened to be around in the vicinity, and the image still haunts the world. At the time, US President George W Bush officially declared that America was under attack. 9/11 made it realise that dealing with terrorism was no child's play. India, on its part, has been dealing with terrorism for over two decades.

Vast improvements in communications have helped terrorist groups organise themselves, plan their attacks and recruit agents. Several terrorist outfits use the Internet to communicate with its members. They are also able to recruit new members and find financial support through the cyber network.

Only recently, at least 153 people were injured and 53 killed in the powerful bomb blasts in front of a temple in Zaveri Bazar, the heart of Mumbai's diamond business, and in a parking lot next to the Gateway of India. Bombs had been placed inside two taxis. The twin blasts were an eye-opener. Bombs can be easily made from common fertilisers and gasoline. They can then be placed inside a bus or taxi, as was done in Mumbai, to cause massive destruction. In the present case though, use of deadly RDX was reported.

Mumbai has been the target of terrorist attacks for the last 10 years. The details of some of the strikes speak for themselves. On March 12, 1993, 13 explosions spread across the suburbs and south Mumbai. The number of casualties was 257 and of those injured 713. On August 28, 1997, blasts occurred near Jama Masjid. One person was injured. On January 24, 1998, there were blasts inside a train near Malad, leaving one injured. Blasts again occurred on February 27, 1998, at Virar, Kandivli and Santacruz in a local train, killing nine.

On December 2, 2002, bombs exploded in Ghatkopar inside a bus, Two died and 31 were injured. On December 6, 25 were injured in similar blasts at Mumbai Central station. On January 27, this year, Vile Parle market was the target. One person died, and 30 were injured. On March 13, there were explosions in Mulund station inside a train, killing 11 and injuring 82. On July 28, bomb blasts took place in a bus at Ghatkopar, killing two and injuring 31.

There was much cause for concern courtesy this trail of terror, when Ganesh Chaturthi -a major festival in Mumbai-approached and went by. It is anybody's guess these blasts were the handiwork of terrorists. And it does not really matter what these agents of destruction call themselves or what they are fighting for. They should be stopped at all costs.

Those involved in the recent blasts have been traced and arrested. The prime suspect, Nasir, has also been killed by Mumbai Police in an encounter. Some analysts have put forth the argument that the attack was in the nature of a "revenge" against the Gujarat carnage of last year. They justify this by saying that the 1993 blasts were meant to avenge the demolition of the Babri Masjid.

One thing should be made clear in this context. Terror has been haunting Jammu & Kashmir for over a decade now, with the people living in perpetual insecurity and fear. Terrorists now seem to have found another soft target in Mumbai, India's commercial capital. The latest bomb blasts are an indicator that the terrorist outfits are well organised and could strike anywhere, anytime. People with vested interests are trying to create communal tensions by blaming one particular community for this. This is to politicise the issue-which is dangerous when terrorism needs to be combated by both a vigilant State Government and a resolute Central dispensation. Dividing the people along communal lines is to merely play into the hands of terrorists. Their main motive, after all, is to undermine the country's secular and democratic fabric.

The inability to prevent terrorist attacks that lead to loss of lives do, however, raise questions about the efficiency of the Government, intelligence agencies and the police. The latter particularly cannot escape such scrutiny. Law and order is a State subject. This is why the police force has to take the responsibility for any lapses in this regard.

Several top officials in Mumbai, both from the police and other departments, are of the view that the performance of law enforcers leaves much to be desired. They also feel that all posts in the police department, right from that of the Commissioner to an ordinary constable, are on 'sale'. Transfers and promotions come only for a price, and definitely not on merit. It naturally follows that those who pay to get plum postings would resort to unfair practices like taking bribes once they hold the posts. Maintaining law and order figures at the very bottom of their list of priorities. In short, rampant corruption has marred the reputation of the force.

Regrettably, this is what most honest officers feel about the prevailing scenario. I myself was faced with the bitter truth three decades ago, when I saw a particular DIG (Headquarters), Karnataka, receiving letters from the Chief Minister's office to post certain constables in chosen stations and to transfer others. I protested that such orders could only come from those quarters with the authority to issue them. My boss laughed at my 'naivete' and said that if he didn't comply, he would be replaced in no time by someone else who would.

I obviously did not agree with his views and his willingness to bend rules. I kept quiet but patiently waited till such time I could change things. When my time came, I firmly put my foot down to such requests. As a result, I had to face transfers quite often. But I preferred that to doing something I have fought against all my life. I know that if the morale of the police force is high, its members can fulfil their duties. Terrorist attacks would, as a result, be considerably reduced, if not be totally eliminated.

Some necessary steps need to be taken. Both the political class and the police should ensure that transfers and postings are conducted on the basis of merit alone, and not on payment of bribes or as a matter of patronage. Caste appeasement should also stop. It has to be borne in mind that the modern-day terrorist may be armed with weapons of mass destruction. Improvement in communications has helped them immensely. Also, encouraged by our neighbour, terrorists have a solid support base. Operations like the one on August 25 in Mumbai could not have been carried out without such backing.

The core issue between India and Pakistan is terrorism. Talk about promoting people-to-people interaction is all very fine. But we should not lose our focus. Even if we assume ordinary Pakistanis want friendly ties with India, the ground realities won't change: Their Government will continue to harbour terrorists. Unless there is a change in Pakistan's official policies, lasting peace would always be elusive. And mass opinion in both the countries would contiune to be shaped by their Governments. In a final analysis, there are no short-cuts in the anti-terror combat. It is a continuous war that requires uninterrupted vigilance on the part of Government and citizens. We have to prepare ourself for a long haul.

7

Security: A Government's Denial

1. Threats and conflicts intensified

1.1. Insecure about security drills

Mr George Fernandes was strip- searched twice at Washington DC's Dulles Airport when he was the Defence Minister, the first time while on an official visit to Washington and the second time while en route to Brazil, according to the former US Deputy Secretary of State Strobe Talbott.

In his recently released book, Engaging India: Diplomacy, Democracy and the Bomb, Mr Talbott says he was told about this incident by Mr Fernandes himself when the former had visited India in February this year as part of a delegation assembled by the Asoen Institute and CII: "Just as we were saying goodbye to Mr Fernandes, a member of our delegation innocently asked him when he would next be coming to Washington. His demeanour abruptly changed. It was as though he was glad to have an excuse to tell us how he really felt about our country. Mr Fernandes regaled us with the story of how he had been strip-searched when he arrived for an official visit in early 2002, and again in mid-2003, when he was passing through the US on his way to Brazil."

The US Deputy Secretary has apologised to the then Defence Minister, for what some may describe as over-zealous checking. To understand the US position, I would like to recall my personal experiences when I visited Washington a decade ago for a bilateral meeting with the State Department officials on Narcotics Cooperation in my capacity as Director General, Narcotics Control Bureau. I was received at the State Department by a Deputy Assistant Secretary of State, who had invited me for the meeting followed by a lunch. As Director General of Police, I had hardly ever been subjected to any security check in India. If any check was carried out; it was done with apologies and very perfunctorily.

I would insist then, as I do even now, that all checks be carried out as required by the law, without exception, and that I should not be shown any leniency. When entering the State Department Building in Washington DC, both my host and I were subjected to a thorough security frisking and X-ray screening. I was a bit surprised when even my host, who had the highest security clearance, was not spared. I asked him out of curiosity as to who were these people conducting security check, and whether they did not know him. He said they were from a private agency and were not United States Government employees. It was part of the agreement that they would not spare anybody from security checks and if they did so, they would be guilty of breach of contract. He clarified that nobody minds these checks as, except the terrorists or other such undesirable elements, nobody in his right senses would object to them.

However, in our country, anybody who is or has been somebody, feels that he or she is above the law and must be exempt from all checks or restrictions. It is more so with the ministers, who feel that people of all ranks or categories should recognise them. Indeed, when one MP belonging to a Northeastern State was told that she could not take her car or her supporters to the tarmac and to the plane stairs, she got enraged. She wanted the Central Industrial Security Force, to whom the security of all the airports has been entrusted, to be withdrawn. It was to be on the ground that the officials were rude as, ostensibly, they wanted to go by the book. Security is thus both thankless and unrewarding, apart from being difficult. Security people are damned if they perform their duty, and damned if they do not.

There has understandably been a lot of hullabaloo about the former Defence Minister being strip searched in the United States, though the Minister concerned could not care less about this. The

VIP culture has become an ingrained part of the political and official existence in our country. Every time an Indian VIP travels by road, everything else stops. Once he goes past, all hell breaks lose. A five-minute stop during peak hours on any road in New Delhi could mean a pile-up of about 5,000 vehicles, which have to negotiate serpentine traffic and compete with snails as to who is faster. Whether entitled or not, even petty dignitaries, including officials, flaunt blue or red light atop their vehicles, as nobody dares check whether the person displaying the light is entitled to it or not. The episode involving the former Defence Minister shows how security checks in India are considered offensive, when it is all part of a drill laid down by the Government itself.

If any Government, whether Indian or America, does not want anybody to be checked or frisked, then it had better issue such orders in advance. It goes to the credit of the US that it does not spare even its own high and mighty from security checks. Law-makers in America are routinely subjected to the same security checks as you and I would be. When US Congressman John Dingel was subjected to a thorough strip down to his under wear, as the metal detector had set off an alarm, he felt hurt as the security personnel would not believe he had a metal hip replacement due to a fall two decades back. He later joked about his search saying they "felt me up and down like a prize steer". When the Transportation Secretary telephoned him to express regret, he replied, "Make sure that the security does, what is necessary and that he gets the same treatment, no better or not worse, than anyone else."

The problem in India is that every little Johnny who perceives himself to be a VIP wants to be treated like one. Worse, he wants to be treated as such both at home and abroad. The so-called VIPs think it is infradig if some body asks them their identity and that it is nothing short of blasphemy if he is frisked or searched. On the other hand, American law enforcement agencies have not been attuned to give an unequal treatment to different categories of people because a person is a minister or a law maker in some other country or for that matter even in their own country. The rich and powerful there get the same treatment like Azim Premji of India or a Pakistani Army corps commander Ali Muhammad Jan Orakzai, who, after his thorough security check, vowed never to go to the US again.

If any Indian VIP on Government account is subjected to a thorough security check or unpleasant frisking, then it is the direct fault of the Indian embassy officials incharge of protocol and reception who failed in their duties of ensuring that proper courtesies are extended to the visiting VVIPs. Probably the embassy officials think that their job is confined to hosting lunches or dinners, or sending a junior official to the airport to receive the VIP. It is amazing that the Defence Ministry has colonels and generals in some places posted as defence attaches.

Put simply, their liaisioning has been poor. Also, Americans, like many Indians, would-by the unstarched and unpressed or crumpled dress, as well as unkempt hair style of Mr Fernandes (with due apologies to him)- have doubted whether he is really the Defence Minister of India. (It happened with him in India, too, when the police in Mangalore, his home town, did not permit him to attend a function with then Chief Minister of Karnataka as he was present there without any fanfare or security hooting sirens). In spite of this incident, there has been no reduction in the number of VIPs wanting to travel to the US.

Checking of so-called Indian VIPs, in the US should be a lesson to our Government that it make sure that nobody is punished for doing his duty. There have been instances in the past when customs and police officials have been transferred from airport for checking the baggage of VIPs who would come loaded with dozens of bags of dutiable goods. Security officials are generally at the receiving end for their so-called high-handedness, when they are only complying with the rules. The Constitution of India ensures equality of all and does not mention anything about anybody being above the law.

Let us do in Rome as Romans do. When we visit other countries, we should be prepared to comply with their laws, and not make a fuss when their checking or laws do not suit us. If it be so, then why take the trouble of crossing seven oceans and then complain that we have been badly treated, when their own citizens get checked the same way and do not grumble about it?

1.2. Strengthen First Line of Defence

All illusions, if there were any, have been junked by the Prime Minister in his speech at the recent Conference of Chief Ministers about the source of terrorism in India and the support of the Government of Pakistan to the same. On January 6, he unambiguously said that the 26/11 terrorist attack on Mumbai was clearly carried out by Pakistan-based outfit Lashkar-e-Tayyeba. On the basis of the investigations carried out, which include inputs by intelligence agencies of foreign countries whose nationals were killed by the *fidayeen*, there is enough evidence to suggest that given the sophistication and military precision of the attacks, they must have had the support of some official agencies in Pakistan.

The Prime Minister added that we face a severe challenge from terrorist groups operating from outside the country, and that many of them act with the support of hostile foreign intelligence agencies. These terrorist forces have been trying to exploit our vulnerability, and at times they have succeeded in their goals, killing and maiming hundreds of innocent civilians.

Our problems are compounded by the fact that we have a highly unpredictable and uncertain security environment in our immediate neighbourhood. The Governments in some of our neighbouring countries are not very stable. The more fragile a Government, the more it tends to act in an irresponsible manner. Pakistan's responses to our various démarches are obvious examples.

This is not the first time that India has laid the blame for the malaise of terrorism at Pakistan's door. For almost every terrorist attack on our soil Pakistan is responsible one way or another, whether it be providing training or logistical support to the terrorists. The only solution, our hawks advocate, is war with Pakistan. But war is no solution to terrorism, as can be seen by the examples of Afghanistan and Iraq, and our own past wars with Pakistan. On the other hand, this doesn't mean that we cannot strengthen our country's security and intelligence-gathering infrastructure to combat terrorism. The Prime Minister has admitted that our defence mechanisms are inadequate and need to be overhauled.

There may be criticism that the range of instruments that we possess to deal with internal security threats is not sufficient. This may not be totally unjustified. There is a pressing need to review the effectiveness of our security set-up for the collection of communication intercepts and human intelligence. The training and equipment provided to our security forces also need careful review.

There is little doubt that our intelligence collection is deficient and so is our preparedness to deal with terror threats. I do not know whether it is due to ignorance or apathy, or a mixture of both. In 2008 the then Union Home Minister, while replying to a question in the Rajya Sabha, had admitted that there were 25 to 30 per cent vacancies in various police forces of the country. Look at Maharashtra, which has borne the brunt of terrorism. According to its then Home Minister, last year 11,000 police posts remained vacant. The current strength of the State Police force is 1,31,000 and there is a need for another 55,000 personnel. Assam, another State severely affected by terrorism, has as many as 7,776 vacancies in different police categories. Similarly, Chhattisgarh has about another 7,000 vacancies.

Not surprisingly, our country has one of the lowest police-to-population ratios in the world. As against a UN international norm of 222 policemen per lakh of population, India has just 143 policemen for the same number of people. This works out to just 14,000 police stations for more than 6.5 lakh villages. In most Western countries, the figure is between 250 and 500. Italy and Mexico, two countries with strong mafia and underworld presence, have 559 and 492 policemen per lakh of their population respectively. According to the latest figures compiled by the Centre, there were more than 1.3 lakh vacancies in the police all over our country. Even out of this nearly 15 to 20 per cent are diverted for VIP security.

New counter-terrorism mechanisms require more information, intelligence and technology, and latest sophisticated weapons. The State police forces, that are our first line of defence against the menace of terrorism, need to be strengthened in numbers as well as in equipment and training to meet the challenge.

The Comptroller and Auditor-General's report for 2006-07 tabled in the Andhra Pradesh State Assembly says: "Given the magnitude of extremist activity in the State, requirement of AK 47, 7.62 mm Self-Loaded Rifle, nine mm carbines, and 5.5 mm pistols for police stations were projected in the perspective plan 2001-05 to improve the striking capability of the police force and Rs. 45.71 crore was sanctioned during 2002-07. Most of the equipment was procured only during 2005-06. In all the police stations of test checked districts it was observed that they continued to depend on outdated weapons like 0.410 muskets and 0.303 rifles, with majority of weapons being kept at the district headquarters. The State Government did not release its matching share (Rs. 98.9 crore in 2002-03 to 2005-06). The percentage of utilisation of funds in the year of sanction was very low at 13 to 38 per cent".

The above report is only an illustration of prevails all over the country. The real problem that India faces in combating terrorism is our unprepared police force. Beyond doubt once a person joins the police force, after initial training it is rare for him to be exposed to a refresher course. But no overhauling of our security system will be effective without improving the capacities and capabilities of our police force.

Thus, instead of searching for elusive terror training camps in Pakistan, we should simply put our own house in order. Before we point finger at others, let us strengthen our own defence mechanisms and start at ground-level policing and then work our way up. We must put an end to terrorism, or terrorism will end us.

2. Issues and Framework of Safeguards

2.1. Scrap the Dangerous Deals

Metal scrap is imported to recycle and reconvert the same to the original metal by many factories in our country. These are imported from all over the world including South Africa, Europe, Asia and West Asia. Metal scraps include spent cartridges, used bomb shells, ferrous and non-ferrous materials like steel, copper, zinc, brass and lead. One estimate puts the import of scrap to a figure of 1,500 tons daily. Imported scrap is in great demand since it is used in the manufacture of secondary products such as steel ingots, billets and bars. The demand for such scrap is estimated at about 6 lakh tons. Only half of this is actually imported.

Scrap is a good source of making money. There is a great requirement of it from low-grade manufacturers of steel who are unable to do away with scrap that is locally generated. Metal scrap is obtained from sources like old machinery items or even from shells and projectiles used by defence forces or by countries engaged in hostilities. But war metal scrap is relatively cheap. Estimates indicate that 60,000 tonnes of stainless steel scrap resulting from the September 11 attack was imported into India for recycling, and for use as building material, furniture and household utensils.

Even by conservative estimate, nearly 315 million computers became obsolete in the US between 1997 and 2004. Two-thirds of these reportedly reached Indian shores as scrap for reconditioning. About 1.38 million computers generate from 1,050 tonnes of electronic scrap every year and there are approximately 40 to 50 major computer scrap dealers in and around Delhi that roughly import 1,500 tons every day compared to about 100 tons of domestic scrap collected by the kabaris from all over including individual houses. Even the Indian defence forces and the police and paramilitary forces sell fired shells, which can be recycled by the industries.

So much so, a case under the Explosive Material Act had been registered on the October 6, 2004, against the Chairman and Directors of Bhushan Steel Company, in Ghaziabad (Uttar Pradesh), following the recovery of munitions and explosive materials from the scrap it imported from Iran. Amongst the explosives found in the steel scrap was a light machinegun, a tank chain and some shells of missiles.

Earlier, the explosions resulting from the metal scrap imported from Iran claimed 10 lives and injured nine on September 30 blast. Since then, it has caught the imagination of the national media and the concerned on this less known but highly profitable trade. It could not have thrived without corruption, slim laws, covert operations and something very basic to countries like India: Cheap labour, cheap life and cheaper death.

Scrap dealers and scrap recyclers have had a comparatively low-profile business life. It was only after the rocket explosions at Bhushan Steel Factory in Ghaziabad that the dangerous side of the trade has been brought to light. To begin with, the customs officials claim that it underwent "thorough" checks at Teheran, Dubai, Kandla Port in Gujarat and then at the Tughlaqabad scrap yard in the heart of Delhi. According to them, nothing incriminating was discovered at any of the checkpoints. This shows that either the officials have neglected their duty, or were in connivance with traders to hurry up clearances and checks for considerations other than efficiency.

In all fairness to the customs department or other checking agencies, they conduct only a visual examination before clearing the entry of scrap. Nobody has bothered to equip the inspection agencies with container-scanning machines, which can detect live shells in scrap. We have the only scanner scanning machine in Mumbai. The writing, on the scrap dump, is portentous. Without any check, or a thorough inspection, any scrap could contain explosives, which can trigger off mishaps. However, the bombs and rockets seized so far are reportedly so rusted that it is difficult to decipher their country of origin. Such scraps have also been found in Khurja Bulandshahr, Mussoorie, Meerut, Aligarh and Mandi Govind Garh in Punjab, Rajasthan, Mumbai and Delhi.

The discovery of so many live munitions has caused consternation and doubts are being raised whether this could be the work of terrorists. How else could live ammunition, rockets and bombs find their way into scrap? The truth is, even in our own country, unexploded shells and ammunitions have caused explosions led to maiming or killing of people who wanted to collect the shells for sale as scrap. So far, no evidence has come forth of the involvement of any terrorist group in selling scrap to any factory.

But there is no convincing evidence to corroborate the theory that terrorist groups have had such wide links that it could manage to mix live shells or explosives, in connivance with the selling, and forwarding agencies in Dubai or Iran and ensure that the consignments containing explosives are sold to India, and then make further sure that the same are sold to industries close to the national Capital.

At the same time it does not mean that all is well with our rules, procedures or methods of either importing or handling such materials. It took 10 lives and scores of people injured for the Government to finally wake up and streamline the existing procedures. According to the new guidelines, the import of scrap would be permitted only in shredded or compacted form. Now, only the unshredded and uncompacted waste would be allowed after total inspection and only through major ports and ICD, Tughlaqabad. For imports from war-affected countries, documents would have to be furnished to the customs.

There is obviously more to be done than just enforcing minimal measures. For instance, there are many more areas in the field of imports or hazardous or unsavoury substances where constant streamlining and vigilance is required. We need a strong mechanism to check import at entry point of any material or waste, which can be recycled or used not only from the safety, security or health point of view but also from the point of revenue loss to the Government. I recall in the 1970s, a vegetable oil manufacturing industry near Delhi (probably in Ghaziabad) imported a lot of beef tallow for mixing in the hydrogenated vegetable. It had created a lot of problems and the Government of the day had some hard explaining to do.

What we need is a comprehensive export import code for materials such as second-hand computers for the purpose of donation or resale, or even for other items. Unscrupulous people can take advantage of the Customs Tariff Act and club old and junk along with other new items. Interpretation of rules lies with one authority and enforcement with others. We need to ensure better coordination and have a responsible and responsive control mechanism. Flexibility in interpretations of rules, consistent with the liberal regime, is the need. It is a difficult to have a balance of the two, but it needs to be done if tragic incidents such as the one that has occured are to be avoided.

We also need to take a second look on the import of junk or scrap items as other. Our trade policy should be so revised that our country is not allowed to become a dumping ground of obsolete technology. If obsolete technology is allowed it should bear correct declaration and accurate labelling. Further, this should be a legal requirement. Some times 'notified goods' (good which are prohibited to be imported without license) are imported, which can be retrieved by paying penalty.

This works as a back-door for obtaining confiscated goods. If any item is not allowed, then it should not be allowed in our country. This will prevent double standards as in the case of imported junk items, including computers and peripheral parts, especially in export oriented zones. We need to have a 'Waste Management Policy' which should embrace and address all issues ranging from import, production and trade to final disposal including technology transfers. If waste or scrap is useless in the country of its origin, it should normally be so for us as well, unless there are exceptional reasons to treat the same on a different footing.

2.2. Vigil on No-citizens

Union Home Minister and Deputy Prime Minister LK Advani has held that illegal overstaying of Pakistani nationals and influx of Bangladeshis pose a serious threat to national security. He has said that as many as "11,500 Pakistanis have come into the country with regular papers and passports but have overstayed". Nobody, at least officially, knows where they are. Mr Advani has also urged the launching of "immediate steps to identify, locate and throw them out". State Governments have been asked to "launch special drives to detect and deport these foreigners". The Central Government's powers to trace and throw out illegal aliens have been delegated to the States. This call has not come a day too soon. In fact, neglect of this crucial aspect of policing and the indifference of State dispensations to the subject are too well-known for comfort.

As Superintendent of Police, Bidar District, Karnataka, from 1965 to 1968, I was keen to give a personal touch to policing in the district. As part of this drill, I would move around in my office to find out what was happening. One day, I noticed a couple of middle-aged men with some burqa-clad women in the my office, talking with Special Branch officers. I asked an officer who the visitors were. He said they were Pakistani nationals who had come to register themselves with the police, in accordance with the law.

This law requires every foreign national, especially a Pakistani, to register himself with the local police on arrival. It is aimed at ensuring all foreigners leave India after the expiry of their visas. Honestly and frankly, I did not realise it was part of my duty to throw out foreigners who had defied visa rules. The simple reason: We were given the impression, during our training, that the Foreigners Act was was a minor Act. Since marks assigned to minor Acts, including the Foreigners Act, were few, nobody at the time bothered much about it, and thought far less of implementing it. The situation is no different today.

As an SP, I felt that if a person had chosen another country as his place of abode, then he had better go away on completion of his social visit. I started making enquires about the number of Pakistani citizens who had outstayed their welcome in my district. The figure came as a shock.

I asked my office whether the Government or the office of the Inspector General (presently Director General-the police chief was called IG at that time) had demanded any explanation or conveyed its unhappiness over non-performance with regard to the Foreigners Act. I was told neither had ever happened and that, in fact, no district police chief had ever shown any interest in this matter. In order to convey the message that this situation would not do, I launched a drive to throw out illegal migrants.

In a rare gesture, the Government of Mysore, now Karnataka, sent me a communication in "appreciation of good work done". The official letter (No GAD 83 SPS 67) bearing the address Mysore Government Secretariat, Vidhana Soudha, Bangalore, and dated July 10, 1967, came from the Chief Secretary to the Government of Mysore. It was addressed to me, "Superintendent of Police, Bidar".

I quote the message: "The Inspector General of Police has brought to the notice of (the) Government that you have been responsible for launching a drive to trace Pak Nationals who had evaded leaving India after the expiry of their permits and that you have made untiring and praiseworthy efforts in tracing Pak Nationals. I am directed, in this connection, to convey to you the appreciation of (the) Government for the excellent work carried out by you, in spite of serious handicaps of difficulties met with in handling such work." The letter was signed K Narayanaswamy, Chief Secretary to the Government.

True, migrants-illegal or legal-often come to India in search of livelihood. Even Indians go to the West, Russia and the Baltic countries as illegal migrants. Unfortunately, this is not the case with people coming from our neighbouring countries. Illegal aliens who have disappeared have done so with a view to instigating riots and disturbances in India, at Pakistan's bidding. True, it is not a good policy to close the doors of one's country to anybody. But it is the lesser of the two evils when denying entry to those who could destabilise and devastate the country.

None can deny that many of the missing Pakistani nationals are agents of proxy war against India. A lot still needs to be done in this direction, such as the preparation of a National Register of Indian citizens and issuance of multi-purpose national identity cards serving as a ration card, passport, driving license and credible individual identification system.

Every individual knows the members of his family. But as a nation we do not know who is our own and who is not. This is why the Government has proposed a scheme for issuance of national identity cards covering, at the first stage, 13 States-Delhi, Rajasthan, Uttar Pradesh, Jammu & Kashmir, Gujarat, Andhra Pradesh, West Bengal, Assam, Tripura, Tamil Nadu, Goa and Pondicherry. It has clarified the card will be different from the Election Commission-issued Voter Identity Card.

We need to examine the arguments in favour of having one card dealing with all facets of Government. A multipurpose card would be economical and create less confusion for citizens as well as the Government. Most illegal immigrants, including the 1.5 crore Bangladeshis (the figure provided by the present Home Minister; the former Home Minister, late Inderjeet Gupta, said it was 2.5 crore in 1996) live in low-cost areas or slums. They naturally eat into the country's resources and take up jobs meant for our citizens. We do sympathise with the world's poor. But surely our first duty is to our own citizens.

National parties need to evolve a consensus on the issue, which must on no account be politicised for the sake of votebank politics. One way to deal with the problem is to consider-since we cannot control slums-the Hong Kong model, which has licensed slums with all modern facilities. But the Government need not make it obligatory for itself to provide land to every encroacher on its property. Most illegal immigrants manage to build ghettos or start living in small slums and then enlarge their size. The Delhi High Court has already ruled the official policy as being illegal, an order against which the Delhi Government proposes to appeal.

India has very generous citizenship laws. In Germany, citizenship is linked to nationality based on ethnicity. In France, citizenship is also linked to nationality and there are near-insurmountable laws for naturalised citizenship. It is relatively easier for the children of foreigners-the second generation-to apply for citizenship rights and status.

Experts of the UN Security Council Monitoring Committee, which oversees the implementation of UNSC Resolution 1373, say that, despite freezing/seizure of terrorist funds and other assets worth $ 112 million since 9/11, the Al Qaeda and its allies in the International Islamic Front still have at their disposal about $ 300 million. Replenishments continue to flow into their coffers.

There has been a spate of terrorist incidents since 9/11 in different parts of the world-including the attack on the Indian Parliament and the Akshardham and Raghunath temple strikes. And there have been sweeping victories of pro-Al Qaeda/Taliban fundamentalists in the relatively recent elections in Pakistan. These prove that terrorists do not as yet face a dearth of funds for their activities, underground (acts of terrorism) or overground (political support to their backers). They would not hesitate to make use of the 11,500 Pakistani nationals who officially entered India and then went missing, apart from millions of illegal immigrants.

Any foreign national who has overstayed his visa and thus broken the law of the land must be deported, without second thoughts or any political or religious consideration. The drive should be sustained and monitored, and end at one statement of the Government.

2.3. Army

2.3.1. Crossing the Thin Line

A Central Reserve Police Force (CRPF) constable who was recruited in 2003 and posted in J&K was not present when his name was called in November 2004. Absence from duty is considered a serious lapse in para-military forces.It can be seen as anything from plain negligence to shirking from work to even mixing with persons of questionable repute or escaping after having committed a crime. Being a new recruit, the CRPF constable was reprimanded and asked to do three days of "fatigue duty".

On November 28, 2004, this constable fired indiscriminately in the CRPF campus, killing a company commander, a sub-inspector, a head constable and four constables before he was himself shot dead. Such incidents, of policemen killing each other are not uncommon. In the last two years even persons of the rank of majors and colonels have been shot dead by their subordinates. In October 2004, a policeman was arrested for shooting dead a truck driver when he refused to bribe. The public has a right to know the reasons for such aberrations in those who are uniformed and are supposedly disciplined and upright. Where do those who are perceived as models of good conduct go wrong?

A number of explanations have been offered for such occurrences among personnel, particularly those involved in combating insurgency. I had firsthand experience of this when I was heading the CRPF in Punjab and J&K 1988 during the peak of insurgency. The security forces are usually fighting invisible enemy who can emerge at any moment. The aim of a terrorist is to cause the maximum possible damage. However, whereas an insurgent can kill mercilessly without any compunction, those in the security forces can retaliate only when attacked.

Often the writ of insurgents is more effective in an area they dominate than that of Government. The local people, in order to ensure their safety, maintain strict neutrality and rarely take a stand against terrorists. They put their lives in peril facing explosives, bombing, shooting and firing to protect those whose attitude to them is one of indifference. Thus, the feeling of insecurity always plagues the mind of those who are deployed in sensitive areas.Each year scores of security personnel lose their lives on duty. Between 2003 and 2004, 991 policemen belonging to the State and Central Police services were killed. In the previous year the figure was 963 whereas in 2001, it was 932.

Those who are lower down in the hierarchy more often than not live in miserable conditions which too adds to their stress. As per the guidelines of the Central Government, it is the duty of the State governments to provide accommodation to the security forces where ever they are deployed in the State. In actual practice, the forces have to fend for themselves and often manage without even basic necessities like adequate water, toilets and accommodation. For this reason, much to the chagrin of local people, schools, rest houses, or even hotels are used to house security forces. In some insurgency affected areas, even vegetables, are not available. When I was posted as IGP CRP in Kashmir, a Union Minister who was supposed to visit the State asked me what he should bring with him. I told him that a plane load of fresh green vegetables would be the best gift for the men.

The uneven, unequal and unexpected fight between the security forces and terrorists, often at places which are known to the insurgents, has them on the edge causing excessive stress. Stress also occurs following exposure to extremely traumatic conditions such as experiencing that involves actual or threatened death or serious injury or physical harm or mental shock after witnessing an event that involves injury or death.

Those deployed in terrorist infested areas are not always familiar with the history, culture, traditions and geography of the area. Before being posted they are only briefed about the anti-terrorist operation in the concerned area. Also, often there are frequent changes in the operational orders by the Government. A simple soldier is not able to understand these complexities. He is left wondering why the Government orders ceasefire one day and reluctantly withdraws it the next day. They cannot explain the authorities' flip-flop-a terrorist becomes a respectable citizen, only to be branded as a terrorist again.

There are times when these terrorists are lionised by the residents of the area where they are active. What bewilders the security personnel most is that at times the government provides protection to secessionists and anti national elements or even those who support them. It is indeed ironical that the same security forces deployed to fighting insurgents are asked to protect these elements supposedly from those who are their supporters.

It happens only in our country that Prime Minister visits J&K and announces a package of Rs 24,000 crore. However, his polite invitation to talk to secessionist leaders is turned down. The same leaders come to Delhi within weeks of the Prime Minister's visit, and wait for hours to meet the second secretary of the Pakistan High Commission, before meeting the Prime Minister of that country.

Swinging from one extreme situation to another adds to the stress and confusion of our soldiers. Working in such circumstances, their nerves are always on the edge. Even a small action can ignite emotions. Moreover, unlike the local police personnel who can stay with their families there is little possibility for the members of the security forces to have their families, with them. Therefore, being away from their near and dear ones too takes a toll on their mental make up. The stress becomes even more acute because all their acts, if they are not within the purview of rules have to be explained to the Government. The rules for fighting insurgency are definitely weighed in favour of terrorists simply because our laws imply that let nine out of ten who are guilty, go scot free.

Thus nine out of ten terrorists in any case escape the dragnet of laws with the tenth also managing to get away. The security forces often feel that their problems are not taken into account by the establishment. Nor are they involved in negotiations or discussions that are held to seek solutions to the problems of insurgency.

While the State should do whatever it can to improve their situation and boost their morale, a close rapport between security personnel and their superiors would do wonders. Some battalions are so large with over 15,0000 men, that it is not possible for those who lead them to be in touch with soldiers who constitute them.

Therefore, having small and self-contained anti-insurgency forces is one solution. Another thing that the government can do is cut the red-tape and provide the basic comfort to men. This will send the message that the Government cares and wants to address the concerns of those waging war on its behalf. Of course, some contradiction of having a fortified state within a democratic polity will always be there, when dealing with separatism and terrorism.

On their part, the security forces need to shed their arrogance which is probably an outcome of carrying lethal weapons, and rid themselves of the feeling that they can get away with anything. Those who lead them must exhibit leadership qualities, sensitivity, understanding and moral character and set an example for their subordinates.

2.3.2. Stressed Out in the Army

Addressing an Army Commanders Conference last month, Union Defence Minister AK Antony said, "All possible steps must be taken to reduce the stress on jawans. A more humane management is needed to tackle these problems." This could be done through enhanced interactions between senior and junior officers, both in qualitative and quantitative terms.

There is no doubt the stress factor is a serious problem. It affects the capability of the Indian Army. The following figures speak for themselves: Since 2004, 282 soldiers have been killed in terrorist attacks. In the same period, 408 soldiers have either committed suicide, or killed colleagues, or died after some colleague opened fire indiscriminately. Out of the 408 soldiers, 333 killed themselves. The Army endures 100 suicides a year.

It is not clear what precisely is responsible for such incidents. The problem faced by the Indian Army is similar to the situation faced by the US Army in Vietnam. We can learn from the American experience.

A study on the Vietnam predicament, "Cohesion and Disintegration in the American Army," was conducted by Richard A Gabriel and Paul Savage. The study made three points: First, senior officers did not oversee and manage their junior officers to the extent required in countering operations that had political implications. Second, the quality of officers was poor with respect to the complexity of the task on hand. Third, the system of rotation through tenures of 13 months in Vietnam for each officer did not permit the development of the required level of cohesion in the teams.

There is always a tendency to pat our defence forces as the best in the world. We should, however, not let praise or criticism get the better of us when we are facing a crisis. It is sheer blindness to get caught up in either of the two extreme views.

A jawan works in precarious situations. He is not sure whether he would come back from the battlefield alive or his body would be brought back in a coffin. Stress, the "wear and tear" the body and mind experience, is thus a natural outcome.

As Inspector General of Police of the Central Reserve Police Force, I had first-hand experience of the stress security personnel are subjected to in terrorism-infested Jammu & Kashmir. In the Valley, the uniform serves like a red rag for the jihadi bull. As Armymen are continuously exposed to negative influences, it results in feelings of distrust, rejection, anger and depression which, in turn, can lead to health problems like headache, stomach upset, skin rashes, insomnia, ulcer, hypertension, heart disease and stroke. It naturally affects their relationship with everybody. Also, excessive use of liquor in lonely places by both officers and jawans has been found to be creating psychological problems.

The demands of the job are such that an Army man or a paramilitary official is exposed to relentlessly inhospitable and hostile conditions. No words can adequately describe those situations. Of course, the authorities make efforts to rotate people between 'soft' and 'hard' postings. Army and paramilitary forces work along borders or in insurgency-prone areas. An official gets to spend between five and eight years with his family while in a comparatively 'soft' posting. Once while inspecting a border checkpost as the Director General of the Indo-Tibetan Border Police, I asked a young officer about his family. He told me that he was waiting for a posting at a place nearer home so that he could get married soon.

In the Army, whose size is much larger, continuous deployment in tough areas can wreck soldiers both mentally and physically. In 2004, as many as 1,263 officials and jawans were discharged from service due to psychotic and neurotic ailments and alcoholism. If the figures of Navy and Air Force are included, the figure rises to 1,415.

In 2006, 508 Army, 35 IAF and 15 Navy personnel were discharged from service for being mentally unsound. The Defence Institute of Psychological Research (DIPR) was asked to conduct a study on the "Psycho-social aspects of optimising operational efficiency of security forces to combat insurgency". It did so for the period from September 2000 to May 2005. It has come to the conclusion that the fear of torture, uncertain environment and domestic stress were mainly responsible for the psychological problems in the armed forces. The hard lives for the 1.13-million strong Army, with soldiers posted either in remote areas or tangled in relentless counter-insurgency operations far away from their families, with no chance of seeing them except once a year and little or no socialisation support systems are undoubtedly taking a heavy toll on the mental health of soldiers.

To tackle this problem, the Army proposes to hire 400 psychologists in the next five years. The truth remains that the job content cannot be changed to cut the stress. But early signs of stress can be identified if the immediate bosses detect the following signals: Chronic fatigue or exhaustion, frequent loss of temper, loss of self-esteem for putting up with undue demands, cynicism, irritability, a sense of being besieged, getting livid at the sight of inconsequential things, frequent headaches and gastrointestinal disturbances, rapid weight loss or gain, sleeplessness and depression, shortness of breath, incredulity, feelings of helplessness, heightened spree for adventure, etc.

It is for the officers to take urgent note of the above signals. However, enumerating the causes of stress can be tricky as there could be innumerable stress factors: Different individuals react differently to an identical condition. What is an extreme stress situation for an individual may be a mild one for another; for yet another person, the situation might not qualify as stressful at all. A stress condition can be genuine or hypothetical. Yet, our brain reacts in the same way to both causes of stress by releasing balancing hormones adequate for the degree of stress felt.

The Army is a closed organisation. What comes out in the public domain is only the tip of the iceberg. The Government is looking after the Army's needs well with concessions and facilities not available to other Government employees - like providing for free ration to all Army personnel irrespective of rank. There are also full medical facilities, with dedicated hospitals, assured leave for two months and travel even by air (at 50 per cent charges). In the canteen facilities, all items are available at much less than the market rates. Of course, if you ask an Army man, he would say the facilities are not sufficient.

The Army has full freedom in its internal affairs. It is for its leadership to rectify the serious lapses.

2.4. Intelligence

2.4.1. What Ails Our Intelligence ?

Every time there is a major terrorist strike, the imprint of Pakistan comes out glaringly. Islamabad, on the contrary, accuses our intelligence agencies of having inspired and perpetrated serious incidents not only in India but also Pakistan.

Washington DC-based Federation of American Scientists (FAS), a privately funded non-profit policy organisation, whose board of sponsors includes half of America's living Nobel laureates, brushes aside such charges as frivolous. It would be unusual for an intelligence agency to mastermind an operation that had the potential of endangering its own country's citizens, it reasoned. If something did go wrong, it would have been an awfully big disaster.

The FAS reveals that Pakistan's Inter-Services Intelligence has become a state within a state, answerable neither to the Army, nor the Government. The result is there has been no real supervision of the ISI. Drug money was used by it to finance not only the Afghanistan war, but also the proxy war against India. It reportedly supplies weapons, besides giving training to terrorists in Kashmir and the North-East.

Are we equipped to deal with the challenge posed by Pakistan? The problem is highlighted by 7/11 serial blasts in Mumbai, which left 200 people dead. Regardless of Pakistan may say, we need to introspect and examine whether our own house is in order. Are our intelligence agencies and Government displaying enough vigilance to prevent the leakage of intelligence? How is it that, in spite of a large number of agencies, terrorists are able to strike at will?

One Union Minister in the previous Government had told a gathering of intelligence officials that the Kargil conflict was a result of the "failure to converge the information into actionable intelligence which led to the subserving of national security."

Have we learnt from our past mistakes? While talking to a police officer, I asked him what was wrong with the intelligence. He said that, with the creation of a plethora of Intelligence agencies, things had gone from bad to worse. Most intelligence officials sit in police stations and send reports based on the information collected by the police. The officer further added that the police station is the key point for interaction with the public and informants.

In our desire to collect more and more security related information, we have not only diluted the responsibility of the local officers in charge of the police stations, but also removed them from the responsibility of gathering intelligence. Apart from the central intelligence agencies, each State has its own intelligence set up. Also, each central paramilitary and defence force has its own system of intelligence gathering, including the Defence Intelligence Agency.

It is the reports collected and collated from different levels and sources that go into the formulation of the national policy on terrorism. Despite everybody trying his luck at collecting intelligence, we do not have an effective management system of intelligence.

Intelligence coordination should be at the heart of intelligence management, which includes gathering and analysis. As each department is an empire unto itself, we do not have clearly earmarked turf and every agency is stepping on the toes of others for inputs to impress their respective bosses. Intelligence relating to national security is provided not only by the IB and RAW, but also military intelligence, BSF, the Customs, Enforcement Directorate, and State police. In a midnight meeting during the VP Singh regime, then Home Minister Mufti Mohammad Sayeed remarked that the intelligence agencies were more keen to inform him as to what was likely to happen, instead of passing on the actionable intelligence to the ground level.

The ideal arrangement would be to have all agencies assemble their information at one point, so that a complete picture is available to the decision-makers. It is best to do so at the district level, whether they are Central or State agencies. Theoretically, the Joint Intelligence Committee and the National Security Council report to the National Security Adviser. But in practice, each agency works independently. The collection, collation and analysis of information are done by each intelligence agency in a veritable vacuum.

Over the years, political parties have misused intelligence and investigating organisations. It is an open secret that governments in power misuse the agencies to bring about changes in political compositions, besides indulging in toppling games and spying on worthwhile individuals. In fact, Rajiv Gandhi had openly accused the Government in 1991 of keeping him under watch. This allegation was repeated in 1996 and 1997 by the then Congress president against the United Front Government.

The bureaucracy, police and intelligence agencies weigh as to what should be reported and what should be watered down. They want to make certain that their bread is buttered on both sides. No wonder they present reports in such a way that they convey only what the bosses would like to hear or believe. This approach proves their loyalty not only to their bosses, but also to ideology. Such stance not only helps them in service, but also after retirement. This fact can be confirmed from the number of Ambassadors, Chairmen of Government Tribunals, Commissions and even Governors chosen from the rank of civil service.

When I was Superintendent of Police, a senior officer told me that the best approach is to guard from all sides and then take action. I told him that he was entitled to his approach and style of working, but putting the facts as they are and not as bosses want would be disloyalty to the nation. He said that sometimes telling the truth could harm one's interest.

We must not only be careful from external enemies, but also from the moles within. Former External Affairs Minister Jaswant Singh has said that there was a mole in Prime Minister Narasimha Rao's office. Besides streamlining external and internal intelligence set up, we must make sure that the country does not leak like a sieve, whether it is about defence or the officials of intelligence agencies deserting their jobs and seeking shelter abroad.

The political executive needs to take more interest in the intelligence and security matters, instead of leaving everything on god and bureaucracy. It was Albert Einstein who once said that the world is a dangerous place not because of those who do evil, but because of those who look on and do nothing.

2.4.2. Intelligence: Spy versus Spy

War in Iraq broke out on March 20, 2003. This highlights the role of Western intelligence agencies, particularly the US's Central Intelligence Agency. Despite talk of human rights, these agencies continue to play a cloak-and-dagger game with the rest of the world.

French intelligence chief Marenches once confessed that, before he took charge, the French external intelligence agency had been engaged in shocking activities. It intervened freely in the internal affairs of other countries. It organised murders and assassinations-for example, the kidnapping and disappearance of the Moroccan leader Ben Barka in 1965, using even the French mafia (just as the CIA has used mafia hitmen) and various gangsters and gunmen.

He claimed he had introduced some degree of morality in his organisation, but went on to proudly narrate how the SDECE (as his outfit was then called) had succeeded in ousting Emperor Jean-Bedel Bokassa of the Central African Republic in 1979. Nations, he held, sometimes had to take actions that might be immoral or even illegal. Such decisions could only be taken by the Head of State. In his case, he said it was up to his discretion whether to go ahead with an action on his own or to consult the President.

In the US, disclosures have revealed that President Eisenhower himself authorised the CIA to scheme the overthrow of President Sukarno of Indonesia. Kennedy too ordered the overthrow of Dr Cheddi Jagan of Guyana, which was achieved by surreptitiousness and manoeuvring. Only recently, President George W Bush literally ordered his Iraqi counterpart Saddam Hussein and his sons to step down or face forcible removal. UN or no UN, world opinion or no world opinion, the US after its success in Afghanistan has embarked on a policy of selecting tinpot rulers of its choice in other countries. It backs up its demands with mighty air power. Morality as a façade is used when it suits its interests, and is given up when it does not.

The Soviet Union and its allies were no different in the heydays of its power. Marenches said the Bulgarians were used by the Soviets frequently "for the worst kind of work-'wet work', or assassination", since the KGB leadership considered them loyal.

The British tried to target Egypt's Abdel Nasser at the time of the Suez crisis. It seems M16 had a plan to kill him using nerve gas. It was abandoned when the then British Prime Minister Eden succeeded in obtaining French and Israeli approval to engage in joint military action. When this alternative did not work out, the plan to kill Nasser was revived. "By this time, virtually all M16 assets in Egypt had been rounded up by Nasser, and the new operation, using renegade Egyptian officers, was drawn up, but it failed lamentably, principally because the cache of weapons which had been hidden on the outskirts of Cairo was found to be defective" (Wright with Green Grass, 1987).

A senior Libyan intelligence official played a crucial role in organising the Panam aircraft bombing over Lock-erbie on December 21, 1988. In April 1993, Kuwaiti police unearthed an Iraqi conspiracy to kill US President George Bush Sr with a car bomb to be planted in Kuwait, at the time of his visit.

Intelligence bodies of various countries have routinely killed the opponents of their Governments who have taken refuge elsewhere. Libya, Iraq and Iran have done it almost all the time. After the murder of former Iranian Prime Minister Shahpour Bakhtiar in Paris in 1991, French investigations showed that Iranian intelligence services had effectively taken part in the criminal conspiracy to carry out the assassination.

The West perceives Islamic terrorism to be as great a threat as communism was 50 years ago. NATO Secretary-General Willy Claes and chief of the British M15 Stella Remington have called radical Islam the geopolitical menace of the future. It is doubtful whether the US has overcome the damage Iran inflicted on it in 1981-1982 by taking 52 American diplomatic personnel hostage and detaining them for 444 dreadful days. Or the car bomb attack on the US Embassy in Beirut in 1983 that left over 240 dead. And, of course, the World Trade Centre blast in New York on September 11, 2001, again the handiwork of Islamic fundamentalists.

Brigadier Imtiaz Ahmed, once head of the Pakistan Intelligence Bureau and a protege of Mr Nawaz Sharif in his earlier term as Prime Minister, was arrested by the Benazir Bhutto Government in July 1994 on the charge he had played an active role in purchasing members of the Pakistan National Assembly to oust the Bhutto dispensation in 1989. The Pakistani media has reported that, as director of Pakistan's Intelligence Bureau, Brigadier Ahmed had planned riots, fake intelligence operations, large-scale tapping of telephones of Mr Sharif's rivals and even setting up a private parallel intelligence agency with secret official funds.

In a testimony to the US Senate on February 10, 2003, the CIA Director revealed that "Pakistan continues to support the groups that resist India's presence in Kashmir, in an effort to bring India to the negotiating table ... Frustration with continued terrorist attacks has prompted India, to reject any suggestion of resumption of dialogue with Pakistan. (The) Al Qaeda continues to find refuge in the hinterlands of Afghanistan and Pakistan, apart from establishing a presence in Iran and Iraq. Osama bin Laden's network is living in the expectation of resuming the offensive".

Pakistan and the ISI have left no stone unturned to create mayhem in India. Apart from freely providing arms and other support to terrorists for the last two decades, it is now directly providing funds and foreign exchange. The Pakistani High Commission in India, the hub of terror sponsorship, was caught with its pants down when it gave a few lakhs to a woman for sustaining terrorism on February 6, 2003. The woman conduit's diary clearly indicated the money was to be passed on to the Lashkar-e-Toiba, Jaish-e-Mohammad, Jammu & Kashmir Liberation Front, J&K Islamic Front, Al-Badr, Hizbul Mujahideen and Al-Umar. The conduit herself was to keep some money for the services rendered. The Pakistani High Commissioner's direct involvement in sabotaging activities left no choice for the Indian Government but to ask him to leave the country.

For India to be strong, we need to stand united and not take partisan positions. At present, there is no federal agency that can tackle crimes that are international or federal in character such as terrorism, drug trafficking, illegal immigration and organised crime.

Chief Ministers, in a meeting convened by the Central Government on February 8, 2003, rejected a proposal for such an agency. This only goes to show that, for these worthies, petty personal interests override the desire to streamline operations in the national interest. They did agree on the need to deport illegal Bangladeshi immigrants. This does not mean much unless backed by action on the ground without being swayed by votebank politics. Bangladeshis have treated India as a dharamshala, where they can walk in at will. The result: 25 million Bangladeshis were illegal residents in India in 1996 (according to then Home Minister). Today, the number must be closer to around 30 million.

Our population is one billion and countless young people are unemployed. We need to strengthen and empower intelligence and enforcement agencies, apart from fencing the 4,100 kilometre-long border with Bangladesh. Every country has its own problems. But the ones affecting us pinch us more.

This is why we need effective leaders. What Burke said about the statesman and the pseudo-statesman is worth repeating: "The great difference between the real statesman and the pretender is that the one sees into the future, while the other regards only the present, and acts on expediency". The true statesman, he asserted, "acts on enduring principles and morality in the true interests of the country and morality".

2.4.3. Intelligence and Accountability

A retired middle-level officer in the country's intelligence agency, the Research and Analysis Wing, has published a book quite critical of the R&AW's functioning. On receipt of a complaint from the Government, the CBI registered a case against him under the Official Secrets Act. There is no power vested in the CBI to decline any Government request to conduct investigation into any alleged violation of law.

As part of the investigation, raids were conducted at his residence as well as the premises of the publisher. Incidentally, such raids are part of investigation to recover any possible incriminating evidence; else, no accused will confess his or her role. The CBI has been severely criticised for conducting raids at his residence. However, a conveniently forgotten point is that no complaint under the Official Secrets Act can be taken up by the premier investigating agency, unless the affected party — this time it's the Government — lodges it.

As long as the 1923 Official Secrets Act is on the statutes, some agency has to act on the receipt of the complaint. The CBI did exactly that. Whether the law is relevant or not, in the light of the Right to Information Act, is a different issue.

In a democracy, no institution should be left without a mechanism of checks and balances. It should regularly be scrutinised to see that it is faithfully pursuing its assigned function. There is some sort of accountability on all Government departments, either departmentally or through CAG or CVC. Ironically, even 60 years after independence, India's intelligence set-up has not been subjected to scrutiny, except by the departmental bosses. This is contrary to the basic norms of democracy.

Intelligence agencies across the world are obsessed with secrecy. It is for this reason that their retired officials are discouraged not only from writing their memoirs, but also speaking in public. In 1977, the British Government deported Philip Agee, an American writer, who had a profound knowledge of the CIA. In 1985, the British Government went to extent of preventing the publication of Spycatcher by a former MI5 operative. I have gone through the book and found it dull and boring. But thanks to the British Government, it became a bestseller.

As for the book of the R&AW officer, it has been in the market for the past five months and has sold over 3,000 copies. Except for talking about the equipment, which India has — or might be contemplating to have — there is hardly anything secret in the book. The writer was a middle-level officer in the R&AW. He may not have all the knowledge about the agency, as all intelligence agencies function on the 'need-to-know' basis.

He talks about the lack of leadership and accountability in the agency and its misuse of funds, as well as some cases of doubtful procurement. The trouble with such books is that they contain a few facts and a lot of gossips. The book also claimed that there were severe lapses by the Government that facilitated the escape of R&AW Joint-Secretary Rabinder Singh, who is believed to have fled to the US in 2004.

He talks about the agency's decision to release the transcript between Gen Pervez Musharraf and Mohammed Aziz at the height of the Kargil war. He says that it was a mistake from the intelligence point of view. He added that releasing the transcript might have served a diplomatic purpose, but it helped Pakistan discover that the Islamabad-Beijing satellite link was being tapped and that source was shut forever. But the truth is that such decisions are taken at the Government level and not the agency's level. It only highlights the writer's lack of knowledge of the working of the Government. However, the book should prod the Government to have a mechanism whereby the so-called sacred cows — our intelligence agencies — are subjected to scrutiny and accountability, as is the case in the US.

The CIA is accountable to the US legislature's Intelligence Oversight Committees; also, it cannot keep its secret files in secrecy forever. CIA files are regularly declassified after 40 years. Unfortunately, there are no such provisions in India. Worse, in R&AW, the recruitment to the senior ranks was limited to the children of the officials working therein. No open system of recruitment was adopted. Right or wrong, it created an impression that favouritism and nepotism work in the country's intelligence agencies.

India's security interests primarily lie in its neighbourhood. According to one report, there are more R&AW operatives posted in Europe and North America than Pakistan, Bangladesh, Sri Lanka, China, Afghanistan, Myanmar and Thailand. The report also says that the R&AW does not have even one Darhi-speaking operative in Afghanistan.

Instead of invoking the Official Secrets Act, it is time an honest appraisal of the country's intelligence agencies was made in the national interest. Indeed, if someone acts as a whistle-blower and exposes corruption, he should not be seen as violating the Official Secrets Act. The RTI Act clearly affirms that it overrides the OSA;

the Second Administrative Reforms Commission, too, wants it to be scrapped. Vital secrets of the country must be guarded. But at the same time, the right of the citizens to get information regarding governance must not be diluted.

It will be in the interest of the nation if, after 20 to 30 years, all papers — except those relating to the operational intelligence — are thrown open for public scrutiny.

A few years ago, it was reported that the Communist countries did not plant any spies in democratic countries, as the newspapers used to reveal their bases and activities. When questioned, a colleague confirmed that the agencies pick most of the intelligence from information published in the newspapers.

As for the book, the very fact that an intelligence officer has written it gives it some value. Still, it is advisable that the members of the secret services do not talk or write about operational matters, as they may reveal some information which may harm the nation. Those in the intelligence agencies must understand that they are in secret services and certain obligations will always remain with their work.

2.4.4. Security and Espionage

Delhi Police has recently arrested two security personnel who were allegedly passing on sensitive information, in the form of documents, pen drives and CDs, about Army establishments to their Pakistani handlers. One of them was caught, carrying sensitive information before he could proceed to Kathmandu to hand it over to his contacts for quick money.

Spying or espionage is not a new phenomenon. Both involve obtaining information by accessing the place where it is stored or developing contacts with those who have some important information. Black's Law Dictionary defines espionage as "gathering, transmitting, or losing information related to the national defence". A spy is a person employed to obtain such secrets.

Incidents of espionage are well known throughout history, as evident from the writings of Chinese military strategist Sun-Tzu to India's Chanakya. About the king's duties, Chanakya says, he keeps his eyes open through spies. All countries - including Egypt, Israel, Japan, the UK, Russia and the US - have used espionage.

Going a step further, the US launched a new six-tonne satellite in 1998 to particularly espy India and Pakistan. "The satellite will be able to spy better than earlier satellites on India, Pakistan, and other countries from West Asia to China and North Korea," according to the Aviation and Space Technology magazine. The satellite, code-named "Orion", is equipped with a 100 feet antenna that can eavesdrop on thousands of communication circuits and frequencies, providing insights into military, political, and economic policies of the targeted countries. "No radio transmission or telephone call will be secure from monitoring by the US," the magazine said. The picked-up data will be interpreted by the US Intelligence services, it added.

Not very long ago, India had beaten the US, despite its sophisticated intelligence system, when it evaded its radar spy satellites overhead to explode a nuclear bomb. This led the US bank on a fleet of smaller spy satellites to cover the world's "trouble spots".

Preservation of secrets is one of the objectives of security of information. However, some people believe that security technology can be more effective, if it is not kept secret. It is a case of security through obscurity.

A person breaking the law of secrecy can be imprisoned for espionage or even executed for treason. Spying is done through various means. The most common is human Intelligence gathered from the operatives working at the ground level. The ISI's operatives in India generally function at this level, though Geo-spatial Intelligence gathered from satellites, aerial photography, mapping/ terrain cannot be ruled out.

Some previous cases of catching spies and recovery of documents in India are given below. On September 20, 1994, four people were arrested with two hand grenades and 44 photocopies of restricted documents. On September 19, 2000, two Pakistanis were arrested with copies of notes on issues that may come up during Parliament's Budget session that was to follow.

Similarly, on November 1, 2001, two persons were arrested while handing over secret documents relating to the Indian Navy to Pakistan's High Commission official, Gulam Shabbir Khan. On December 22, 2001, Ajay Kumar was arrested from a restaurant in

New Delhi where he had gone to get information on defence. On March 2, 2002, Wasi Akhtar Zaidi was arrested while handing over defence documents to Pakistani High Commission officials. Likewise, on April 16, 2002, Corporal Tripati Kumar Mahapatra was arrested from Paharganj while passing on information to Ali Abbas, a Pakistani High Commission official. The list is quite long; the latest incident took place on October, 23, 2006, when two Armymen - Anil Kumar Dubey and Ritesh Kumar Vishwakarma - were arrested and charged under the Official Secrets Act, after they were caught passing defence secrets to their Pakistani handlers.

Apart from the above, there was an attempt to pass on naval data in December, 2005, in which Commanders Vijendra Rana, Vinod Kumar Jha and Captain Kashyap Kumar, who headed the Directorate of Naval Operations (DNO), were accused by the Navy of being behind the leak. According to a Defence Ministry note, "They (the three officers) have collectively, as well as individually, compromised the security of classified naval information and thereby jeopardised the interests of the state. The above acts of omission and commission can be summarised as copying/obtaining/retaining/disclosing classified information that is likely to adversely affect the interests of the state. They failed to take reasonable care of information, likely to affect the security of the state. They accepted gratification other than legitimate remuneration." Despite all these accusations, the Navy refused to court-martial the officers on the ground that "since a trial by court martial could have led to considerable delays, the Central Government has decided to terminate their services forthwith".

The Central Bureau of Investigation, in July 2006, arrested businessman Abhishek Verma in connection with the Navy War Room leak case for his alleged involvement in the leaking of classified military information. Seven people have been arrested so far in this case.

Gohar Ayub Khan, son of Ayub Khan, recently made some sensational revelations regarding the 1965 India-Pakistan conflict. In his autobiography, he wrote that an Indian mole of the rank of a brigadier allegedly handed over Indian war plans in 1965 for a monetary consideration. The cat-and-mouse game goes on all over the world in trying hard to cultivate moles in the most sensitive areas of their adversary's establishments. The ISI is not immune to such practices.

There is no doubt that Pakistan's ISI network is rather extensive and has a number of modules to foment communal tension and terrorist attacks. Then Defence Minister Pranab Mukherjee, and now Foreign Minister, said that the ISI had moles in different defence organisations. Some of them operate via Nepal and Bangladesh.

In this game, we have to be one up; otherwise, all our beans would be spilled. Access to most confidential papers should be restricted to those who have a vital role to play in operations. We need keep revising and upgrading our systems, rather than saying all is well. Greed and amassment of wealth is the main temptation for moles, intelligence agents, double agents, spies, etc.

Let us not be contemptuous to our hostile neighbours, but take all possible measures to prevent our vital secrets from falling in their laps. Constant vigilance by every citizen is the price we must pay for the freedom that India won after a thousand years of slavery. Small leaks, if not checked in time, turn into gaping orifices.

2.5. Security and VIP

3. Congress general secretary Rahul Gandhi recently visited a Maoist-infested tribal village in Koraput district, Orissa, with minimal security cover. As the protection of a VIP is the responsibility of the State Government, Koraput District Superintendent of Police said; "Although I physically tried to prevent Rahul from visiting the place, his security personnel engaged me in arguments for about 15 minutes." The police advised him against the visit, but Mr Gandhi was in no mood to listen. His SPG escorts, too, resented any move to prevent him from visiting the sensitive village.

This is not the only case of Mr Gandhi giving his security escorts a slip. On the same day, he had also slipped out of his Z-category security ring and rushed into a crowd of thousands at Bhawanipatna in Orissa's Kalahandi district.

It naturally gave the local police a major scare. On the face of it, the entire episode may look a non-event, as no harm was done to the VIP. But the truth is that as long as things go normally, nobody bothers. If nothing happens, some people take the view that they knew that nothing would happen. But if something untoward happens, then hell breaks loose and the heads start rolling. Sometimes, even riots take place to avenge the killing of a VIP.

Security, evidently and obviously, is a nuisance. It puts too many restrictions on the protected person. As long as there is a requirement of safety, people have difficulty in pursuing what matters most to them. It is more so in the case of politicians who cannot achieve their objective unless they meet people without hesitation.

The VIP security is one of the most important duties of the Intelligence Bureau. It is responsible for assessing the threat perceptions to important persons, including the Prime Minister, President and other national dignitaries. The threat perceptions by it are categorised as extremely serious, very serious and serious on the basis of intelligence inputs received from various sources, including the local police. The extent and dimension of threats are decided on the basis of this evaluation.

The threat assessment to various protected individuals is reviewed periodically. It may look 'courageous' to defy the restrictions necessitated by the requirements of security, but many tragedies have been faced due to such negligence. Moreover, the situation in the country is not the same as it was a few decades ago. There are a myriad of problems — terrorism, insurgency and even espionage operations conducted by external agencies hostile to the country.

To a normal person, force is not a remedy. Terrorist outfits, however, believe that this is the only solution. They believe that the essence of their fight against the present system is violence.

Several important personalities have been assassinated since 1947. Mahatma Gandhi (1948) tops the list. He was followed by Mrs Indira Gandhi (1984), Rajiv Gandhi (1991), Beant Singh (1995), etc. Besides, several MPs and Ministers were killed either in the country, including Jammu & Kashmir and Jharkhand.

Our neighbourhood, too, has been the victim of terrorism. The most shocking incident took place in Nepal on June 1, 2001, when the entire family of King Birendra was assassinated. In Pakistan, the Bhutto family has been the victim of terror; Benazir

Bhutto has been the latest entrant in this list. Other important victims were Egyptian President Anwar Sadat (1981), US President John F Kennedy (1963), Robert F Kennedy (1968), Martin Luther King Jr (1968), Sri Lanka's President Ranasinghe Premadasa (1993) and SWRD Bandaranaike (1959), Swedish Prime Minister Olof Palme (1986), etc. Even Bangladesh was not left untouched and Sheikh Mujibur Rahman was assassinated on August 15, 1975.

The above list is only illustrative and is not exhaustive. People in public life are the face of the country. But there are some who are more than equal and that is why there is a different gradation of security and provision of different agencies for guarding them. The concern for accessibility to the public has to be balanced with the need of the security. After all, it is true that security can be an intimidation for the public.

Security is a vital matter of a sovereign state. There can be no alibi for failure of a state to provide protection and security to its citizens, as well as to those who are concerned with the affairs of the state. It is also true that this duty cannot be discharged without the support of the citizens as well as the protected ones. Moreover, it's better to err on the side of caution and advice of all those who are in the know of things, rather than face unfortunate incidents.

On a number of occasions of breach of security guidelines, political considerations have outweighed all other considerations. Basically, security is a two-players' game — between the protector and the protectee. It also involves accepting legal limitations, formal and informal. The protected person has to become conscious of the security needs. After all, security personnel are the employees of the political master and they cannot enforce security regulations except by making polite requests. As Inspector General of Police, I had once to take away the key of the car of a Union Minister to prevent him from going and meeting terrorists in Srinagar in the 1990s. But after I went away, I learnt next day that he had got the terrorist's car to go to them.

It should be understood by the protected person that the intention of the security is not to isolate him from his constituency, but to ensure his safety.

It must be said to the credit of Ms Sonia Gandhi that she once cancelled her visit to the terrorist-affected area in February 2008 during her visit to Jammu & Kashmir, when she was apprised of likely *jihadi* attack on her. Even BJP leader LK Advani cancelled his participation in the rallies on the advice of security apparatus in January 2008.

The security of the SPG protectees is not a matter of party politics, but an issue of national importance. Any harm to them will encourage terrorists and other anti-national elements.

3. Policies and New Checkouts

3.1. Just Intent is Not Good

With a lot of fanfare, the government has announced a supposedly tough anti-hijack policy. The policy says that any hijacked plane, intended to be used as a missile for targeting vital installations, would be shot down.

The policy says that any negotiation with hijackers will only be aimed at preventing loss of life, or ending the incident. The Defence Minister says that if hijacking takes place on Indian soil, the aircraft will not be allowed to take off, and the talks will be aimed at rescuing the plane and passengers. If the plane is hijacked to a third country, negotiations will be conducted with the authorities concerned, the Minister added. Besides, the Indian Air Force will be employed and the hijacked plane can be shot down in extreme circumstances of national security.

The policy also provides for death penalty to hijackers. The IAF has been empowered to scramble fighter jets to guard and guide the hijacked aircraft and force it to land in an Indian airport. The policy lays down procedures to ensure that NSG commandos, accompanied by a central negotiating team, are airborne within two hours of hijack. The BJP and the CPI (M) have welcomed the anti-hijack policy, saying that it would strengthen the country's internal security.

Hijacking has happened 12 times in India. The last one was on December 24, 1999, when IC-814 from Kathmandu to Delhi was hijacked to Kandahar via Amritsar and Lahore. It has taken almost five years for the government to make up its mind as to how it will deal with hijacking. The Kandahar hijacking was retrieved when the then Foreign Minister - jokingly called by some people, "Minister for Release of Terrorists" - exchanged the passengers in lieu of five dreaded terrorists. It is surprising that in spite of all the noises made by the NDA government against terrorism, it meekly surrendered to the terrorist demands. It did not even formulate any policy, though it was in office for over four years after this incident. It cannot be faulted more than other government as the instinct to kill even those who harm the country is not there in any government. All are willing to wound, but afraid to strike.

Organised terrorism (which includes hijacking) as an instrument of policy by Pakistan is quite different in scale, nature and consequence than the activities of stray individuals and groups. All hijackings of Indian planes had their source, support or landing in Pakistan. Sustained terrorist violence is not possible without sanctuaries, training, financing, encouragement and assistance by some countries. Government patronage gives terrorist groups and individuals enormous resources and safe haven. In fact, one of the Kashmiri terrorists - now turned peacenik - spilled the beans in Pakistan a few months back when he thanked Pakistan's current Information Minister for supporting them in cash an kind.

The anti-hijacking policy is only a pious expression of intent. It is like a letter issued to somebody for starting an industry, but it is not a license. If any policy is to be effective, it needs to have the backing of the law in the form of a legislation passed by Parliament. Otherwise, it remains a matter of convenience and expediency that any government can change at will. The intent of the announced policy is good, but it is still not good enough.

A former Director General of Punjab Police once told me during discussion that he was getting phone calls from Delhi to make sure that the hijacked plane, which had landed in Amritsar, is not allowed to take off and he should try to rescue the passenger. When he asked whether he could use force that could lead to some casualties, he was not given clearance by the Crisis Management Team headed by the then Cabinet Secretary. The policy talks about the hijacked plane being shot down, if it heads towards sensitive areas like Rashtrapati Bhavan or Parliament. Pray, how is one going to fathom the intentions of the terrorists, if one does not have any information about the likely hijacking?

Hijackers are determined to commit suicide and they know what lies in store for them. Hijacking transcends international boundaries. In case of fool-proof deterrents, a hijacker might blow up the flight in frustration as an entry fee to whichever heaven he is trying to enter.

There is no such thing as a "perfect" anti-hijacking policy. Loss of life and property is likely in any hijacking situation. Suicidal frame of mind is tricky to guard and defend against. Incidentally, Ethiopian Airlines always sends two armed assassins on every flight to make sure that no hijacker lives to tell his tale. They never have had a successful hijacking. I have seen our sky marshals on duty. They behave as if the whole thing is a picnic. Most of them insist on sitting and eating in Club Class and, with a few exceptions, are rarely alert.

What is required when dealing with hijacking and potential hijackers is a high sense of commitment, sound and clear laws, well-defined chain of command and responsibility and quick response. Also, one should not forget the willingness on part of the government to accept some losses, if they are inevitable.

3.2. India needs a Federal Agency

3.3. In the era of improved communications and a plethora of gadgets, terrorists —*jihadi* or otherwise — do not feel inhibited in executing their nefarious designs. What is good enough for one age, time or generation becomes redundant for the next. Nobody can predict the future. When a law is passed, it is in response to a given situation. When situation changes, laws, rules, regulations and even customs become redundant and they need to be drastically changed.

We are governed by the laws framed more than 145 years ago by the British. There was no need for the British to have a federal investigating agency, as all the top authorities right from the Viceroys to the District Heads were Britishers. Their objective was to rule India. There was no question of working at cross-purposes as sometimes happens now. As absolute foreign rulers, they did not have to indulge in vote-bank politics, as is the case now.

There was no need for a federal investigating agency for the first 30 years of independent India, as there was one political party ruling both the Centre and the States. Also, at that time, the country did not have problems like terrorism, hijacking and drug-peddling. Now, no country can be said to be safe from them.

Terrorists take advantage of a deficient and ill-trained police force, and an extremely pro-criminal and pro-accused, 'liberal' legal framework. Loopholes in the criminal justice system, especially the delays in investigation and the judicial process, help them enormously.

India was among the countries worst hit by terrorism in 2007, with more than 2,300 deaths. The Government's counter-terrorism efforts remained hampered by "ill-equipped" law enforcement machinery and "slow and laborious" legal systems, as the recent US State Department report has said. It has added, "The Indian court system was slow, laborious and prone to corruption. Terrorism trials can take years to complete. Many of India's local police forces were poorly staffed, lacked training and were ill-equipped to combat terrorism effectively." The report also said that the Indian Government's counter-measures remained hampered by outdated and overburdened law enforcement and legal systems.

At present, the country faces a series of low intensity conflicts, which includes tribal, ethnic and extremist movements and ideologies. This is apart from the proxy war conducted by our unfriendly neighbours, who provide training and logistic support to several terrorist outfits.

For eradicating terrorism, a focussed response, which includes intelligence gathering, data processing, investigation and counter-terrorism operations on a national scale, is required. Currently, these tasks are carried out by a multiplicity of agencies, which are keen to protect their turf and score brownie points with the powers-that-be. A federal investigating agency can be effective only if there are proper intelligence inputs.

With different political parties ruling different States, perception of the above problems varies from one leader to another. The recent Jaipur bombings have again brought to the fore the need for a federal investigating agency. The reasons for such an agency are obvious, thanks to advanced means of transport and communications. In the wake of the Jaipur bombings, Prime Minister Manmohan Singh has come out in favour of the creation of a federal crime agency. However, the proposal for the same had failed to materialise in the past mostly because of "reluctance" of States to "surrender" their authority.

The Union Government is responsible for the sovereignty and integrity of the country. Under Article 355 of the Constitution, it is the responsibility of the Union Government to protect every State against internal disturbances and to ensure that the governance of every State is carried on in accordance with the provisions of the Constitution.

If the UPA Government is serious about setting up of a federal agency, it can pass a law like The Delhi Special Police Establishment Act, 1946, as amended by the Central Vigilance Commission Act, 2003. This is the law under which the CBI derives its powers. The CBI functions with the consent of the State Governments. No State has denied its consent to the functioning of the CBI. Some have given blanket sanction, while others give sanction from case to case. The Union Government did not seek the consent of the State Governments while framing the Delhi Special Police Establishment Act, 1946; surely, now also, it does not need the consent of the State Governments for creating a Central agency for dealing with terrorism, hijacking and drug-peddling.

Nothing will ever be attempted or achieved if all possible objections were first to removed. Once a law is in place, hardly any State will object to the Central investigating agency taking up cases of terrorism. If anything, they will welcome, in due course of time, the opportunity to pass on the responsibility of crimes of all-India nature to this agency.

No two men ever think alike on the same issue. It is impossible to find two persons having exactly similar opinion at the same time. Theoretically, the VIP security, including that of the Prime Minister, is the responsibility of the State Government. But no State has ever objected to the Special Protection Group providing security to the Prime Minister and some other VIPs. The responsibility of the air port security used to be under the State Government, but after the hijacking of IC-814 from Kathmandu in 2001, all States have accepted the security provided by the Union Government. Besides, if some States do not accept the law made by the Union Government, they will get the blame for encouraging terrorism.

In February 2001, the NDA Government decided that the Home Ministry should be proactive in ensuring internal security safeguards. Unless that decision is abrogated by the UPA Government, it is legitimate for the Centre to implement it.

3.3. The Need Met: A Review

(**Note**: The author must write an article on the 'National Investigative Agency' Act (NIA Act) recently passed- and the other security measures practically formed after the latest Bombay terror attack- with features of salience, prospects and lapses. The author is again duly requested to write for Para 3.3.).

8

Police: Internal Security Weakened and Perplexed

1. The Mentors of the Precipice

1.1. Matter of Uniform Disgrace

The degeneration of standards in the institutions of power, authority and governance seems to be all-pervasive in the country. It can either be found in the form of disorder in the UP Assembly, or the strategic shift of power from the husband to the wife in Bihar. It is also manifest in the murder by a trigger-happy policemen of his colleague or a civilian. Even the Armed forces have not remained immune to it. The jawans threw five people out of a train on January 25 merely because they refused to vacate their seats at their order. All these prove the same - the institutional decline in the country.

Theoretically, the men in uniform are duty-bound to protect their countrymen. But the reality is quite different. They have been transformed from protectors to predators. This is more because of the failure of the state's machinery to punish those involved in crime. In fact, the man in uniform deserves the most stringent punishment. Besides, the cops have an additional problem, which is psychological. Being in uniform and having weapons makes them vain. Some of them, at least, tend to believe that they are the masters, which leads to their transformation into uniformed monsters.

There have been numerous such instances. Four persons, including a woman and a child, were allegedly killed by a drunk police constable in Begusarai, Bihar, in November 2004. Their only fault was that they resisted his attempt to rape a widow. The incident sparked off violent protests in the area with demonstrators setting the nearby police outpost and the Begusarai railway station on fire. The mob also attacked a police station with bombs and stones.

Let us take the Delhi Police which has "With you, for you, always" as its motto. It has a strength of about 56,000 personnel. In the last four years, the Delhi Police has tried to police itself by punishing, through departmental proceedings, one assistant commissioner of police, 63 inspectors, 1,385 sub-inspectors, 724 assistant sub-inspectors, 1,569 head constables, 3570 constables and 54 class four of its employees. The punishment includes dismissal, forfeiture of service, reduction in rank, withholding increment and censure for gross misconduct and misuse of position.

Of the 7,755 police personnel punished during the past four years, 293 were dismissed or terminated from service, 931 faced forfeiture of service, while the ranks of seven policemen were reduced. Ninety-four police personnel faced reduction in pay, while annual increment of 343 were held. A maximum of 6,087 police personnel faced censure for their crimes. Till June 2004, 35 police personnel were dismissed, while 192 faced forfeiture of service. Four-hundred cases were registered against 517 Delhi Police personnel during the period for their involvement in corruption and crimes, of which 47 were done by the Anti-Corruption Branch, 55 by the Central Bureau of Investigation and 298 by the police itself.

Obviously, more needs to be done by the police as any misconduct on the part of its personnel involves the public. The more transparent and responsive their functioning becomes, the greater goodwill and cooperation they will enjoy from the public. The man on the street fears the man in uniform so much that he does not want to have anything to do with the police.

The high profile Army, which gets the best of perks in the country, can afford from free food rations, to subsidised canteen and housing facilities, travel at half the cost six times a year both by train and air, is not very far behind in the institutional decay. It has its own share of disgrace in the form of fake encounters, fake claims of skirmishes for medals and honours, and rapes. The worst was revealed by the Tehelka sting operation which proved there was corruption even among the top brass. One person said, "Army officers may be referred to as gentlemen cadets during their training period, but the jawans under them treat us civilians like animals." This is the common perception of the soldiers.

Whenever any serious incident involving a uniformed person occurs, the standard reply is that stern action is being initiated, or that the guilty will not be spared. But the ground realities continue to be almost unchanged. There is no doubt that the menace is increasing by the day. In 2003, a division bench of the Bombay High Court, by overturning an earlier judgment, sentenced 11 policemen to life imprisonment for a custodial death that occurred seven years ago. However, some alleged murderers are still hiding behind their uniforms.

The British Government in India set up a commission in 1902-03, which observed after examining witnesses and the performance of the police: "There can be no doubt that the police force throughout the country is in a most unsatisfactory condition, that abuses are common everywhere, that this involves great injury to the people and discredit to the Government." But the situation did not change as the Dharam Vira Police Commission (1977-1981) too came to a similar conclusion. No amount of public relations, or patting oneself on the back, is going to help improve the image, unless the uniformed forces, including the police and political leadership, take up cudgels on behalf of those affected.

The common man believes that the police indulges in favouritism. The enforcement of laws by them is selective, anti-poor and pro-rich. They function only when the cases involve influential and powerful person. They are generally discourteous and mostly use abusive language. Even the aggrieved and complainants are not spared. The result is that even honest citizens avoid doing anything to help the law enforcement agencies. They think that it is best to avoid the police and keep them at a distance even for redressal of their genuine grievances.

Professor David H Bailey says: "In India today, a dual system of criminal justice has grown, the one of the law and the other of politics." With respect to the police, decisions made by the police officials about the application of law are frequently subjected to partisan reviews or direction by the elected representatives. People accused of crimes have got into the habit of appealing to political figures for remission from the law. Police officials have grown accustomed to calculating the likely political effect of any enforcement action they contemplate.

Then the question arises: How do we improve the situation? Policemen are expected to uphold the rule of law. As professionals, their only interests should be the law of the land and its enforcement at all costs. This, however, is only an ideal situation and we are far from it. The job ethos and various pressures, including politics and caste, play a major role in establishing the standards in an organisation. The general collapse of professional standards, disposition, temperament, poor leadership and integrity due to the deterioration of values has led to this situation.

We get the Government we deserve, and the same is true of our uniformed services. People need to gather together to form pressure groups, which should compel reforms. Obviously, some political leaders are also involved in crime. It does not matter, as long as the vast majority is able to stand up to them. At the same time, it is equally important to have leaders in the police and other uniformed services, who are willing to be unpopular for doing the right thing. There should be the strictest possible standards of discipline, which need to be maintained. The Government should allow the police to be run by the police hierarchy. It should enforce strict accountability.

Dr. Martin Luther King Jr once said, "Is it safe?" Expediency asks the question, "Is it politic?" Vanity asks, "Is it popular?" But, conscience asks, "Is it right?" The time has come when one must take a position that is neither safe, nor politic, nor popular, but which is right. Do we need any other wake up call?

1.2. Police, Probe and the Need

2.The gruesome murder of Aarushi Talwar is becoming increasingly mysterious by the day. At the time of her murder, there were only four persons in the house, including Aarushi and a domestic help, Hemraj. Two of them are no more. The only survivors are her parents.

Dr. Rajesh Talwar has been arrested by the police as the likely suspect in the murder of his daughter and the domestic help. The initial investigation done by Noida Police was so perfunctory that it led to the media pointing fingers at it.

At the instance of Dr. Talwar, Noida Police lapped up the theory that the crime was committed by Hemraj. It took his word for granted and did not even search the house for the murder weapons or other clues. It was only a day later that a retired police officer, who visited the house to condole the 'grieving family', noticed bloodstains and the locked terrace, leading to the discovery of the body of Hemraj.

Ironically, basic investigation was not done, which should have entailed summoning the dog squad, photographing the victim's position at the scene of the crime before being removed, collecting physical evidence from the victim, as well collect the victim's clothing and personal materials. The police should also have prevented people from entering the house. Its failure to follow up on collecting items from the crime site can cause their loss or render them useless as evidence.

It is the job of the investigator to mark and photograph the location of crime and objects discovered there. The spot should have been secured to prevent the entry of any unauthorised person in order to prevent any possible destruction of fragile evidence, such as fingerprints, footprints or other clues. The idea of a thorough investigation is to find out how, when, where and why of a crime. Ironically, the investigation done by Noida Police was full of loopholes. No wonder when the dead body of Hemraj was discovered, the top brass got busy attending Press conferences rather than ensuring that the case was thoroughly investigated and all possible clues were collected.

Noida Police, then, seemed to have made up its mind that Dr Talwar was the culprit and it went all out to buttress its claim. Maybe, what it said was true. But the criminal justice system runs on the basis of evidence and not on anybody's personal feelings, however right one may turn out to be. The case was transferred to the CBI, after two weeks, as the family of Dr Talwar expressed doubts about the fairness of the investigation by Noida Police.

The first investigator of any crime has the opportunity to collect all the clues. He can either make or mar the case. The CBI, on receipt of the case, was hard put to gather the clues, which had been either messed up or whitewashed — deliberately or unconsciously. Not surprisingly, the CBI has asked the television news channels to hand over the footage of the crime.

The Aarushi case depends on the circumstantial evidence. Nothing can be ruled out about anybody's guilt. The CBI faces an uphill task and it may take quite a few days or months to unravel the mystery of the case. Two lie detector tests have already been done on Dr Talwar.

The CBI, in its submission to the court, has said that for now it does not require custody remand of Dr Talwar. Incidentally, the CBI can question Dr Talwar even in jail as and when required, with the permission of the court. The future course of investigation will now depend on what evidence the agency gets from the forensic examination of blood samples, computers, laptops and other materials seized from the spot, as well as the reports of two lie detection test.

This case has highlighted the working of the police, which has been almost the same for the last 147 years. The First Police Commission (1902-1903) had this to say about the police: "There can be no doubt, that the police force throughout the country is in a most unsatisfactory condition; that abuses are common everywhere; that this involves great injury to the people and discredit to the Government; and, that radical reforms are urgently necessary."

The National Police Commission of 1977-81, set up under the chairmanship of Dharmavira, observed: "The basic and fundamental problem regarding the police today is how to make them function as an efficient and impartial law enforcement agency fully motivated and guided by the objectives of service of the public at large, upholding the constitutional rights and liberty of the people. What the Police Commission said in 1903 appears more or less applicable to the conditions obtaining today." Among other things in its report, it recommended the separation of law and order functions from the investigation of crime so that full-time attention could be paid to the investigation.

As happens with the reports of several commissions and committees of the Government, the reports of the National Police Commission have remained in cold storage in the name of examination. It continued till September 2006 when the Supreme Court, in a landmark judgement, gave direction for separating the law and order and investigative functions. It also said that it should be ensured that there is full co-ordination between them.

The apex court also added that the process may be initiated in towns/urban areas with 10 lakh or more population and then extended to smaller towns. This was apart from a number of other directions regarding tenure of officials, selection of State police chiefs called Director Generals of Police and insulating the police from unwarranted political influence or pressure. The directions were to be complied with before December 31, 2006.

But almost all State Governments, which are responsible for policing in the country under the Constitution, are either indifferent or are dragging their feet. They do not wish to give even a modicum of independence to police.

The Aarushi murder case has again highlighted the need to bring about the reforms in the police, besides paying attention to the training of the policemen in the latest techniques of investigation. Handing over any case to the CBI, which is a very small organisation, is just like applying a band-aid and not a solution to the problem of poor investigation.

1. Of Police and Encounters

2.1. Challenge Fanged

Police is always in the news, but mostly for the wrong reasons. The death of a policeman, overrun by a rash driver or killed by criminals, rarely invokes public sympathy. If a terrorist is killed by the police or security personnel, he becomes an instant martyr among his own fellowmen. But if a policeman is killed, he is a mercenary.

People sit in judgement, in the comfort of their air conditioned rooms, on policemen and pronounce them guilty of either killing criminals in fake encounters or using excessive coercion. It is no secret that the police does not shed tears if a notorious gangster is killed in an encounter. It is more so because the law enforcing agencies are disillusioned when a gangster or a rapist walks free because he or his henchmen have been able to intimidate witnesses.

In this murky scenario some policemen use their office to fill their coffers because of the powers they enjoyed. Recently, a police officer in the Capital, whom newspapers referred to as 'encounter specialist' was accused of functioning as a 'henchman' for some property dealers. In a sting operation which was shown on a number of television channels, the officer in question reportedly intimidated the person at the other end declaring " tumhara encounter kar doonga".

The police has merely ordered a departmental probe. Obviously, such a chastisement for brazen misuse of office does not go down well with the public. Whether the departmental probe clears the official or not, the damage to the image of police has been done.

Terrorism has come in handy for policemen who either use violence to settle scores or make a fortune for themselves. As Inspector General of Police of the Central Reserve Police during the days of terrorism in Punjab, it was a painful to see policemen indulging in extortion. They would threaten that if they were not paid, Anti-Terrorist Act would be used against their children. The then Director General of Punjab Police told me that he had dismissed 110 policemen during his tenure to curb this practice. But he also hastily added that he could not open war on two fronts, one against the terrorists and the other against the corrupt in his department.

In a case of mistaken identity, a few years ago, Delhi Police had shot a businessman at Barakhamba Road and then declared that he was a terrorist. The 'trigger-happy cop' has become the norm rather than exception. Notwithstanding, the fact that we have been independent for over five decades, the approach of the police towards citizens is as highhanded as it was in the colonial past.

Having been in police myself, I have been extremely concerned about this fact. From my first district posting onwards as police chief of Bidar in Karnataka, and even later, I had made it clear to all my subordinates that cutting corners with the law was not allowed. Also, if anybody was found guilty I would personally ensure that he was dismissed. When questioned by some of my colleagues as to what could happen to criminals and detection of cases, my answer was simple. I told them that if the law of the country wants us to follow a given procedure and give the benefit of the doubt to suspects, then why should we assume that what we do is for the greater good of the country even though it might be against the law?

Senior police officers by their conduct and approach need to convey the message to their subordinates that the use of force or extra constitutional methods in field operations does not necessarily deter criminals. If policemen show contempt for the law then they should expect the same from the citizens as well as criminals. The problem in our country is that if a mistake is committed by someone in the police, the top brass is not willing to accept it. It is unlike the London Police which honestly admitted killing a Brazilian whom it mistook for a terrorist.

In our country people expect the police to catch a criminal in the morning, have him tried in the afternoon, and sentenced to imprisonment or any other form of punishment in the evening. Unfortunately, this happens only in the movies. It would not be wrong to say that the country's middle class is indifferent to encounter killings unless the person who is killed is dubbed a terrorist. There is not even a thin line that differentiates a deliberate killing from an encounter. No civilised society can afford to give anybody a license to kill. Otherwise, there would be no difference between gunmen belonging to a group of gangsters, and the police indulging in encounters as a short cut to dispensing ready and prompt justice.

The aberrations in the country's law enforcing system are too many to be recounted. On January 1,1998, the UP Government identified 850 policemen who had alleged nexus with criminals. The list included two officers of the rank of additional director general of police, and one of them became director general of police later. In Calcutta, a police commissioner had maintained close links with the underworld. In Haryana, an officer of the rank of director general of police was caught accepting bribe and another was involved in getting a person killed in custody. A third one was accused of molesting a teenaged girl who subsequently committed suicide in Delhi.

There is a silent consensus among the policemen on the use of third degree methods to extract confessions. The use of force on those suspected to have violated the law -or caught red handed doing so-is considered by our society a clever way of bringing relief to victims of the crime.

The perceived obligation and necessity of rendering prompt and natural justice on the spot dominates not only the mindset of most policemen but also of the entire society. The public quite often in sensational and not so sensational cases, not only demands but hails strong police action including 'encounter' killings against anti-social elements. This is precisely what happened in Bhagalpur a couple of years back.

Prof Bailey believes that, "Policemen violate law consciously, knowing that what they are doing is wrong. They rationalise it subsequently saying that this is required to render justice to victims. What compounds such behaviour (interestingly referred to by some scholars as "noble cause" misbehaviour or "blue-coat crime") is that it is abrupt and instantaneous and often reckless. It is meant to drive home two points; first, the police are efficient and action-oriented, and second, they are quicker purveyors of justice than all other state agencies put together."

The police must realise that it is not the sole guardian of law and that the responsibility to control and keep crime in check crime is not its exclusive responsibility, but of the entire criminal justice system. The same is true of the fight against corruption which is not the exclusive concern of the CBI but of the entire community.

While training in ethics is definitely welcome, we must also remember that it is the educated people, with the ability to differentiate between right and wrong, who indulge in unlawful activities. In fact, ethics in itself is not enough. It must be accompanied by down to earth procedures and quick retribution in case of any breach. Ultimately, the ball lies in the court of government, which must do all it can to make the police not only more responsive but also an institution that respects the law of the land.

2.2. Fishing the Ulternatives

On Diwali eve, November 3, two Lashkar-e-Toiba (LeT) terrorists were shot dead by Delhi Police in an encounter at the basement of Ansal Plaza at about 7.20 pm. These men had targeted the shopping mall to inflict massive damage and casualties. The intelligence agencies had warned of massive strikes during the festive season. So Delhi Police was on the alert. It won a lot of kudos initially for averting a tragedy. The Home Minister said the terrorists were Pakistani citizens and even asked Pakistan to take back their dead.

Yet, as it generally happens, even if things go well, no one gets credit for doing a good job. If there is a terrorist incident, all hell breaks loose and questions are asked as to why the police were not tough. When the police are tough, it is said that they 'fake' encounters. Terrorists, meanwhile, have a free run of the country, particularly the National Capital, as the details of the incidents in Delhi described below will show.

On January 14 this year, one Hizbul-e-Islami and four LeT militants were arrested, along with three hawala operators. Police recovered 13 kg RDX, electronic detonators and other explosive materials and Rs. 39 lakh in cash. The terrorists' target was the Republic Day celebrations. On March 9, two Pakistan-trained militants involved in the Red Fort shootout were killed in an encounter and three others arrested. One AK-47 assault rifle with 30 live rounds and Chinese-bore Star pistols with spare ammunition were recovered. On July 2, one LeT militant and two other operatives were caught and Rs. 7 lakh recovered. On August 28, two LeT militants and four others were apprehended. The haul: Four kgs explosives and live detonators.

Going backwards, December 13 last year witnessed the attack on Parliament. Before that, there were the Red Fort assault and killings. The year 2001 also saw the arrests of Pakistan's ISI's operatives on a number of occasions, too numerous to be recounted.

Go farther back. On January 6, 2000, 25 people were hurt in an explosion at the Old Delhi Railway station. On February 27, eight were injured in a high-intensity explosion in a guest house in Paharganj. On March 16, seven people were hurt when a low-intensity bomb exploded in Sadar Bazar. And on June 18, two people were killed and 12 hurt in twin explosions near Red Fort.

In 1999, a powerful bomb exploded inside a train at Holambi Kalan railway station, killing two and injuring five on April 16. On June 3, 37 people were injured after an explosion in Chandni Chowk.

On January 9 the previous year, one person was killed and 55 injured in an explosion 50 metres from the police headquarters. On June 27, 1998, a bomb, thrown from a moving Gypsy by men in police uniforms, exploded outside a club in Greater Kailash-I, injuring two. On July 26, two people were killed and three hurt after a high-intensity blast ripped apart a bus parked at the Kashmere Gate inter-State bus terminus. On August 31, a bomb exploded in the crowded Turkman Gate area of central Delhi. One person was killed and 17 hurt. On December 19, a crude bomb went off inside a Bhajanpura temple at night. This time, no one was hurt.

Coming back to November 3, 2002, a homeopath who calls himself a Doctor-and who has a couple of cases registered against him at Agra and Tappal, near Ali-garh, for attempt to murder and culpable homicide-jumped into the fray after the Ansal Plaza incident, saying it was not a genuine encounter but murder by the police.

There are always two opinions on every subject and incident. The one easily lapped up is that police actions are fake, all encounters are stage-managed and innocent people are killed. People look for a rational pattern in the behaviour of terrorists, where none exists or can be possible. Why only terrorists? Even an ordinary person's conduct is unpredictable in different circumstances. There is bound to be lack of explanations for many incongruities, as human beings do not react in the same way to any given set of circumstances. Dog-bites-man is no story, but man-bites-dog is. In my case, a monkey biting me when I was Director, CBI, during my walks in Lodi Gardens was a big story. Its headline was: 'Monkey bites Tiger'.

Anyone indulging in police-bashing-a mediawala, a human rights-wala, a TV channel or a politician-becomes an instant celebrity. People dislike the police, often because they have been exposed to certain incidents, or because of the unpleasant experiences of their near and dear ones.

The reasons could vary. One, the arrest or non-arrest of a person, against whom a case is taken up for investigation by the police. Two, deliberate handcuffing of a person in police custody, merely to humiliate him. Three, release or non-release on bail after arrest. Four, suppression of material evidence found during searches. Five, inclusion or non-inclusion in the chargesheet placed in the court on conclusion of investigation. Six, police posting or non-posting in an area of apprehended trouble to give the advantage to one party or another. Seven, foisting of false criminal cases against political functionaries for political ends.

Eight, discretionary enforcement of law while dealing with public order situations, with emphasis on severity and ruthlessness in regard to persons opposed to the ruling party. Nine, taking persons into preventive custody to immobilise them against legitimate political activity in opposition to the party in power. Ten, manoeuvring police intervention by exaggerating a non-cognisable offence or engineering a false complaint to gain advantage over any party in a situation which will lie outside the domain of police action in the normal course. Sometime this is done to extort money and indulge in corruption. Eleven, preparation of malicious and tendentious intelligence reports to facilitate action against an opponent, or the alleged involvement of innocent people in false cases or indulging in false killing.

One of the main source of news is the police personnel themselves-including the juniormost functionaries in every organisation-who are euphemistically called 'reliable sources'. Yet some of them may not have known anything at first hand. Sometimes it is asserted that the police say contradictory things about a case to the media. This problem arises due to loose talk and ill-informed people at different level, giving their versions of the case. The police do need to put their house in order and ensure the media is fully briefed and all questions are answered by a sufficiently senior official or a spokesman. Any doubt is likely to leave a question mark on the force's credibility. Investi-gative journalism has come to stay. It will be naïve for police officers to be think they can get away with wrongdoing. In a free country, a criminal has the same rights as any other free citizen, though the police may feel uncomfortable about this.

However, it is surprising that, by insinuations and other means, it is being suggested that Delhi Police committed cold-blooded murder at Ansal Plaza and the encounter was a fake one. If the police were to stage a fake encounter, pray, why should they choose a place bustling with Diwali shoppers? They could have chosen some isolated spot if the intention was to eliminate anybody. It needs to be understood that the police force has no personal animus against anybody. These are difficult times. As Prime Minister Atal Bihari Vajpayee said, "Human Rights are no doubt a lofty concept, but we live in an imperfect world and this reality imposes practical difficulties in living by the ideal standards of human rights."

In India, terrorism has claimed 60,000 lives in Kashmir and Punjab. Tough decisions to combat it may temporarily infringe on freedom and abridge human rights. But they are essential for preserving the country's integrity and sovereignty and, in fact, to ensure the overall freedom of all Indians. Let us have human rights by all means, but they should be for human beings and not for demons.

2.3. Cop and Killing

A sub-inspector of Maharashtra Police - who has been subject of Hindi films like Ab Tak Chhappan and Kagaar and is considered an encounter specialist in killing criminals - is facing an encounter of a different kind. This official began his life as a canteen boy in Mumbai's Udupi hotels, attended night schools and qualified to join the Mumbai police. He was regarded as an 'encounter specialist' with a record of having gunned down 80 criminals - mostly gangsters. Now he has been cut to size for having amassed assets disproportionate to his known sources of income. He has been on the run and even approached the court for anticipatory bail.

The Bombay High Court had ordered the Anti-Corruption Bureau to submit a report on a former journalist's allegation that the official had underworld connections as well as assets disproportionate to his normal income. The official had reportedly built a college at the cost of Rs. 1 crore in his village in Karnataka.

He flew down with Amitabh Bachchan and few other Bollywood celebrities for the inauguration of this institute. It is surprising that the then police commissioner gave him a clean chit. According to the journalist, the encounter specialist had amassed assets worth Rs. 4 crore in less than 10 years of service. Only a miracle can make this possible with Government officials of his rank getting a salary of merely, Rs 1 lakh plus annually.

The Maharashtra Government has suspended the 'encounter specialist' after Mumbai's anti-corruption bureau conducted raids on the official's three flats in Mumbai. It unearthed jewellery and cash worth more than Rs 41 lakh. The official has been accused of accepting money from gangsters to kill their rivals. His wife has also been charged with helping her husband in parking his funds in finance companies, in which she is reported to be a director. In innumerable instances, the official position that people hold is nothing but a means to amass wealth and legitimise it through a labyrinthine of laws, court appeals or by using political influence in case they are convicted.

Sometime back in the Capital this, "encounter specialist" (he has reportedly killed 60 persons) had been accused of functioning as a gun-for-hire for some property dealers. In a sting operation, which was shown on a number of television channels, the officer in question reportedly intimidated the person on the other end by declaring, "tumhara encounter kar doonga" (you will be killed in an encounter). The police top brass has merely ordered a departmental probe apart from transferring him to another post. Obviously, such a step, for an alleged serious misuse of office does not cut much ice with the public. Neither has the Central Government, under whose nose this happened, batted an eye lid.

The law-enforcing agencies create a hell-like situation. Many people who do not have the money to bribe their way out of troubles are conscious of the fact that they could be killed in a fake encounter. The police in our country, due to laxity and tolerance, or in connivance with their senior officers have developed a reputation for extra-judicial killings in which suspects are shot in what is officially termed as 'retaliatory fire'.

There are some suspects for whom there is an option list with the police including provisions like 'gentle' arrest, nominal punishment and freedom afterwards. Even the dreaded dacoit Phoolan Devi, who later became an MP, decided to surrender in Madhya Pradesh instead of her home state, Uttar Pradesh. She feared that she would be killed by the Uttar Pradesh police in a fake encounter if she surrendered there.

The situation is no better in most States, whether in Bihar or Jharkhand. An Additional DGP was suspended and spent considerable time behind bars for allegedly being party to killing three people including his son's NRI business partner. Haryana has half a dozen Directors General and Inspectors General of police involved in crimes ranging from molestation to murder to smuggling.

Join the police and be above the law is the current joke making rounds. But people in khaki cannot escape public scrutiny. Cases of corruption and custodial deaths and blatant encounters are on the rise. It is common to find the names of policemen associated in many rape, murder, robbery and kidnapping cases. In fact, some of them do it with such finesse that they would put habitual criminals to shame.

It is true that criminals have become bolder and do not hesitate to use automatic AK series weapons. Gangs has proliferated and kidnapping for ransom has become an industry. The opening up of the Indian economy has not only created new problems for the underworld but also given it new opportunities.

The number of cash rich builders all over the country, including Mumbai, has increased considerably, thus giving criminals a chance to extract a part of their wealth. Soft targets like doctors, hoteliers and industrialists are galore. Quite often police officials have to use weapons in self defence. However, there is no justification for the police to step outside the law as they are only one wing of the criminal justice system.

The parliamentary Standing Committee on Home Affairs previously headed by Mr Pranab Mukerjee had asked the Home Ministry to "make an effort to depoliticise the institution of police before it becomes too late to retrieve it from the morass of degeneration". All members were of the view that the country's intelligence gathering machinery and their performance would improve greatly if a "proper system of accountability is evolved". It hit out at the police system and described it as a "pawn in the hands of its (political) masters". It found that policemen get political "patronage essential for their survival and police personnel are found to be divided in camps having distinct political leanings".

It further observed that "this connivance of the police with those in power is giving rise to cynicism among people. These are, by all means, very dangerous signs for the continuance and survival of democracy." Recommending preparation of a blueprint for a "model police force" to be followed by all States, the Committee asked the Home Ministry to ensure modernisation and accountability by following a "definite plan of action" that would establish "unity of command and direction". Dealing specifically with police encounters, the National Human Rights Commission had issued the following guideline to all State Governments:

- All encounters should be probed properly and without bias.
- Any death caused in an encounter with any local police force or paramilitary force in peace area would amount to culpable

homicide unless it is established that the action was taken in self defence

- The probe report must be submitted to the Commission within six weeks.
- Investigation should be independent and policemen involved in encounter should be kept out. But all this has hardly had any impact.

After all is said and done, it ultimately revolves around on the Government of the day as to the sort of administration it wants. It has to make up its mind whether it will let the situation go from bad to worse. It can either hide behind alibis or it can stride forth and set matters straight.

It is time to take what Calvin Coolidge said to heart: "Nothing in this world can take the place of persistence. Talent will not; nothing is more common than unsuccessful people with talent. Genius will not; unrewarded genius is almost a proverb. Education will not; the world is full of educated derelicts. Persistence and determination alone are omnipotent. The slogan 'press on' has solved and always will solve the problems of the human race."

3. Makeover Needed

3.1. Policing India is a Tough Job

A six-decade-old democracy, our country is facing a unique problem. Agitations, *dharnas* and protests have become the order of the day. No State is free from clashes between law enforcement authorities and protesters. The allotment of 40 hectares of land to the sacred Amarnath shrine led to violent protests against the order of the Jammu & Kashmir Government. Separatists and secessionist elements, aided and abetted by Pakistan and some local politicians, were at the forefront of these protests. An impromptu strike to protest the death of a demonstrator in police firing on June 23 virtually paralysed Srinagar.

Even the PDP, a coalition partner in the State Government, joined the protests. Then again, the PDP did advocate the use of both Indian and Pakistani currency as well as a dual power-sharing arrangements between New Delhi and Islamabad in Jammu & Kashmir. It is the same political party whose leading light, a former Home Minister, wanted Jammu & Kashmir to have a Governor elected by the State legislature. Following the withdrawal of the PDP, the coalition Government in Jammu & Kashmir has collapsed. In an act of abject surrender, the Government has cancelled the allotment of forest land.

The allegations against the allotment of land were based on the false premise that it would change the Muslim majority character of the Valley. Ironically, in the ethnic cleaning of Hindus and Sikhs around 3.7 lakh of them had to leave the Valley just to survive. There were no complaints about changing the demography then.

The cancellation of the allotment of land might have led to jubilations in the Valley, but has had repercussions in the rest of the country, including Jammu. In the country-wide strike that followed the Government's capitulation, there have been riots and police firings to control the rioters. In fact, in our country tempers can rise on any issue. Instead of peacefully drawing attention to their grievance, agitators make it a life and death issue. No decision or action is universally acceptable. What is acceptable to one section, whether it is a Gujjar agitation or riots in Gurgaon against the allotment of land for a Special Economic Zone, is anathema to others.

Ultimately, when the police try to separate the warring groups or ensure law and order they become the bad boys. In fact, the police in India is like a jack of all trades and is called upon to perform different roles at different times. And if it fails to do so, people do not spare a single moment's thought before lambasting it for negligence of duty.

There is no fixed method of dealing with a crowd. In our country nobody wants to stand in a queue or obey orders. On the recent occasion of the Rath Yatra in Puri, six persons lost their lives and hundreds were injured because of a stampede caused by frenzied devotees competing with each other to get near the rath. A million people had gathered for the celebration. In a situation like this, a few hundred or thousand policemen cannot do anything to control the people without using force.

Similarly, during the Gujjar agitation when the police had fired upon the rioting mob to control the situation, it led to the punitive transfer of the Director-General of Police. In such circumstances, the hands of our law-enforcement authorities seem to be firmly tied behind their backs. The truth is that no policing is possible without public cooperation. Without which it becomes impossible to control chaos and prevent the destruction of public property and at the same time save innocent lives.

An impression has gone around the country, based on past and present experiences, that if any section of the society wants anything then the best way to get it is to launch a violent agitation. The idea of a peaceful agitation has long been given a burial. It has been replaced by *bandh*s, bullying, beating, killing and destroying. Whether it is a question of cancellation of allotment of a piece of land or the demand of a community for reservation, only violence has brought the Government to its knees.

Needless to say, the police gets caught in the crossfire. Since the police is the visible symbol of the Government, it is the easiest target to vent one's anti-establishment frustrations. Indeed, all anti-Government protests become a free for all between the police and the agitators. It is all very easy for armchair theoreticians to assess the police's performance while sitting in air-conditioned comfort. But the reality for our police force is quite different.

If people are injured or killed when the police is trying to bring a riot-like situation under control, it is accused of using unnecessary or unwarranted force. If it does not take action, it is accused of inaction or playing it safe. The police has to literally walk a tightrope. The National Police Commission has observed, "The dividing line between the objectives of the Government in power on one side and the interests and expectations of the ruling political party on the other, gets blurred in actual practice and the image of the police as an impartial law enforcement agency suffers as a consequence. The concept of ministerial responsibility has given an impression to the political masters that they are authorised to guide and intervene in all functions of the police in all areas. Most often, interventions take the form of only oral directions, which are difficult to prove later on in a court of inquiry or in case the politicians set up commissions of inquiry to look into the conduct of the police."

Prof. David H Bayley says, "In India today, a dual system of criminal justice has grown up, the one of the law and the other of politics. With respect at least to the police, decisions made by the police officials about the application of law are frequently subject to partisan review or direction by the elected representatives. The autonomy of the police officials in specific and routine application of law has been severally curtailed... Police officials, throughout India have grown accustomed to calculating the likely political effect of any enforcement action they contemplate. Fearing for their careers and especially their postings, they have become anxious and cynical. But everywhere officers are expected to be held personally accountable by the politicians, even more than by their superior officers, for enforcement action taken in the course of duty."

Ultimately, it boils down to what kind of police the country wants and what kind of police our rulers are willing to give us. Governments bear the final responsibility for the state of the nation, both internal and external, and for the well-being of its people. The Government should remember what Pearl S Buck said, "All things are possible until they are proved impossible — even the impossible may only be so, as of now."

3.2. Police Need a Makeover

Laws and rules are generally framed in such a manner that those responsible for enforcing them, irrespective of their departments, can convert them into money-minting machines. Sometimes ago, a Delhi Police officer, known in public parlance as an 'encounter specialist', was killed in Gurgaon by a property dealer.

The accused surrendered to the local police and confessed his crime. The police officer had gone to meet the property dealer after instructing his securitymen to stay behind. Incidentally, he had used the police vehicle for his private work. The self-confessed killer has said that the killed police officer had given him money for investing in properties. His investment had sunk and he was not in a position to pay back the amount, which ranges between Rs. 40 lakh and Rs. 95 lakh.

The truth of the amount invested and its source by the deceased police officer will never be known. It is impossible to earn so much money honestly for an officer who joined as Sub-Inspector and later rose to the level of Deputy Superintendent of Police, even after assuming that he had saved all his salary. If the killer is to be believed, the weapon he used to kill him was provided by the policeman. Incidentally, this weapon was 'lost' in an encounter!

The killer says that the policeman had threatened him that he would kill him if he did not return the money. He also added that he wanted to commit suicide, but was persuaded by his family not to do so.

This is not to down play the role of the highly decorated police officer. But if the previous complaints involving him in property disputes and the present case are put together, an unsavoury picture emerges. However, the 'encounter specialist' is not alone in amassing wealth. Not long ago, another Delhi Police ACP-rank official was arrested by the CBI on "extortion" charges lodges by a businessman.

In 2004, as many as 7,755 Delhi Police personnel were punished in departmental inquiries for their involvement in corruption and various other crimes. Among those punished were one Assistant Commissioner of Police, 63 Inspectors, 1,385 Sub-Inspectors, 724 Assistant Sub-Inspectors, 1,569 Head Constables, 3,570 Constables and 54 class-IV employees.

The punishment included dismissal, forfeiture of service, reduction in rank and pay, etc. About 2,312 police personnel were punished in the departmental proceedings and penalties were imposed on them in 2001, while at least 1,972 were punished in 2002. In 2004, about 400 cases were registered against 517 Delhi Police personnel during the period for their involvement in corruption and other crimes.

Unfortunately, delay in criminal justice is not conducive to quick punishments or acquittals of the innocents. A whopping 2,276 long-pending cases investigated by the CBI are awaiting trial. While 244 have been pending trial for more than 20 years, the remaining 2,032 have been gathering dust in different courts for over 10 years. In all, 8,297 CBI cases are awaiting trial after completion of investigation.

Sadly, criminalisation is not confined to corruption. There is ample evidence of increasing police deviance, as can be seen from the reports of incidents of brutality, murder, rape and other cases by the policemen. The problem is not confined to flouting of departmental rules and regulations or in indulging in peccadilloes, but to committing heinous crimes like rapes, dacoities, extortions, murders, etc.

A DG-level officer of Bihar is under investigation for possessing assets worth over Rs. 60 lakh. A former Punjab DGP has been suspended and chargesheeted by the State Government for "buying" *benami* property. The fact is that criminalisation of police cannot be de-linked from criminalisation of politics. It is the criminalisation of politics that allows a bad policeman to get away with mistakes.

Corruption or criminalisation is not a monopoly of any political party. No political party can say it has not patronised the corrupt and the criminals and given them a certain degree of respectability. They denounce it publicly, but accept the same privately. The induction of charge-sheeted Ministers in the Government headed by one of the 'cleanest' politicians in the country confirms what has been known for decades.

Even in Parliament, as per the affidavits filed at the time of contesting elections, the following number of elected MPs had cases pending against them. The number comes to 100 out of 543 members of the Lok Sabha. In other words, almost every fifth Lok Sabha MP has had a brush with the law, with cases pending against them.

Corruption and lack of morality, however, are not just India's problems An American had this to say about his country and its leadership, "I have, in my life time of 79 years, lived through and with: Two Presidents who had mistresses unknown to their legitimate wives. One President whose mother did not know who was the father was of her child. One President who shouted from the rooftops about drugs, but was on them himself. One President who accumulated illegal cash in White House. One President who lied under oath to a grand jury. Two Presidents who had sex in White House with women other than their wives. A Vice-President who was found guilty of tax evasion. A Secretary of Defence who lied to the Congress and was charged with improper conduct and got off only because a President pardoned him! What else can you expect from a generation of Americans who have lost their way? Our culture sponsors them, generates them and teaches them to be thieves, liars, cheats and crooks."

Whatever may be the situation in the US, Indians have enough of mal-administration and misgovernance. In the earlier years of independence, we could blame the British for our mess. But now after 61 years, this excuse does not hold water. A survey about the police, by the country's leading publication had this to say: About 77 per cent say the police have become less trustworthy; 84 per cent think they open to political interference; 80 per cent believe corruption is a problem with the police; worse, 75 per cent will think twice before filing an FIR.

At the same time, it is futile to put the entire blame on police. In the words of a former London Commissioner of Police, Sir Robert Mark, "The police are the best reflection of a society. If the society is tolerant, literate, human, the police will act accordingly."

There are big speeches on police reforms, but at the end of the day, the result is zero. It is so because no political party is willing to improve the police and shed its control over them. It is time to act and improve the sagging image of the police force.

3.3. Levelling the Playing Field

In a landmark judgement on police reforms in the country, the Supreme Court has directed the States to constitute a Security Commission to ensure that the Government of the day does not exert unwarranted influence, or pressure on its police. Its functions would also include giving directions for the performance of preventive tasks and service-oriented functions of the police, evaluation of performance of the State police and preparing a report for the legislature. This body shall be headed by the Chief Minister or Home Minister, as chairman, with DGP as its ex-officio Secretary.

The Supreme Court has observed: "The DGP shall be selected by the State Government from amongst the three seniormost officers of the department, who have been empanelled for promotion to that rank by the Union Public Service Commission on the basis of their length of service, good record and range of experience. Once a DGP is selected, he should have a minimum tenure of at least two years, irrespective of his date of superannuation."

The court has also directed a fixed tenure of two years for IGPs, superintendents of police and even the station house officer, unless "cogent reasons" warranted their removal midway. It has also directed the setting up of several institutions, which include National Security Commission for the selection of Chief of Central police organisations, CBI, ITBP and CISF, with the chiefs having a minimum tenure of two years each.

The reforms in the police system have been overdue for over 100 years. The British, who had created the Indian police and the existing Police Act in 1861, set up a commission in 1902-03. After examining the performance of the police, the commission observed: "There can be no doubt that the police force throughout the country is in a most unsatisfactory condition, that abuses are common everywhere, that this involves great injury to the people and discredit to the Government, and that radical reforms are urgently necessary."

The British did not have the police reform as priority, as they were in India only to rule. Thirty years after Independence, the Government set up a police commission under Dharam Vira, which observed: "Functioning under the constraints and handicaps of an outmoded system, the police performance has undoubtedly fallen short of public expectation. The present culture of the police system appears a continuation of what obtained under the British regime when the police functioned ruthlessly as an agent for sustaining the Government in power. In public estimates, the police appear as an agency, more to implement and enforce the objectives of the Government in power, as distinct from enforcing laws as such as an independent and impartial agency. The dividing line between the objectives of the Government in power as such on one side, and the interests and expectations of the ruling political party on the other side gets blurred in actual practice, and the image of the police as an impartial law enforcement agency suffers in consequence."

A number of committees and sub-committees were set up to examine the reports of the Police Commission, and almost all of them unanimously recommended that reforms were essential. In fact, Prof Bailey said: "In India today, a dual system of criminal justice has grown up - the one of the law and the other of politics. With respect at least to the police, decisions made by police officials about the application of law are frequently subject to partisan review or direction by the elected representatives. The autonomy of police officials in specific and routine application of law has been curtailed. This is not only true of the law and order situation. People accused of crime have got into the habit of appealing to political figures for remission from the law. Police officials have grown accustomed to calculating the likely political effect of any enforcement action they contemplate."

The note observed that the Government would impress upon the Chief Ministers that efforts should be made "to ensure that there is no unlawful interference in the exercise of statutory powers. Second, in the matters of posting and transfers, States should seek to restore leadership and effectiveness of the official hierarchy with a view to ensure that the requisite rapport between the officers and men is not eroded". At the end of the deliberation, the participants agreed that the "problem arising out of interference will bear effective solutions at the political level". Unfortunately, even decades after the discussion, the position has not only remained unaltered but has gone from bad to worse.

The above observations indicate that the police are being used by the political masters, irrespective of the parties in power, for their gains and ends. In fact, transfers have become an industry. In Uttar Pradesh, for example, Mayawati set a record in 1997 by transferring over 1,400 civil and police officers in six months of her rule. Kalyan Singh had transferred 521 officials in 1991-92 and the SP-BSP Government headed by Mulayam Singh transferred 814 official in 1993-95.

An Administrative Reforms Committee appointed by the Government of Rajasthan, under the chairmanship of late Harish Chandra Mathur, had observed: "In the matters of transfer and posting of Government employees, there has been considerable undue interference by senior authorities in the powers of the subordinate authorities in this respect. The interference of this nature is one of the major causes of indiscipline and frustration and demoralisation."

In his first letter to the Chief Ministers in July 2004, Prime Minister Manmohan Singh said: "Maintenance of law and order is critical in providing an atmosphere conducive to economic development and social harmony." Frequent transfers of public servants have a debilitating impact not only on their performance and morale, but also on the whole process of governance. Development administration also depends on the regularity of tenure. "Therefore, I urge you to ensure stability of tenure to officials in key positions in order to ensure effective administration and proper delivery of public services," he wrote.

Unfortunately, politicians of the day were loath to shed control of the police. As police reforms were not a vote-netting problem, nobody was interested in improving it. As one swallow does not make a summer, so one Prime Minister, however honest and sincere, cannot transform the police governance. He, along with the people of India, should be thankful to the Supreme Court for doing something that nobody has been willing to do in the 59 years of Independence.

It is, however, not enough to insulate the police from political pressures. It is equally important to make its functioning transparent and accountable, which is necessary for good governance and sustainable development. In their absence, corruption and mismanagement is bound to rule the roost.

1.1. Police Reforms Long Overdue

The police are always in the firing line. As if our police forces were not burdened enough, another important duty has been added to their list of charter. It is to maintain internal security and fight terrorism. Till a few decades ago terrorism was an unknown phenomenon. This was also the time that the laws under which our police functions today were also framed. The job of the defence forces is to protect the country against foreign aggression. It has a unified command and clear standard operating procedures. Nobody questions the Army when jawans kill infiltrators or those who attack the country. They do not have to give any explanations as long as they achieve their objectives.

However, the war against terrorism is quite different. The reason is that terrorists operate in different States for which separate police forces are responsible. Theoretically, law and order being a State subject, the Union Government may well say that it is the State's responsibility to maintain peace and harmony. The result is that no unified approach is adopted to deal with terrorism.

The problem gets further aggravated as the Centre, except for periodical sermons, does not play any pro-active role in tackling terrorism. However, the issue is so grave that on an average seven persons were killed in terrorists attacks every day in 2007. India is third on the terror toll list, after Iraq (13,611) and Afghanistan (4,673), as per the report of the National Counterterrorism Center of the US.

The modern day *jihadis* are technology savvy. They could be computer experts, software engineers, electricians, hoteliers or management experts who have been thoroughly indoctrinated to kill all *kafirs*. Following the Delhi terror bombings of September 13, two of the Indian Mujahideen were killed in a police encounter a week later. In the operation one inspector of Delhi Police lost his life and two other police men were seriously injured. Still there are people who contend that it was a fake encounter. The allegation is laughable. But for the fact the credibility of the police is so low, some people will believe anything said against the police.

A survey conducted by a leading newspaper has revealed that eight out of 10 people in Delhi approve and support encounters. It is because most people think criminals deserve to die and, that our courts are rarely able to convict them. Delhi's mood perhaps has something to do with its rising crime situation and also the spate of recent terror bombings.

And here is the odd thing: Delhiites support encounters despite knowing that a lot of them are not genuine, that criminals at times do not open fire first or threaten the police. Still, Delhiites favour encounters.

It is true that bigger the criminal, the harder it is to convict him. Either the witnesses don't depose in court or they keep on delaying the trial. People get fed up and, therefore, heave a sigh of relief when they hear that the criminal has been killed in an encounter.

Unlike the other wings of the Government, the police have maximum visibility. Visibility takes away anonymity. Accountability of the police means performing of duties to the satisfaction of the party for whose benefit duties are being discharged. Here both the patient and the doctor is the Government.

Reforms in the police system have been overdue for over 147 years. The British, who had fathered the Indian Police and the present Police Act in 1861, set up a commission in 1902-03, which observed: "There can be no doubt that the police force throughout the country is in a most unsatisfactory condition, that abuses are common everywhere, that this involves great injury to the people and discredit to the Government, and that radical reforms are urgently necessary. These efforts will cost much, because the department has hitherto been starved, but they must be effected."

Thirty years after independence, the Government set up a police reforms commission under Dharam Vira, which observed:

"Functioning under the constraints and handicaps of an outmoded system, the police performance has undoubtedly fallen short of public expectation. The present culture of the police system appears a continuation of what obtained under the British regime, when the police functioned ruthlessly as an agent for sustaining the Government in power. In public estimates, the police appear as an agency more to implement and enforce the objectives of the Government in power, as distinct from enforcing laws as such as an independent and impartial agency. The dividing line between the objectives of the Government in power as such on one side, and the interests and expectations of the ruling political party on the other side, gets blurred in actual practice, and the image of the police, as an impartial law enforcement agency, suffers in consequence."

Politicians are not only unwilling but totally opposed to improving the police. The Supreme Court orders of September 2006 also calls for reforming the police, which includes a fixed tenure for key officials, separation of crime from the investigation wing and having open and transparent norms in transfers and postings.

Supervision by politicians in the name of democracy has eroded the foundations upon which impartiality rests in a criminal justice system. The police are allegedly being used by their political masters for their gains. Only, when a party is out of power it talks about police reforms. In fact, police reforms, notwithstanding the Supreme Court directive, is not even on the election agenda or manifesto of any political party.

The result of all this is that it is the common man who is the victim, as he does not get redressal of his grievances. The rich do not bother as they can bribe their way out of any case or crime. The poor, however, cannot pay bribes.

Still, when all is said and done, despite the restrictions and Government indifference, it is up to the leadership within the police to ensure that the force upholds the law of the land. If the law enforcers themselves were to violate the law, then who would respect their sanctity? Many police officers look upon human rights activists as stumbling blocks in their working. Let these people put themselves into the shoes of the innocent victims and then honestly ask themselves whether the emphasis on human rights for the perpetrators of crime is justified. The police may not like the laws for dealing with terrorism, but as long as the laws are on the statute book they have to be followed.

The police should work in a way so as to win public approval. If there is even remote suspicion about any of its operations, including encounters and in the killing of terrorists, it should have the courage to come clean so that the right message is sent out to the public. As Winston Churchill said, "Courage is rightly considered the foremost of the virtues because upon it, all others depend."

3.5. Time to Reforms Long Overdue

Police reforms in India have been the subject of discussion right from the day it was passed and implemented in 1861. The founder of British Police, Robert Peel, the then British Prime Minister, propounded the following nine basic principles to govern all police actions:

- To prevent crime and disorder as an alternative to their repression by military force and severity of legal punishment
- To recognise that the power of the police to fulfil their functions and duties is dependent on public approval of their existence, actions and behaviour, and on their ability to secure and maintain public respect.
- To recognise that to secure and maintain the respect and approval of the public means also the securing of the willing cooperation of the public in the task of securing observance of law.
- To recognise that the extent to which the cooperation of the public can be secured diminishes, proportionately, the necessity of the use of physical force and compulsion for achieving police objective.
- To seek and preserve public favour, not by pandering to public opinion, but by constantly demonstrating absolutely impartial service to law, in complete independence of policy, and without regard to the justice or injustice of individual laws; by ready offering of individual service and friendship to all members of the public without regard to their wealth or social standing; by ready exercise of courtesy and good humour; and, by ready offering of individual sacrifice in protecting and preserving life.

- To use physical force only when the exercise of persuasion, advice and warning is found to be insufficient to obtain public cooperation to an extent necessary to restore order; and to use only the minimum degree of physical force, which is necessary on any particular occasion for achieving a police objective.
- To maintain at all times a relationship with the public that gives reality to the historic tradition that the police are the public and that the public are the police; the police being only members of the public who are paid to give full-time attention to duties which are incumbent on every citizen in the interest of community welfare and existence.
- To recognise the need for strict adherence to police executive functions and to refrain from even seeming to usurp the powers of the judiciary of avenging individuals or the state and of authoritatively judging guilt and punishing the guilty.
- To recognise that the test of police efficiency is the absence of crime and disorder, and not the visible evidence of police action in dealing with them."

Our police force, however, did not come up to the expectation of both the Government and people even during British rule. The Police Commission (1901-03) was set up to look into its working and suggest reforms. It said, "There can be no doubt that the police force throughout the country is in a most unsatisfactory condition, that abuses are common everywhere, that this involves great injury to the people and discredit to the Government and that radical reforms are urgently necessary." The National Police Commission of 1977-81, set up under the Chairmanship of late Governor Dharma Vira, observed: "What the Police Commission said in 1903 appears more or less equally applicable to the conditions obtaining today."

Studies after studies and commissions after commissions have highlighted the problems affecting the police. Professor David H Bayley has aptly summed it up by saying, "In India today, a dual system of criminal justice has grown, the one of the law and the other of politics. With respect at least to the police, decisions made by the police officials about the application of law are frequently subject to partisan review or direction by the elected representatives. The autonomy of the police officials in specific and routine application of law has been curtailed. This is not only true of law and order situations, but people accused of crimes have got into the habit of appealing to political figures for remission from the law."

"Police officials, throughout India, have grown accustomed to calculating the likely political effect of any enforcement action they contemplate. Fearing for their careers and especially their postings, they have become anxious and cynical. The frame, upon which justice hinges, has been undermined by the rules of politics. Supervision in the name of democracy has eroded the foundations upon which the impartiality depends in a criminal justice system," added Prof Bayley.

In a landmark judgement on police reforms, the Supreme Court, on September 22, 2006, asked the State Governments to set up state security commission by December 31. It wanted DGPs to be selected from a panel of three officers to be finalised by the UPSC. Those who are selected must get a two-year term. The apex court also wanted police officers on operational duties in the field to have a minimum tenure of two years.

There should be separate investigation and law and order duties. Police Establishment Board must decide all transfers, postings, promotions and other service-related matters of subordinate officers. Also, the police complaints authority at district and State levels has to hear complaints from the public.

Almost all the State Governments have filed affidavits either asking for more time or pleading that under the Constitution, law and order is a State subject and this order would go against the constitutional provisions. Some States have also sought more time from the apex court to bring in the desired changes. Police reforms, particularly the recommendations that the DGPs have a two-year fixed tenure and that they be chosen from a panel of officers drawn up by the UPSC have been opposed by most States.

Meanwhile, the Union Government, in its affidavit, has stated that it constituted, on January 2, a Committee on National Security and Police Welfare, which would have the Union Home Minister as its Chairperson for recommending the names of chiefs to be appointed to various Central police organisations.

Thus, the Governments are mostly reluctant to bring about the much-needed changes to reform the police. Neither would they do it themselves, nor would carry out the orders of the apex court, which has only tried to provide a level-playing field to all citizens and ensure that the fundamental right to equality is observed both in letter and spirit. It is time to remind them that it is in the interest of all that the police in India are reformed.

3.6. Police Outsourcing: Checking Cruelty

In Shakespeare's Hamlet, the prince of Denmark says there is something rotten in the state of Denmark. In the first two decades of Independence, we in India used to hold the British responsible for all our ills. But now there is none else but ourselves to blame. These days, there is hardly any section in our public life that is free from corruption. The genesis of corruption lies in the politician-bureaucrat nexus. Unprincipled businessmen also stand to benefit from this unholy bonding.

There is Hindi saying: Behti Ganga main hatth dho lo (Wash your hands in the running Ganges). Thus have criminals too joined their kindreds in the bureaucracy and politics. Alleged murderers, dacoits and rapists have made it to the Centre and State assemblies. Lack of transparency, coupled with red tape and time consuming obsolete rules and procedures, encourage the tendency to make quick money. More than that, the cushion of legal safety, in the form of appeals after appeals, and the principle, "Everybody is innocent till proved guilty", leads to the charge-sheeted persons escaping for one reason or the other.

Such persons hire the best legal brains. They are thus able to easily get out of the reach of the law. Shakespeare, in his play Measure for Measure, says: "Laws are like scarecrows." They are initially installed to scare the birds. Once the birds know they are stuffings, they do not even give them a second glance.

In the second week of April, 2004, the Delhi police cracked the CBSE paper leak case. The paper was leaked to a coaching institute for an astronomical sum of Rs. 50 lakh. Even small functionaries, whose total salary for a number of years would not amount to much, also made their millions. The lure of money was too strong even for the investigating officer, who demanded a "cut" to spare some people. He was trapped by the CBI on April 30 along with his other police associates for demanding Rs. 8 lakh.

Corruption, to some degree, exists in every society. But in our country, public servants routinely accept, demand or extort money for work. Corruption has become an all-pervasive phenomenon. Public service has been substituted with unabashed avarice. Campaign or warfare against corruption is not an end in itself. This crusade is not just on moral grounds. A struggle against this malaise is necessary for an effective, fair and efficient government, which, is the professed aim of all political parties. It is true that corruption cannot be totally eliminated. But it should not be forgotten that it has a negative impact on development schemes. Even otherwise, it is necessary to reduce corruption as it will leave more money for development.

There is only one model for dealing with corruption. The Government must accept the fight against graft as its moral and ethical responsibility. In fact, maintenance of law and order is also a function of the state. But this function has been privatised to some extent. Finding that the state is not able to look after the individual or even the collective needs of society, private industries have started hiring security agencies. Due to shortage of policemen, it has been reported that some police stations too have requisitioned for private guards. Where Government cannot provide protection, the security agencies slip in to do their job. In fact, chaukidari is nothing but policing though it is without the power to prosecute the offenders.

I led an Indian delelgation to the US during my service period. I was surprised to see that the privte agencies were performing the job of security and guarding in the State Department as well as the Central Intelligence Agency. In fact, even under the existing Indian laws, every individual has certain powers to defend himself, his property and the life of others. The right of private defence permits killing if no other course is available.

Corruption should be unacceptable in any civilised society. The police's inefficiency and corruption directly affect a common man's right to life and liberty. Like the Government's disinvestment policy, it is time serious thought was given to divesting the police service as well. Monopolies play havoc and the police's monopoly must be broken. It is this lack of recourse that has resulted in a conviction rate of six per cent in corruption cases. In other words, anybody without money or contacts faces both a difficult and sometimes, impossible situation.

The alleged involvement of senior police officers in murder, land-grabbing, extortion and other similar crimes is symptomatic of the increasing criminalisation of the police force. Their delinquency is not confined to mere violations of the code of conduct or discipline; rather, it includes serious offences.

On January 1, 1998, the Uttar Pradesh Government identified 850 policemen who had alleged nexus with criminals. The list of policemen included two officers of the rank of additional director general of police. In Calcutta, a police commissioner had maintained close links with the underworld. In Haryana, an officer of the rank of director general of police was caught accepting a bribe. A third one was accused of molesting a teenaged girl, who subsequently committed suicide.

In Karnataka, senior officers were charge-sheeted in murder cases. In Assam, two senior officers were involved in rape. In Rajasthan, an officer of the rank of DIG was allegedly accused of raping his orderly's wife a few years ago. He has been absconding for the past many years.

In Delhi, a senior officer of the UT cadre grabbed land illegally. Some time back in Bihar, an SP was reportedly dealing in stolen cars. It may be argued why should only the police be singled out when standards of public morality have plummeted in politics and other departments of the Government as well. But this claim ignores the fact of the power of "life and death" is wielded by even the lowest police functionary.

A policeman, on committing a crime, violates the trust of the community. It is a fact that there is a correlation between crimes committed by police and the growing criminalisation of politics. The nexus between criminal policemen and politicians subverts and undermines the authority of the police as well its discipline.

If the number of complaints received by the National Human Rights Commission is any indication, the police has a lot of explaining to do. In one year, the NHRC generally receives between 425 to 627 such complaint against the police. This is only the tip of the iceberg. The condition in other places is worse. This can be judged from the police top brass's involvement in various scams like the Telgi stamp scandal. It is time a new approach to policing was evolved.

Surely, there is scope for the private sector to take up duties like traffic management, normal watch and ward functions, illegal distillation, patrolling in the night, and simple cases of cheating or bounced checques or even property disputes or giving of summons and warrants. The administration's resistance to change and its inability to discard that which has outlived its utility is another reason for corruption and malpractices in the police sysytem.

The British have discarded their old administrative system in favour of a more responsive one. But India is still fanatically sticking on to the model given by them. It is time the Government made a reappraisal of the problem and did something to improve the situation.

4. CBI: A Review

4.1. CBI: The Spirit of Inquiry

Normally, when ordinary people do not trust investigative agencies, and the Central or State Government or the judiciary wants an impartial investigation, the latter turns to the Central Bureau of Investigation. Right or wrong, the CBI is looked upon as an agency which delivers the goods, because it is seen to act without fear or favour. In fact, there are more demands for CBI inquiries than for any other type of probe.

The CBI was set up by an executive order of the Government on April 1, 1963. The Delhi Special Police Establishment (the CBI's legal name) was created in 1939. Its primary objective was to deal with corruption and economic offences arising out of World War II, involving federal government employees and funds. It was a very small organisation at the time, with a limited charter of duties.

The CBI is now the nodal police agency in India, meant to coordinate investigation on behalf of other Interpol member countries, and pursue India's cases outside. It is the only Central agency that has been credibly probing cases entrusted to it by the constitutional courts- that is, the High Courts or the Supreme Court. In fact, when even the Central or State Governments do not want the agency to take up a matter, the judiciary often steps in to stem the rot.

For instance, in the case of the Bihar fodder scam, the State Government opposed a CBI inquiry. It was the Supreme Court which upheld the High Court's ruling of 1996 stipulating that the scandal be investigated by the CBI. The rest is history-a serving Chief Minister and President of the then ruling party had to leave office under a cloud. This could not have ever occurred without the direction of the Supreme Court and the High Court.

Similarly, under the Delhi High Court's instruction, the CBI took up investigations into the Jharkhand Mukti Morcha bribery case in 1996, which led to the conviction of a former Prime Minister and a former Home Minister. Of course, these politicians were acquitted when they subsequently moved court, and the present Government, in its wisdom, chose not to file an appeal against the acquittal.

More recently, the breaking of the Taj Heritage Corridor scandal, now being investigated by the CBI, led the Supreme Court to order the registration of cases against former Uttar Pradesh Chief Minister Mayawati. It is widely believed that the CBI probe into the Taj Corridor project was the cause of the break-up of the Mayawati-led BSP-BJP coalition Government.

It is, therefore, evident that CBI investigations can have a major impact on the political and economic life of the nation, depending on who is being investigated.

The CBI is headed by a Director of the rank of the Secretary to the Government of India. Other police ranks in the agency are Special Director/Additional Director, Joint Director, Deputy Inspector General of Police, Superintendent of Police, Deputy Superintendent of Police, Inspector, Sub-Inspector, Assistant Sub-Inspector, head constable and constable, The sanctioned police strength-inclusive of all ranks-is 5,944. In addition, the CBI has a permitted strength of 230 Law Officers, 194 technical posts, 140 posts for scientists in the CFSL and 208 Group D posts.

The investigation of cases by the CBI is done only by officers of the rank of Inspectors or Deputy Superintendents of Police, numbering about 1,100. Those below are only meant to assist in the investigation; those above-like the Superintendents of Police, DIGs, IGs, Special Directors or Additional Director Generals Of Police, Director or Director General of Police-are supervisory officers.

Law and order is a State subject. The basic jurisdiction to investigate crimes lies with the State Police. Besides, due to limited resources, and with nearly 30 per cent vacancies in the ranks of the investigators and prosecutors who form the backbone of CBI cases, the agency cannot take up all matters which come to it. The CBI can function in any State with its consent. There have been instances in the past of its being asked to close shop, bringing a halt to its operations in the States concerned.

A CBI draft act prepared and sent to the Government about two decades ago is gathering dust. The main reason for this is that State dispensations do not want a super agency over which they have no control. The result is that we do not have a federal law enforcement agency for the investigation of federal crimes. Indeed, there is no concept of a federal crime in India. Despite so much apparently well-meant debate on the need for zero tolerance of corruption, rhetoric has not been followed up with action. The CBI is still beholden to the Government for its infrastructure. It has no independent status of its own. It is, in fact, no more than a wing of the Government. It has its masters in the Central Vigilance Commission, who have been given the power to supervise all cases of corruption.

The CBI is answerable to the judiciary, since the results of its investigations are to be placed before the courts. Yet it depends on the Government for sanctions and infrastructure, and has to seek its permission to prosecute the guilty. It cannot complain against the Government in the courts or to anybody else for any problem that it might face.

Despite the Supreme Court ruling on the Single Directive-under which the Government's permission is required to take up cases against officials of the rank of Joint Secretary and above-the Central Vigilance Commission Bill, which has now become law, has restored it. Thus, there is built-in insulation in the system to prevent inquiries from being launched against the higher echelons of the bureaucracy. Such is the law passed by Parliament. Unless the Supreme Court strikes down the illegal section, as it did in the case of election laws, it will continue to be in force.

Well over 100 cases are entrusted to the CBI annually by the apex and high courts. With a strength smaller than that of a single big district police force, the agency has the capacity to take up about 1,200 to 1,300 cases per year all over the country. Those entrusted to it by the courts are given the highest priority, as they are generally timebound. The CBI is a full-time investigative agency. The yearly workload of one investigating officer is 2.5 cases of general offences and 1.75 cases of economic offences. A normal police station in the country handles over 80 to 100 cases per year.

It is not that States cannot have their own equally efficient investigative agencies. The problem is that, at every step, the 'political masters' of these organisations use inquiries to suit their needs. An unheard of situation, in fact, arose with regard to the Madhumita Shukla murder scandal that broke in UP in May. The entire CB-CID investigative team, including the Director General of Police, was placed under suspension, ostensibly for not completing the probe on time. The real reason seemed to be their failure to adequately stonewall a case against a former Minister in the Government of the day and thereby act as his saviour.

The case was referred to the CBI by the State Government and it is on the way to solving it-with the help of the former Minister himself, who is in police/judicial custody. The same police officers, when on CBI deputation, do a wonderful job!

Pressure on the agency to take up more and more cases, whether due to public pressure, or courtesy the direction of the Government or the courts, is bound to increase. Unfortunately, the Government seems to have no roadmap with regard to how strong and efficient it wants the CBI to be at the end of five or 10 years. With greater liberalisation and the opening of economy, we can look forward to more scams and more defalcation. If the present set-up or approach continues, I fear that the CBI will find itself stretched beyond acceptable limits where maintaining the same level of efficiency is concerned. It is time the Government acted in advance.

4.2. Who is Afraid of the CBI ?

Whenever a high profile accused involved in a CBI case is acquitted, the favourite whipping boy is the CBI itself. Everyone seems to have a love-hate relationship with the agency. CBI investigation into cases faces greater public outcry-and quite often court orders-than judicial inquiries.

The CBI was set by an executive order of the Government on April 1, 1963. This simply gave a new name to the Delhi Special Police Establishment, which had been created in 1939 by the British Government. Laws governing the working of the CBI are the same as those that created the Delhi Special Police Establishment, the primary objective of which was to deal with corruption and economic offences concerning Federal Government employees and involving the federal funds during World War II. It was a very small organisation at that time, as it is even now. The British Government in India did not aim at rooting out corruption. Its objective was to safeguard its interests. Nor was corruption an issue immediately after Independence.

Corruption raised its head in a big way with the first LIC scam called the Mundhra scandal in the 1950s, when the then Finance Minister TT Krishnama-chari resigned. None other than Feroz Gandhi, Indira Gandhi's husband, raised the dust of the scandal. He was the firebrand son-in-law of the then Prime Minister, Jawahar Lal Nehru, and the father of late Prime Minister Rajiv Gandhi.

However, corruption mostly remained in the background, because Indian leadership still demonstrated some measure of idealism. Senior leaders led comparatively clean lives. The example they set percolated downwards. In the 1950s, even the slightest suspicion of corruption was enough to finish a man politically. A stalwart like Sardar Partap Singh Kairon, the then Chief Minister of Punjab, had to demit office only on the ground that he ought to have been responsible for the moral guidance of his family members, though technically and legally he was not responsible for the actions of his grown- up children.

In the 1970s, banks were nationalised with the laudable objective of utilising the country's resources for the greater good of society. But this soon degenerated into loan melas with electoral encashment in view. Non-performing assets of banks today stand at more than Rs. 110,000 crore.

The vigilance set-up of the Union Government, including the CBI and departmental vigilance, with regard to Central Government and public sector employees numbering eight million, does not exceed 8,000. And that is a very generous estimate. Even at the best of times, watchfulness is appraised as an unavoidable but necessary evil, yet the CBI itself is misunderstood on that count. However, the agency is a tool that aids the Government. Its objective is the same as that of the latter: To ensure that all public servants perform their duties as laid down by the rules, and that Government money is spent for the purpose for which it is sanctioned and not siphoned off. When action is taken against somebody for defalcating or plundering the state treasury, a cautionary message goes down to all concerned to beware.

A critical situation arrives when action is sought to be taken against those in power. Sometimes it is the same set of people who have been responsible -either by collusion or negligence-for a crime or action which is sought to be inquired into. No support for strengthening the vigilance set-up can be expected from such people with influence in the Government.

That is one reason the CBI-the only multi-purpose investigative agency for all kinds of crimes-has remained unsatisfactory in terms of composition, jurisdiction and performance. The basic law has remained unchanged from British times. Unlike the US's Federal Bureau of Investigation the writ of which runs in the entire country, the CBI functions at the sweet will of State Governments.

No action can be taken against Central Government employees posted in States where the CBI is not authorised to operate. Even if consent has been given for it to function in a particular State, no action can be taken against a State employee without the approval of the State Government concerned.

Income tax, Central customs, and railways officials are posted all over the country. Even if they defalcate or play hell with Central revenues, a State Government can withdraw its consent to CBI operations and nullify its probe. In case of a clash with the Central Government, States have withdrawn their sanction to the functioning of the Special Police Establishment in their territory. States like Karnataka and Haryana had at one stage or the other revoked consent, forcing the CBI to close shop. Later, some of them relented. Some States give consent on a case-to-case basis. Surely it is essential for the Central Government to have vigilance jurisdiction over its employees no matter where they are posted.

It is difficult for the CBI to draw a road map for its functioning, given that it is not a constitutional body or institution like the Election Commission or the judiciary. There is no Central law governing CBI investigations. The matter pertaining to the formation of a CBI Act has been gathering dust for over two decades now.

The truth is, catching and punishing the corrupt is the Government's last priority, notwithstanding its high and mighty proclamations about "zero tolerance" for corruption. The reality is that there is a zero intolerance for dishonesty and graft. How else does one explain the fact that corrupt leaders, known dacoits and notorious criminals are lionised in society, some of them entering the country's legislatures? The proverbial Page Three of newspapers is full of such worthies, who attend court cases involving corruption in the morning, only to attend fabulous high society parties with glamourous women in tow at night.

Despite the massive size of the country, the CBI has been kept lean and trim. It is not as if there is not enough work or no need for extra staff. It is that any proposal sent to the Government takes ages to be cleared, that is, if it is not rejected. Endless queries to the babus who refuse to reply to the proposals achieve little. Hence, matters have remained static. This stems from the basic fact that vigilance is not and has never been the focus of any Government. In fact, the Government's headache has been the other way round: How to prevent vigilance from being vigilant?

This can be gauged from the fact the CBI has no authority to inquire into the misconduct of all-India services officers belonging to the Indian Police Service and Indian Administrative Service officers working for State Governments. In the case of the all-India services officers, the appointing authority is the President. They cannot be dismissed, removed or reverted by State Governments, whether or not they are working in connection with the affairs of the latter. In their cases, all reports of misconduct have to be sent to the Central Government. The Central Government, in turn, consults the Union Public Service Commission or the Vigilance Commission.

It is a travesty of justice when the system is such that, quite often, CBI reports end up on the table of the accused! The only way to improve matters is for the Government to make up its mind on how strong it wants the vigilance set-up to be. That, of course, depends on how heavily it wants to come down on the dishonest who are looting the country left, right and centre. There is a mistaken belief that taking action against malpractices will demoralise the bureaucracy. On the contrary, it will make it work as per the rules and ensure good governance.

It is wise to remember that eternal vigilance is not only the price of liberty, it is also the guarantor of good governance. There is no escaping the fact that good governance means using Government money for the welfare of the people.

4.3. CBI is Short of Staff.

The shortage of staff in the Central Bureau Of Investigation has recently come into focus again. On an average, there is a shortage of 25 per cent to 33 per cent of the strength of staff sanctioned under different categories. The CBI has some permanent staff of its own in the ministerial cadre as well as other ranks - constable, sub-inspector, inspector, DSP, legal officer, etc. To make sure that the staff available represents a cross-section of society, a substantial quota is earmarked for deputation from State polices. Without the deputationist, the CBI would not be able to deliver and take up cases of national importance. The case of Rajiv Gandhi's assassination, for example, would not have been solved but for the availability of Tamil-speaking staff who could question and talk to the local people in Tamil. The result is that there is some staff from every State in the country.

The CBI's legal power to investigate is derived from the Delhi Special Police Establishment Act, 1946. In fact in legal parlance, there is no such thing as the CBI, as the CBI draft act sent to the Government for its approval has been gathering dust for the last two decades. The CBI was created by an executive order of the Union Government. Legally, the investigation agency continues to be officially called the Special Police Establishment. The above Act confers concurrent and coextensive powers, duties, privileges and liabilities upon the members of DSPE (CBI) with police officers from Union Territories. The Central Government can extend the power and jurisdiction of members of the CBI to any area, including the Union Territories, to facilitate investigation by the agency. This is possible only if the concerned State Governments consent for the functioning of the CBI in their territory. There have been instances where, for political reasons, or to avoid investigation by the Central agency, some State Governments have withdrawn their consent, rendering the CBI officers deputed there redundant.

The CBI normally investigates cases that concern the affairs of the Union Government, those relating to breaches in Central laws, or the ones that may be referred to it by State Governments, big cases of fraud, cheating, embezzlement and the like - relating to companies in which large funds are involved - and similar other cases when committed by organised gangs or professional criminals having ramifications in several States. The CBI also takes up cases with inter-State and international ramifications and those involving several official agencies where it is considered necessary that a single investigating agency should be in charge of the investigation. As law and order is a State subject, it basically falls under the jurisdiction of the concerned State Police to investigate a crime in its area. Though the CBI takes up cases involving Central Government employees only, some States like Karnataka give permission to the CBI to investigate a few cases off and on. Of course, the State has no say in matters of Central Government employees.

Procedural delays, too, are an impediment in the fight against corruption. The latest CBI report highlights the position of cases in the country. In 2006, a total of 8,297 CBI cases were awaiting trial even after the completion of the investigations. The figure of pending trial cases was 6,898 in 2005. More than 2,276 cases have been pending trial in various courts all over the country for more than 10 years; 244 cases are pending trial for over 20 years. This also includes cases which are more than 25 years old. There are 438 cases in which chargesheets have been filed but the designated courts have not framed charges for over 10 years.

The CBI, incidentally, is one wing of the criminal justice system, the others being the prosecution department and the judiciary. How wide and high-level corruption has pervaded can be gauged from the fact that in 2006, CBI booked 1,917 cases against public servants. Nearly half of them (941) charged were gazetted officers, of whom 25 were of the level of joint secretary and above. Out of the 1,156 cases registered in 2006, the highest was reported from the customs and central excise departments (68) followed by the department of post (57), railways (54) and MCD (37).

Another factor highlighted in the CBI report is that the left hand does not know what the right is doing. On the one hand, Governments have been talking of zero tolerance of corruption. On the other, 113 cases were pending at the end of 2006 for want of sanction for prosecution of corrupt public servants.

In a reply to a question in Parliament on May 7, 2003, then Deputy Prime Minister LK Advani said that out of the 186 cases pending against IAS and IPS officers, the "overwhelming majority related to corruption charges". This number, four years later, must be much more.

All cases that State Governments find embarrassing to handle are passed on to the CBI. Nandigram was a simple case of rioting and so was the disturbance in Madurai in May, 2007. However, both West Bengal and Tamil Nadu Governments decided to hand over the respective cases to the CBI. Most Governments find it easier to pass the buck to the CBI instead of tackling the problem themselves.

Ironically, the same police officers, including the IPS, come on deputation from the State Government to the CBI, to investigate cases referred to by their States. They are able to work impartially and honestly because they are allowed to.

Even where State Governments have competent officials or agencies for investigations, the officers are circumspect to ensure that their reports would be in accordance with unexpressed - but clearly understood - expectations of the powers-that-be. It was the same Gujarat Police, which after post-Godhra riots brought the situation under control when it was given a free hand under the leadership of a retired DGP from Punjab as the Security Adviser. It is the same Gujarat Police which, in response to the Supreme Court's directions, has indicted its own senior officers in encounters.

Expertise can be developed if officials are given a free hand. Most control-freak State Governments are trotting excuses for not bringing in the much-needed reforms in the police and fixing tenure for officers despite such orders of the Supreme Court.

Many a time, a CBI investigation is not to the liking of the State Governments. When the CBI raided some IAS officers of the

Punjab cadre during the investigation of a case ordered by the High Court, the then Chief Minister of Punjab expressed his unhappiness about the raid that was conducted without his permission. The angry Chief Minister also said he would take up the matter with the Prime Minister. Such political interference is an extra burden on CBI.

9

Jails and Indian Position

1. Some Major Issues

1.1. Some Major Points Jails can't Wait to be Broken: Security

In what may be regarded as the biggest incident of jailbreak in the country, at least 303 prisoners, many of them Maoists, escaped from the Dantewada district jail on December 16. At least 105 Maoists were among the escapees along with many others who are believed to have been in custody for related offences. The jail is about 9 km away from the Dantewada town and is located at a secluded spot. There were just four guards on duty (instead of the usual 16) when the prisoners escaped.

The incident occurred in broad daylight at about 5 pm and not in the dark of the night. The prisoners looted half a dozen rifles from the security personnel in the jail. The police chased the prisoners and, in the process, 12 policemen went missing after an encounter with Maoists in Dantewada's forests. They were killed by the extremists. The extremists also looted 11 self-loading rifles and an AK-47 rifle from the policemen. Among the killed were eight Chhattisgarh Armed Force personnel and four from the district force who got separated when a 28-member police party came under attack from the Maoists in the Golapalli forest 450 km from Raipur, the State's capital. The 16 who survived reported back to their base camp in Golapalli with the weapons.

The Maoists had publicly vowed to free their jailed comrades. In February, the Maoists in their ninth congress on the Jharkhand-Orissa border had resolved to free their comrades languishing in jails in several States.

Encouraged by their successful jailbreak operations in Jehanabad, Bihar (November 2005), and R Udaigiri, Orissa (March 2006), the Maoists said in the resolution that they intended to carry out similar strikes in Chhattisgarh where their comrades were behind the bars. The resolution said; "This congress resolves to strive to carry out every possible means to free our comrades from jails... with support from the masses we had carried out historic actions such as the Jehanabad and R Udaigiri jailbreaks."

According to an estimate, there are 15,000 Maoist activists with 10,000 firearms. They pose the biggest inner security challenge to the country. They wield influence in 170 of the 602 district of the country. Their sphere of influence covers 16 of the 32 States.

Bihar has a total of 54 jails including the six central prisons which house over 42,000 prisoners against the total capacity of 19,000. None of the jails in Bihar has jammers, close-circuit cameras or X-ray scanners. The security personnel do not have even basic equipment like walkie-talkies. In Beur Jail of Patna alone, there are over 2,600 prisoners against a capacity of 1,400. Only 100 guards are deployed to supervise the hardcore inmates even though the total sanctioned strength is 200. Around 300 Maoists including some dreaded commanders were lodged there. They virtually took charge of Beur prison on the outskirts of Patna for nearly eight hours on December 18. The tragedy began early around 6:30 am when 150-odd inmates went on a hunger strike demanding action against officials responsible for the recent suicide by a Maoist. They stormed into the jail's five kitchens, damaged the vessels and roughed up security men and hounded them away. The administration literally yielded, agreeing to pay compensation for the family of the prisoner who committed suicide. As a result of negotiations, including a judicial inquiry and action, the prisoners agreed to call off the protest.

Among scores of cases of jailbreaks, there was the scandalous escape of three persons accused in the assassination of Punjab Chief Minister Beant Singh from the Burail Jail in Chandigarh in 2004.

Inspection of the jail showed that the high profile prisoners were not only leading a luxurious life but also had enclosed their cells. This was used to dig a tunnel to escape.

The pitiable condition of Indian prisons is not beyond remedy. The number of prisoners in our jails is small as compared to that in many other countries.

India's prison population is a little under 340,000. It is not a big deal for a country of a billion plus. The US has nearly 1.5 million prisoners and another three million under penal control outside the prison. In 1995, Russia had 687 prisoners for 100,000 people; in India there are about 25 prisoners for 100,000 people.

The most disturbing aspect of Indian prisons is the presence of under-trials. They constitute 75 per cent of the country's prison population. In many jails they constitute about 90 per cent of the prison population. In Meerut, the NHRC found that against the authorised capacity of 650 prisoners, there were 3,000 prisoners and 90 per cent of them were under-trials.

Indira Gandhi had appointed the Justice AN Mulla Committee to review the jail system nationally though law and order and jails are State subjects. The committee recommended in 1983 that the Constitution be amended to shift the subject of prisons from the State to the Concurrent List. That never happened. The Centre at present has no say in the matter of State's jails. In Union Territories including Delhi, where the Union Government is the authority, the jails are far from being models. Jails continue to be governed by an outdated law enacted by the British in 1894. We have no national policy on prisons.

A recommendation of the Mulla Committee was to classify prisons into special security prisons, maximum-security prisons, medium-security prisons and minimum-security prisons. Such a classification can safeguard against the kind of jailbreaks and jail riots seen all over the country. If terrorists and all those accused of similar offences can be segregated for special security arrangements, the mortification of seeing high profile prisoners escaping would become a near impossibility. But the recommendations of the committee are gathering dust for the last 24 years.

Official indifference and lethargy emboldens the criminals. We need to decongest the prisons with the help of a responsive judiciary. Unfortunately, that is not the priority of the Government. Chief Justice of India KG Balakrishnan said, "India has only 12,000 judges — 2,000 short of the sanctioned strength of 14,000. As a result, there are over 2.5-crore cases pending in the lower courts, 37-lakh in High Courts and 46,000 in the Supreme Court. He added, "We need one judge for (every) 500 cases to clear the backlog — that would mean 77,664 judges. At best, however, the judges' strength can be pushed up a few thousand more. We need more courts and more Budget (allocation) for the judiciary." It is time for the introduction of jail reforms as well as a guarantee of prompt justice.

1.2. Locked Away and Forgotten: Human Rights

Not only is there a heavy pendency in the criminal justice system - the backlog of cases that have not reached their legal conclusion as on February 27, 2006 in Supreme Court was 33,635, in all High Courts taken together, it was 3,341,040; for subordinate courts, it was 25,306,458 - but administration of our jails, too, is in a mess.

Only when some VIP is sent to jail does the Government wake up to the need to ensure minimum humane conditions for prisoners. For instance, when a former Chief Minister of Bihar was sent to the Beur Central Jail of Patna, the building construction department spent Rs 2.52 crore on renovating the prison. There was a virtual scramble among the department's staff to get a posting in Beur so that they could get easy access to the former Chief Minister whose party was ruling the State at that time.

Whatever funds were sanctioned to provide the 'humane' conditions dried up as soon as the VIP prisoner left Beur Central Jail. This is something not exclusive to Bihar; the same story is repeated all over the country in greater or lesser degree.

Taking suo motu cognisance of the scenario, the Delhi High court has set up a five-member committee in June. The committee members are to visit Tihar Jail and submit a report on the medical facilities available there. This follows the death of half-a-dozen prisoners in one week. Curiously, the jail authorities are attributing the deaths to the extreme hot weather in Delhi during those days. On an average, at least 24 prisoners die in this jail every year.

For one, the infrastructure to handle the pressure of increasing prison population is inadequate. Tihar Jail, situated in the national capital, has a capacity of 6,250 inmates. But as of now, it houses some 13,750 prisoners. Naturally, when the infrastructure - medical facilities, living space or supervision - is stretched thin, incidents worse than the recent deaths could happen. And if such is the condition of a high-profile jail in the national capital, one can imagine the condition in the States. Prison is a State subject and jail reform is no State's priority. For that matter, even the Union Government is not bothered.

I overheard a conversation at the next table in a restaurant a few days ago. An apparently well-off person was narrating to his friend his experiences in a jail. He said; "I spent a month in jail and had the best of life there. I paid Rs 1,000 a day for staying in a separate air-conditioned room." This package, however, did not include the use of mobile phone, TV, DVD, meals of his choice and meeting people privately, for which he had to pay separately.

But for ordinary prisoners, a ward meant for 40 to 50 people has only five to six fans. These prisoners suffer from various ailments, erratic water and electricity supply, inadequate or rudimentary facilities and scarce medical attention. The last, if and when available, is no better than first aid.

Doctors deputed in jails and the prison administration treat prisoners as the scum of society. There are 90 doctors for 13,750 inmates in Tihar - much worse than the 100:7,000 doctor-prisoner ratio in 1995. People are sentenced for breaking the law. Death in the course of serving a jail sentence is certainly not part of the penalty, but that often appears ordained.

The Bible says that there is an inscription at the entrance to hell: "Abandon hope, all ye who enter here." That is the condition of Indian jails. The Government needs to streamline the procedure of detention applicable to an undertrial till the case(s) against him or

her is/are disposed. The rich people, including politicians, despite being convicted and sentenced to jail, manage to stay outside prisons, while their appeals are pending in higher courts. On the other hand, there are cases where people have spent a lifetime in prison for crimes that merit a maximum sentence of five to 10 years by law.

In 2002, it was reported that some three quarters of all prisoners held in Indian jails had not been sentenced but were undertrials. The largest number of undertrial or remand prisoners were in the jails of Uttar Pradesh, Manipur and Meghalaya, where more than 90 per cent of the prison population had reportedly not been tried in courts of law. According to a National Crime Research Bureau study, "Crime in India 2002", nearly 220,000 cases took more than three years to reach the courts, and about 25,600 exhausted 10 years before they were completed.

Too many laws tend to turn ordinary citizens into criminals. Out of 525 sections of the Indian Penal Code, only about 100 are put to use. It is time to revise the penal laws so that most cases are disposed of through summary trials. We have a jail system devised, developed and implemented by the British. It has failed to provide basic justice to the inmates before they are convicted. If a prisoner wants humane treatment, he or she has to bribe the staff at every second instance.

Moreover, the lacklustre jail staff cannot handle terrorists attacking jails. In some States like Chhattisgarh, Orissa and Bihar, criminals have succeeded in freeing their fellow travellers from jails. This is the age of privatisation. Why does the Government not think of privatising prison administration? The experiment can begin with undertrials involved in ordinary crimes.

What Ayn Rand says suits the Indian prison scenario: "Do you think that we want those laws to be observed? We want them broken. There's no way to rule innocent men. The only power the Government has is the power to crack down on criminals. Well, when there aren't enough criminals one makes them. One declares so many things to be a crime that it becomes impossible for men to live without breaking laws. Who wants a nation of law-abiding citizens? What's there in that for anyone? But just pass the kind of laws that can neither be observed nor enforced nor objectively interpreted and you create a nation of law-breakers."

1.3. Five Stars Jails of India: Criminality Upheld

In a raid on Meerut Jail led by the DIG of Agra Jail to recover and seize cell phones and other unauthorised and prohibited items, there was a fight between the jail police and inmates of the high-security prison. It left six police officials and four inmates injured.

The raiding DIG said, "It could not have happened without the connivance of jail officials. We had special instructions from the home department as Meerut Jail is known for its lawlessness. But we were shocked when a thou-sand-strong mob attacked us with sticks and stones. We were trapped and could only escape after we charged towards the gate."

The prisoners snatched away all the mobile phones and contraband recovered during the check that was ordered at the instance of the State Government. The DIG has accused the superintendent of Meerut Jail of "inciting the jail inmates to attack us so that we could not find prohibited articles in the jail".

On the other hand, the jail superintendent has accused the DIG of demanding illegal gratification. Some staff has been suspended. The other form of corruption reported from the Meerut Jail included unauthorised sale of items at exorbitant prices. Cigarettes were being sold for Rs. 20 per stick. It cost Rs. 500 for a meal of choice. A local call could be made for Rs. 20, an STD call cost Rs. 100. The Meerut Jail, built to house 700 inmates, now has 1,850 prisoners.

A former Uttar Pradesh Minister, serving his sentence in Lucknow Jail for the murder of his mistress Madhumita Shukla, freely hosted a wedding anniversary bash for a co-accused in the murder case inside the jail premises. A sitting Minister when asked replied, "No one is born a criminal and the Samajwadi Party believes in transformation of criminals. You can't stop anyone from celebrating an occasion concerning him, his family or near and dear ones - within the premises of the jail. As per my knowledge, there was no violation of the jail manual."

In 2004, three accused involved in the assassination of Punjab Chief Minister Beant Singh escaped scandalously from the Burail Jail in Chandigarh. Inspection of the jail showed that the high profile prisoners were not only leading a luxurious life, but they had also enclosed their cells in a way that their activities inside could not be kept under vigil. Once the cell was turned into a virtual fortress, the prisoners dug a tunnel to escape.

The escape of terrorists involved in one of the most high-profile assassinations could not have materialised simply through a nexus between corrupt jail staffers and the prisoners. Vast sums of money as well as a pattern of internal and external intimidation was necessary to create the conditions for the eventual breakout and a significant network of support was essential to make sure that the fugitives could evade the police system once they were out.

The escape of Phoolan Devi's killers from high security Tihar Jail and other similar escapes of prisoners highlight the ineptitude and complicity of jail staff. Tihar Jail is actually a complex of seven prisons, having a capacity of 4,000 prisoners. But actually there are more than 12,000 prisoners lodged there. Regrettably, there is no fixed rule as to how many prisoners can be lodged in a particular jail.

The following is the existing jail system. There are two categories of jails - district jails normally built for 400 prisoners each and central jails for 750 each. The jail staff members are not from the police and have their own distinct hierarchy. There are different categories of under-trial prisoners depending upon their education and social status. Courts have directed jails to do away with the colonial, vintage classification of under-trial prisoners into Class I, II and III, based on their socio-economic status, but Government continues to stick to the old practice.

Selected prisoners are used for the internal management of jails - to make up for manpower shortage - as well as administrative work. The convict- supervisors become a link between the prisoners and jail officials. They are given an incentive for their work. Any wrong placement or selection can lead to the escape of prisoners or other crimes going unchecked inside the jails.

The Indira Gandhi Government had set up a high-powered panel in 1980 to propose prison reforms. The apparent cause was Mrs Gandhi's first-hand experience of the conditions in Tihar where she was lodged in 1978. Mrs Gandhi appointed the Justice AN Mulla Committee to review the national jail system even though jail is a State Government subject.

The Mulla Committee, 1983, recommended that the Constitution be amended to shift the subject of prisons from the State List to the Concurrent List. That never happened. The Centre at present has no say in the matter of jails except when they are in Union Territories where, again, jails are far from being models. The result is that jails continue to be governed by an outdated law enacted by the British in 1894. The position is that the jail conditions vary greatly from one State to another or even from prison to prison. There is no national policy on prisons.

A sensible recommendation of the Mulla Committee was to classify prisons into special security, maximum, medium and minimum security prisons. Such a classification can serve as a safeguard against jailbreaks and jail riots.

Much before sting operations became a norm with the media, a hard-hitting report had shown that in the Tihar Jail, officials mixed with notorious inmates like Charles Sobraj who ran an extensive drug and liquor racket with impunity. This led to a secret visit of the then Home Minister Giani Zail Singh to Tihar Jail. He was stunned to see a drunken prisoner offering him a bottle of liquor. A mortified Government finally suspended two jail officials.

Criminalisation of politics has produced a strange phenomenon. Criminals have contested elections from behind the bars and some of them have won. Given such topsy-turvy world of politics, prison officials are often either unmindful of the crimes being committed regularly inside the prisons, or sometimes they are the ones to provide prisoners with mobile phones, drugs and food. These jail staffers also organise kavi sammelans and mushairas and help prisoners run extortion rackets and criminal gangs from inside the jails. A prison for some prisoners has become a home away from home.

The next issue is that of under-trials. According to the statistics compiled by the Custodial Justice Cell of the National Human Rights Commission, 225,817 of 304,893 or 74.06 per cent of the total prison population in the country comprises those awaiting trial. The total jail capacity in India is 232,412 prisoners, which makes the total prison population 31 per cent higher than capacity, clearly emphasising the urgent need for a speedier justice mechanism.

Only when politicians go to jail do they talk about reforming the jail system. They forget the issue the moment they are out. We must be clear as to what kind of confinement or jail system we want. The time to make a beginning is now before things get worse. There must be a Central law to be followed as a model by all States.

10

Bureaucracy: Demagogues at Second Line

1. The Red-tape Tangle

Any riot, or an act of corruption, or a complaint about the same, is a sure sign of misgovernance. The riots in Gujarat in 2001 which left at least 700 people dead and over 90,000 displaced, or the violence in Maharashtra, or the fake stamp scam which has affected 22 states, are a manifestation of not only the breakdown of the system, but also the extent to which the rot has affected the polity. It also shows how some citizens, including politicians and criminals, have been treated as more than equal.

In a welfare state, the Government becomes the favourite whipping boy and is blamed almost for everything which goes wrong, whether due to natural causes or human failure. The functioning of any organisation or Government depends on its priorities and the persons heading it. In fact, all grievances are against the government of the day, whether it is the killing of over 100 civilians in Assam in November and December 2000, or the attacks on Biharis living in Assam in November, 2003. First of all, this is an assessment of the Government of the day, which can always be doctored.

In the police, there are numerous complaints of burking of cases, so that a rosy picture of the area or of the officers working there can be presented. The same is equally applicable to any economic picture. It has been claimed that the growth rate of India is six per cent. The acid test is, what is the situation on the ground? By the same standards, Pakistan has claimed a growth rate of 18 per cent and China 16 per cent. The following figures, as per a UNDP report, reveal a telling tale. The population living below $ 1 a day in India is 34.7 per cent as compared to 13.4 per cent in Pakistan and 16.1 per cent in China. In India, 24 per cent of the people are undernourished as compared to 19 per cent in Pakistan and nine per cent in China. The percentage of female literacy per 100 literate males is 82 per cent in India, 60 per cent in Pakistan and 98 per cent in China.

The present is an era of numerically delicate coalitions. Some partners have been rather mercurial and have threatened to walk out on the filmiest of grounds. The expected election in 2004 is also likely to throw up a coalition Government at the Centre. The strong regional parties in states like Tamil Nadu, Andhra Pradesh, Bihar, Maharashtra, Punjab, Uttar Pradesh and Jammu & Kashmir, would not cede majority of seats in favour of the national parties. They know that if they do, they would lose their clout at the Centre. It is immaterial which party or parties win, as the real winner is the bureaucracy, unless there is a strong Chief Minister or Prime Minister, who can effectively monitor what is happening in the state or the country.

The Government, or to be precise, the bureaucracy, adopts a circuitous mode of functioning so that those desirous of doing anything lose their steam. Babudom costs 84 per cent of Rs. 2,50,000 crore of government spending. In 2002, the bill for salaries, perks and allowances of Union Govern-ment employees totalled Rs 38,659 crore or nearly $ 9 billion, almost equal to the cost of the oil imports in that year.

High salaries and better pay cheques alone will not make the bureaucracy honest. Officials need to be made accountable by ending the system of automatic promotions and unlimited discretionary powers.

The Government of India has around 150 departments and 180 secretary-level officers even for subjects which fall within the purview of the State governments according to the distribution of powers in our Constitution. At least 100 unwanted departments and hundreds of unwanted super bureaucrats, are superfluous.

During one of my stints in the Government, a Joint Secretary working under me complained of not having even half-an-hour of work. When I mentioned this to the then Home Minister, he said jocularly that at least some bureaucrats are not complaining about being terribly overworked! He skirted the issue. Even after serious bank and stock scams, not a single senior officer has been punished or has been sent to jail. In terms of integrity, India was the 83rd most corrupt country in the world according to the corruption perception index prepared by Transparency International, the world's unofficial anti-graft watchdog.

In reality, the rules of business are framed in such a way that quite often, ministers get to know what is happening in the country only when newspapers highlight something which is obviously wrong and glaring. A parliamentary committee noted a staggering Rs. 43,401 crore cost overrun of 461 central projects. "We are distressed to note that the cost of these projects with respect to originally approved cost, had increased from Rs. 1,21,345 crore to Rs. 1,64,746 crore, a 33.6 per cent increase. The committee members are confident that if the projects are monitored with seriousness both time and cost overruns can be drastically brought down," the committee noted. The top five of the 43 Central PSU5 consistently running into losses during 1991-2001 were Hindustan Fertiliser Corporation, Fertiliser Corporation of India, Rashtriya Ispat Nigam, Indian Iron and Steel Company and Indian Drugs and Pharmaceuticals Limited.

These five PSUs recorded accumulated losses of Rs. 6,132.69 crore, Rs. 5,467.56 crore, Rs. 4,429.26 crore, Rs. 1,575.87 crore and Rs. 1,414.50 crore, respectively, over the last 10 years. It has also been observed that the top five loss-making units accounted for 76.12 per cent of the total loss incurred by the 43 PSU5 over the decade. The cumulative losses of these 43 central PSU5 stood at Rs 34,261 crore on March 31, 2001.

It would not be out of context to remind India's governing elite of what Jaya Prakash Narayan once said: "I know politics is not for saints. I am no saint myself, presuming to preach a sermon to other. But politics, at least under a democracy, must know the limits which it may not cross."

In an astonishing disclosure, the Union Finance Minister told the Lok Sabha in December 2003 that he ordered the dismissal of a senior Finance Ministry official for his suspected links with scamster Abdul Karim Telgi, but his order remained unimplemented because of the bureaucratic tangle. "I feel frustrated that my order for dismissal (of this official) has got so bureaucratically entangled that I have not been able to achieve his dismissal", he said, adding in anguish, that his order for "dismissal requires approval of a committee of secretaries." The so-called Committee of Secretaries has not accepted the advice so far.

Even in the latest Pravasi Divas, the major demand was to cut down the bureaucratic tangle. Good governance cannot be ensured by an unresponsive and literally unaccountable and overprotected bureaucracy. It is time job retention was linked to performance and not simply because one has joined Government service. Otherwise, good governance will remain a distant dream.

Controlling the bureaucracy and assessing its performance for fulfilling the targets should be the top priority of the Government, both now and after the elections. The Government-whether at the Centre or in the states-must make it clear that it is earnest and will not equivocate or compromise on good governance.

1.1. Trouble with Bureaucracy

Every Government wants to change the administration for the better. It is a noble ambition, but most of them flounder as the initial enthusiasm gets overtaken by the day's pressing problems. It is more so since the compulsion of coalition and the desire to keep the partners happy takes precedence over every other necessity, however pressing it may be.

Mr Manmohan Singh's Government is contemplating a number of initiatives aimed at re-inventing the administrative system in the country. The latest is to begin the process of civil service recruitment right after a student passes Class XII tests, on the pattern of National Defence Academy examination.

The idea is that successful candidates would join the "National Academy" for a five-year course. It is suggested that two committees, under the chairmanship of the Cabinet Secretary, will study the recommendations of the two earlier committees-the Surendranath Committee and the PC Hota Committee-to suggest systemic changes in the administration, as well as consider ways to improve probity, efficiency and transparency in the Central and State governments. Having said this, should one really believe that the present Government does not know why has the administration has deteriorated and why corruption, dishonesty and inefficiency are dogging the country at every step?

The rot began when one former Prime Minister said what the nation needed was a "committed" bureaucracy. For, the bureaucracy took it as a call for "personal commitment" to a leader. Almost all bureaucrats are naturally bothered about their advancement, and every thing else becomes secondary. So, from 1970s onwards, they have vied with each other for being more loyal than the king. Those who have showed resistance, or have refused to fall in line, were left to sulk in insignificant postings.

The politician, once having tasted blood, cried for more. A commission set up by a previous Government observed that when bureaucrats were asked to bend, they crawled. A former Lok Sabha MP, who was shot dead in July 2001, only represented the larger issue of criminalisation of the Indian polity. Many criminals like her have joined politics and one MLA from Gujarat was sentenced to life imprisonment for murder in August 2004. Such elements have been encouraged by political parties for their "winnability". The situation has become so bad that some charge-sheeted individuals have found berths both in State and Central governments.

Another question which the political class has seldom asked itself is how someone born in poverty, including former chief ministers or central ministers have accumulated property worth tens of crores of rupees in brief political careers. Whatever is said about the bureaucracy, it is a fact that both criminalisation of politics and politicisation of the State has become much worse in the past few decades. From a mere trickle of complaints about a few criminals entering the legislature in each State, 40 sitting members of the Lok Sabha and around 700 of the 4,072 members in the various State Assemblies had a criminal record in 1997 according to an Election Com-mission study. Even in the 14th Lok Sabha, more than 100 MPs are involved in criminal cases.

The bureaucracy is a tool to implement the policies of the Government. It is not the master. It is just like a horse, which is to be guided by the rider. In the present case, the political masters are the riders. The horse will go in the direction it is spurred on, by the rider. According to rules bureaucracy is debarred from criticising the Government. It has been specifically debarred from approaching the press. So whatever be the doings or misdoings of the political masters, the same remain buried in "classified" Government files. In his first letter to all chief ministers, the Prime Minister, in July 2004, minced no words.

He pointed out that the failure of the Government to tackle the menace of "transfer and posting industry" will have a "debilitating impact not only on their performance and morale but also on the whole process of governance". This is the right stand, but contrary to the most famous speech of then president of the All Indian Congress Committee, Jagjivan Ram, in 1969, in which he argued that "the so-called neutral administrative machinery is a hindrance, not a help" and that the philosophy of a neutral administration was "hardly relevant to Indian conditions". His remarks were replicated by other senior Congress leaders of the time, including then Prime Minister Indira Gandhi.

According to media reports, Uttar Pradesh Chief Minister Mulayam Singh Yadav, within 40 days of taking charge, ordered transfer of over 650 administrative and police officers, much less than the 1,000 mark in transfers established by his immediate predecessor in ffice, Ms Mayawati. But it will be unfair to single out Ms Mayawati or Mr Mulayam Singh.

Similar zeal was displayed by their predecessors in UP as well as in the rest of the States. Mass transfers all over the country take place with such regularity that they have ceased to raise eyebrows. Such postings have reduced administration and good governance to an exercise of placing favourites in strategic positions, who not only bend themselves, but also the rules and laws to please their political masters.

In 1947, Sardar Patel had said in the Constituent Assembly: "You will not have a united India if you have not got a good all-India service which has the independence to speak out its mind and which has a sense of security." "As a man of experience I tell you," warned Sardar Patel, "do not quarrel with the instruments with which you want to work. It is a bad workman who quarrels with his instruments..." I doubt whether teenagers selected after their Class XII exams will have the necessary maturity and will prove better material than what is available now. In fact, being trainees without any security, they will turn out to be only "yes men", arguably better yes-men than the contemporary breed of civil servants.

It is impossible for the Chief Minister (or any Central Minister) who orders such mass transfers to possess direct knowledge of the work and worth of most of the transferred officers. It is also impractical on the part of a Chief Minister to asceratin personally the quality of work or the reputation for fairness and honesty of hundreds of transferred civil servants. Such transfers are ordered because an influential MLA or party functionary wants a particular officer in or out for his own reasons.

This pernicious practice forces many officers to seek political patronage to stay where they are, or to get posts or places which they wish to have. This, in turn, leads to the notorious politician-civil servant nexus, which is the main cause of corruption and poor governance in public services in our country today and not the method of selection of civil servants.

The problem of mass transfers is not so acute in the Central Government as it is in the States, which have more than 80 per cent of IAS and IPS officers working for them. The Central Government has only three million plus employees, whereas the States put together cross 15 million. The truth is that political masters do not want to be shown the rule book.

They regard anybody who quotes the book as a trouble-maker. Uprightness and integrity requires that the political master must decide as to what kind of governance he wants to give to the country. With the best of men, and the worst of system, almost anything will work or can be achieved. But with the worst of men and the best of system, you can create a mess anywhere.

Setting up committees and commission will not help in improving the system of governance. What is required is fewer rules, lesser inspector raj, greater transparency and a quicker judiciary. We honestly do not require committees or commissions to do that, unless the intention is to give sinecures to retired politicians and loyal former bureaucrats.

1.2. Professional Longevity: A Curse, a Crime

The bureaucracy has been the biggest beneficiary of increased professional longevity. It managed to sell an idea to the Central and some State Governments that increasing the retirement age from 58 to 60 would lead to huge savings. The reason? Experienced staff would be available to deliver the goods. So, across the board and whether a person was physically or medically unfit, the Government made 60 the new age of superannuation. Obviously, nobody realised it would be impossible for a lineman at age 60 to climb a pole to repair phone lines or an electric fault, or for officials in other categories to do their job with full mental and physical agility.

Due to poor health, most officials can hardly function actively after the age of 58. Even dishonest and inefficient employees gained from the enhanced retirement age, since there was no rider for scrutiny of records to disqualify them. The result: Another bonanza for the corrupt to make hay while the sun shone for another two years. The bureaucracy is in any case never satisfied with what it has. It keeps asking for more whether the country can afford it or not.

Government employees in Tamil Nadu, already the best paid and most privileged, went on strike in July. They wanted more goodies and perks. They paralysed Government functioning, without caring a fig about whether the public was inconvenienced. The Supreme Court, in continuation of an earlier ruling of 'no work, no pay', held that Government employees had no fundamental right to strike.

At present, automatic promotions and security of service-whether employees perform or not, whether they are active or deadwood-are the hallmark of much of the bureaucracy. The present system does not match qualifications of competence and work experience to assignments. For the last four years, the Prime Minister has been eloquently talking about downsizing the Government. It does not need an insider to reveal the huge surplus staff that is supported by the taxpayer. But, despite promises and exhortations, very little has been achieved.

The Government, waking up to the need to weed out the deadwood, should therefore call for cautious optimism. Indian Railways is introducing a voluntary retirement scheme so that 20,000 old engine drivers could retire. This was prompted by a spate of train accidents. If the past is any indicator, the plan will be a non-starter. In parliamentary session this year, the Government had replied to a question by saying that, out of a total employment of 3.3 million, only 23 had opted for VRS.

The Expenditure Reforms Commission, which looked into the working of 36 Ministries/departments, had arrived at the conclusion there was surplus manpower of 42,200 in a total sanctioned staff of 865,000. That is, nearly five per cent of employees is redundant, and their exit can have no adverse impact on Government functioning. Nothing has been done to get rid of even idle hands. Bureaucrats have had the best of both the worlds, irrespective of the party in power.

In fact, senior ex-bureaucrats never retire. They angle regulatory or other post-retirement jobs. It is amazing how Governments after Government recycles retired bureaucrats to jobs in commissions or committees, irrespective of their track records. This is not to say that some of the old hands appointed are not talented, or that it is not for the political executive to take a decision in this matter.

Sometime ago, a former Commerce Secretary and a Company Affairs Secretary were appointed as Chairman and member respectively of the proposed Competition Commission of India. Such appointments are bound to reinforce unease in trade and industry, fuelling suspicion that the Government does not want to part with bureaucratic control over economic activity, liberalisation and globalisation notwithstanding. Almost all regulatory jobs -whether the Central Election Commission, State Election Commissions, Central Finance Commission, State Finance Commissions, banks, Insurance Regulatory and Development Authority, the Central Electricity Regulatory Commission, the Telecom Regulatory Authority of India, the Securities and Exchange Board of India, the Central Vigilance Commission or the Union Public Service Commission-are cornered by retired bureaucrats.

Post-retirement jobs mean another two to five years of extension in service. Even postings such as India's Executive

Directors with the World Bank and the International Monetary Fund have been taken up by retired bureaucrats with or without economic specialisation.

With bureaucrats heading almost all regulatory authorities in the country, they consciously or unconsciously bring in the 'bureaucratic mindset' that a liberalised economy is expected to discard. This can negate the benefits of having an independent regulator, whose objective is to ensure a level-playing field between private players and the Govern-ment if it is also in the same business.

It may be asked why those governing the country cannot seem to find talent anywhere else except in retired bureaucrats. In the US and elsewhere, economists, lawyers, bankers and financial experts shift freely between the academia, business, various thinktanks and the bureaucracy. Professional experts fill about 2,000 top bureaucratic posts in America. The President can fill up those posts by nomination. He is free to bring specialists directly into the Cabinet. There have been instances where top economists or professors have been appointed as Treasury Secretary (finance minister).

If India has to keep pace with the 21st century, it has to break with tradition. It must revamp the bureaucratic set-up given to us by the British. We should have a system in which the bureaucracy looks after the people rather than itself. The Government should immediately consider rolling back the retirement age to 58, so that a younger and more enterprising lot can fill the slots. Rules still provide for taking outsiders into Government service, either at the level of Joint or Additional Secretary. Induction of outsiders, on an extremely limited scale, has been a success. Montek Singh Ahluwalia, who joined as Joint Secretary dealing with the economic affairs and later on became Finance Secretary. He rose to greater heights even in the international financial sector as the IMF evaluator. The same is true of Dr Vijay Kelkar, who also joined as Joint Secretary and has won laurels as a distinguished economist both nationally and internationally. Of course, both were regarded as intruders by the established bureaucracy.

The present bureaucracy which surrounds the political executive has successfully brainwashed it into almost banning the entry of the outsiders in the Government. The result is the mess the country is in, with its bureaucracy warring with the political executive. Amateurs and small-timers, with the mentality of municipal politicos, occupying posts whose importance they do not understand, are no match for a wily bureaucrat. The latter has an attitude of self-righteousness in defending the indefensible, be it corruption or inefficiency. The conduct of our mandarins can only lead to cynicism on the part of the people, who know the truth and are concerned about the future of the nation.

The truth is, there is no systemic counter to redress the grievances of the people, when their complaints are against bureaucracy. There is no threat to the latter of competition from outside, as you cannot appoint someone not part of the bureaucracy basket so as to replace the inefficient and the incompetent. Nor is there fear of dismissal from within.

It is time the Government did a reality check. Without performance and competence as criteria, the deadwood in the bureaucracy will be a drag. Deadwood is best used for the purpose it serves best-firewood. If the Government does not go in for a ruthless spring-cleaning, it will have a liability on its hands rather than an asset. It is, in fact, not an exaggeration to say that, with friends like self-serving bureaucrats, the Government does not need enemies in the Opposition.

1.3. Bureaucracy Needs a Mending

Everybody wants a Government job in our country so that he or she could become a part of governance. For governance, departments are required so that specific Government functions can be performed. In some countries, officials are elected up to some levels, like in the US, along with the non-elected officials. But in India, only the political executives are the members of legislatures.

Max Weber, a proponent of bureaucracy, argued that working to the rules in a hierarchical offices in which appointment and promotion went by merit was more rational than making appointments on other bases such as patronage, favouritism and recommendations.

Noble ideas indeed, but they have been turned upside down. Bureaucrats are more powerful than everybody else. Powers once assumed are never relinquished. So jobs or bureaucracies once created never die even after their need is over.

With the politicians busy running fragile coalitions and more keen to stick to power at any cost, the bureaucracy, including its retired personnel, had never had it so good in India. Despite the claims that the Government service is not attracting the best talent, only eight officers from the IAS have quit in the last four years, that also after earning their pension for life. More than half a million try every year to enter this elite service.

A little known and scarcely used rule in the past is now extensively used to enable officials to have their cake and eat it too. Under Article 312, Rajya Sabha has the power to create an All India Service (AIS) like the IAS, IPS and Indian Forest Service. In its 93rd report, a House Committee on Subordinate Legislation noted that IAS officers should be sent to non-Government bodies only in "exceptional circumstances" for reasons to be "recorded in writing". The department of personnel and training (DoPT), which controls the IAS, notified this in July 1993.

This rule is in Section 6(2) of the IAS (Cadre) Rules 1954, which allows officers to take up non-Government assignments. A parliamentary committee had observed that the Section was to be used sparingly. It was meant to give officers the needed experience to make their contributions to Government more useful. This rule is being used by the officials with clout to enjoy the best of the two worlds - being in service while taking up lucrative assignments with up to hundred times their pay in the Government in the private sector, NGOs, and international organisations.

Approximately 115 members of the 5,000 plus IAS cadre are hanging on to non-Government assignments. At last count, 64 IAS officers were working with private firms or NGOs while 51 were on foreign assignments including those with India offices of international organisations. At the same time, the Government claims that there is a shortfall in the IAS and it needs more officers. So it has decided to enhance recruitment - 110, 120 and 130 IAS officers will be recruited respectively in 2008, 2009 and 2010.

If a private firm is paying you an average of five or six lakhs per month - in some cases, it's Rs. 20,00,000 per month - as against the highest Government salary of Rs. 26,000 per month plus other allowances, you would be beholden to it. You would naturally safeguard or even promote its interest when you are back in Government. When such people reach the level of policy making, it's human to slant policies to favour the organisations which have been extremely generous to you.

The present Government believes that it has salvaged its conscience after it has set up a committee. A joke doing the rounds in Delhi is that there is no favourite left to appoint in any more committees. Everyone who needs to be given some perks is a member of some committee or the other. The bureaucrats and politicians on such committees are has-beens or wannabes and those on the fringes in Delhi. Age or experience has no relevance to their appointments to any office or committee.

The following Committees have been set up since 2001 to improve the administration: In 2001, Alagh Committee recommended reforms in the recruitment procedures. In 2003, BN Yugandhar Committee was instituted for in-service training programmes of IAS officers. In 2003 again, Surinder Nath Committee worked on the system of performance appraisal promotion empanelment and placement for All India services and higher civil services of Union Government. In 2004, PC Hota Committee delved into civil service reforms. In 2007, R Vaidyanatha Ayyar Committee worked on revamping the curriculum for induction training of the Indian Administrative Service.

As per an NGO, the cost of governance of India by 800 odd politicians at the Centre, the 6,000 in the 30 States and the 197 million employees of the Central and State Governments cost the country about Rs. 1800 crore per day or Rs. 650,000 crore per year. About 1.87 per cent of Indians (mis)govern 1,020 million people! This comes to about $ 138 billion or nearly 30 per cent of India's GDP. The figure must be at least 20 per cent more now with periodical almost automatically enhanced Dearness Allowance.

The real problem is that of quid pro quo between politicians and bureaucrats, which continues even after the latter's retirement. It is mainly for this reason that the delivery system, whether it be in the NREG Scheme, Sarva Shiksha Abhiyan or poverty alleviation schemes, has failed abysmally.

The rot started when a late Prime Minister said that the country needed a committed bureaucracy. Bureaucracy took it as a call for personal commitment to a leader. So from the 1970s, they have been vying with each other for being more loyal than the king. Those who showed resistance were left to sulk in insignificant postings. To fall in line with political diktats, manipulation and cultivating the powers-that-be becomes the rule rather than the exception.

Despite worthy candidates joining the civil services, the country remains awfully corrupt and poor. The Central Government finds itself too weak to enforce its will as its very survival depends on the sweet will of its allies in power in different States.

Training, retraining and bringing about reform in the curricula or tinkering with the recruitment of the higher civil service is no substitute for reforming governmental mindset. The recommendations are prescriptive in nature like the Brahminical dos and don'ts. Favouritism has become an important factor in the governance of our country. Pressure is always built for the appointment of obliging bureaucrats and friends of friends.

Government should remember that bad administration can destroy good policy; but good administration can never save a bad policy.

11

Travesty of Justice

1. The deity defiled

1.1. Veto of the Influential

On the intervening night of January 9 and 10, 1999, Sanjeev Nanda, scion of a rich family, allegedly mowed down six people, including three policemen, in Delhi, while he and two of his friends were returning from a party around 3:45 am. Though more than eight years have passed since then, the case is nowhere near conclusion, as one witness after another has turned hostile.

The case took a new turn recently with a sting operation conducted by a 24x7 news channel. The exposé culminated with witness Sunil Kulkarni meeting a person allegedly offering to cut a deal with the family of the accused for Rs. 2 crore. The testimony of Kulkarni is crucial, he being the only witness who stands by his testimony that a black BMW, and not a truck, with the accused as one of its occupants, was the vehicle that ran over the victims.

The Delhi High Court observed on May 31, taking suo motu cognisance of the case: "What is caught (on camera) is very bad and a cause of concern for the criminal justice system in the country... It is in the fitness of things and interest of the justice system that the facts be brought to light at the earliest."

The Delhi Police has dropped the counsel working as the public prosecutor in this high-profile case for his alleged collusion with the defence. However, both the lawyers in question have denied any collusion between them. The defence lawyer has gone a step further, threatening to sue the television channel for defamation, demanding Rs. 50 crore as damages.

The problem is not new. The Supreme Court had on January 10, 2005 ordered an inquiry committee to investigate the Zahira Sheikh/ Best Bakery case. The committee in its report called Zahira Sheikh a "self-condemned liar". On this, the apex court observed, "This is a classic example of a case where evidences were tampered with and witnesses won over... We find people have started feeling that criminal trials are like cobwebs where small flies get caught and big people dash through."

It is not that the Government does not know what is wrong and how it can be rectified. The Law Commission, in its 177th report, had noted: "Where the accused happens to be rich and/or influential persons or members of mafia gangs, the witnesses very often turn hostile either because of the inducements offered to them or because of the threats given to them."

The public outrage over the failure of the criminal justice system in some high profile cases, as reported in the media, has failed to improve the work ethic in the system. The Government has failed to revamp the whole process. The Government feels that in due course of time, the uproar in media will be forgotten.

The laws that Government enacts to punish criminals are hedged between ifs and buts. The result is that there are few laws capable of delivering punishment to the guilty. The laws of the land are the people's greatest grievance. They are expensive and dilatory.

The latest television sting operation has highlighted what was already common knowledge. As is usual, in this case too, the players have followed the American saying: "In God we trust, all others must pay cash."

Knowing something is different from procuring hard evidence for proving the same in a court of law. What has been exposed is only the tip of the proverbial iceberg. Media reports what happens in Delhi or any State capital, but incidents of corruption in other parts of the country go unnoticed. As improvement in the criminal justice system would not fetch any votes, this vital aspect of governance is put on the backburner.

The Uttar Pradesh Police Commission (1970-71) had noted that the performance of the prosecuting machinery was far from satisfactory. Then Chief Justice of Allahabad High Court SK Verma had deposed before the Commission, saying, "At every level, the prosecution of the State cases is of poor quality and that is generally responsible for the large number of acquittals."

Another witness, a former Advocate-General of the State told the Commission: "At most of the places today, the District Government counsel and the Assistant District Government counsel are unsatisfactory... Generally, the prosecution of serious cases at the level of Magistrate and (in) the Sessions Courts is unsatisfactory... Recommendations made by the District Judge and the District Magistrate... are based on political influences... There have been cases in which a Minister appointed a person as the District Government counsel who had no pending case in court either on civil or criminal or revenue side at the time of his appointment... Both at the High Court and at the Sessions Court, there exists system of panel of lawyers who attend to the overflow of work, which the Government counsels cannot attend to personally. We have received innumerable complaints about the working of the panels of the Sessions and High Courts both from the judges and the Bar. Generally brief-less lawyers are put on panels and failure of many Government cases are due to their inefficiency" (UP Police Commission Report 1970-71).

What I have quoted are observations made over 36 years ago. But if I had not mentioned the years, it would have looked as if I were talking about present times.

Another matter of concern is the Transparency International Global Corruption Report 2007, which deals with graft in 32 countries. The report claims that Indians paid Rs 2,630 crore in bribe to lower judicial officers in 2006. It also mentions the huge backlog of cases, which compels people to seek redressal outside the formal legal system. The report also talks of the poor judge-to-population ratio of 12 to 13 judges per million people, which is at the root of the huge pendency of cases.

It is to be noted in this context that the Law Commission had recommended a ratio of 50 judges per million people in 1988. The problem of a huge pendency, a late justice delivery, witnesses turning hostile, bribery and collusion between the defence and prosecution are interlinked and make justice prohibitively expensive.

We have listened to a lot of homilies on the need of improving the justice delivery system from almost every Prime Minister and other Government functionaries, but seen little action. As Buddha said, "All know the way; few actually walk it."

1.2. Politics of Clemency

Broadly speaking, all crime is against the state because it disturbs public order and tranquillity. It is not so only in India, where the criminal justice system is patterned after Anglo-Saxon law. Most countries, including the US, have adopted the system of public prosecution undertaken by a Government prosecuting attorney.

In India, any crime - from pick-pocketing to murder - is regarded as having been committed against the state. The unfortunate and deplorable consequence is that the victim's version is only treated as evidence against the accused. He is, at best, considered a witness to the crime committed against him. He is not even accepted, or acknowledged, as a party to the case. As the laws stand, the victim has little or no involvement in the process of bringing a wrongdoer to justice. A number of committees, including that of Justice Malimath, have urged that the victim's rights must be acknowledged. However, unlike the US, here we have no basic rights of the victims of crime and no state protection is extended to them.

The selective grant of pardon to many convicted criminals in several States like Haryana, Punjab, Andhra Pradesh, etc, has put a question mark on the political motive of the powers-that-be. Most pardons are based on political considerations.

A pardon is defined as forgiveness granted by a sovereign power for a crime and the penalty associated with it. Unfortunately, quite a few criminals who have been granted pardon for ghastly crimes include relatives of former Ministers, workers of political parties and other influential people.

Every country has a provision for pardon. In the US, the power of granting pardon in federal crimes is vested in the President by the American Constitution. Section 2 of Article II states that the President "shall have power to grant reprieves and pardons for offences against the United States, except in cases of impeachment".

Some people argue that pardons have been used more often for the sake of political expediency than to correct judicial error. One of the most famous pardons was granted by then President Gerald Ford to former President Richard Nixon on September 8, 1974, for the Watergate scandal. Polls showed a majority of Americans disapproved of it and Ford's public approval ratings plummeted subsequently. He was narrowly defeated in the presidential campaign, two years later. As President, Mr Bill Clinton pardoned 140 people, on his last day in office, including millionaire fugitive Marc Rich and his brother.

In Canada, pardons are decided by the National Parole Board under the Criminal Records Act, the Criminal Code and several other laws, after making suitable recommendations, and clemency is granted by the Governor-General of Canada or the Governor-in-Council. In England, the power to pardon is a royal prerogative - it depends on the monarch's mercy. In France, the President has the power to pardon and is the sole judge of the propriety of the decision. The right to grant clemency in Germany lies with the President.

In Italy, the President of the Republic can pardon or commute their punishment. Under the Constitution of Ireland, the President of Ireland can pardon convicted criminals. But the President cannot pardon people without the Government's consent; to do so would spark a constitutional crisis that may lead to the impeachment of the President.

The President of the Russian Federation has been vested with the right to pardon by Article 89 of the Constitution. The Pardon Committee manages the list of people eligible for pardon and directs them to the President for signing. While former President Boris Yeltsin frequently used the institution of pardon, his successor Vladimir Putin is much more discreet. He has not used this power yet.

So, it is seen that most countries have vested the power of pardon in their respective heads of state and that it has been mostly used to pander to sectional, personal or political interests.

A terrorist who masterminded the attack on Parliament on December 13, 2001, has garnered political supporters who only care for their vote-banks. This was quite aptly manifested when former Chief Minister of Jammu & Kashmir Farooq Abdullah threatened that if Mohammed Afzal Guru is hanged, it will endanger the life of the judge who delivered the verdict. He has the cheek to say that the death sentence is too extreme and the temerity to demand clemency for the terrorist. This is, to say the least, an indirect threat to the judiciary to abstain from punishing terrorists. Mercifully, such politicians have no absolute power to play politics of appeasement.

The advocates of mercy fail to understand that if Mohammed Afzal Guru is not hanged, terrorism will not end. Moreover, he is not the only person sentenced to death; there are 333 convicts awaiting execution, according to the recently released Prison Statistics of India, 2003. Fifty-six people have been given the death sentence in nine months, of whom only three are terrorists.

The Supreme Court, in its October 2006 judgement, has clarified the compelling grounds citing which the judiciary can be moved, challenging a decision of the President or a Governor to pardon a convict, reduce his prison term or even reject his mercy plea. It has ruled out grounds like religion, caste and political loyalty while the President or a Governor exercises his or her power to grant clemency to a convict. At the same time, it has laid down guidelines for questioning the rationale behind the decision to pardon a condemned prisoner or remit his or her prison term.

The apex court has clarified that it is a well-settled legal principle that the Supreme Court and High Courts have a limited judicial scrutiny of exercise of clemency powers. And a convict can also question the rejection of his mercy plea. Exercise or non-exercise of the power to pardon a convict is not immune to judicial review, the bench has said. Thus, while the grant of relief to terrorists may be questioned before the Supreme Court, in turn, the accused and his well-wishers, too, may question the rejection of the mercy petition moved by him or his relatives.

The Supreme Court has observed: "The position, therefore, is undeniable that judicial review of the order of the President or the Governor under Article 72 or Article 161, as the case may be, is available." Their orders can be challenged on the following grounds: That the order has been passed without application of mind; that the order is mala fide; that the order has been passed on extraneous or wholly irrelevant considerations; that relevant materials have been kept out of consideration; that the order suffers from arbitrariness.

"Let the law take its own course", is a cliché. But it is apt in the Mohammed Afzal Guru case. If the Government were to falter now, it would owe an explanation to the judiciary and the nation.

1.3. Fractured Will for Justice

A court in El Dorado, Argentina, has rejected the CBI's request to extradite Ottavio Quattrocchi, the Italian businessman and last principal accused of receiving payoffs in the Bofors deal. This is the second such rejection. Earlier, a Malaysian court rejected a similar request in 2003. However, the CBI says that it will study Friday's verdict for a possible appeal to the Argentine Supreme Court.

The correct legal position is that the CBI plays only a marginal role in taking a decision in this kind of cases. The final decision is taken by the Union Law Ministry in all cases wherein an appeal is to be filed either in a High court or the Supreme Court in India. It is the same with cases filed abroad for which all sanctions are to be accorded by the Law Ministry.

Confidential records, obtained and published by a newspaper, show that long before he was detained in Argentina on February 6, Quattrocchi had already been given a clean chit by the senior-most law officers - from the Attorney-General to the Law Secretary, from the CBI's Director of Prosecution to the Additional Solicitor-General.

It was this clean chit that Quattrocchi's lawyer Alejandro Freeland used in the El Dorado court to his client's advantage - a fact he admitted to the newspaper soon after Judge Hachiro Doi dismissed the agency's request. The CBI has until June 20 to file its appeal; Quattrocchi has been asked not to leave Argentina until June 18.

Freeland has told the newspaper that among the papers he presented to the judge was the opinion of CBI's Director of Prosecution SK Sharma - who was, ironically, present in the El Dorado courtroom - that the entire Bofors investigation had become untenable and that "there was no case".

The newspaper claims that it has a copy of Sharma's confidential opinion, though Freeland has refused to divulge how he got a copy. Freeland also added, "I showed (the judge) Sharma's opinion, as well as the two High Court judgements but the CBI did not even bring the High Court judgement of RS Sodhi with them. They withheld so much information that the judge saw through their game."

If the CBI withheld information, it perhaps had reason to - its record of being over-ruled by law officers at almost every step: From the High Court rulings to the decision to defreeze Rs 21 crore parked in his London accounts, which the agency said was linked to the alleged Bofors payoffs.

Other points quoted from the official records include:

On September 2, 2005, Sharma argued against challenging the High Court (Sodhi) verdict. He noted, "It would really be a travesty of justice and fair play, if accused (the Hindujas) are forced to face trial without any definite time and then at the end of the day - say after 15/20 years - the court passes an order of not guilty."

• He also said he was against the CBI filing its first chargesheet (in 1999): "...we had no case under the Prevention of Corruption Act or for any offence under the Indian Penal Code or at least our case was very weak." Subsequently,

- Law Secretary wrote on July 5, 2004: "The Bofors case was examined in this Department (the Law Ministry) vide notes produced and a view has been taken that it is not a fit case for filing an SLP in the Supreme Court."
- Attorney-General of India wrote on the same day: "I have perused the papers; in particular, the careful summary prepared by ... Law Secretary. I agree with the view of the Law Secretary that this is not a fit case for filing a Special Leave Petition."
- Additional Solicitor-General argued for defreezing of Quattrocchi's UK accounts on October 7, 2005, saying: "The CBI was unable to show that the funds had any link with the offence alleged. It is clear, that even as regards Quattrocchi, on a parity of reasoning, there is no authentic evidence to connect him with the alleged offence and the case against him cannot stand in a court of law."

Another Additional Solicitor-General B Datta, in a reported e-mail to CBI on December 23, 2005 (after his London visit where he asked for the defreezing of Quattrocchi's accounts) wrote: "The conclusion is that there is no likelihood of the case against Quattrocchi ever succeeding and thus he should not be prosecuted any further is founded on the factual position that the CBI does not have in its possession the necessary relevant and admissible evidence as required under the provisions of the Indian Evidence Act."

Another shocking revelation is that law officers deputed by the Government of India to Britain kept the CBI in the dark on defreezing Quattrocchi's London accounts. Datta's e-mail reached 17 days later by when the money had been withdrawn. At the same time, the deputed law official told Crown Prosecution Service (CPS) officials in Britain to allow the defreezing of the accounts.

The CBI separately kept sending repeated reminders to the CPS that the accounts should remain frozen and was pushing diplomatic channels to uncover the money trail from Lugano, Switzerland, to London to connect the Rs. 21 crore with the alleged Bofors kickbacks. The CBI has no authority over the law officers, whose term is co-terminus with the tenure of the Government.

These officers include the Attorney-General, Solicitor-General, and a host of Additional Solicitor-Generals. The Law Ministry assigns them work. The system in the Government is that in any case the CBI takes a final decision after getting all the legal inputs.

There have been cases where legal officers at different levels have tendered conflicting advice and the Director has taken a final decision. But nowhere in the world the legal officer is the final authority. Here it appears that the legal officer became the final authority.

There may be difference of opinion on any issue between two law officers. In a way, this is healthy, provided it is an honest opinion based on facts and not on extraneous conditions or circumstance or considerations. In any event, if things go wrong, the fall guy is the CBI, which normally is made the scapegoat for the failures of others.

Agreed that there may have been two different opinions on the Bofors issue. But how did Quattrocchi's lawyer get hold of the confidential opinions of the Government law officers? Do we then have somebody in our system who smuggled all the papers to him so that Quattrocchi could use them to his advantage? In the entire exercise, the CBI was kept out of the picture except, perhaps as, the fall guy!

Obviously, Quattrocchi has friends in powerful places who have apparently gone out of the way to provide him with file notings. That there are people who, for love or money, can pass original notings to help an accused indicates that the country is facing a grave danger. Beginning with this, it can extend even to the defence of the nation.

Despite all the legal quibbling and hair-splitting by the Law Ministry officials, including CBI's Director of Prosecution, nobody has looked at the agreement entered into by AE Services with Bofors in November 1985 —— that it would secure the contract before March 31, 1986. The contract was signed on March 24, 1986. Nobody has asked why Bofors transferred \$ 7.34 million to Quattrocchi.

Documents showing all this and more were personally brought by me in January 1997 to India from Switzerland. The case against Quattrocchi is still strong as it is based on bank records. He can still be extradited, provided the Government has the will and deputes outstanding lawyers and not Government lawyers whose sole objective may be not to displease anybody in power.

1.4. And Criminal Justice for None

Fourteen persons were burnt to death at Best Bakery, a bread-making unit in Vadodara, in the post-Godhra riots in Gujarat. They were employees and members of the Sheikh family which owned the bakery and lived above it. Zaheera Habibullah Sheikh, the 19-year-old girl who survived the night of March 1, 2003, when a mob attacked Best Bakery, was the main complainant and prosecution witness. She had initially described the attack and named the accused in her statement to the police. But, during the trial, she denied she had named the accused or witnessed the incident. Before her testimony, her elder sister Sahera and brother Nafidullah also denied any knowledge of the incident and were then designated to have turned hostile. Other family members too backtracked, saying they were unable to identify any person in the mob.

Of 120 witnesses, only 73 deposed, of whom 41 did an about-turn on their police testimonies. The judge ruled that, although the details of the incident were known, there was not enough evidence to prove the accused had committed the crime. However, in a reversal of her court testimony, Zaheera said after the judgement had been passed, "What I said in court was not true. I said it after pressure was put on me. In fact, I recognise all those who attacked us that night."

The Indian public, the media and the National Human Rights Commission have been grumbling ever since about the acquittal, saying a dastardly crime has gone unpunished. The NHRC filed a petition for retrial of the case outside Gujarat in the Supreme Court, following which the State Government approached the Gujarat High Court to appeal against the acquittal of the Best Bakery accused.

In its order of August 8, the Supreme Court declined the NHRC's plea for transfer of the case outside Gujarat, on the grounds it could not "undermine our Courts and the High Court of Gujarat". It also asked the State Government to provide adequate protection to victims and witnesses. It had to be ensured, the court observed, that the Gujarat Government's appeal to the High Court did not become a "mere eyewash". The bench directed the State dispensation to report within three weeks "the steps, if any, taken by it for extending protection to ... victims, their families and their relations", and "whether any action has been taken against those who are said to have extended threat or coercion to the witnesses".

It also observed that "criminals often have access to the police and influential persons" and that "trial in most of the sensational cases does not start till the witnesses are won over". Given this, the court stated: "We are prima facie of the opinion that the criminal justice delivery system is not in sound health."

In this context, it wanted to know what steps the Central Government had taken to implement the recommendations of the Malimath Committee report. Justice Malimath had recommended enactment of laws to protect witnesses. The Committee had also suggested that the concept of 'proof beyond reasonable doubt'-the usual getaway route for offenders-be done away with. The only standard would be a court's conviction that proof sufficed, again a Continental concept adapted in Australia with success. Regrettably, the records of punishment in riot cases has been dismal.

To prevent witnesses from turning hostile, the Cabinet recently approved a Bill to amend the Criminal Procedure Code. Under the amended CrPC, the police would be asked to record statements of witnesses in sensitive cases before magistrates.

Witnesses turning hostile afterwards would face charges of perjury, since their earlier testimony would be treated as final.

In the din created over the acquittal of the accused in the Best Bakery case, the basic flaws in the Indian legal system have been lost sight of. The British had once said about the present criminal justice system: "It will be neutralised if all parties act in harmony together for the good of the public service" (Minute 11-4-1851, parliamentary papers 162 of 1853, pages 63 to 95). One of the magistrates mentioned that the police had been "greatly neglected everywhere."

It was said: "The root of the whole evil is useless expenditure in legislation, neither homogenous to the character of the people, nor suited a code of laws, that delights the thieves, rogues, and vakeels. It is a stumbling block and rock of offence to all, and grievous hindrance to the efficient administration of justice. The people may have some confidence in our honesty and desire to do justice but they hold our courts in contempt. Look through the country and see who thrive and make fortunes; but a greater evil ... is the court of Sadar Adalat and their incessant fault finding with the Magistrates and reversal of decisions for defect of form ... and so it will be to the end of the time, as long as the Bombay Judge tries the pursuant robber, and lets him off because his mother's name is said to be Managua instead of Lingo. It may be very good law, but it is very bad justice ... Penal laws loosely enforced are lotteries in which the offenders speculate, and it is remarkable how accurately they calculate their chances of prosecution and escape."

The British had toyed with the idea of changing the criminal justice system. But, of course, their priority was preservation of the British raj, not providing justice to the people. Moreover, there was no separation of powers between judiciary and executive. There was sufficient authority vested with the executive to deal with any serious disturbance or law and order situation. In a flush of enthusiasm, the judiciary was separated from the executive after Independence.

The Indian criminal justice system is based on one principle: Let the nine guilty escape, rather than one innocent be convicted. This has led to the acquittal of all the nine guilty, along with the innocent!

Whenever any sensational case ends in acquittal, there is a hue and cry. Yet in variably, after some time, the matter is forgotten. Nobody has undertaken the task of improving the criminal justice system. Unfortunately, there seems to be no punishment for perjury and no punishment for misguiding the stream of justice.

The present Attorney General, who is the highest legal advisor and officer of the law of the Government, has said: "Criminal justice is on the verge of collapse. Because justice is not dispensed speedily, people have come to believe that there is no such thing as justice in the courts. Justice delayed will not only be justice denied, it will be the rule of the law destroyed. This perception has caused many a potential litigant who has been wronged to settle out of court on terms which are unfair to him, or to secure justice by taking the law into his own hands, or by recourse to a parallel mafia-dominated system of 'justice' that has sprung up in metropolitan centres like Mumbai."

In the 1984 riots, 2,733 innocent Sikhs were killed after Prime Minister Indira Gandhi was assassinated by her Sikh bodyguards on October 31. All the accused have been acquitted, and only a few have been awarded some sort of punishment. In fact, the Best Bakery case and other riots in Gujarat pale into insignificance when compared to the 1984 massacre.

Unless the basic law is changed to enable discovery of truth and punishment of the guilty, the present state of affairs will continue. Bandaid-type remedies will not do. We need to bring about a balance between the rights of society and the rights of crooks and criminals. This would demand that we not go overboard with the abstract concept of rights, which often boil down to letting the crooked escape by hiring expensive advocates who quote the devil's scriptures to prove their case. In other words, "innocence" or other wise becomes a matter of sophistry. It is time for our rulers to overhaul the legal system so that criminals, however high or low they may be, do not escape the punishment they deserve under the law.

1.5. Terrorism vis-à-vis Law

Even the most die-hard democracies like the US, the UK and France have been compelled to enact laws for dealing effectively with the threat of terrorism. Having stringent anti-terrorism laws to protect the integrity of the country is not inconsistent with democratic values.

Dealing with terrorists broadly involves identifying the terrorist organisations, their members, sympathisers, infrastructure, methods of raising funds and channels of command and communication. The next step entails dealing with individuals involved in the terrorist organisations.

Unlike terrorists who are uninhibited by any limitation of working within the confines of the law the counter- terrorists agencies whether police or other security forces, have to act within the parametres of law. It is not within the ambit of security agencies to punish terrorists or their sympathisers.

This lies only within the purview of the judiciary. The present Indian laws were framed in 1863 when there were no crimes like terrorism, hijacking and threat to the security of the State. Assassination of its state functionaries was unheard of.

Terrorists these days are also adept at using information technology. They use improved communication methods like the internet for effective links with followers, fellow terrorists, potential donors and recruits who may be located over a large geographical area. Pakistan has reportedly enlisted over 31,000 Indian spies.

Over 10,000 Pakistanis and other foreigners have infiltrated into India. Over the last decade, 30,0071 civilians and 6077 defence personnel have been killed in the country by different militant groups and more than 3,50,000 rendered homeless. The ordinary laws of the land are hardly adequate to deal with terrorism. Hence the introduction of TADA followed by POTA. And now the Unlawful Activities Ordinance.

In France and the US not only the executive and legislative branches but even the judiciary have recognised the need for special powers and procedures to deal with terrorism. In August 1994, Carlos, a notorious terrorist, was allegedly drugged and kidnapped by the French external intelligence from Khartoum with the help of the Sudanese intelligence. Carlos's contention that this violated his prosecution and trial, was rejected by the judiciary.

In the US, the judiciary had upheld in the 1980s the right of the US counter- terrorist agencies to kidnap an international terrorist for offences against US nationals or the country if, in the assessment of the agency, there was no other way of bringing him to justice.

On the other hand, we in India keep tinkering with the instruments that deal with terrorism and go on debating whether terrorists' rights are being violated. It is a well-known fact that the effort of the terrorist is to leave no track and survive so that he continues to create problems. It is the terrorists who force the Govern-ment to bring anti-terrorist laws. If there were no such problems there would have been no need for such legislations.

The President of India, on September 23, promulgated an ordinance that scrapped POTA. The new law, called the Unlawful Activities (Prevention) Amendment Ordinance, 2004, defines terrorism the same way as POTA. It has dropped Section 4 under which the independent MLA from UP, Raja Bhaiyya, is charged.

Under the amended law, carrying unauthorised arms in a notified area and possession of bombs, RDX, dynamite, biological and chemical weapons is not a terrorist act. The ordinance has done away with POTA special courts and the provision where an accused could not apply for bail for one year. Bail provisions as laid out in the Criminal Procedure Code will apply to those charged under the amended law.

The POTA (Repeal) Ordinance has provided for setting up of one or more review committees to revise all existing cases both at the investigation and trial stages within a year. The amendments to the Unlawful Activities (Prevention) Act also discard the POTA provision of a confession before a police officer admissible in court and shifts the onus of proof on the prosecution besides providing for forfeiture of proceeds of terrorism.

However, it allows any investigating officer (POTA only allowed officers not below the rank of SP) to make an order, with prior approval (in writing) of the DGP of the State concerned to seize or attach a property representing proceeds of terrorism. The ordinance allows evidence collected through interception of wire, electronic or oral communication as admissible evidence against the accused in the court during trial.

However, the POTA safeguards providing for a one-year punishment or fine to a police officer who intentionally intercepts communication or gets any person to do it, have been deleted. There is a POTA like provision on checking funding of organisation. Similarly, terrorist organisations proscribed under POTA remain banned under the amendment ordinance as well. There are no special courts to try suspect terrorists.

Doubtless, the use of POTA against MDMK leader Vaiko may have been a major reason behind its repeal, but the Unlawful Activities (Prevention) Amendment Ordinance very much retains Section 21 of the scrapped law under which he was charged with a rider that the offence should have been committed "with intention to further activity of a terrorist organisation".

Section 21(2) and Section 21(3) of the repealed law have been reproduced verbatim in Section 39(l) (b) and Section 39(l)(c) of the amended Unlawful Activities (Prevention) Act. According to Section 39(l) (b) a person commits the offence relating to support given to a terrorist organisation if he knowingly arranges, manages or assists meetings in support of a terrorist organisation. The Unlawful Activities (Prevention) Amendment Ordinance (2004), also retains the punishment for such an offence, which is imprisonment for a term not exceeding 10 years or fine or both.

However, the BJP, the main Opposition party, feels that the newly promulgated Unlawful Activities (Prevention) Amendment Ordinance that replaces POTA not only shows the Government's political motives but also its "naive" approach towards terrorism. It says, "It is naive of the Government to believe that the fidayeen will honour bail and judiciary." Under the new law, the bail provisions against terrorists would be much less stringent compared to cases involving crimes like smuggling, black-marketing and narcotics. The normal rule that bail is the rule and jail the exception will apply to terrorists as well.

The Unlawful Activities (Prevention) Amendment Ordinance has a clause under which organisations like the Bajrang Dal and VHP could be banned. Extremist groups like the Peoples' War or an outfit like the SIMI, which was banned under POTA can no longer be declared unlawful.

Section 2, sub-clause O&P of the ordinance defines "unlawful activities and association". Sub-clause (11) says, "which has for its object any activity which is punishable under Section 153A or Section

153B of the Indian Penal Code, o~ which encourages or aids persons to undertake any such activity." Section 153A and 153B of the IPC deal with provisions to punish for "promoting enmity between classes in places of worship and promoting enmity between classes".

Nevertheless, we must realise that there is no quick and decisive result to the war against terrorism. We should be determined to engage in a protracted conflict. It is a tough battle because ultimately democracy survives on civil liberties and the rule of law. Unfortunately, such anti-terrorist measures can erode the very basis of democracy.

Moreover, rather than inspiring, the track record of the agencies enforcing laws against terrorism has at times been lackadaisical and partisan. We must gather all we have to fight terrorism. The rule of law must be held at all costs and the rules of the games must be respected by the state.

2. The Breach Favoured

2.1. Outdated Laws, Modern India

Under the Constitution, criminal jurisdiction belongs concurrently to the Union and the States. Our basic law on crime prevention, punishment and evidence is embodied in three principal statutes: The Indian Penal Code, the Code of Criminal Procedure of 1973 and the Indian Evidence Act. These laws take precedence over State legislations. No State can alter or amend them.

The Indian Penal Code came into force in 1862. Based on British criminal law, the code defines basic crimes and punishments, applies to resident foreigners and citizens alike and recognises offences committed abroad by Indian nationals.

It classifies crimes under various categories — crimes against state, armed forces, public order, human body, property; crimes relating to election, religion, marriage, health, safety, decency and morals. Crimes are cognisable or non-cognisable. Six categories of punishment include fines, forfeiture of property, simple imprisonment, rigorous imprisonment with hard labour, life imprisonment and death. The Criminal Procedure Code lays down as to how the cases will be investigated and how their prosecution and trial will be conducted. Though the Code of Criminal Procedure of 1973, which came into force on April 1, 1974, the basic framework given to us by the British has remained unchanged. The Indian Evidence Act lays down as to how and what kind of evidence will be collected to prove any crime.

Law says that a person cannot be compelled to give evidence against himself. In high-profile cases, sometimes it is reported that the accused has confessed his crime before the police. The law has clearly laid down that no confession made before any police officer will be admissible in the court of law. Only confessions made before a magistrate are legally valid.

Time changes, crime profile changes and even the approach of society changes. New circumstances necessitate the change in laws. Recently, the Union Cabinet has approved amendments to the Code of Criminal Procedure (Amendment) Bill, 2006. The changes proposed in the Bill include use of technology like video-conferencing and camera recording during trials; steps to prevent witnesses from turning hostile; and, compensation for victims of crime.

The CrPC has been amended nine times since it was enacted in 1973. The other approved packages include the steps to lessen the agony of rape victims. Completing trial of rape cases in two months, having women judges hear rape cases "as far as practicable" and recording statements of victims at places of their choice are some of the other changes to the Criminal Procedure Code that have been approved.

The changes related to rape seek to provide protection to victims, many of whom dare not come forward to complain — or in the case of the brave ones who defy the stigma to report the crime — to long endure police investigations and still longer trial proceedings. If the proposed changes become law, the investigation of rape cases will be conducted at the residence of the victim and "so far as practicable, by a woman police officer". The changes also provide for a victim to be questioned in the presence of her parents or a social worker of the locality. These provisions will spare the victims of the agony of visiting police stations and answering inconvenient — obscene in many cases — questions in the presence of unknown persons.

The suggestion for the presence of women trial judges will also cushion against the insensitive inquisition by the defence counsel. In the case of child victims, a provision will be made for completion of investigation within three months from the date on which the information was recorded by the officer-in-charge of the police station and not from the date of offence.

The other vital change approved by the Cabinet is giving the victims the right to appeal against acquittals. This provision is aimed at acting as a deterrent against frequent allegations of collusion between the prosecution and the accused.

Anything that promotes justice in the country is welcome. The reality, however, is disheartening. A young engineer, working for the National Highway Authority of India, was murdered by the mafia in November 2003, when he blew whistle on the corrupt practices going on in the Golden Quadrangle Project in Bihar. The murder led to an outrage and all political parties then seemed supporting the Witness Protection and Whistle Blower Bill. However, even after five years, there is no sign of progress on the issue.

It is not that the expert advice or reports were not there with the Government. A lot of commissions and committees have been set up with fanfare to bring about reforms. But unfortunately, our laws have remained static since the British times. A number of commissions and committees have been set up, apart from permanent bodies like the Law Commission, whose full-time job is to update laws.

Eight reports of the National Police Commission, produced between 1979 and 1981, have suggested several measures to minimise political interference in the functioning of the police, reduce the incidence of torture in police custody and make the police accountable by withdrawing the immunity they enjoy against prosecution.

Justice Malimath Committee (2001-03) has concentrated on the rights of the victim. It mentions the need to formulate a witness protection programme, reclassify offences and involve the victim in all stages of the trial. The committee has addressed the issues of compensation to victims. Justice Malimath also says, "The present criminal justice system had totally collapsed and was not acting as a deterrent for criminals... With the rate of conviction on criminal offences being low, there was very less risk factor for a person committing an offence. A national survey shows the conviction rate around seven per cent. Ninety-three per cent of people get acquitted, resulting in criminals moving in the society without any stigma."

Regrettably, even the amendments to the Criminal Procedure Code, approved in 2006 by the Cabinet, are still to be brought on the statute book. Nothing new is being done in the country so far as its laws are concerned. Pious intentions and resolutions are not enough. What is required is a time-bound action to translate all Cabinet recommendations into law. Early implementation will help litigants and Government in reducing court pendency.

2.2. Restructure the Judicial System

A female model who worked as a part time bartender at a fashion designer's restaurant was shot dead on April 30, 1999, by a young man with strong political connections. His accomplices were equally influential. The fault of the bar maid was that she refused to serve him a drink because it was past the prescribed hours for serving them. The main reason for the acquittal of the accused and other co-accused was that the eyewitnesses did not support the prosecution's charges. The sister of the deceased model says, "Money and muscle-power played an important role. We couldn't do anything, it's a terrible feeling. You can't fight against so much money and power."

Our legal system is such that unless you have an eye witness you cannot expect a conviction. This system has to change otherwise such verdicts will continue to be given. Commenting on the case former Chief Justice VN Khare, whose landmark order re-opened the Best Bakery case and set the norms for dealing with hostile witnesses, says that the same standards should have applied to the murder trial.

He said, "If a witness turned hostile during trial proceedings, it is the duty of both the prosecution and the trial judge to cross-examine (him or her) to ascertain whether the witness turned hostile because of greed or fear or any other ulterior consideration... If it is so then the statement should be ignored and re-trial should be ordered."

He added, "Our criminal jurisprudence, borrowed from (the) British (is) heavily loaded in favour of the accused... In such a situation what I said in that (Best Bakery case) context was, give protection to witnesses." He also said that, "Indian Evidence Act provides for cross examination of 'hostile witnesses' and on this ground, too, the prosecution and the victim's family could move the high court."

On the one hand we take pride in being citizens of a country with great tradition while on the other we come across sordid crimes like a bartender being shot point blank in the middle of a swinging party throbbing with about 400 people. Yet nobody has the courage to depose about this reckless criminality. I must add that if the trial of a case drags on for seven years, as it did in this case, it is only the witnesses bestowed with immense patience who would be willing to come to the court repeatedly, depose at various stages of the case and be subject to humiliating cross examination.

Turning hostile is not a new phenomenon in our country. There is no punishment for perjury or changing statements. It is a common occurrence which the lawmakers are not willing to accept and rectify. In fact, it is naïve to expect otherwise as out of 542 MPs in the present Parliament as many as 119 at the time of filing affidavits before contesting and winning elections had disclosed their involvement in some case or the other. With a substantial number being involved in cases, it is foolish to expect them to put a noose round their own necks and make it difficult if not impossible to manipulate witnesses.

French writer Andre Gide has said, "Everything has been said already, but as no one listens, we must always begin again." The same is true of the Indian criminal justice system which is in a shambles. With a huge backlog of cases, it is no surprise that the murder of the model turned bar tender took seven years. The backlog at various levels at the end of 2005 was 33,635 in the Supreme Court, 33,41,040 High Courts and 2,53,06,458 in subordinate courts.

The Supreme Court of India has 26 judges. There are 21 High Courts with a total sanctioned strength of 719 judges; and there are a total of 12,360 subordinate courts functioning in India. On an average every year the Supreme Court of India decides about 40,500 cases out of 42,000 cases filed, the High Courts decides 11,23,500 cases out of 12,41,000 cases, and the subordinate courts decide 1,32,22,000 cases out of 1,42,29,000 cases filed. In spite, of such high disposal numbers the figures of cases pending has been rising due to increasing influx of cases.

As streamlining the criminal justice system will not fetch votes and on the contrary may prove detrimental for tainted politicians, reforming the system is not a priority with the political class. President APJ Abdul Kalam has observed that there are innumerable instances of court cases dragging on for more than 10 years.

The reason for the delay includes inadequate number of courts and judicial officers, dilatory tactics by litigants and their lawyers who seek frequent adjournments and delay in filing documents. The backlog of cases can be cleared through age analysis of cases, alternative dispute redressal mechanism, fast-track courts, introduction of e-judiciary, capacity enhancement and continuous training of judges, lawyers and the judicial staff. A grouping of cases similar from the legal point of view could be placed before a particular judge or bench for disposal.

The problem of witnesses and even complainants turning hostile during a trial is going to persist unless the Government shows the will to tackle the issue. Suggesting a way out, the Law Commission in its 178th report had suggested that for all serious offences punishable for 10 years or more of imprisonment the statement of important witnesses be recorded under oath at the earliest by the magistrate concerned before commencement of trial.

Apart from this there is the question of the protection of witnesses who turn hostile to avoid the wrath of the high and mighty, whether they are politicians, extortionists or dons. Intimidation and vulnerability of witnesses is an issue which has been neglected and left untackled. Several countries have an extensive witness protection programme but in India this is not being thought of as an option. Witnesses are aware that they have to eventually live in the same society and deal with the same people once the case is over. Therefore, they first think of post-trial and post persecution protection.

When it comes to assessment of the failures in delivery of justice in high profile cases the so-called experts blame the prosecution as well as investigative agency for their ineptitude in bringing the guilty to book. But no amount of thorough investigation can make up for an eye witness account.

Says a law professor, "Our system is such that while dealing with an influential person, the law is applied differently, as compared to the common man, be it at the time of arrest, investigation or trial." Prolonged trials make witnesses to lose interest or turn hostile. "People get fed up running around in courts and waiting for justice," he says. "The longer a trial, the greater the chances of witnesses failing to recall the incident. They then get exposed during cross-examination. This is an outcome of procedural delays caused by our system," says a senior advocate.

Ultimately, it all depends on those at the helm as to what sort of criminal justice system they want to give to the people. Do many more Jessica Lals have to be shot dead before the Government realises the mess the country's investigation and legal system is in? It is not too late even now to heed the wake up call for reforms in the judicial system.

2.3. Injustice: the Policy of State

A quick recapitulation of the well-known details of the Best Bakery case. On March 1 last year, 14 persons were burnt to death in the wake of post-Godhra riots in Gujarat. They were workers and members of the Sheikh family, which owned Best Bakery in Vadodara, and lived in its top floor. During the subsequent trial, 19-year-old Zaheera Sheikh, the main complainant who survived the night the mob attacked the bakery, denied having previously named the accused or even witnessing the incident. Her family members who also lived through the tragedy denied making police complaints and previous statements as well. They said they were unable to identify anyone from the mob that had set the place on fire. Of 120 witnesses, 73 deposed. Of them, 41 turned hostile. The judge ruled that, though the details regarding the incident were true, there was not enough evidence to prove those accused had committed the crime.

Throughout the trial, the prosecution remained ineffective and weak. It was not surprising that in a dramatic reversal of her court testimony, Zaheera said on July 7 in Mumbai, "What I said in court was not true. I said it after pressure was put on me. In fact, I recognise all those who attacked us that night."

The witnesses who had turned hostile said later they did so since they would never get justice in Gujarat. This was because-it was alleged-the public prosecutor, the police and politicians were all protecting the accused, who owed allegiance to the ruling BJP. During the hearing of an appeal by the National Human Rights Commission seeking transfer of the Best Bakery case, the Godhra carnage case and two other riot-related cases outside Gujarat, the Supreme Court on September 12, told the Gujarat Government to resign if it was not able to punish rioters. So anguished was the Chief Justice that he said, "I have no faith left in the prosecution and the Gujarat Government. I am not saying Article 356. You have to protect people and punish the guilty. What else is Rajdharma? You quit if you cannot prosecute the guilty."

The Gujarat Government had filed an appeal in the High Court against the court judgment acquitting all those accused in the Best Bakery case. The apex court stated, "It appears to us that it (the appeal) is an eyewash." It was thus forced to declare, "We will not be silent spectators. There is no cross-examination as to why so many witnesses turned hostile. This shows the nature of the prosecution." Chief Justice VN Khare further said, "Democracy does not mean you will not prosecute anyone".

When the Additional Solicitor General cited shortcomings in the criminal justice system, as a result of which not many rioters had been punished, including the 1984 anti-Sikh rioters, the bench asked him: "Are you saying that the rioters in Gujarat should also be acquitted. What else are you saying? Just because nobody had been punished for the last 40 years, it does not mean, that we should shut our eyes? We do not take any pleasure in doing so. But when we are forced to do, what else can we do?"

The 'Rajdharma the court talked of was the duty of the state to protect the weak and punish the guilty. In so far as this duty applies to all office-holders, the court was right in rapping the knuckles of the Gujarat dispensation. However, the fact remains that all political parties have given Rajdhar-ma a new meaning. They have interpreted it as the dharma of sticking to the Raj at any cost, and building up or retaining their existing votebanks.

This corrosion of the meaning of public duty is the reason why investigation of cases and prosecutions are hardly ever satisfactory, as has been mentioned by various commissions. Consider the observation of the Delhi Police Commission (1966-68): "Political interference is another rich source of corruption.

Allegations have been made before us that some politicians resort to the device of securing the assistance of goondas and bad characters who are given protection by the police."

A study was conducted sometime ago by the Indian Institute of Public Opinion at the instance of the Home Ministry regarding "The Image of the Police in India". It came up with the following conclusion: Political interference is seen by the public as a major factor contributing to the poor image of the police, and manifests itself in the misuse and abuse of police powers and disregard of the law by law enforcers themselves.

There are some typical ways the police is pressured by the political class or other extraneous factors. For instance, pressure may involve the arrest or non-arrest of a person against whom the police are conducting an investigation. Pressure may also be put on law enforcers to suppress any material evidence that may become available during search operations. The inclusion or non-inclusion of such evidence in the chargesheet placed in the court on the conclusion of investigation may, by extension, be influenced. Discretionary law enforcement while dealing with public order situations is another area political interference may force ruthlessness vis-a-vis persons opposed to the ruling party.

Transfers or suspensions are used as weapons to make officials toe the line of their political masters. Almost all political parties have done it, some with finesse, some crudely. Most of the time, the first casualty of a new government coming to power in a State is the Chief of Police and the Chief Secretary. They are transferred to make room for more pliable officers. Many obliging subordinate officials develop such clout with the political leadership that their seniors lean on them to retain their jobs. Such is their influence on the political leadership that, if any senior official tries to control them, he gets transferred. Such politically-motivated transfers seriously damage the discipline and morale of the bureaucracy.

Once the case is sent to the court, it is for the prosecuting agency to properly marshal evidence, law and other aspects of the case. Efficient investigation alone cannot bring offenders to book. It needs to be followed up by an equally efficient prosecution. The UP Police Commission (1970-1971, pages 512-517) noted that the performance of the prosecuting machinery was far from satisfactory.

The then Chief Justice of Allahabad High Court, SK Verma, deposed before the Commission saying: "At every level, the prosecution of the State cases is of poor quality and that is one of the reasons for the scandalous number of acquittals in the districts." Another witness, a former Advocate General in UP told the Police Commission: "At most of the places today, the District Government Counsel and the Assistant District Government Counsel are unsatisfactory."

One witness deposed by saying, "It is a fact that appointment of the District Government Counsel and the Assistant District Government Counsel has in recent years become a matter of patronage by the Minister of local people. Both at the High Court and at the Sessions Court, there exists a system of panel of lawyers who attend to the overflow of work which the Government Counsels cannot attend to personally. We have received innumerable complaints about the working of the panels of the Sessions and High Courts both from the judges and the bar. Generally briefless lawyers are put on panels and the failure of many Government cases are due to their inefficiency."

The Supreme Court's observations on Rajdharma are, thus, timely. They should be treated as a wake up call to rectify the deficiencies in the investigation and prosecution of cases. The recommendations of several police commissions and the Law Commission appointed after Independence have been pending with State and Central Governments for more than three decades. It is time to dust those files, so that the guilty are brought to book. No price is too high to ensure justice is done and people's faith in the criminal justice system is not eroded.

3. The Needs Undermined

3.1. Enforce the Amendments

There is a popular Hindi saying: "Der aaye durust Aye" (late arrival, but to the right place). The Union Cabinet has reportedly cleared a large number of amendments to the Criminal Procedure Code (CrPC) based on the recommendations of the Law Commission of India, that are expected to improve the functioning of the criminal justice system.

The law is a drab subject, apart from being non-vote catching. So it does not interest the powers-that-be. It's only the collapse of a high profile cases, duly highlighted by the media, that has led the Government to dust up some reports and recommendations, which otherwise had no chance of seeing the light of day. A major problem is that witnesses are too scared to depose independently, especially when powerful interests are involved.

The Supreme Court has repeatedly urged the need for a law on various aspects of witness protection. In its judgement in the PUCL Vs Union of India, while dealing with the validity of section 30 of the Prevention of Terrorism Act, 2002, the Supreme Court referred in detail to the subject of protection of the witnesses. It stressed on the need to maintain a balance between the rights of the accused for a fair trial and to enable prosecution of witnesses whose identity is known to the accused to give evidence freely without being overawed by the presence of the accused in the court. It also called for protection of the identity of witnesses who are not known to the accused by devices, for example video-screen which precludes the accused from seeing the witness even though the court and defence counsel will be able to observe both their demeanours.

In Sakshi Vs Union of India, the Supreme Court, while dealing with the plea for enlargement of the definition of the word 'rape', and protection of minor victims of sexual abuse, observed that in matters relating to such sexual offences there is need to provide victim protection at the time of recording statement made before the court. Though the particulars of the amendments have not been made public, it has been stated that that the amendments were based on the recommendations of three Law Commission Reports - the 154th, 177th and 178th reports.

One of the recommendations accepted is that victims of crime, or their kin, can appoint a lawyer in the prosecution of cases. Public at large feels, rightly or wrongly, that the role of the prosecution in both Jessica and Priyadarshini Mattoo murder cases was suspect. Friends of the victims also feel that the outcome of the cases would have been different if the victims' kin had been legally allowed to appoint a lawyer.

The present position is that all crime is considered "crime against the state". For this reason, the state appointed prosecutors alone are allowed to take up cases on behalf of the victims. There have been cases registered by the CBI in which unscrupulous Government prosecutors have colluded with the counsel of the accused. In fact, in major CBI cases I noticed that the CBI's counsels had not even read their briefs.

In some cases where I was present in superior courts, I had to pass small slips of papers to the Government advocates, gently pointing out that they were missing the crux of the problem. Even assuming that all public prosecutors are honest, the workload on them just does not allow them to thoroughly devote themselves and prepare their cases. In Delhi, there are only 87 public prosecutors to counter expert defence counsels and argue in 14,000 pending cases of heinous crimes.

A most desirable amendment is that women judges would try rape cases. As it is, rape is a traumatic experience and in the case of minors, they are not expected to understand the complexity of the law. Often they are overawed by the court's atmosphere. Since sex is a closed subject, the victims, either out of shame or reluctance, cannot recount and relive the experience. So sometimes they can blunder with some details.

Despite the Supreme Court's rulings, defence lawyers occasionally add to the embarrassment of the victims by asking inappropriate questions. The presence of a woman judge would work as a deterrent to such counsels, apart from giving confidence to the victim that one of her own gender will look into her humiliation sympathetically. However, the amendment needs to be backed by increasing the number of women judges all over the country so that there is at least one or more woman judge available in each district.

Another amendment envisages that a witness who makes a statement before a magistrate under Section 164 of CrPc can retract from it only at the risk of inviting perjury charges. The smoothness with which eyewitnesses turn hostile has led to the failure of many cases. The 178th Report of Law Commission had suggested an amendment so that in all cases punishable with imprisonment for a period of 10 years or more (with or without fine) including an offence which is punishable with death, the investigating police officer shall forward all persons whose evidence is essential for just decision to the nearest magistrate for recording their statement.

The magistrate shall record the statements of such persons forwarded to him under sub-section (1) on oath and keep such statements with him. However, copies of such statements shall be furnished to the investigating officer. Incidentally, Terrorist and Disruptive Activities (Prevention) Act, 1987, and Prevention of Terrorism Act, 2002, provided for protection of witnesses. The prosecution, as also the court, could direct that the identity and the address of the witness be kept secret. The court could even avoid mentioning the names and addresses in its order or judgement.

These provisions now being incorporated in the Indian laws have been in place for decades in countries like the United States, Australia, UK, and other Western democracies. These may not solve all the problems of the criminal justice system or the judiciary. However, at least the Cabinet has approved these changes. The big question is when will these changes be introduced as our august Houses are adjourned repeatedly for one reason or the other. Moreover, in the era of coalition governments, any party lending support can put a halt to the process of legal amendments, as happened with the divestment plans of the Government. Early implementation will help litigants and Government must not lose the momentum out of a good initiative.

3.2. Make Perjury a Serious Ofence

Montaigne once said: "Lying is a hateful and accursed vice. We have no other tie upon one another, but our word. If we did, but, discover the horror and consequences of it, we should pursue it, with fire and sword and more justly than other crimes." The Indian public and press grumble, whine and criticise incessantly - and rightly - whenever any high profile case ends in acquittal or other serious crimes go unpunished. The crimes range from fraud, abuse of office, scams, looting the state treasury, corruption, embezzlement, rape, murder or criminal riot. However, the cause of this state of affairs, which is perjury, has not attracted attention from the quarters that matter.

Perjury naturally affects the quality of justice, as a judge has to decide only on the basis of evidence presented in the court. In fact, the law as it stands only makes it incumbent on the citizen to depose truthfully in a court of law. However, there is no punishment for lying. The only way to make our countrymen see the beauty of justice is by showing them, in simple and plain terms, the consequences of injustice. Time and again the prosecution in some of the most significant cases has failed, because the witnesses - after giving initial evidence supporting a particular theory about a crime - recanted when examined in the court.

This has happened in a majority of cases registered in several states under TADA. In sensational scenarios like the BMW case in which a rich youth crushed to death some poor people sleeping on the pavement, or even the famous Jessica Lal murder case in which a bar hostess was shot dead by the brats of high and mighty, and, most recently, in the Best Bakery case in which the NHRC intervened when the witnesses changed their statements in the court, the same story of perjury has been repeated. While it is not possible to pinpoint the exact cause of witnesses turning hostile, there have been cases where money-power, intimidation and fear for their lives have led individuals to change their stand. Both lying to sentence the innocent and dishonesty deposing to convict the guilty are condemnable.

However, whenever such cases are acquitted, the police and the CBI are held responsible for poor investigation. This is not to deny that investigations can be occasionally slanted or motivated in some cases, because, after all, it is the same Indians who commit perjury and it is their brethren of the same category who are a part of the criminal justice system. The expectation of the people is that the guilty should be arrested immediately after the crime, the case investigated instantly, full evidence marshalled, and, by evening, the criminal should be put behind bars. This kind of crime, investigation, and punishment unfortunately happens only in the Hindi cinema. Real life is full of potholes and is different from the reel life.

Perjury is a fact of life and more than perjury, acquittals on technical grounds equally play havoc with the criminal justice system. Wherever the accused can take a technical plea to get of, they do. Even former US President Bill Clinton took shelter of a technicality to escape the charge of sexual misconduct with one of his aides. He literally escaped the charge of perjury in the trial by Senate. Many believe that the results would have been different if he had been tried in a judicial forum or if the trial court had not taken a partisan view. The condemnation of either perjury or poor investigation is no justification for the malaise, which exists in our society.

People have come to accept this "institutionalised" tendency to tolerate perjury. Also, in some cases of extortion, or when criminal gangs are involved, the accused are able to intimidate witnesses because there is no law or a system under which, after the assessment of the need for protection to a particular witness, the administration could give him or her the requisite security cover.

The Supreme Court has also observed that perjury is widespread in the country. In the latest reported case of perjury decided a few months ago, the apex court said: "Unscrupulous litigants are found daily resorting to utter blatant falsehood in the courts," while "most of the witnesses...make false statements to suit the interests of the parties calling them." The perjurer in the instant case was advocate R Karuppan, then president of the Madras High Court Advocates Association.

Ordering a complaint of perjury to be filed against Karuppan before a magistrate, the apex court warned: "If the system is to survive, effective action is the need of the time." The perjury committed by Karuppan was that he filed a petition questioning the authenticity of Anand's date of birth in spite of knowing full well that the issue had already been settled by the President of India. Significantly, the Supreme Court even acknowledged that perjury in the Karuppan case was "not an exception to the general practice being followed by many of the litigants in the country."

In our courts, any action contemplated on the charge of perjury, like contempt trial, is only a derivative of the main case. Starting of perjury proceedings will mean burdening the system, which already has huge mounting arrears of cases. Only in an ideal situation, when we have sufficient number of judicial officers, can taking up of perjury cases be feasible. The offence of perjury and dealing with it expeditiously can only be a part of the overall reform to speed up the justice delivery system. This approach will mean breeding more perjury, thereby causing immense harm to straightforward litigants.

In April 2003, a high level committee headed by former High Court Chief Justice VS Malimath was appointed by the Home

Ministry to reform the criminal justice system. The commission recommended a the Witness Protection Programme. It generally emphasised the growing trend of hostile witnesses. One simple way to check perjury is to make any charge by any person in a serious cases a sworn deposition before a magistrate. If the witness then turns hostile, it should be treated as perjury, with no defence, and the judge should be free to convict such a witness on spot. This will ensure that witnesses find lying far less profitable than truth. This simple legal reform can do wonders.

Police perjury in the fabrication of their reports, which is done with a view to see the guilty brought to "justice", should equally be treated as criminal offence. The most charitable explanation for such lying is, as law enforcement officers, the police do not want a person they know to be a criminal to escape conviction simply because of a "technical" violation of the Constitution, or a procedural formality, or even a trivial "exculpatory" fact. For this, responsibility should be cast on superior officers, that they will be held personally responsible for any misdemeanour on the part of their subordinates. Deterrence to lying while testifying in court should lead to stiff punishment. Government can make a rule that a perjury conviction would automatically lead to dismissal of a policeman from the force.

Police too needs to be sensitised, especially at the level of constables and inspectors - which is the investigating and intelligence collecting level - to the immorality and dangers of perjury. Prosecutors should be warned to take their ethical duty to not support any case which, in their view, depends on perjury - either by the police or witnesses. At the same time, it needs to be emphasised that archaic laws coupled with anachronistic enactments have created the present anomalous situation. In short, our legal systems needs a thorough overhaul to meet the aspirations of the people. Justice is the great and simple principle which is the secret of success of all governments. It is as essential to the training of the infant as it is to the control of a mighty nation like ours.

3.3. Needed Investigative Excellence

Investigation is the first step towards finding out the truth behind any complaint made to the police. While trying to ferret it out, the truth some angularities slip in, which bring disrepute to police. It becomes more pronounced when high profile cases involving powerful people are taken up. In fact, there is a strange kind of pressure on the complainant.

There is usual apprehension about the way a high profile case should end especially if the person concerned is connected with senior officials or holds a high position either in government or society. It has also been seen that if, after investigation, a case does not throw up evidence which supports the complainants' case, a campaign of vilification against the investigator or the investigating agency is started for their alleged failure to prove the case in the court of law.

According to present laws any statement given to police or investigating officer need not be signed. Any confession made to police officer has no value in the court unless such statement leads to the recovery of items incriminating the accused. In fact, telling one thing to the investigating officer and another to the court has become the norm. The interesting case involving a Minister from Kerala illustrates well how witnesses change their stand.

The same is true of the JMM bribery case involving late Prime Minister PV Narasimha Rao and present Governor of Bihar Buta Singh along with many others. Out of 48 witnesses, 47 turned hostile. Apart from this the investigation agencies, whether the police or CBI or Customs or Directorate of Enforcement are part of Government. They do not enjoy independent status. They were conceived in this manner by the British whose main objective was to rule the country and not to necessarily ensure that justice was delivered.

All political parties pay lip service to the concept of independent, fearless and unbiased investigation. But when they come to power they do not want to let go of their hold on them. In fact, referring the cases to an investigating agency by the party in power against its adversaries who may have been in power in the past is common. At times such cases are referred after a few years as was done in case of Tehelka or the case against former Chief Minister of Punjab by the present Chief Minister. Due to delay, it is possible that either the witnesses would not be forthcoming or evidence would have become diluted if not eliminated during this interregnum.

Another problem that has been noticed while investigating cases is that a large number of complaints are made to settle scores and not for the purpose of getting justice or redressal of their grievances. Determining the truth and procuring evidence is of utmost importance. But in the absence of any legal mechanism to protect witnesses, it becomes almost impossible to get independent witnesses who can be persuaded to depose.

It is for the Government of the day to ensure of the investigating agency succeeds in its objective. However, such expertise must be accompanied with respect for principles enshrined in the Constitution, especially fundamental rights and freedoms, knowledge of the law, and fairness and objectivity in decision-making. It means increasing professionalism within the investigating agencies and developing a new attitude of cooperation among different wings responsible for speedy administration of justice. There is no point in having a complex and lengthy police investigation if the evidence gathered during the process is declared inadmissible in a court of law. Excellence and innovation require cooperation at all levels.

In today's world of interdependence, cooperation is probably the only sustainable answer to increased complexity of crime. Cooperation is a matter of common sense. It is about rationalisation of limited resources. On it depends the survival and reputation of investigating agencies. Investigative excellence is neither a programme nor an initiative. It is a set of principles fundamental to ensuring safe homes and communities for all Indians through fair, lawful, ethical, informed and clever application of the best investigative and prosecutional techniques, practices, strategies and training available.

To put it simply, striving for excellence means professionalising policing by adopting rigorous standards like: * Clear accountability, * more intelligence-led investigations, * increased integration through building partnerships among international, State and Central law enforcement agencies, * better and more timely sharing of both intelligence and best practices, * furthermore innovative and creative investigative training, practices, strategies and techniques.

The biggest problems facing criminal investigations can be listed as under: * Weak case mismanagement, * investigative tunnel vision, * lack of accountability * poor leadership, * inconsistencies with legal requirements and not strictly following the legal provisions and * lack of respect for the criminal justice system, by some investigators.

Another serious problem is avoidable acquittals of known criminals caused partly due to sloppy handling of cases, poor leadership and inconsistent legal advice during investigations. Weak court preparations also contribute to the failure of these cases. Professionalism begins when the top leadership starts looking for ways to improve current investigative practices and enforcement strategies. It also involves improving investigation standards with better supervision and more strategic approaches to crime.

Once I asked a State Director General of Police how much time he spent in supervising investigation. He replied that 95 per cent of his time was spent on transfers, postings, meetings with political leaders, three per cent in meeting his own officials and other meetings and two per cent in attending to office work.

Effective training is one aspect of achieving investigative excellence and professionalising police. On a broader front investigative excellence also depends on seamless, integrated policing and intelligence-led policing. Improving policing and investigative excellence is only one side of the story. Decluttering the criminal justice system is equally important.

The list of the following pendent cases in courts across the country will show: * 33,635 cases pending in Supreme Court, * 39,41,040 cases in High Courts, * 2,53,06,458 is the case backlog in the subordinate courts.

The enormity of the problem can be gauged from the large number of posts of judges lying vacant. * Out of the sanctioned strength of 26 judges, the Supreme Court has four vacancies. * The Madras High Court has been functioning at less than half its capacity - 27 out of 49 posts are vacant. * Out of the sanctioned strength of 726 judges in all High Courts, 189 have been lying vacant across the country. * Out of the 71 new posts created over two years in High Courts, only 20 have so far been filled.

The greatest challenge before the judiciary is the numerous cases still pending in the courts waiting to be settled. The enormity of the crisis can be viewed by a quick look at statistics. The Supreme

Court has 26 judges; there are 21 High Courts with a total sanctioned strength of 719 judges; and there are 12,360 subordinate courts functioning in India. On an average every year the Supreme Court of India decides about 40,500 cases out of 42,000 cases that are filed, the High Courts decide 11,23,500 cases out of 12,41,000 cases that are filed, and the subordinate courts decide 1,32,22,000 case out of 1,42,29,000 cases that are filed.

In spite of such high disposal figures, the number of cases pending in courts is on the rise due to their influx. Also, however finely investigated a case may be, if it remains pending for years, the interest and enthusiasm of the investigator is bound to flag and dampen. Good policing and good governance go together. The road may be hard and difficult, but there is no alternative to it. What is required is a committed will to tackle the massive problem of ensuring justice to the poorest of the poor in the shortest possible time.

3.4. Sting to Ensure Justice

Sting operations are generally carried out to trap the corrupt, the underworld dons and spies. They are also undertaken to establish adultery. Sting operations can also be useful in the arrest of terrorists and anti-national elements. The gadgets generally used are camera, recording instruments, audio and video equipment. Generally, the media has used it to expose shocking acts of politicians, officials and others, who are allegedly guilty of subverting the rule of law. In the last week of January 2004, in a sting operation to expose the alleged sale of judicial warrants, a television channel recorded shady proceedings involving a court of justice.

The Supreme Court of India and the High Court of Gujarat acted promptly by suspending with immediate effect the presiding magistrate of the concerned court in Gujarat, and ordering a CBI inquiry into his conduct. The CBI immediately registered an FIR against three Ahmedabad-based lawyers who allegedly struck a deal with the magistrate to secure the warrants for R.s 40,000. The case was filed under Section 120-B (criminal conspiracy) of the Indian Penal Code and Section 8 of Prevention of Corruption Act. The Chief Justice of India remarked, "Look at what is happening. You can get an arrest warrant for Rs. 40,000. The time has come to take strict action, otherwise nothing would remain."

The Supreme Court ordered that all the records summoned from the High Court and the videotapes and other documents submitted by the television journalist be handed over to the CBI. The journalist claimed to have conducted a sting operation to expose corruption in subordinate judiciary in Gujarat. The Ahmedabad lawyers involved in the case had assured the journalist that once Rs. 40,000 was paid, "he should not bother about anything". They had also assured him that the substance of complaint, the complainant and witnesses would be their "bother".

On the court's request, the Attorney-General of India agreed to put forth suggestions to improve the judicial system. Earlier, the journalist's counsel had pointed out that a similar incident occurred in 1999, when a court at Dakor, in Gujarat's Kheda district, issued a non-bailable warrant against the then Chief Justice of India. There is no doubt that a few black sheep have tarnished the fair name of the judiciary. In May 2003, a judge was arrested in Chandigarh by the CBI in a corruption case. Along with him, a Jalandhar district and sessions judge, on whose behalf a judicial magistrate had allegedly demanded Rs. 11 lakh from a litigant, was also arrested. Clearly the morals of people in positions of authority, in alarming number of instances, are at their lowest ebb.

Around the same time, a former Delhi High Court judge who resigned following the DDA scam, was arrested and booked under the Prevention of Corruption Act. A household survey conducted by Transparency International (TI) in December 2002 reported high levels of corruption in public institutions across South Asia. Of the seven major public institutions, the police emerged as the most corrupt in all the five countries surveyed. The judiciary was identified as the second most corrupt area in all countries except Pakistan, where land administration and the tax authorities were identified as the second and third most corrupt respectively.

Land administration figures prominently in the list of the most corrupt sectors in four out of the five countries. The latest report by TI, entitled "Corruption in South Asia: Insights and Benchmarks from Citizen Feedback Surveys in Five Countries", identifies high levels of corruption encountered by citizens attempting to access seven basic public services. The survey results show that even when public services are meant to be freely available, bribes and delays keep many from receiving them, and it is most often the poorest in society that suffer the most.

Former Chief Justice of India SP Bharucha publicly expressed that "eighty per cent of judges in the country were honest and incorruptible and that a small number of corrupt officials were bringing the entire judiciary into disrepute." Over the years, some judges of different high courts have been hauled up or advised suitably by the Supreme Court, for alleged misconduct and impropriety affecting the discharge of their judicial functions. Some of them resigned or have been transferred.

It is a matter of great satisfaction that whenever any misdemeanour has been brought to the notice of the superior courts, they have lost no time in stemming the rot. Superior courts have been prompt in disciplining judges guilty of any misconduct. However, as matters stand, the procedure for disciplining deviants is not only too unwieldy, it is also cumbersome- especially when it comes to impeachment in Parliament. How can Parliament, which has some members facing scam charges judge the members of the judiciary? That politics in our democracy is at its lowest ebb, was first indicated through the video recording by Tehelka, exposing corruption in defence deals. Later, the Samajwadi Party in Uttar Pradesh showed the former Chief Minister, Ms Mayawati, asking her party legislatures to contribute to the party fund, from the MLA Local Area Development Fund. Miss Mayawati is said to have countered:"Every MLA gets Rs. 75 lakh as his constituency fund.

For MPs the figure is Rs. 2 crore. Whatever work is carried out from this development fund, and how it is done, depends on the MLA. So if you make five lakh out of this development fund, do not keep everything for yourself. Use four lakh for your constituency and give at least a lakh to the party. The same stands for MPs. After all, the BSP has made you an MLA or an MP. You should give something back to the party. Am I saying anything wrong?"

Then came the infamous "cash-on-camera" scam involving a former Central minister, followed by the "cash for MLAs" scandal, involving the outgoing Chief Minister of Chattisgarh, who was caught on the audio tape, striking an odious deal with senior members of the BJP to effect a split. The Union Law Minister, Mr Arun Jaitley, had organised the audio part of the sting operation with the approval of the Deputy Prime Minister. There is no law at present in our country to regulate or legitimise sting operations. Police do it for prostitution cases, corruption cases, as well as catching drugsters and spies. Decoys are used to trap offenders.

Many would question the legitimacy of sting operations on the ground that it is unethical, or not approved by law or, broadly speaking, is illegal. They may even say that sting operations do not change anything or there is no dividing line between sting journalism and yellow journalism. A Chinese proverb is apt; "Going to the law is losing a cow for the sake of a cat". About laws, it is said they are like cobwebs, which may catch small flies, but let hornets and wasps break through. However, sting operations keep the guilty on tenterhook, as well as the Government on alert.

The fact remains there has been a tremendous deterioration in public morality. Regrettably, the systems do not seem to be working as the common man would like them to work. The public is already aware of the wrong doings in the country. For instance, the right to information acts are hedged by many "ifs and buts". These acts, wherever passed or promulgated, have failed to bring about transparency or shake the bureaucracy, or induce accountability in governance. Anything which promotes maximum good of the maximum numbers should be welcome.

In fact, the right to sting operations should be guaranteed legally not only to the Press, but also to any private individual. Sting operations should be legitimised only where public interest or public money or public figures are involved. These can catch some of the offenders, but they do not necessarily induce honesty. Moreover, with the arrival of new technology, it would be unfair not to use the same for effective enforcement of the law, and to ensure the highest standards in public life in the larger public interest.

3.5. Plea- bargaining Makes Senses

Our judicial system has been congested with cases which take between a quarter to half an individual's life to reach its logical conclusion. A National Crime Research Bureau study, 'Crime in India - 2002,' reported that some three quarters of all the inmates held in Indian prisons had not yet been convicted but were still "under trial".

Nearly 220,000 cases took more than three years to reach court. About 25,600 exhausted 10 years before the final decision could come. A staggering number of accused, awaiting trial, have already spent more time in jail than the sentence that would have been awarded to them had they been convicted. As on February 27, 2006, the Supreme Court had a backlog of 33,635 cases, whereas the high courts and the subordinate courts had a backlog of 33,41,040 and 2,53,06,458 cases respectively.

Our country has a lethargic criminal justice system. Prisoners spend years in jails without being tried. Pierre Joseph Proudhon's apt description of law rightly suits the Indian legal system: "We know what they are, and what they are worth. They are spider webs for the rich and mighty, steel chains for the poor and weak, fishing nets in the hands of the Government".

To ease the pressure from the system, the Government has enacted the law of plea-bargaining. The law is likely to benefit those awaiting trial and are imprisoned. The law aims to pre-empt the trial of such offences that are punishable with imprisonment of up to seven years. The system has been in vogue in the US where over 90 per cent of the cases are disposed of under its provisions.

In some legal systems such as those in England and Wales - and Victoria in Australia - plea bargaining is permitted to the extent that the prosecutors and the defence are able to reach an agreement that the defendant shall plead guilty to some charges and the prosecutor would, in that case, drop the remainder. The courts in these countries have made it clear that they will always decide the quantum of penalty to be paid and that the penalty cannot be bargained.

Many jurists believe that our criminal justice system has almost collapsed because of its inability to cope with the ever-mounting figures of pending cases. Trials are sluggish, cumbersome, and prolonged. The prosecution and defence counsel demand a lot of time to prepare their cases. It has become difficult to schedule and ensure the presence of all the witnesses. The delay during the arrest and trial of an accused, thus, adversely affects the conviction rates.

Under the mechanism of plea-bargaining, an accused in a criminal case, may now plead guilty in exchange for a reduced sentence. This will help in reducing the pressure on the courts. Moreover, an accused may get a lighter sentence by pleading guilty. He may pay some compensation if necessary. The most important part of this law is that both the parties should mutually accept the plea bargain made by the accused.

Plea-bargaining would not be applicable in cases related to heinous crimes such as murder and crimes against women and children. Though the law was introduced in July 2006, its results have started trickling down only now. Recently, special courts were organised in the overcrowded Tihar Jail, where about 83 per cent of inmates are undertrials.

To begin with, the authorities have chosen prisoners booked under the Excise and Arms Acts because the complainant in most of these cases was the Government and hence the cases were thought to be less contentious. As such, 187 cases were heard and 71 out of them were disposed of. Twenty-seven were found unfit for plea-bargaining. The rest are pending till the next hearing. The Delhi Legal Services Authority took the initiative for organising such camps within the jail's premises.

Plea-bargaining has become possible with the amendment of the Criminal Procedure Code. Under Section 265 thereof, prisoners charged with offences that entail a maximum imprisonment of seven years can be shown leniency if they fulfil a set of criteria laid down by the law. The accused and the victim, or his family, are brought to a magistrate court to settle the case amicably.

Equally important, the "mutually satisfactory disposition" envisaged by the amendment requires the culprit to pay compensation for no more than half the minimum sentence he is liable to serve. The accused, in this case, will have to file an application for plea-bargaining any time before the commencement of the trial. The court will consider the application only if it is accompanied by an affidavit stating that the accused has "voluntarily" opted for plea-bargaining and that he had not been convicted previously on the same charge. On this, the court will issue a notice to the prosecutor or the complainant.

The court will further examine the accused in camera to satisfy that he has filed the application voluntarily. If the court is satisfied that the application is indeed voluntary, it shall allot time to the parties to the dispute in order to work out a mutually satisfactory disposition, which may include a compensation to be paid to the victim by the accused.

However, the court will have to ensure that the process of working out a satisfactory disposition is also voluntary and allow the accused, too, to participate in it. If a satisfactory disposition has been worked out, the court will prepare a report that will have to be signed by the judge and all the parties involved in the case.

While disposing of the case, the court will direct the accused to pay the compensation, as has been agreed upon, to the victim and hear the parties on the quantum of punishment to be awarded to the accused.

If the accused is a first-time offender, the court will have the option of releasing the accused on probation despite his conviction. Alternatively, it may sentence the accused to half the minimum punishment prescribed for the offence in question. The judgment based on plea-bargaining shall be final and there will be no statutory right of appeal against it. The accused who pleads guilty as part of a plea bargain gives up his constitutional right to confront and question the accusers, and the right to refuse self-incrimination.

Plea-bargaining, as it would put a check on the crime, is welcome. Delhi's example needs to be replicated all over the country. It should be made mandatory for all States to hold such camps. Moreover prisoners should be apprised of the new law and how they can take advantage of it.

4. Assisting Death: Law and Opinion

In December 2004, a terminally ill man requested the High Court of Andhra Pradesh for permission to die. The patient who was dying of muscular dystrophy in effect pleaded for mercy killing. The High Court asked for medical opinion. However, even before the matter could come up before the court the next day, the applicant had expired. Permission for the act was tantamount to gaining permission for committing suicide-an offence punishable under Section 309 of IPC. There have been other cases as well of people suffering from incurable diseases seeking legal sanction to choose the time of their death. But the legal status of such cases remains the same: These would be treated as a person wanting to commit suicide.

In reality, the fundamental question propounded by euthanasia or assisted suicide is: should a person, who is terminally ill, and (a) who feels that life is not worth living because of intractable pain, and/or loss of dignity, and/or loss of capability; (b) who repeatedly and actively asks for help in committing suicide; and, (c) who is of sound mind and not suffering from depression, be provided assistance in dying?

Mercy killing is of the following types. One, euthanasia is intentional killing by act or omission of a dependent human allegedly for his own benefit. The key word here is "intentional". In case death is not intended, it is not euthanasia. Voluntary euthanasia can be defined as killing a person at his own request. On the other hand, non-voluntary euthanasia is killing someone without his consent. Involuntary euthanasia occurs when the person who is killed has also made an express wish to the contrary. Whereas euthanasia by action means intentionally causing death by performing an act such as giving a lethal injection. Finally, euthanasia by omission can be understood as intentionally bringing death by not providing necessary and customary care or food and water.

What does not constitute euthanasia? There is no euthanasia unless death is intentionally caused by what was done or not done. Thus, some medical actions that are often labelled as "passive euthanasia" are not a form of euthanasia, since the intention to take away life is lacking. These acts include not commencing treatment that would benefit the patient, withdrawing treatment that has proved to be ineffective and burdensome or is unwanted, and giving high doses of pain-killers that may endanger life but have been shown to be necessary. All these actions are part of good medical practice and lawful if carried out properly. Oregon is the only state in the US which allows a physician to assist in suicide. The number of people availing themselves of the law in 2002 doubled since 1998, when the law was enacted. However, in India, the law frowns upon euthanasia just as it considers suicide a punishable offence. It is, in fact, a complicated question and even religions do not sanction it. The Bible explicitly says, "thou shall not kill." While the justifiability of the right to die with dignity cannot be denied, yet there are tremendous possibilities of the misuse of this provision, if any legal sanction is given to such contingencies. There have been cases where brothers have killed brothers and children have killed parents for petty financial gains or property. There have also been cases in India where unscrupulous doctors have certified sane women mad simply for monetary considerations or to help the husbands to contract second or third marriages.

In some cases the line between murder and suicide is very thin. If a person is pushed from the top of a multi-storeyed building, then it is murder. If he jumps to death, then it is suicide.

All the same, it is true that sometimes for the indigent and sick senior citizens, old age does become a curse. Our country of 1000 millions has about 700 recognised old age homes in India and another 300 that are run by religious organisations. Each home may have 70 to 100 inmates. Hence, at best, there is provision only for 100,000 senior citizens. The cost of accommodation in such homes would be anything from Rs. 4,000 per month and above. There are 95 million old people in India, at present. Thirty per cent of these live below the poverty line and 80 per cent reside in the rural areas. As many as 93 per cent are illiterate. In Delhi alone there are 1.5 lakh couples over the age of 60. What is more, 70 per cent of Delhi's real estate, running into thousands of crores of rupees, is owned by persons above the age of 70.

Those who are sick and can claim to possess suicidal tendency need protection and support from society, not imprisonment or sophisticated methods to bring death. Die all us have to, but the way to reduce suffering of others is to teach them to lead a meaningful existence and die with dignity. There is a need to tell patients that doctors can, at most times, cure, but on few occasions comfort. Moreover, the hospital staff, especially the doctors and nurses, must acknowledge that patients go to them only for treatment and cure, and that they should be attended to with all devotion and understanding.

Life is a gift from God and each individual is its custodian. Only God can give life and only He should take it away. The almighty does not put us in situations that we cannot handle. He supports us all through our suffering. To actively seek an end to one's life would be showing our lack of trust in Him. An individual who commits suicide is committing sin both against God and man.

Indeed, no religion, be it Hinduism or Christianity or Islam, supports assisted killing or murder. The Quran states, "Take not life which Allah made sacred otherwise than in the course of justice" The concept of a life not worthy of living simply does not exist in Islam." However, a growing number of so-called agnostics, atheists, humanists, secularists and liberals rubbish such religious injunctions. In Switzerland, altruistic suicide with the assistance of a non-physician is considered legal. Swiss law does not recognise the concept of euthanasia. "Murder upon request by the victim" (Article 114 of the Swiss penal code) is dealt with less severely, than murder without the victim's request. However, it remains illegal. The Netherlands passed a law in 2000 allowing voluntary euthanasia and physician assisted suicide took effect. Prior to this law, for 20 years this had been permitted under prescribed guidelines. In 1990, physicians in the Netherlands were involved in 11,800 deaths that constituted nine per cent of all deaths in the country.

Belgium passed a similar law in 2002, allowing both voluntary euthanasia and physician-assisted suicide. Assisted suicide and euthanasia raise questions that cannot be answered from the perspective of medical opinion alone. There is an incompatibility between the act of bringing death voluntarily and the professional ethos of physicians. For most physicians in India, it would mean that they should not assist in speedy death. The average life expectancy in 1900 was about 30 years. Now a child born in Japan lives to the age of 80. Life expectancy in the US is 77 years whereas in India it is 68 years. Nobody has ever said that living such a long life is not worth it. Moreover, there are moments of weakness or stress when persons can take wrong decisions.

Our Constitution sanctions right to life. Article 21 states a person cannot be denied right to life "except in accordance with procedures defined by law". The right to die is not inherent in the right to life. Assuming for a minute euthanasia is permitted, it will be almost impossible for any court to precisely adjudicate whether the murder of a human being was carried out for reasons claimed as unselfish or self-seeking. In a survey conducted by a leading magazine in India in December 2004, to ascertain the views of Indians on the question of mercy killing, a surprising 76.92 per cent voted in its favour and 23.08 voted against it.

However, I would like to emphasise once again that we have in our country the right to life, but not death. Committing suicide can be painful but medical assistance in curing the ailments can make death less tortuous. The Supreme Court, in one of its earlier rulings, held decriminalising suicide as "unconstitutional". In another ruling, it said the provision against suicide was "constitutional, necessary and proper". It is best to render unto God (human life) what is of God.

12

Woman: The Better Half of Society

1. The Gains

1.1. Gain of Justice

The Supreme Court in a landmark judgement on February 14 gave the Central and State Governments three months to enact a legislation to make registration of marriages compulsory. According to the court's order, the proof of a traditional religious marriage ceremony is not adequate. Earlier, the Union Government had rejected the National Human Rights Commission's proposal for compulsory registration of Hindu marriages - as had the PV Narasimha Rao Government in 1994 and the HD Deve Gowda Government in 1996.

The National Commission for Women had put before the court its views favouring registration of marriages. According to the commission, such a law would help ensure a minimum age for marriage, prevent marriages without consent of both parties, check bigamy and polygamy and deter people from buying and selling young girls in the guise of marriage. Women, whose marriages are registered, can easily claim alimony in case of divorce or separation.

At present most marriages in India remain unregistered as people are married according to their religious rites. The Convention on the Elimination of All Forms of Discrimination Against Women

(CEDAW), which is considered an international bill of rights for women, was adopted in 1979 by the UN General Assembly. India became a signatory to the convention on July 30, 1980, and ratified on July 9, 1993, with two declaratory statements and one reservation.

Article 16 (2) of the convention says: "The betrothal and the marriage of a child shall have no legal effect, and all necessary action, including legislation, shall be taken to specify a minimum age for marriage and to make the registration of marriages in an official registry compulsory." India, at that time, while agreeing to the principle of compulsory registration of marriages, said: "It is not practical, in a vast country like India with its variety of customs, religions and level of literacy."

It is believed that registration of marriages is only an urban phenomenon and married couples register only to meet special requirements like getting passports or visas. There is no doubt that there have been a lot of social reforms which were pioneered by reformists like Raja Ram Mohan Roy in the 19th century. There has been a concerted effort to bring an end to sati and child marriage. Moreover, our Constitution guarantees equality to women. So far it had not been made compulsory to register marriages in India. However, there are a number of legislations on the issue in the country which transcend religion, caste and community.

Under the Special Marriage Act 1954, which is valid for any Indian citizen regardless of the religion of the marrying couple, each marriage can be registered by officers specially appointed for the purpose. Registration of marriage is compulsory under the Indian Christian Marriages Act, 1872. Parsi Marriage and Divorce Act 1936 makes registration of marriages necessary. According to Muslim law, a marriage is regarded as a civil contract and the qazi or officiating priest records the terms of the marriage in a nikahnama, which is handed over to the married couple.

Under Section 8 of the Hindu Marriage Act 1954, there is a provision for registration of marriages. However, it is left to the marrying parties either to solemnise the marriage before the sub-registrar or register it after performing the ceremony in conformity with Hindu beliefs. Regardless of caste, creed or religion Goa's family laws provide for compulsory registration of marriage to avoid multi-marriages. There is a provision for penalising the civil registrar if any marriage is registered in contravention of the provisions of the civil code.

The following enactments by the State Governments have provided for uniform compulsory registration of marriages:

- The Bombay Registration of Marriages Act, 1953. This Act applies to the States of Maharashtra and Gujarat.
- The Karnataka Marriages Act, 1976 in force since 1983.
- The Himachal Pradesh Registration of Marriage Act, 1997.
- Andhra Pradesh passed the Compulsory Registration of Marriage Act, 2002.

It is women who are affected the most by non-registration of marriages. In the absence of registration of marriages women become victims of bigamy and property disputes. They face enormous hardship as they have no proof of their marriage. It is worse in cases of bigamous marriages as women can lose their cases because of their failure to prove the first or second marriage of their husbands.

Another serious national problem that can be tackled through the compulsory registration of marriages is that of child marriage. It is estimated that in half of all the marriages which take place in the country, the girls are underage. According to the Rapid Household Survey conducted across the country, 58.9 per cent women in Bihar were married before the age of 18; 55.5 per cent in Rajasthan; 54.9 per cent in West Bengal; 53.8 per cent in UP; 53.2 per cent in Madhya Pradesh; and, Karnataka 39.3 per cent.

Jammu and Kashmir has the lowest percentage of underage marriage - 3.4 per cent followed by Himachal Pradesh 3.5 per cent and Goa 4.1 per cent. Despite high female literacy, close to one-tenth of women in Kerala are married off before the legal age of 18. Despite Child Marriage Restraint Act 1929, which prescribes minimum marriageable age of 18 years for girls and 21 years for boys, child marriages are rampant in Rajasthan, Madhya Pradesh, Uttar Pradesh, Haryana, Orissa, Chhattisgarh, Jharkhand and Bihar.

There have been cases of foreigners especially aged Arab men paying for young brides from poor Muslim families in Hyderabad. There have been well-known cases of old Arab men marrying girls and deserting them after a couple of days. Such marriages are arranged by brokers and solemnised by recognised Muslim clerics. Laws for registration of marriages will act as a deterrent to the problem of such marriages to wealthy Arab men looking for perverse gratification. Prajwala, an NGO, that is devoted to stop traffic in women reports that "every month nearly 35 such marriages take place in Hyderabad".

It also claims to have "identified at least 75 families that have married off their daughters to Arabs for a price". Less than one-fifth of them actually hear from their daughters later to know that they are well. The NGO has also found out that many of the girls are sold to prostitution after their husbands leave them or become domestic workers once they reach the Gulf.

The only solution to this complicated state of affairs is to insist on registration of marriages. Religious ceremonies can follow for those who want to go through them. The registering officer should be empowered to demand a signed declaration that neither party has a living spouse. This order will also deal with child marriages. The law against child marriages itself is weak. Parents can be theoretically sentenced to three months' imprisonment.

But it happens rarely. A survey in 2001 found that there were never more than 89 attempted prosecutions across India in any one year on this count and much less convictions. According to UNICEF, 82 per cent girls in Rajasthan, where the practice is particularly widespread, are married when they are 18 years old; 15 per cent of girls in rural areas across the country are married before 13; and 52 per cent of girls have their first pregnancy between 15 and 19 years of age.

The Supreme Court's order making registration of marriages compulsory will both strengthen and regulate the institution of marriage. The order when put to effect will, among other things, prevent child marriages, check bigamy and polygamy, help widows to claim inheritance and deter men from deserting their wives. The significance of the Supreme Court directive, asking Government to compulsorily register all marriages, is enormous and revolutionary. The court's order has furthered the cause of gender empowerment. The passing of the order was an extraordinary moment in the history of free India.

1.2. Gain of Emancipation

In our country, there is a general belief-bordering on the ridiculous-that reservations are the panacea not only for poverty alleviation, but also for social uplift. The present position is that the initial reservation for Scheduled Castes and Scheduled Tribes, which was to last only for a decade, has been put on a permanent footing. It is also felt that quotas for other categories have been included, taking the total reservation percentage to 50 per cent. For vote-catching needs or sustaining votebanks, political parties left to themselves would have gone to the outrageous extent of dividing the whole of society into reserved categories.

One thing is clear. Quotas are only meant to create an illusion in the targeted section that a particular party espousing its cause is its true messiah. But no politician in the current dispensation has the guts to call a spade a spade.

It would be useful to look at the statewise representation of women in Parliament (Lok Sabha). Take, for example, the number elected in the 1998 election: In UP, they accounted for nine out of a total of 85; from West Bengal, five of 42; from Bihar four of 54; from Maharashtra three of 48; from Tamil Nadu one of 39; and Kerala, one of 20. No other State sent any woman MP to the Lok Sabha.

Politicians of all hues feel' that it is better to keep the carrot dangling in front of the likely beneficiaries. There is no doubt that women for historical and other reasons, or for being dubbed the 'weaker sex', have not moved ahead in many fields. Existing legal remedies have failed to protect them from the most common crimes in this country: Dowry, bigamy, kidnapping, desertion, rape, refusal of shelter and denial of nourishment. But this is not because of lack of reservations. Quotas or no quotas, these perceived 'nature'-assigned and society-apportioned roles are not going to change easily, either in India or abroad.

This country has, however, taken tremendous strides in ameliorating the conditions of women. Earlier, a woman joining the Indian Foreign Service could be asked to resign. The doors of the defence services, police and paramilitary were shut to them. But with more and more women opting for these professions, some have actually broken into traditional male bastions on the basis of merit. Still, their presence in these services, where entry is by open competition, is only slightly better than marginal. Even in services in the private and Government sectors, their total number is just less than five per cent.

It is worth noting that women belonging to the reserved category of 50 per cent could, if competent and qualified, corner all the jobs. With equal ease, they could get the rest on the basis of merit. Reservation divides, it does not unite society. Yet there has been a rising demand that women should get 33 per cent seats reserved in State legislatures and Parliament. It will be interesting to go through the history of this proposal.

In June 1996, the then Prime Minister, Mr HD Deve Gowda, promised a Women's Reservation Bill. In May 1997, his successor IK Gujral faced a party revolt on the Bill. Law Minister Khalap introduced it, but shortly after, the House was adjourned. In August 1997, Mr Gujral gave up, citing lack of consensus. In December the same year, the Lok Sabha was dissolved, and the Bill lapsed again.

Then, in December 1998, the legislation was reintroduced amid stormy scenes in the Lok Sabha. In April 1999, the House was dissolved, and the Bill fell through. In May 2003, it was reintroduced for the third time. But the Samajwadi Party, the RJD, the Samata Party, the Shiv Sena, the JD(U) and the IUML stalled proceedings. Matters, therefore, remained where they were in 1996, after Parliament was adjourned on May 9, 2003.

During the last effort to stall the Bill, its opponents demanded a quota-within-a-quota for SCs/STs, OBCs and minorities. The BJP, the Congress and the Left as well as regional parties such as the Telugu Desam, the DMK and the AIADMK, promised to support the Bill. However, the lung power of a small section thwarted what probably the silent majority wanted-or should we say actually did not want? This helped the NDA Government, divided as it was internally over the Bill, disown the responsibility of ensuring the passage of the Bill.

A number of MPs, whose parties were self-professed backers of the Bill, congratulated the shouting brigade for successfully scuttling it. The convenient justification trotted out was the quest for consensus on alternative proposals.

If the major parties genuinely uphold the cause of women's empowerment, why do they not have a compulsory quota in party nominations? If they voluntarily accept the underlying principle, they can make a beginning by fielding at least 20 per cent women candidates. In fact, party quota is the route taken by most democracies where women have succeeded in securing a decent political representation.

However, many women have done extremely well the world over not on the basis of quotas, but merit. It is true they were aided by circumstances. Most women in prominent political positions attained office in succession to a male relative, perceived to be heroic and usually martyred. SWRD Bandaranaike was assassinated in 1959. His widow was swept into political prominence after his death. Her daughter, Ms Chandrika Kumaratunga, is now Sri Lanka's President.

Nehru died in 1964 and, in 1966, his daughter Indira Gandhi became Prime Minister. Zulfikar Ali Bhutto was executed in Pakistan in 1979. In course of time, his daughter Benazir Bhutto became Prime Minister for the first time in 1988. She continued to be in and out of power, before going into exile in the UK.

In nascent Bangladesh, Sheikh Mujibur Rahman was assassinated along with his wife and five children in August 1975. One of his surviving daughters eventually became the leader of the Awami League, and finally Prime Minister in 1997. President Ziaur Rahman was likewise killed in May 1981. Ten years later, his widow was sworn in Prime Minister. Bangladesh is the first country to have had two women Prime Ministers in succession, belonging to rival parties.

In the only South American member of the Commonwealth, Guyana, Cheddi B Jagan was sworn in on October 30, 1992, in succession to Hugh Desmond Hoyte. Cheddi Jagan died in March 1997. In December 1997, his widow Janet Jagan was elected President amidst charges that, as a Chicago-born White American, she was not qualified to be Head of State.

The one remarkable woman leader who did not acquire power on account of a male relative was Britain's Margaret Thatcher. She became Prime Minister in May 1979, and continued at the top for 11 years. Another leader, Dame Mary Eugenia Charles of Dominica in the West Indies, was Prime Minister from July 1980 till 1994. Canada also had its woman Prime Minister when Brian Mulroney resigned in favour of Kim Campbell in 1993. It was not an appropriate time obviously. In the election, her Progressive Conservative Party suffered the worst defeat any ruling party had faced. Its seats shrank from 153 to two members in the House of Commons. She was Prime Minister for a mere 134 days, and resigned as party leader on December 13, 1993.

The point is that no developed country talks of reservations. The deserving get what they deserve, by dint of merit. It is pertinent to note that Switzerland gave women the vote only in 1971. In the US, only 13.6 per cent seats in the Senate and House of Representatives together are currently held by women. A token reservation for women exists in Bangladesh, France and the Scandinavian countries.

According to a political thinker, "Nothing can stop an idea whose time has come." Clearly, it is not the opportune moment for India to have women's reservation in legislatures. Let us continue to experiment with reserving seats for them at the grassroots levels, like in Panchayats and municipalities over the next 10 to 20 years. If the experiment proves successful after two decades, it could be extended to the national and State Legislatures, but only after building a consensus.

2. The Taboos

2.1. Violation of Women Rights

Domestic violence has plagued marriages since the dawn of history. Forty per cent of divorces granted during the Victorian era in the UK were the result of "marital cruelty", indicating that women and society were intolerant towards such acts. In lectures and speeches, our leaders pat themselves on the back that we have always treated women as equal and protected them. The latest figures, however, disclose a totally different story.

According to the latest figures of a Government organisation, the National Crime Records Bureau, crime against women takes place every 17 second. Similarly, one dowry death is recorded every 77 minute and one arson case every hour. Worse, in India, one rape case takes place every 27 minute.

In Delhi, crime against women has increased by 45 per cent. Women in the city do not feel safe at their workplace, as per the first Human Development Report of Delhi. Delhi leads the four metro cities in crime against women. The report says, for every 10,000 people, 14 cases of crime against women are reported in Delhi. In this list, Chennai stands at seven, while Mumbai and Kolkata remain at five.

Even Delhi Chief Minister Sheila Dikshit has declared, "Delhi has emerged as quite an unsafe city for women." According to the report, "One-third of the people in the survey have confessed personal safety in the city was poor. Opinion of half of the people that the city was unsafe for women is another concern." Only 24 per cent people feel Delhi Police has been doing a good job in terms of public safety.

Religious beliefs and traditions, coming down through ages, have promoted women's subordination not only in the household, but also places of work. Religious subordination implies that for a woman to be virtuous, she must follow the lead of her husband and accept him as he is. Violence against women is only a continuation of male domination over his wife. Illiteracy, foeticide and treating girls as burden further worsen the situation. How else can one explain the honour killing of girls by their fathers for marrying outside the community?

Several women victims keep quite because they are economically dependent on their husbands. Such crimes go unreported and unregistered. The actual figure could be much higher, as only those crimes that are reported to the police become the basis of analysis.

The Constitution provides equality to all, but the reality is that even the modern women have to struggle with circumstances to prevent their being exposed to hardships and crime.

"Gender-motivated crimes", like the sexual harassment, is considered a "violation of women's rights", but they continue not only at work places, but also public places like the public transport. In our country, women are subject to discrimination not only on the basis of gender, but also other factors such as caste, community, religious affiliation and class. Poor families have generally no interest in educating their daughters. They will marry them off even as children to ensure that they are taken care of economically.

Levels of crime, including rapes, kidnappings, dowry deaths, mental and physical tortures, sexual harassments and traffickings show that the Government, despite their proclamations, has failed to enforce the law regarding the protection of women. Laws against dowry, domestic violence, sexual harassment and child marriages, if enforced properly, can mitigate the hardships to a great extent.

Another crime for which there is no classification is that of attacks on the "honour" of women. There have been cases where women have been stripped and paraded naked on the ground that they have broken the community's norms. Sometimes they are killed after being branded as witches. It is believed that most women killed as witches are, in fact, targeted because of property disputes. And, most of them are widows.

In India, only determined women can break the shackles to win universal acclamation. Indra Nooyi has been ranked as the fourth most powerful woman and Congress president Sonia Gandhi occupies 13th position in the list of 100 most powerful women in the world.

The country was expected to witness tremendous changes when the 73rd Amendment was passed by Parliament. There is no doubt that there is definite improvement, but it is marginal.

Molestation and sexual harassment of women and girls are not new. Women students have often complained of sexual harassment. Sometimes back, a college professor of Wilson College, just prior to his retirement, had to face the wrath of students for allegedly misbehaving with a girl student. The students paraded him with a garland of slippers before handing him over to police. This kind of punishment and public humiliation is more effective than jail sentences. One may question the legitimacy of the students' act, but even as per the law, the students would have been guilty only if they had caused any grievous hurt to the professor. What they have done is only a non-cognisable offence of putting a chappal garlands around the neck of an erring professor.

Despite sporadic incidents of crime against women, like a constable raping a girl and teachers misbehaving with his their students, Mumbai remains the safest city in India according to many Mumbaikars. Some say that Mumbai is safe because it was never unsafe. They feel that even the shadiest parts of Mumbai are safe for women. However, with public morality being hostage to politicians, chances are that it may soon become a heaven for the depraved. After all, perversion breeds best where there is repression.

The truth is that any place, whether it is Delhi or Mumbai, is safe for a woman if she decides to become a "Durga" and not the traditional suffering Indian woman. There are no free lunches in life. It equally applies to women who should know what their rights are - first as a citizen and then as women. It is the duty of the Government and the organisations working to empower women to make them aware about their rights. More than anything else, women should be persuaded to learn martial art for self-defence.

The women in Mumbai are comparatively bolder and dynamic than others. It is also for this reason that men in Mumbai do not dare to harass them. This is what makes Mumbai a reasonably safer place.

Women should keep in mind what Eleanor Roosevelt once said, "Nobody can make you feel inferior without your permission."

2.2. Prestige Threatened

The figures of National Crime Research Bureau indicate that the incidents of rape have increased from 15,330 in 1997 to 16,496 in 2000. This includes custodial rape which is worse because it is done by the guardians of the law who are duty bound to protect people from such heinous crimes.

At times, the authority vested in men in uniform seems to go to their heads encouraging them to commit the gravest of offences such as rape. The latest to join the ranks of a uniformed rapist is a constable of the Mumbai Police who allegedly raped a girl inside a police post at Mumbai's Marine Drive on April 21, 2004, purportedly under the influence of alcohol. Since then, the constable has been arrested, remanded to police custody and dismissed from service.

However, this is hardly a consolation to the victim, her family or even the public at large. Moreover, neither is this the first nor the last case in which deeds of people in authority have tainted their own image. Indeed, we have countless instances of policemen being accused of sexual harassment.

On September 6, 2003, a 22-year-old private nurse was raped by a ward boy at Delhi's Shanti Mukund Hospital in East Delhi. The rapist, Bhura, has been sentenced to life imprisonment. Earlier, he had made a despicable offer to marry the victim, pretending as if he wished to save her from ignominy. However, his offer was nothing more than a ploy to escape punishment.

Once again on September 23, 2003, a 15-year-old girl was allegedly sexually assaulted by a doctor in the Holy Angels Hospital in Vasant Vihar, New Delhi. A 17-year-old Delhi University student was raped by four jawans of the President's Body Guard the same year near the Capital's Buddha Jayanti park. Incidentally, these jawans are supposed to be among one of the best in the Army and are handpicked to take care of the President's security.

A sex scandal rocked judicial circles in Rajasthan in November 2002 when a deputy registrar of the High Court was suspended for seeking sexual favours for himself and a couple of judges from a woman litigant. Another woman had complained in August 2004 against the then serving director general of Meteorological Department. She accused him of sexually harassing her over a period of 10 years. According to her, she had got the job by using his influence and did not want to lose it. She alleged that she was forced into a physical relationship with the accused.

She claimed that the accused prevented her from getting married. In a similar case, an aspiring actress called Preeti Jain filed a complaint in July 2004 against film director Madhur Bhandarkar for allegedly raping her 16 times between 1999 and 2004 and even threatening to kill her. In yet another shocking incident of sexual assault, a 29-year-old teacher was arrested for allegedly raping a minor student over a year.

It is obnoxious that those on duty-who are supposed to protect people-do exactly the opposite. However, it is society which is responsible for the prevailing situation in which sexual harassment takes place brazenly.

Also, to downplay such heinous crimes is unjustifiable. The fact that the society attaches stigma to rape indicates that the victim is victimised further. Cases of sexual assault are kept as guarded secret by the guardians of victims so that it does not jeopardise their marriage prospects.

On an average, rape cases take anywhere between two and ten years to be decided. In one such instance, it took 15 years to wrap up a case. According to a report released by Delhi Commission for Women, "Only 20 per cent of rape cases are reported." The conviction rate in the last four years has never exceeded more than 20 per cent. In most cases, it has been revealed that the police acts as a mediator between the accused and the victim-often for monetary considerations. This is one reason why victims are reluctant to file cases with the police.

According to the Delhi Police, statistics of the last four years in the Capital reveal the following. Out of a total of 561 cases of rape in 2004, the rapist was known to the victim in 503. In 242 of such cases, the rapist was a neighbour. In 201, the rapist was a doctor, servant or priest. A large number of perpetrators were also teachers. In 39 cases, the offender was a relative, father, stepfather, father in-law, brother in-law, etc.

All existing laws are framed with the objective of deterring such crimes as well as punishing the guilty. However, they need to be harsher to cause the most hardened criminals to think twice before committing any crime. Once a crime is committed, the judicial verdict must be passed expeditiously and the perpetrator punished swiftly.

On both these counts, the current laws and their implementation leave much to be desired. Such loopholes in our legal system do not check the men from committing such crimes. They do so brazenly because they know from the past that there have been only a few instances when such cases reach their logical conclusion. Although there are various reasons for this, the foremost is lack of cooperation from victim and her family members. It requires uncommon courage and effort on the part of a rape victim to wait patiently for the conclusion of the case.

Apart from the above handicaps, rape victims or their guardians not only have to humour but occasionally bribe the investigating or medical officers to treat the traumatised sufferer with empathy and courtesy. At times, victims are examined by male (instead of a female) doctors, which adds to their woes. According to the police, most rapists go scott free because victims turn hostile in court. This may be due to the fact that the guilty is usually known to them. The foremost problem of the victims is protracted litigation. The primary concern of parents is to help their child recover from the trauma. However, a lengthy litigation does not permit that. Also, it affects the victim's marriage prospects.

Whenever an outrageous crime like rape occurs, those at the helm issue statements and order formation of committees. However, tall promises of curbing such incidents are forgotten till the next rape. Piles of reports are lying with the Government to bring about the desired changes in the law concerning rape but no concrete step has been taken so far.

A committee formed under the aegis of the Home Ministry on March 2005 went over the recommendations made by the National Police Commission, the Padmanabhaiah Committee on Police Reforms, Malimath Committee on Criminal Justice System and suggestions of various State Police Reforms Commission to improve the criminal justice system in the country. However, the record is woeful in terms of implementation.

Meanwhile, rape victims and their families continue to endure pain and misery. Till we have stringent laws against sexual assault as well oppression, the only remedy for women is to guard themselves against unwanted male attention. They must stay vigilant and observant and avoid going to deserted locations. A potential rapist is on the prowl in a quiet and lonely place where he can pounce upon his prey. Intuition is a good guide. If a woman senses something fishy, she must quickly be on alert. She should think twice before relying on a person, no matter how trustworthy or familiar he may be. This is because a majority of rapes are committed by those known to the victim. However, an assertive and strong woman would discourage a potential rapist.

God forbid, if a lady is confronted with such a situation, she must raise alarm to draw the attention of passers-by. Children-especially girls-are advised to seek help from women, preferably the elderly. They should also be discouraged from talking to strangers and not allow entry of men in their hearths even if they are acquaintances, when they are alone. After all, prevention is the best way to deal with such crimes.

2.3. Crimes of Passion and of Honour

Of late, there has been a spate of criminal incidents wherein, instead of outsiders, family members themselves have been responsible for the killing their near and dear ones. In Delhi a father killed his daughter because she married against his wishes. A wife got her husband killed to prevent him from marrying another woman. A lover threw acid on a girl who was presumably his beloved for spurning his advances.

In other words, there have been numerous crimes of passions. Crime passionale in the usual sense of the term, is a crime in which the perpetrator commits a heinous offence, especially assault or murder, against spouse or another loved one due to feelings of sudden jealousy, rage or heartbreak. In other words, it is not a premeditated crime. A characteristic or representative crime of passion might involve a jealous husband who comes to know that his wife is cheating on him. He might then proceed to murder her and/or her paramour. Although this concept has no legal acceptance, the defence lawyers often use it due to the fact that popular opinion, if not courts of law, sometimes view the commission of murder or grievous bodily harm involved in the crime of passion with sympathy and acceptance.

In some countries, notably France, crime passionale has been a valid defence of murder cases. Until 1975, the French Penal Code commuted the sentence of a husband who found his wife in the act of committing adultery and killed her. India's most celebrated crime of passion, involving pati, patni aur woh took place on April 27, 1959, when a Naval Commander Nanavati murdered a glamourous romeo who had enticed his English wife. Such an incident was unheard of in the higher echelons of Bombay society. It was called the original crime of passion. It immediately caught the imagination of the people in Bombay and other parts of the country.

The case swept the judicial system of the country like a tornado and was a landmark in India's legal history. Jury trials in India were abolished after this case, as it was alleged that the jury had been influenced to give a verdict in favour of Nanavati.

Human Rights watch defines 'honour killings' as follows: Honour crimes are acts of violence, usually murder, committed by male family members, against female family members, who are perceived to have brought dishonour to the family. A woman can be targeted by her family for a variety of reasons including refusing to enter into arranged marriage, or being the victim of a sexual assault, or seeking divorce from an abusive husband or committing adultery. The mere perception that a woman has acted in a manner that brings 'dishonour' to the family is sufficient to trigger violence. In fact, crimes of passion have nothing or little in common with honour killings which come across frequently not only in our country but also elsewhere. Those responsible for honour killings are supposed to be prosecuted, under ordinary murder, but in practice police and prosecutors often ignore it.

Reports submitted to the United Nations Commission on Human Rights show that honour killings have occurred in Bangladesh, Great Britain, Brazil , Ecuador, Egypt, India , Israel, Italy, Jordan, Pakistan, Afghanistan, Morocco, Sweden, Turkey, and Uganda The question is, can anything be done to control or reduce crimes of passion, since the police force has not been able to curb it? Police forces all over the world are patently uncomfortable with any rise in crime. Logical and methodical efforts are made by some of them to underplay the crime in order to give an impression that all is well.

In some countries cold blooded murder as well as in flagrante delicto (in the act of committing adultery) are not punished. These countries include Jordan; where a part of Article 340 of the Jordanian Penal Code states that "He who discovers his wife, or one of his female relatives committing adultery and kills, wounds, or injures one of them, is exempted from any penalty."This was twice put forward for cancellation by the Government, but was retained by the Lower House of the Parliament. Countries that allow men to kill female relatives in flagrante delicto (but not in cold blood) include: Syria.

Article 548 of the Syrian Penal Code states: "He who catches his wife or one of his ascendants, descendants or sister committing adultery, (flagrante delicto) or illegitimate sexual acts with another and he killed or injured one or both of them benefits from an exemption of penalty." Countries that allow husbands to kill only their wives in flagrante delicto (based upon the Napoleonic Code) include Morocco, where Article 418 of the Penal Code states: "Murder, injury and beating are excusable, if they are committed by a husband, on his wife as well as the accomplice, at the moment in which he surprises them in the act of adultery."

Consequently, on October 26, 2004, Pakistan's lower house of Parliament passed a bill that would make honour killings punishable by a prison term of seven years and death penalty in the most extreme cases. Thousands of women are murdered by their families every year in the name of family 'honour'. It is difficult to get the precise number of honour killings; because such murders frequently go unreported. Hence, the perpetrators remain unpunished. Most honour killings occur in countries where the concept of women as a vassal of the family prevails.

In Muzaffarnagar district of Uttar Pradesh, at least 13 honour killings occurred within nine months in 2003. In 2002, while 10 such killings were reported, 35 couples were declared missing. All India Democratic Women's Organisation estimates that Haryana and Punjab alone account for 10 per cent of all honour killings in the country. Caste panchayats have come to play an increasingly important role in Haryana and elsewhere, especially in view of the vote-bank politics.

Fundamental to the subject of honour and violence, is the subordinate position of girls and women in all castes and communities. A woman's chastity is the 'honour' of the community. A woman does not even have right over her body at any point of her life. In our country, more than 5,000 brides are killed annually because their dowries are considered insufficient and a disgrace to family's honour according to the United Nations Children's Fund (UNICEF). Says Widney Brown, Director for Human Rights Watch. "In countries where Islam is practiced, they're called honour killings, but dowry deaths and so-called crimes of passion have a similar dynamic in that the women are killed by male family members and the crimes are perceived as excusable or understandable. The practice, goes across cultures and across religions."

There are several attributes to the issue of crimes of passion and honour killings. First, the sheer geographic size of the country and the spread of this phenomenon. Second, there are personal and family reasons behind people perpetrating honour or crime for passion killing. Though there is no religious sanction to the phenomenon, society looks upon it with an amused tolerance and at best something that affects others and not it. The truth is not much can be done unless the world treats women with equality. Women have to take the lead in educating their own ilk.

It is disturbing to see mothers, mothers-in-law, sisters, and cousins frequently supporting attacks on women in the name of honour and thereby abetting crimes of passion. It is also a question of change of community's mentality. These incidents are occurring among the uneducated and illiterate people whose attitudes cannot be changed. Even the educated do not come out against this practice forcefully. More than that, a strong political will is a pre-requisite to tackle this abominable issue.

2.4. Sexual Harassment

In March 2008, an allegation of sexual harassment levelled against Orissa's Assembly Speaker by a woman marshal not only led to the adjournment of the House, but also his resignation. A Minister of Orissa, too, lost his job for allegedly engineering the conspiracy against the Speaker. Terming the allegation as baseless, the Speaker said that it was the fallout of actions initiated to discipline employees and also part of a "conspiracy in which important persons were involved".

This is not the only case of sexual harassment involving a high-profile celebrity in the country. In September 2004, former Kerala Minister A Neelalohithadasan Nadar was sentenced to one-year imprisonment in a sexual assault case. This was the result of a complaint filed in 1999 by a Divisional Forest Officer, in which she had alleged that the Minister attempted to molest her after summoning her to his room at a guesthouse on the pretext of an 'urgent' meeting. Another case was filed against him by Ms. Nalini Netto, an IAS officer, who had complained about his misbehaviour to the then Chief Minister on February 9, 2000. Following the complaint, he had to resign from the Ministry.

An inquiry conducted in 2007 by the Ministry of Women and Child Welfare found the UNICEF India Chief guilty of sexual harassment. It requested the Ministry of External Affairs to withdraw his diplomatic immunity, though a UNICEF inquiry had absolved him of the charge. An Army court of inquiry found an official of the rank of Major General guilty of sexual harassment of his subordinate woman officer of the rank of Captain. He would now be court martialled.

Sexual harassment and rape are two sides of the same coin. Both have one victim - women. Often, sexual harassment cases have hit the headlines in our country. Such cases are not confined to the Government sector. They are equally rampant in the private sector.

The Supreme Court has defined sexual harassment, which "includes such unwelcome sexually determined behaviour (whether directly or by implication) as: Physical contact and advances; a demand or request for sexual favours; sexually coloured remarks; showing pornography; any other unwelcome physical, verbal or non-verbal conduct of sexual nature". It has emphasised that the guidelines and norms being laid down by it have to be duly observed at all workplaces or other institutions until a legislation is enacted for this purpose and that these should be treated as law under Article 141 of the Constitution.

The apex court has also observed that employers should take appropriate steps to prevent sexual harassment. These include: First, express prohibition of sexual harassment at the workplace should be notified, published and circulated in appropriate ways. Second, the rules and regulations of Government and public bodies relating to conduct and discipline should include rules and regulations prohibiting sexual harassment and provide for appropriate penalties in such rules against the offender. Third, appropriate work conditions should be provided in respect of work, leisure, health and hygiene to ensure that there is no hostile environment towards women at workplaces. No woman employee should have any reasonable ground to believe that she is disadvantaged vis-?-vis others.

Whether or not such conduct constitutes an offence under law or a breach of the service rules, a mechanism should be created in the organisation to redress the complaint made by the victim. In other words, any action of a superior or a senior against a female employee which is against accepted moral norms and does not stand the test of decency and modesty amounts to sexual harassment.

The truth is that women desist from complaining against superiors not only because they fear losing their jobs, but also because there is an element of doubt and disbelief against their complaint. In certain cases, women who have complained have had allegations made against them that they invited it by being 'too friendly' with the accused. Some have had their antecedents dug up, leading to trivialisation of complaints. In many cases, such complaints are seen from the male point of view, according to women rights activists.

In India, according to a survey, a woman is reported to be sexually harassed every 51 minutes and every 26 minutes a woman is sexually molested. Several studies indicate that the magnitude of unreported cases is several times over the estimate. The report of a study conducted by the Gender Study Group of the University of Delhi showed that 91.7 per cent of all inmates of women's hostels had faced sexual harassment on the roads and within the campus.

According to a study by the International Labour Organisation in 23 countries, between 15 per cent and 30 per cent of working women had been subjected to sexual harassment, which varied from explicit demands for sexual intercourse to offensive remarks. One out of 12 women surveyed had to quit her job; some of them were dismissed. The issue of sexual harassment has been in the forefront of Western women's movements for equality and efforts have been made to make educational institutions and workplaces safer.

A study has found that 45 per cent of Czechoslovakian women have been sexually harassed in the workplace, but the real numbers are higher. The Czech term for sexual harassment, "*sexualni haraseni*", implies a tacit understanding that whoever complains about harassment is making an unnecessary fuss.

Till now no law has been passed which considers sexual harassment as a separate legal offence in our country. The fact is that it is not less serious, but it is always taken less seriously. France is the only country that has passed a criminal law related to sexual harassment. The statistics released by Delhi Police in January 2008 has reinforced Delhi's image as a city where women are unsafe. The reported molestation cases rose to an all-time high of 835 in 2007, as against 713 in 2006. And this number may just be the tip of the iceberg, as a large number of cases go unreported.

It is high time for the Government of India to pass a law aimed at curbing this social evil.

3. Beyond Tokenism: Challenges to be Met

Last Monday, March 8, was observed as the International Women's Day. On this day, everybody who is somebody tries to show his concern for the fair sex. This is so right from the street level politician to the President, the Prime Minister, governors, and chief ministers, at the top levels. Concerned bureaucrats dealing with women try to beat the other in their expression of love and concern for women. The first International Women's Day, or IWD, was observed on March 19, 1911, in Germany, Austria, Denmark and some other European countries. This date was chosen by German women because on this day in 1848, the Prussian king faced with an armed uprising had promised many reforms, including an unfulfilled one of votes for women.

It was during International Women's Year in 1975 that IWD was given official recognition by the United Nations. From then on, several governments which had previously not known of its existence, started observing it. International Woman's Day has inspired many women's movements in the world. It was in 1982 that women in Iran courageously discarded their veils on IWD. Though its impact has not been uniform, it still has its influence. Women in Taiwan are awarded an extra day's holiday by the government as part of a new "Gender Equality Act". Under new legislation, women are entitled to take a day's holiday every month during their menstrual period, and those who suffer miscarriages can take five days to four weeks off. Men and women can apply for up to two years' maternity leave.

In India, though the position is not as it should ideally be, women are occupying some of top-of-the-line managers' jobs including governors, chief ministers, chief secretaries, secretaries to the Government, additional secretaries, income tax and customs commissioners, inspectors generals of police, deputy commissioners, the superintendent of police. However, in all sectors and Government jobs, women will always have to prove themselves. They have to work doubly hard than men to carve a niche for themselves. It is a fact that men traditionally have enjoyed greater position of prestige and power than women the world over. The opportunities in the world largely belong to men. But still Women's Day celebration is not a meaningless exercise, though one day's token observation does not change their status. Nevertheless, it is an occasion when women all over the world share their thoughts and feelings leading to greater empowerment, self-respect, status and identity as a person, as well as greater bonding. It is also a fact that women are women's best friends, as well as their worst enemies.

Mr. Kofi Annan, the Secretary General of the UN, has affirmed the organisation's commitment "to build on the contribution of women in managing conflict and building peace".

Indian political parties have still not been able to forge a consensus to guarantee a third of the seats in the Indian Parliament and State legislatures for women. The idea of reserving seats for women was first mooted in 1995. It has been blocked in successive parliamentary sessions. It has never been put to vote. However, some states have declared reservation for women in panchayats and municipalities. Although India had the world's first woman Prime Minister, Indira Gandhi, there were only 44 female MPs in the 545-member in the 13th Lok Sabha and just 17 in the 247-seat Rajya Sabha. The BJP had 15 women Lok Sabha members and the main opposition, the Congress, which is headed by a woman, had only 10. The two main Communist parties accounted for a total of five women members.

The National Family Health Survey (NFHS-2) conducted between 1998-99 by the International Institute of Population Sciences revealed the following startling facts: 40 per cent women felt neglecting the house or children was reason enough for the husband to beat up his wife. Another 36 per cent felt if a woman goes out of the house without informing her husband, she needs to be thrashed. The other reasons which women think justify domestic violence include the wife's inability to cook properly or her failure to respect her in-laws. The survey also revealed that women in patriarchal societies in India have been conditioned not only to silently accept and tolerate violence as part of their lives but also rationalise it.

Interestingly, while women justify violence on trivial issues like the wife not being a good cook, they feel dowry-related violence is unjustified. While 90 per cent of Meghalaya women have experienced domestic violence, 40 per cent of Tamil Nadu women say they had been physically mistreated by family members since the age of 15. Women's exploitation, irrespective of their education, continues. Sometime back a sex scandal in judicial circles in Rajasthan came to light in which one deputy registrar of the High Court was suspended on the charge of seeking sexual favours for himself and a couple of judges from a woman litigant. Women suffer handicaps even after scoring high marks. They receive less approval and recognition from male bosses and are slower to be promoted. Ninety-one per cent women work in the private corporate sector and only nine per cent in the public sector.

Another survey shows 46 per cent of women between age group of 22 to 35 years work as executives or assistant managers. Only 10 per cent are managers and two per cent general managers, while only one per cent are vice presidents. The data analysed shows 59 per cent of women work in Indian companies while 41 per cent in multinational corporations. The reason for such small representation of women in the age group of 45-60 years in management positions in the corporate sector is the non-acceptability of working women by Indian society at that point of time. In 1987, the percentage of working women was 13; two years ago, it was 20; today, it is 28.

Women in India are still subjected to sexual harassment and rape. This is because of the very difficult position in which victims are put in. A large number of accused are well-known to the victims. Though India has been independent for over five decades, real independence and emancipation of ordinary women is still distant.

It will come about only if the woman is able to stand on her own in terms of economic equality with man. We cannot have 50 per cent people enjoying all the fruits and the other 50 per cent almost living like serfs. It is a kind of battle between the haves and have-nots. Women's organisations should encash on election time for a better deal for their folk.

The best we can do towards the cause of women is ensure that they are treated with respect and concern in our own families and in the families known to us, and that they are given the opportunities of the best education. Only then will their emancipation come about. It is time we got rid of gender inequality in our country. It is a fact that whatever women do, they must do twice as well, and if possible better than men, to be thought of as half as good. This is a challenging situation. This challenge must, among other things, include gender sensitive policies, an efficient and quick criminal justice system and, above all, education of the girl child without which she will always remain dependant on a patriarchal society.

13

Policies: Mending on the Rags

1. Opinion of the Unchecked Might

1.1. Of Reservation and the Dread

Prime Minister Manmohan Singh, while addressing the conference of State Minorities Commissions in the first week of November, called for a fair share for minorities in Central, State Government and private sector jobs. Before we ponder the statement, it is important to be clear as to what constitutes a minority community.

It is the numbers that count, which determines the majority-minority division. The minority being numerically less, is perceived weak and has to be empowered separately through special measures to make it equal to the majority. This is a hypothesis.

Some Government functionaries have expressed concern over the fact that a section of the minorities were lagging behind other communities in respect of many socio-economic indicators. In India, minorities include Muslims, Sikhs, Buddhist, Jains, Christians, Zoroastrians and a few others. Out of the total population of 102.8 crore in the country as in the 2001 Census, the Hindus were 82.7 crore in number and constituted 80.5 per cent of the population of the country. The Muslim population stood at 13.8 crore comprising 13.4 per cent of the population. The next in size are Christians (2.4

crore), followed by Sikhs (1.9 crore), Buddhists (79 lakh), Jains (42 lakh) and those following other religions and persuasions including the tribal religions (66 lakh).

Hindus population growth declined over the previous decade, their population grew by 20.3 per cent during 1991 and 2001 as compared to 25.1 per cent during 1981-91. Muslim population on the other hand, grew by 36.0 per cent during 1991-2001, compared to 34.5 per cent during 1981-91. Among Buddhists too there has been a sizeable decline in the growth rate from 35.3 per cent during 1981-91 to only 24.5 per cent during 1991-2001. Also, though there is slight increase in the growth rate of the Christians (from 21.5 per cent to 22.6 per cent), there is a noticeable decline in Sikh growth rate from 24.3 per cent in 1981-91 to only 18.2 per cent during 1991-2001. Most prominent in the 2001 Census data released is the growth rate of Jains (26.0 per cent) during 1991-2001 as compared to their growth of only 4.6 per cent during the previous decade 1981-91.

The real problem is that the Government is the biggest employer and it is a craze in middle India to go in for a Government job. A Government job with a security of tenure till the age of retirement and a lifelong pension thereafter is the cherished dream of a vast majority of people. Other attractions include virtual permanence in career irrespective of performance. Moreover, an unwritten, howsoever unethical, perk is of the income over and above the salary.

Muslims have not been adequately represented, says the following data collected by a Committee headed by former Chief Justice of High Court Rajinder Sachar. 94.9 per cent of Muslims living below the poverty line (BPL) in rural areas do not receive free foodgrains. While only 3.2 per cent of Muslims get subsidised loans, just 1.9 per cent of the community benefit from the Antyodaya Anna Yojana Scheme, a programme meant to prevent starvation among the poorest of poor by providing food grains at a subsidised rate. 60.2 per cent of Muslims do not have any land in rural areas. National average: 43 per cent. Just 2.1 per cent of Muslim farmers have tractors. With 15,25,000 tractors, India ranks no. 4 after the US, Japan and Italy. In school attendance, the national average is 40.8 per cent in rural areas and 19.9 per cent in urban areas. Only 0.8 per cent of Muslims in rural areas are college graduates.

Although nearly 40 per cent of Muslims now receive modern education in urban areas, only 3.1 per cent of the community in urban areas are graduates. Just 1.2 per cent is postgraduate. India has acceded to a number of treaties and declarations, including one that reiterates India's commitment to abiding by the provisions "in conformity with its policy of non-interference in the personal affairs of any Community without its initiative and consent."

The status of personal laws of minority communities and the plurality of religious laws in general are much debated in the country. Article 44 of the Constitution gives a commitment to the gradual establishment of legal uniformity in India. The aim is that the state "shall endeavour to secure for the citizens a uniform civil code throughout the territory of India." This directive is believed to be a threat by some elements in some religious minorities that continue to be governed by their own personal laws in family matters as applied within the structure of the Indian legal system.

Article 26 also guarantees freedom to manage religious affairs for every recognised religious denomination or sect. Complexity arises in reconciling the constitutional protection of the rights of religious minorities and the Directive Provision of Article 44. It means that legal uniformity for all citizens will continue to be a chimera.

This difficulty of integration of the secularity of the Republic and the objective of having a legal uniformity with the protection of minority rights (also enshrined in the Constitution) has meant that, 59 years since the adoption of the Constitution, the goal of the directive principle in Article 44 is still far from being realised.

No matter how much Government tries to improve the lot of minorities, it wouldn't improve without their zeal. The condition for prosperity is education and only those communities flourish that emphasise on it. The literacy rate among Hindus (65.1 per cent) is slightly better than the national average (64.8 per cent) for all religious groups combined. Among Muslims, the literacy rate is 59.1 per cent, which is below the national average. The highest literacy rate recorded is among the Jains (94.1 per cent), followed by Christians (80.3 per cent), Buddhists (72.7 per cent) and Sikhs (69.4 per cent).

In a competitive environment, one cannot survive without competence, a quality that comes from education. Even assuming that 15 per cent funds are earmarked for development of the minorities, it will be only a trickle. Even job reservation from amongst Government and semi-Government employees, including about five million central Government employees, is not good enough to address the problem.

How does one compare the gulf in economic progress between authoritarian yet fast-growing China and democratic, economically straggler India? Prof Amartya Sen says that India, with its massive neglect of public education, basic health care and literacy, is poorly prepared for a widely shared economic expansion; China on the other hand has made substantial advances in those areas, and was thus able to capitalise on its market reforms. In fact, what he says should be the starting point for development of minorities, rather than providing sops here and there and making big pronouncements.

1.2. Of Commissions and Inquiries

There are certain holy cows in the country. If you take action against them or even say anything about them, it would be considered blasphemy or contempt of their institution. Tehelka, for instance, exposed corruption in the Defence department. The Government of the day predictably set up a commission. When one judge who headed the commission resigned, another was appointed. This process continued for more than three years. The truth as well as the legal stand on the subject is that inquiry commissions have little to do with law and justice. Since they are not courts of law, they do not have the authority to punish the guilty.

Moreover, the common perception is governments are not required to act on any or all of their recommendations. Therefore, setting up an inquiry commission is the best way to "investigate" a matter. In this way one can postpone the handling of problem for which, ostensibly, the commission was set up. Even after a commission presents its report, the document can be conveniently put in the cold storage. The Vajpayee Government had set up a commission to review the Constitution, knowing well that it did not have the majority to bring about changes, however suitable they might have been for the country.

So who benefits from such commissions? Obviously not the aggrieved party. They are generally individuals who constitute these bodies. Thus, while the people wait expectantly for such committees to come up with their reports, the exercise of playing politics through forming them continues endlessly. Prior to the Tehelka episode, the Defence Ministry was considered above board. However, the web portal, by revealing graft in defence procurements, showed the extent to which this Government wing was steeped in corruption.

It revealed a systemic decay that was often concealed behind the pretext that any exposure of corruption in the Army would demoralise it. However, no sensible person would claim that if one brought to light the underhand dealings in some institution it would adversely affect its personnel' mental make up and efficiency. Before the Tehelka tapes were shown on television, they were screened privately on March 13, 2001, at a five-star hotel in Delhi, for which I had been invited. What I saw disgusted me so much that I walked out in the middle of the show.

When asked as to why I was leaving, I replied that I had never imagined the video clippings would be so bad. In reality, the video had captured what had already happened. The report of a study on corruption in urban services by the Centre for Media Studies reveals, "Nearly half of those who avail the services of the most frequently visited public departments of Government in the country, have had first-hand experience of giving bribes at one time or the other." So deep has corruption seeped into the Government that now the bureaucracy is referred to as "steal frame" and not "steel frame"!

The Government of the day, in all its wisdom, set up a commission of inquiry to look into the matter. Two committees were set up for over three years. Generally, such bodies in our country are formed to diffuse red-hot unmanageable crises. These are techniques that help in diverting attention from issues for which they are constituted temporarily. Once they are set up, they can take as much time as they want to produce a report. However, the present Central Government decided to kickstart the legal process by asking the CBI to register criminal cases, which it has done. In another case of cash on camera and audio tapes, involving Mr Ajit Jogi and newly elected MLAs of Chhattisgarh, the same party that was in Government both in Delhi as well as Chhattisgarh decided to ask the CBI to investigate the cases.

Many people ask, why does the CBI not act on its own? The answer to this is, unlike the judiciary or the Election Commission, the CBI is not a constitutional or an independent wing of Government. While it is true that the judiciary upholds its investigations, the body cannot do much if the cases are not even allowed to reach the courts. This can be done by delaying the sanctions as the following chart will show. It is eventually for the Government of the day to order investigation into any malfeasance or be selective in its approach. Even otherwise, there are a lot of shackles on the functioning of investigating agencies.

In the CVC Bill, passed by the Government and made effective since September 2003, the CBI cannot investigate cases against corrupt and dishonest public servants who are of the rank of joint secretary and above. Forget investigation, it cannot even inquire into misconduct of any such official without the Government's permission. It is almost as if one takes the permission of a thief to inquire into his crime. This is one way to a have quid pro quo system. Thus a bureaucrat understands that if he keeps his political bosses happy by carrying out their orders, he would be safe. Incidentally, this law which existed in the form of a single directive was struck down by the Supreme Court, on December 17, 1997. However, a PIL has been filed against it and the matter is pending in the Supreme Court.

Often people accuse the CBI of taking action against only the small fry and ignoring the influential. They say that criminals, if they are "important personages", can even operate from behind bars. I must says the people expect a bit too much from the law enforcing agency. Catch a person in the morning, trying him in the noon and sentencing him by the evening is not feasible. To achieve such alacrity is virtually impossible. The CBI finds itself unable to deliver for the reasons quoted above.

Nearly one-fifth of MPs in the present Lok Sabha are involved in one criminal case or the other. In a situation when law breakers become law makers, it is obvious that they would go to any extent to keep themselves safe from the long arms of the law. They would leave no stone unturned to defang independent agencies like the CBI. Being an MP or an MLA is considered an immunity against judicial action, especially if one is from the ruling party. It becomes easy for politicians to overcome their legal troubles by trading their support to those in power. Recently, a jailed MP enjoyed all the trappings of his office while he was in judicial custody in Bihar. The Supreme Court has taken cognisance of it and tried to ensure that judicial custody is not misused by people who have clout in Government circles.

The CBI cannot function or take action against anybody, including a Central Government employee, unless the State Government gives its consent to the agency to operate there. In October 2004, the Goa Government withdrew its consent to the functioning of the CBI, as it disapproved of the agency's searches on one of its Cabinet ministers. Politicians may say that the law is supreme; however, they leave no opportunity to escape it if it does not suit their interests.

The CBI has frequently been used as a whipping boy by the Opposition. It is ironical that the party under which the agency was working when it was in power only a few months ago, goes all out to malign it when in the opposition. Parliament's right to censure any action of the Government or its agency is undeniable. However, in the prevailing circumstances, what the CBI has achieved so far is not to be underestimated. As against the general conviction percentage of 6.5 per cent, the CBI has a conviction rate of over 70 per cent. The figures speak for themselves.

However, it is equally a fact that the CBI has no control over cases pending in the law courts. It is for the Government of the day to ensure that not only is justice done, but is also seen to be done. Ultimately, the responsibility lies on those at the helm to decide the kind of governance, or even an investigative agency like the CBI, they would like to have for the country.

1.3. Of Tinkering with CBI

In a proposal to the Ministry of Personnel and Training, which is the administrative department of the CBI, the Law Ministry has proposed to set up another department of prosecution for scrutiny and review of all cases of the CBI. The Law Ministry's argument is that it wants to establish an independent directorate with an independent budget and its own cadre of lawyers. It also wants that the directorate, on the lines of the British Crown Prosecution Service, should be independent of both the CBI or the Law Ministry.

At present, the CBI has its separate prosecution wing headed by the Director of Prosecution, who is a Joint Secretary-level officer on deputation from the Law Ministry. Director of Prosecution, who was earlier called as the Legal Advisor of the CBI, is the highest legal functionary in the organisation. He also heads the prosecution cadre consisting of public prosecutors, senior public prosecutors, assistant, deputy, and additional legal advisers. The CBI's law officers take the cases in the courts of special judges and magistrates, and occasionally in higher courts. Private counsels are hired with the approval of the Law Ministry and the Department of Personnel for conducting cases in the Supreme Court and the High Courts.

The CBI has a panel of advocates for fighting cases in courts. It has a sanctioned strength of 230 law officers. There are 32 courts of special judges and nine magistrate courts, functioning exclusively for the trial of CBI cases in the country.

Government officials, irrespective of being good, bad or excellent, are fitted in a Government pay scale. However hard working or brilliant they may be, what they earn as law officers is a pittance. The result is a perennial shortage of law officers.

As the head of the CBI, I was once invited by the Union Public Service Commission to sit on the board for selecting law officers for it. For four vacancies, only three candidates turned up for interview. Two of them were uninformed lawyers and one candidate, who could answer some questions, was selected. A fact which came out clearly during the discussion after the interview was that meagre salary offered for Government prosecutors attracted only those who had little or no practice and hence very small income.

The Law Ministry's argument it wants to establish an independent directorate, sounds hollow because without conferring an independent status — like that of the Election Commission — how can there be an independent department? In fact, nothing moves in the CBI without the permission of the Government. Whether an appeal should be filed in higher courts or not, how much private counsels should be paid, etc, are all decided by the Government, not the CBI. There have been a number of incidents, including the JMM bribery case, wherein the lower court convicted former Prime Minister Narasimha Rao, but the High Court acquitted him. The Government, however, decided not to challenge the verdict in the Supreme Court.

Over the years, the CBI has been subverted by politicians. In 1988, then Prime Minister Rajiv Gandhi made it mandatory for the CBI to seek prior consent of the departments concerned for a probe against officers of the level of Joint Secretary and above. However, in 1997, the Supreme Court quashed this order. Then the Government brought forth a CVC Bill, in which it reintroduced the same order, which, too, was struck down by the apex court. A PIL on this issue has been pending in the Supreme Court for the last three years.

The Law Ministry says that the creation of an independent directorate of prosecution was one of the directions given to the Government by the Supreme Court in 1997 in the Vineet Narain case. What is being contemplated, in reality, is not an independent directorate of prosecution, but an attempt to weaken the CBI. With law officers directly under the Law Ministry, it will be easy for the Government to bury any case it wants. All kinds of obstacles are put on the working of the CBI in the name of 'supervision' and 'legal advice'.

It will be of interest to cite one case. In 2006-07, it is the Law Ministry which was responsible for de-freezing Ottavio Quattrocchi's account, having more than Rs. 24 crore in London. In a bizarre statement, the same department claimed that the CBI did not have any evidence to prove Quattrocchi's involvement in the Bofors case. It sent an Additional Solicitor General of India to tell the Crown Prosecutor in the UK to do so, when a registered case is still pending against him in Indian courts. Again in 2007, when Quattrocchi was detained in Argentina, a deliberate attempt was made to weaken the CBI's case. The unkindest cut of all was to come later when the Law Ministry refused to pursue the case in the Supreme Court of that country. It is strange that instead of strengthening the apex anti-corruption agency of the country, efforts are being made to enfeeble it.

If the Law Ministry is serious about improving the criminal justice system in the country, it should heed to what the Chief Justice of India has said; "India has only 12,000 judges, 2,000 short of the sanctioned strength of 14,000. As a result, there are over 3.5 crore cases pending in the lower courts, 37 lakh in High Courts and 46,000 in the Supreme Court. We need one judge for 500 cases to clear the backlog — that would mean 77,664 judges. As the governance is not good in this country, we suffer. Our system is encouraging litigation."

There have been reports of disposal of civil and criminal cases after 20 or 25 years. These are the urgent matters which need the attention of the Law Ministry, rather than tinkering with the CBI.

1.4. Of Election and Less Governance

The election process which started on April 20 has ended. Frenzied behind-the-scene negotiations amongst the likely coalition partners has led to the formation of the new Government. It is welcome that most political parties agree on economic reforms. Of course, the degree and thrust of reforms will depend upon the individual agendas of the coalition partners.

The focus on development as an electoral issue was a first in the history of Indian elections. If the NDA focussed on "India Shining", the Opposition shot it down saying the country was as corrupt and as mal-administered as ever. Now that the elections are over, it is time to bury recriminations and carry the development process further. This is most desirable in national interest as a government touches the life of every citizen with its policies. Its economic and other policies regarding rationing of food, transport, electricity, health services, income tax, etc., determine the kind of goods and services the citizens will have.

Whatever be the common minimum programme for governance, the efforts of the new Government should be to enhance the delivery of services. Even a marginal increase can make a lot of difference to the lives of the common people. The first belief that the Government must shed is that it should have a finger in every pie. I am reminded of the time when a committee was set up to identify obsolete laws. The committee listed over 1500 laws which could be deleted from the book without any damage to society. Its report is gathering dust and the old laws are still in position. Overhauling governance with the sole objective of less government will rid the country of corruption and other malpractices.

The mot significant complaint of a person dealing with government offices relates to the number of officials and agencies the person has to run to in order to get his legitimate work done. If the number of times a person has to go to the government offices is reduced, the chances of corruption too will correspondingly reduce. Everybody who wants to improve the functioning of the government talks about simplification of forms, procedures and processes. These are no doubt major stumbling blocks.

During my stint as a Director in the Commerce Ministry, during the regime of permit and quota raj, I discovered to my dismay that an importer had to fill 132 forms and applications for procurement. When this was sought to be reduced to 28 on the recommendation of a committee, it was made out as if the heavens would fall. Now with a liberalised economy, heavens are still where they were. In fact, there is now a increase in revenues and a lessening of trouble that a businessman has to go through. The effects of liberalisation are only visible in select departments like the customs, excise, telecommunication and petroleum. These reforms have hardly touched other departments of the Central or State governments.

The new Government should concentrate on having less of governance in non-vital areas and where the private sector can suffice. With losses of over Rs. 32,000 crore, the Delhi Government obliged, rather impelled, was under obligation to privatise the distribution of power. Some political parties protested vociferously when the private distributors were given the power to enter and search premises where there were possibilities of theft of electricity. It is this attitude, which has led to over 50 per cent of power theft and transmission losses. Good governance requires that events, circumstances and other matters be controlled before they become unmanageable. The new Government should identify such areas and ensure that a leakage of revenue or corruption is controlled before it turns into a torrent.

The new Government should take care to not reverse all the policies of the previous Government. Instead, it should continue to accelerate and upgrade programmes for improving power, roads, airports, ports, water supply, building highways, etc., besides paying the highest attention to agriculture. With all parties swearing by liberalisation, it is important that the size of the Government be reduced.

It should exit from areas in which it has no role. There was reportedly a more than 30 per cent increase in fresh recruitments by the Staff Selection Commission and Union Public Service Commission last year. It may have been an election driven exercise, but it has led to jettisoning of course suggested by the Expenditure Reforms Commission (ERC).

Any further increase in the Government's strength is totally unwarranted as indicated by the ERC. It also makes political sense to cut down on unproductive investments. It will be better to allocate more funds for the creation of infrastructure, to create an environment in which the private sector can operate with ease. The private sector is imperative to meet the unemployment situation. Nearly 30 to 50 million people in the country are unemployed.

Only an expanding private sector would be in a position to absorb these unemployed people. The more money the Government can save by cutting on unproductive expenditure like subsidies to IIMs etc., the more it will have to spend on essentials like infrastructure, health services and education which are vital for the growth of the country.

We need to create a climate that encourages people to develop entrepreneurial spirit. People should not look upon the Government as a provider of jobs. Overhauling governance should be an ongoing exercise rather than a sporadic volition indulged in to garner votes or nurse a constituency. The reforms process hits a bottle neck when those asked to implement it find excuses to delay its implementation.

This happens almost with every commission or committee where retired bureaucrats find new parking slots for themselves. The new Government should change the old policy of rewarding retired civil servant with extensions of two to five years in various commissions, committees or regulatory bodies. If a person is deemed unfit for any government work at age 60, how can he be considered fit for working for another five years in another Government job? Equally capable exists outside the Government.

It is time the Government itself practiced some outsourcing. Till now, the bureaucracy has been the real beneficiary from any party coming to power. In one instance, when the new Competition Commission was sought to be set up with a bureaucrat as its chairman, the then Law Minister volunteered to suitably amend the Competition Commission Act to accommodate a particular bureaucrat, instead of a judge. It is time the new Government changed the old bureaucracy serving policy and appointed only deserving bureaucrats. This will also help the Government in cutting down on unnecessary expenditure and reducing the size of the bureaucracy. The new Government should bear in mind that the country's prosperity lies in discarding ideas which have become redundant.

The new Government should work towards instilling trust and confidence in the people. This can be done through increased productivity for within all sectors including agriculture, trade and commerce. Social harmony, communal concord and the maintenance of law and order is the first requisite before any development. These should be the topmost concerns of the new Government. It should take all steps to ensure that any thing which divides the country or promotes social disharmony, is discarded. The Government would do well to remember Abraham Lincoln's words: "Let us have faith that right makes the might, and in that faith, let us to the end, dare to do our duty, as we understand it."

1.5. Of CAS and Conditionality

There is a lot of talk going round about the Conditional Access System (CAS), at least in the quarters concerned with television viewing and broadcasting. The Indian CATV industry has grown from near-zero in 1990s to the current estimate of over four million subscriber homes. Penetration of cable in the residential sector exceeds that of telephones. Cable, in fact, can be an alternative choice for the delivery of various services into residential homes.

It would be pertinent to consider the salient features of the Cable Television Networks (Amendment) Bill, 2002, which is expected to be applicable from July 14, 2003. It would make the introduction of addressable systems mandatory, and pay channels would be delivered only to these systems. All free-to-air channels would be part of the basic package, related to which the Government will specify the rates and minimum number of channels. There is to be monthly reporting by cable operators on the subscribers' base for free-to-air and pay channels. A period of six months would be given to the operators to introduce CAS.

One expected benefit of CAS for customers is that there will be freedom of choice with regard to channels, and people will make payments only for those they actually watch. Basically, therefore, CAS is a gadget allowing customers to pay and receive only those channels they want. The apparatus allows a viewer to choose between different bouquets comprising one channel or or a group of channels.

A sample of the bouquets and their charges in May 2002 are as follows:

Star package: 40.00, for Star Plus, Star Movies, Star News, Star World, Star Gold, National Geographic; the ZEE package: 40.00, for Zee TV, Zee News, Zee Cinema, 4 Alpha channels, Zee MGM, Zee English, Asianet Kaveri, Nickelodeon and the complimentary channels of Zee Music, Asianet Bharati, UTN and Zed TV; ESPN and Star Sports: 24.00; the Sony package: 40.00, for Sony, AXN, SET Max, CNBC; the Turner Package: 20.00, for Cartoon Network, HBO, CNN; the MEN package: 38.00, for DD Sports, Hallmark, B4U, Ten Sports, FTV; and Discovery, Animal Planet: 06.25.

With copyright at 20.00 and entertainment tax at 20.00, the total comes to 248.25. Add to this Maintenance of equipment at 15.00, salary of maintenance staff at 10.00 and electricity and other such expenses at 5.00, and the grand total comes to 278.25.

This excludes the profit of the cable operator. In case he is affiliated to a multi-services operator (MSO), there is an additional burden of franchisee charges.

CAS is supposed to arrive in the country's four metros on July 14, 2003, and thereafter in other cities. This would bring the industry in line with the globally accepted "pay per view" practice. But it could also make watching TV a more expensive pastime. If CAS is actually introduced despite the demands for its deferment, it will roll out in phases. The second phase, September-October, will cover Bangalore, Hyderabad, Pune and Ahmedabad. Bangalore alone has over 11 lakh cable and satellite homes serviced by over 1,000 cable operators. And it has five multi-system operators like Siticable, Hathway Cable and Datacom, In Cable, ICE and Atria Communi-cation Technologies.

In all, cable TV networks generate a monthly turnover of Rs 25,000 crore. However, this figure is only an estimate, since hardly any cable operator will admit to being affluent or pays taxes.

In India, there is no system of issuing geographical franchising/ licensing areas to MSOs/cable operators. Thus, cable TV operators have the opportunity to expand beyond their existing cities of business. MSOs in the country have grown primarily through a system of entering franchise arrangements with local cable operators. The latter are the ones who provide low-cost yet fairly responsive customer care to CATV customers.

At present, thousands of independent operators coexist with a few national and regional players. Cable operators have been primarily concerned with the provision of video services. In the absence of CAS and addressable set-top boxes in customer homes, all channels are delivered in free-to-air form to the customer.

Currently, MSOs are the ones feeling the pinch. The reason is that franchise operators do not give them the correct accounting. Introduction of CAS will give them a better hold on and position within the distribution chain. As said earlier, with CAS and set-top boxes, people can choose the programmes they spend on, thus linking payment to actual viewership. This contrasts with the current model in which a plethora of unwanted and unwatched channels are paid for.

However, the underlying purpose of CAS is only to deal with the issue of under-declaration of connectivity prevalent in the CATV industry, which is causing losses to pay channels and MSOs. There was no public demand for the new system of TV viewing. Installation of set-top boxes will enable MSOs to deliver services such as Internet-on-TV, Pay per View, Home Banking and Home Shopping etc. These will come at a cost to the customers.

The introduction of CAS will entail investments in the new system by subscribers. Big broadcasters like Rupert Murdoch's STAR TV accuse cable operators of not divulging the total number of their subscribers. STAR group's Chief Executive, Mr James Murdoch, was in Mumbai sometime ago to address 'Frames 2002,' a seminar on the entertainment sector. He accused the operators of compromising on quality on the one hand, and cheating broadcasters by under-declaring the number of subscribers enrolled by them on the other. He alleged that the under-declarations were as high as 85 per cent in some areas.

Mr Murdoch also pointed out that the broadcaster received only five per cent of subscription revenues, as against the global norms of 20 per cent. The cable access system might help channel owners to get the correct picture on their accounts.

But, in this battle, the real loser would be the consumer. He would continue to be fleeced by both, apart from having to spend between Rs. 2,000 to Rs. 7,000 on a set-top box. All devices for receiving cables channels would be imported. Assuming the cost of the same to be Rs. 4,000, the outgo in foreign exchange would be Rs. 16,000 crore. Import of millions of set-top boxes would mean generation of thousands, if not lakhs, of jobs in other countries that would be selling these items to India.

Nowhere does the amendment Bill propose to deal with cable operators violating laws in an exemplary manner. For instance, I am paying Rs. 180 to my cable operator for all the channels he beams, including the ones I do not want. He will now charge Rs. 282. Nowhere does the Bill or the rules say what will happen for overcharging. It will, therefore, only benefit big operators, certainly not the common viewer. All the people-unfriendly implications of CAS have obviously not been considered; the only thing that has been is that it will help big operators and pay channels.

Besides, CAS technology is actually old and there is no guarantee that, after one or two years, cable operators may not dub the technology prevailing then as outdated and ask cable receivers to replace the same with other, more expensive gadgets. We have seen how last year's mobile telephones have already been junked. It is still not too late to ensure that only a 'made in India' system is used. This will help generate jobs and boost industry.

Finally, it has not been indicated which authority will enforce the Act. It would be advisable to keep police sub-inspectors and thanedars out of the enforcement proceedings. If customs and income tax can have their own enforcement agencies, it is time the police were not drawn into enforcement of social or semi-social legislation. It should, at the same time, be clearly spelt as to who will redress customer complaints. In view of these grey areas, it would be better to defer the introduction of CAS till all the issues concerning it are sorted out.

1.6. Of Extradition: Looking Before and After

Extraditing criminals, wanted in India from other countries, is an area where political compulsions, diplomacy and a country's standing in the world play a dominant role, irrespective of the existence or otherwise of any bilateral extradition treaty. Indeed, no country needs any treaty to expel an undesirable alien, from within its jurisdiction.

Where there is a duly executed bilateral extradition treaty, it is open to the states to use the same. However, the process of extradition usually involves the judiciary in the countries concerned. International law regulating extradition acknowledges the following points as a basis of exercise of criminal jurisdiction by a sovereign state-namely, territoriality (the state where the offence has been allegedly committed); nationality (the nation to which the offender or the accused belongs); the protective principle (the state whose essential economic or other interests have been directly and adversely affected by the offence); and universality (the offence being an international crime).

Extradition or deportation is simply handing over of a person accused of an offence by the country where he might have run away, to the country that has made a request that he be handed over. Neither any national law nor international law imposes any obligation on countries to extradite. Neither has any special procedure been prescribed, for handing over such a person or persons to the requesting state.

Mr Ottavio Quattrocchi, an Italian power broker and self-proclaimed friend of late Rajiv Gandhi, had received $7.34 million through his company AE services for clinching the AB Bofors deal with the Government of India for the purchase of 155 mm Howitzer guns. He has been chargesheeted for his role in the deal by the CBI in what has come to be known as Bofors case. This case is now on to the second decade. It is important to recapitulate quickly a few details, for a full understanding of the case.

The Government of India was on the look out from 1980 onwards for a suitable 155-mm gun system to meet the country's defence operational requirements. The choice was short-listed to M/s Sofma of France, M/s AB Bofors of Sweden, M/S IMS of UK and M/S Voest Alpine of Austria in December 1982. In November, 1985, further short-listing focused on Sofma and Bofors. Finally the order was placed by the Government with Bofors on March 24, 1986, for supply of 410 numbers (400 plus 10 free) of 155 mm field Howitzer

77-B gun system/spare guns for a total amount of SEK 8410.66 million (Swedish kroner is the official currency of Sweden) In Indian rupees, this was equivalent to around Rs 1437.72 crore at that time.

Earlier, the Ministry of Defence had set up a seven-member negotiating Committee in May, 1984 with the defence Secretary as the Chairman. At the meeting held on March 12, 1986, the Committee felt that the offer of Bofors was the better of the two. It recommended that, pending finishing touches to the contract, a letter of intent might be issued to Bofors, to the effect that the Government was willing to award the contract to them. It was subject to their satisfying the Government of India on all aspects of the purchase, license production, credit and other arrangements.

These recommendations of the Committee were approved, first by Ministry of Defence and then Ministry of Finance Officials, and then by Minis-ters: By RRM (Rajya Raksha Mantri Sukh Ram), RRM (Rajya Raksha Mantri Arun Singh) and RM (Raksha Mantri KC Pant) on March 13, 1986, and then Finance Minister (VP Singh) and RM (Raksha Mantri-PM) on March 14, 1986.

The letter of intent was promptly issued to Bofors on March 14, 1996. Further negotiations were continued. It was an unusual case, where negotiations continued even after a letter of intent was issued. Bofors submitted revised offers on March 21, 1986, in a hurried exercise. The correct procedure would be to issue a final letter after all the negotiations were over and not halfway.

Bofors, despite their clear knowledge-from May 1984 and definitely from May 3, 1985 onwards-that agents were prohibited, employed them. Huge payments were made to these persons throughout 1986 and even as late as March 30, 1987. The "agents" did not do any purported service to get the contract in favour of Bofors, as per the views of Defence Ministry. Yet they were paid large sums as "commission". Bofors paid an amount of SEK 50,463,966 to Mr Quattrocchi's AE Services Ltd on September 2 and 3, 1986. Obviously, no businessman pays any money without a quid pro quo.

Bofors consistently declined to disclose the names of the actual beneficiaries of the remittances made by them to three companies. The Government of India had set up a Joint Parliamentary Committee to look into the question of kickbacks. In the report of the JPC, Lars Eric Thunholm, then Chairman of Nobel Industries (Bofors was its subsidiary), had stated that so far as he was aware, payments had been made to Indians or to an Indian company in connection with the contract. He had also stated that he could not guarantee that bribes had not been paid. Mr Quattrocchi, an Italian power broker, was arrested on December 20, 2000, in Malaysia and was later on released on bail.

Mr Quattrocchi's had earlier lost his legal battle with the CBI in India while contesting the Interpol Red Corner notice as well as his unsuccessful challenge to the non-bailable warrant issued by the Delhi Special Court. Despite the undertaking given by his counsel, Mr Quattrocchi refused to obey the Supreme Court order to cooperate with the CBI for investigation of the Bofor's case within 15 days. The Supreme Court had directed CBI not to arrest him.

What legal battle he lost in fighting his case in the Indian courts, he won in Malaysia through the intervention of the Italian Prime Minister, who pleaded his case with Malaysian Prime Minister. The dropping of proceedings against Mr Quattrocchi has more to do with the compulsions of international politics than the nitty-gritties of evidence.

If Malaysia wanted to help India, as it has done in the case of the United States, it would have simply deported Mr Quattrocchi to India. Rumours were rife in Malaysia that, with ill-gotten money in his pocket, he was able to purchase a lot of influence in that country. It may be recalled that the Malaysian Foreign Minister had announced some time back that if India wanted to enter into an extradition treaty with Malaysia only to get Mr Quattrocchi extradited, then his country would not enter into such an agreement. Such was the clout of Mr Quattrocchi.

Now the bird has flown and there is no likelihood that he will come back from Italy to Malaysia to face an Indian appeal. There is hardly anything judicial about the Malaysian judge's decision in Mr Quattrocchi's case. Much less evidence, given to Switzerland, was sufficient to get bank papers from that country. When the bank and other strong evidence was given to Malaysia, the judges rejected the case.

Obviously they have taken the cue from their country's Foreign Minister. After all, an extradition court is not concerned with punishing a criminal. It is concerned only with examining whether or not a case has prima facie evidence to back it up. We live in an flawed world and one man's goose is doubtless another man's gander. But I have no doubt that, sooner rather than later, somewhere the Italian escape artist will meet his nemesis. For, God evens out things in this life itself.

1.7. Of Kashmir and the Concern

The CRPF Inspector-General was transferred from Srinagar on August 13 after an uproar in the Kashmir Valley, led by terrorists and their supporters, who alleged excesses by the Central paramilitary force. He was also denied the President's police medal for fear of controversy and wider protests. There is nothing new in this kind of approach as the decision-makers are far removed from reality. Meanwhile, it is the police and the security forces that continue to face life-and-death situations, standing between chaos and order.

In 1990s, the then Governor of Jammu & Kashmir lost his job for taking a tough stand against anti-nationalist elements. That did not help the situation, nor will the recent transfer of the CRPF Inspector-General restore peace. On the contrary, it will embolden separatists and terrorists who will now think that they can get away with anything.

Wherever the Government of the day has pursued the policy of appeasement and has compromised on basic values, it has invited trouble. Terrorism in the Valley flourishes in direct proportion to the political will to deal with the same. It commenced with the kidnapping of Ms Mehbooba Mufti, the daughter of Mufti Mohammed Sayed, former Home Minister, who is now a former Chief Minister of Jammu & Kashmir. To secure her release, the then Government had freed five dreaded terrorists. This emboldened the separatists and the terrorists, and was enough to start a series of chain reactions in the Valley from 1988 onwards. I am an eyewitness to these events as I was the InspectorGeneral of the CRPF in Srinagar at the time.

The Government's tendency to sweep such incidents under the carpet has today resulted in terrorists openly dictating terms to the people; enforcing the *purdah* system for women, closing down beauty parlours and cinema houses, etc. The Prime Minister, like many before him, gave a laudable speech from the ramparts of the Red Fort on Independence day this year as he appealed to the masses to shun communalism.

But unfortunately, the whole agitation in the Kashmir Valley is based on a communal ideology. The truth is, communalism in one community generates communalism in others. Otherwise, how could hordes of people led by terrorists start a rally with the declared aim of crossing the LoC into Muzaffarabad? The Government should have responded that those who cross the LoC illegally will not be allowed back into the country.

A series of misconceived policies, or the so-called people-to-people contact, have brought about this situation. Otherwise, how could a mainstream political party demand that Pakistani currency be declared legal tender in Jammu & Kashmir? It would be wrong to say that 'transferring' 97 acres of forest land to the Sri Amarnath Shrine Board has led to the present crisis. The separatists and terrorists have been going all-out to create disturbances and problems as per the following report of the Jammu & Kashmir Government:

"A total of 42,147 people, including 20,647 militants and 5,024 security personnel were killed in the State between January 1990 and the middle of February 2007... Violence left 33,885 people, including 12,124 security personnel and 21,659 civilians injured during the same period in the State... 11,221 civilians were killed by militants and another 1,678 lost their lives in grenade and Improvised Explosive Device explosions, while 173 civilians were killed when they were caught in clashes between militants. A total of 3,404 civilians were killed in cross-firing incidents between security forces and militants... The highest number of 1,438 civilians were killed in 1996, the year elections were held after a gap of seven year, while the highest number of 3,602 Army and other paramilitary personnel lost their lives fighting militants in the same year. Jammu and Kashmir Police lost 537 personnel since January 1990. As many as 438 Special Police Officers engaged by the police in counter-insurgency operations were killed. 127 Village Defence Committee members were killed fighting militants in the State. 613 security personnel were killed in a single year in 2001, which was again the highest."

Now, the question arises as to what can be done. Also whether what is being done is sufficient. In 1990, the midnight protests were sparked by the call given by 1,100 mosques, which had installed loudspeakers to call the faithful to prayer. Loudspeakers in Kashmir's mosques, then as now, are used to give calls for anti-national activities, asking the people to gather in the streets or at a particular spot to stage demonstrations. The then Governor had ordered the disconnection of these loudspeakers, which itself led to protests.

It is a fact that many terrorists take shelter in places of worship. During my recent visit to the US I was told that the police had, with the co-operation of the Muslim community and their religious leaders, installed CCTV cameras in mosques to monitor any criminal activity. In a situation like that which prevails in the Kashmir Valley, which has been highly communalised, it is impossible to get any kind of evidence to prove anti-national activities as no witness will be willing to come forth to depose. Mrs Margaret Thatcher used to say publicity is the oxygen of terrorism. Any publicity which eulogises terrorism should be discouraged, if not completely banned.

Terrorist leaders, their supporters and sympathisers should be immobilised by using the present laws and detained outside Jammu & Kashmir. The Government has announced financial assistance for the families of terrorists on the grounds that it is not their fault if the only earning member of their family becomes a militant. This approach is fraught with danger and the sooner it is given up the better. It should not become a scheme to help traitors.

Many so-called intellectuals talk about a referendum in the Valley. With Pakistan having hijacked the anti-India movement, any referendum or election will be irrelevant at this point of time. The first priority is to drive the Pakistani terrorists out of the Valley and send them to the country of their origin. The Government should stop all dialogue with these militants who are nothing more than agents of Pakistan. Only a tough approach will send the right signal that the Government means business.

1.8. Of Overseas Employment

People have historically left their homes and countries in search of greener pastures. The search for El Dorado or hidden treasures has fascinated generations across the world. It was Columbus who first sailed in search of India, and ended up discovering America.

It is the same spirit of adventure which has led 20 million people of Indian origin to spread across 107 countries of the world. At the same time, there are innumerable stories of people cheated and lured into paying hefty sums for going abroad and abandoned later to either die in the high seas, or end up in prisons as happened with 281 Punjabi youths in 1997.

There is nothing new or strange about people seeking fortune abroad. The number of Indians working in UAE and Kuwait is more than the population of these countries. This is equally true in other West Asian countries. The natives of affluent nations use people of Indian origin for jobs they are reluctant to perform or are not equipped or trained to do.

For instance Iraq, which has been the scene of a bloody war, has been almost in a state of anarchy for the last one year. Various Iraqi groups are reporting about their existence with daily car bomb attacks on allied soldiers and other foreigners. So far India, despite pressure, has neither supported US presence in Iraq, nor has it in any way approved of American action of toppling the former Iraqi regime headed by Saddam.

However, on July 21, seven truck drivers, which included three Indians, apart from an Egyptian and a Kenyan, working for a Kuwait-based company, were kidnapped by a little known group in Iraq which demanded the company stop working for Americans and pull out. The group also asserted that if their demands were not met, they would begin beheading the kidnapped persons.

The kin of kidnapped Indians have demanded the Government intervene to save their lives. It is a legitimate demand as, in a democracy, it is the duty of the country to intercede on behalf of its citizens. Of course, the private sector will say that persons working abroad do so at their own risk and cost, and it is not its business to intercede on their behalf.

The fact is whatever be the public demand, or demands of the relatives of the unfortunate victims, or even of the kidnappers, India has little or no leverage in the matter except putting up a request with the Americans for help, as they are the effective rulers of Iraq. But even the American writ runs only in a few parts of the country.

Americans themselves have been proved wrong in that no Iraqi WMD was found. CIA chief George Tenet had to leave in embarrassment for having fed inaccurate intelligence to the President. The White House itself has acknowledged that the President was relying on incomplete and, perhaps, even inaccurate information from US intelligence agencies when he declared, in his State of the Union address, that Saddam had tried to purchase uranium from Africa.

This statement undercut one of the key pieces of evidence that the US President and his aides had cited to back their claims made prior to launching an attack against Iraq in March 2003, that Hussein was "reconstituting" his nuclear weapons programme. Those claims added urgency to White House version that military action to depose Saddam needed to be taken quickly, and could not await further inspections of the country or additional resolutions at the UN. Despite having captured Saddam, America's enemy number one, it is obvious to the meanest intelligence that the war on Iraq not only brought privation and suffering to millions of Iraqis, but has itself cost over $229 billions so far.

One result of America's war in Iraq is that the US President asked, on August 2, for the creation of a National Intelligence Director who will be appointed by him with the advice and consent of the Senate and hold office at his pleasure. He will serve as the President's Principal Intelligence Advisor and will oversee and coordinate all foreign and domestic activities of the intelligence communities.

However, the CIA will be managed by a separate Director. The US President, in the same message, also asked for the creation of a new counter-terrorism centre to coordinate and monitor activities of all Government agencies and departments "to ensure effective joint action and that American efforts are unified in priority and purpose". The US has spent more on wars than in helping others in alleviating poverty, disease and suffering.

It has a history of chasing red herrings, which quite often has proved counter-productive. In recent years, the US reported Al Qaeda and Osama bin Laden of having caused devastation in the US on September 11, 2001. Afghanistan was ravaged and when Americans found the going tough, they quietly handed power to select Afghan leaders and withdrew. The result was chaos and a situation worse than what obtained under the Taliban, according to many observers.

Of course, the Americans throw a few millions dollars here and there as salve to their conscience, like peanuts thrown to monkeys to keep them quiet. Now the same story is being repeated in Iraq. I am no supporter of dictators, least of all of Saddam who was ruthless and who had territorial ambitions on neighbouring countries like Kuwait.

But it must be mentioned that he generated national pride in most Iraqis, which enabled them to withstand economic sanctions for nearly a decade. In the meantime the fate of Indian truckers, along with four others taken hostages and used as gambling pawns, hangs in balance. The dice is loaded against them as all cards are in the hands of the abductors. As it is, it appears the kidnappers have an upper hand, since all concerned including the Kuwait-based company KGL, is willing to meet all their demands, which includes ending its operations in Iraq.

The despair and apprehension of the family members of the kidnapped Indians is both understandable and justified. But notwithstanding the protests and the media coverage, there is nothing that the Indian Government can do save make pious appeals and requests to the negotiators to expedite the release of the hostages.

Indian governments have never taken a tough line against kidnappers, abductors or extortionists, whether it was the case of the release of Rubaiya Sayeed, the daughter of then Home Minister abducted in 1990, or the freedom of an IOC official kidnapped by ULFA, or even the release of Kashmiri terrorists to get the hostages of IC-814 from Kathmandu to Delhi released in Kabul in 2001. Indeed, the one thing the family members of the kidnapped truckers cannot accuse the Government of is that it is guilty of not conceding the demands of the kidnappers or having taken a firm stand against them!

Meanwhile, those who go abroad in lure of dollars must bear in mind that nothing comes without risks. There is a price to be paid for everything, which can sometimes be with life, blood or simple sweat. It is also time the Government created opportunities for increasing employment potential in the country.

If equally good jobs are made available at home, then a contingency like the current one would never arise again. Reservation in the private sector is no answer, as it will amount to killing the goose which lays the golden egg. The Government should also not make the blunder of increasing staff as there are already too many men doing too little job. Let us indulge in some fresh thinking and act resolutely on employment generation so that the kind of incident which has happened in Iraq leads to positive developments at home.

14

India and the Others

1. Of Nepal

1.1. Nepal at a Crossroads

2.Nepal evokes memories of a country full of beautiful scenery, high mountains and spiritual places. Till recently, the King of Nepal was regarded as god. However, the image of King Gyanendra has taken a beating, thanks to Maoists who have bullied the seven-party alliance into submission. Moreover, neither the King nor his crown prince has done anything to win the hearts of the people. In all fairness to Maoists, they have never hidden their ambition of removing the monarchy from the centrestage of Nepali politics.

Instead of begging and appealing to the King to become a titular head, Maoists went straight for his head. If they have their way in the election scheduled for April 10, the days of the King are numbered. Maoists have been — and they still are — in the forefront of a movement to abolish monarchy.

Nepal, one of the few monarchies in Asia and the only Hindu kingdom, has a population of 26.3 million, which is less than the population of Mumbai and Delhi put together. However, it has an area of 147,181 sq km. In Nepal, a landlocked country, tourism is the primary source of income.

During my recent visit to Nepal, I tried to gauge the ground reality in that country. One thing which came out clearly was that people were afraid to express their opinion openly. When pressed the most they would say was that all political leaders are keen to amass wealth for themselves.

In Nepal, petrol and diesel are being sold at Rs 50 per litre; after some time, even their availability will be a problem. Due to strikes, *bandhs* and non-payment of previous dues to Indian suppliers for petroleum products, 10 litres a day is the petrol sold to cars and five litres to two-wheelers. There was an interesting slogan put in the market in Nepali language, "*Petrol chhenna, mitti taail chhenna, paani chhenna, bijli chhenna, sarkar chhenna*" (there is no petrol, no kerosene, no water, no electricity and no Government).

There are power cuts in India, but the day I reached Kathmandu the power was off between 7 pm and 12 pm. I was told that we would have electricity between midnight and 5 am, and again between 9 am and 1 pm next day. This would be followed by no electricity between 1 pm and 5 pm and the cycle would continue till further notified.

When one visits Nepal, one is back to the candle age even in the best hotels. You need candles in the bathroom, in your living room and even dressing room. Normally, it is considered stylish to have a candlelight dinner. But it is not comfortable to live for eight hours in the hotel with candles lighting your room.

Due to political uncertainty, along with lack of basic facilities like water supply and electricity, many foreign companies are treating Nepal as a punishment posting. No wonder hardly any new industry has been set up in that country; worse, even the present ones are facing difficulties in their functioning. The first annual report of the RNA Human Rights Cell, 2006, has recorded 10,725 abductions and 72 killings by Maoists during the past six months of the year. It has also recorded 65 cases of explosion, 40 cases of extortion and looting and 30 cases of threats issued by Maoists. More than 12,000 civilians, Maoists and security personnel have been killed in that country since the rebels began their 'people's war' in 1996.

India, mostly for wrong reasons, occupies the front page of Nepal's media. The kidney scam king, Amit Kumar, who was recently arrested in Nepal, hogged the limelight in that country. On his arrest, Nepal Police recovered Euro 145,00, $ 18,900 and a bank draft of Rs 936,000. He was also guilty of possessing foreign currency — the amount recovered from him was above the ceiling prescribed under Nepal's laws. Had he been convicted, he would have got up to 10 years of imprisonment and a fine of Rs 2 lakh. But at India's request, he was deported to New Delhi.

Today, Nepal stands at a crossroads. This strife-ridden nation is all set to implement a new 'deal' worked out between the current interim Government and Maoists. One of the conditions for arriving at the understanding is to abolish Nepal's more than 200-year-old monarchy after the election to the new Constituent Assembly is held on April 10. In the election, the electorate will also decide whether Nepal will become a democratic republic or retain ceremonial monarchy.

So far Prime Minister GP Koirala is the only SPA leader who has openly expressed his support for ceremonial monarchy. But now in the interest of peace, he has agreed to its abolition after the Constituent Assembly election. Most people in Nepal, however, will be happy to see King Gyanendra go, but not the monarchy.

Maoists may sweep the election as their writ runs in rural Nepal. Most people will vote for them to avoid any reprisals. The handful supporters of retention of constitutional monarchy will not be able to stem the anti-monarchy drive of Maoists. Of course, what Nepal does with monarchy is its internal matter, but a friendly Government in our neighbourhood is in our interest.

Bordering China and India, Nepal offers a geo-political advantage to any country that is influential there. Though one does not foresee any major conflict in the near future, India feels that the military capability of China will increase if it gets a foothold there. Also, we have to be respectful of the sentiment of the people of Nepal.

Winston Churchill once observed: "The monarchy is extraordinarily useful. When Britain wins a battle it shouts, 'God save the Queen'; when it loses, it votes down the Prime Minister." Only the future will indicate whether Churchill's statement is relevant to Nepal or not.

1. Of Pakistan

2.1. Ballistic Missiles

Pakistani dictator Pervez Musha-raff's nuclear bluff is nothing new to India. He recently said that, had there been a war in 2002, he would have used nuclear weapons against this country. As is usual with liars, he subsequently denied this, saying he was misquoted. He is the fourth armyman who, by sheer force, threw out the democratically-elected Government of Mr Nawaz Sharif in October 1999, to take over as the ruler of Pakistan. He did not do so for love of Pakistan. He did it to save his job from which he had been dismissed in absentia by Prime Minister Sharif.

General Ayub had first opened the army's account by taking over Pakistan, on October 7, 1958. His rule lasted nearly 10 and half years. General Yahya, who dethroned him, ruled Pakistan for two years and nine months. When Pakistan lost the 1971 war with India, leading the creation of Bangladesh, he handed over power to Zulfikar Ali Bhutto. Bhutto lost his job to General Ziaul Haq on July 5, 1977. General Zia got Bhutto hanged and was himself killed in an air crash in 1988. Neither poor economic conditions nor other evils disappeared with the Generals, during their over two decades of rule.

Smarting under successive defeats at the hands of India, Pakistan has always nursed the ambition to cow it down, both by military might and in international forums. The nuclearisation of Pakistan is only one step in that direction. The Indian missile programme for self-defence is not only transparent, but also by and large indigenous. India's nuclear doctrine clearly enunciates 'no first use'. But it also emphasises building and maintaining a minimum deterrent. It also warns adverturists that nuclear retaliation to the first strike will be massive and designed to inflict unacceptable damage.

Unlike in countries ruled by Generals, India's nuclear retaliatory attacks can only be authorised by mature civilian political leadership, through the nuclear command authority. Both India and Pakistan have a ballistic missile capability to hit each others targets. India announced its indigenous integrated guided missile development programme in 1984. Pakistan suddenly claimed possession of ballistic missiles in 1989. It will be interesting to compare the Indian and Pakistani missile programmes, as reported in an American publication.

India's Prithvi-I carries a payload of 1,000 kilogrammes and has a maximum range of 150 kilometres, while the figures for Prithvi-

II are 500-750 kgs and 250 kms. Prithvi-III has a payload of 500-750 kgs and a maximum range of 350 kms. The figures for Agni-IA are 1000 kgs and 700 kms; for Agni-I, 1,000 kgs and 1,500 kms; for Agni-II 1,000 kgs and 2,000 kms; and for Agni-III, 1,000 kgs and 5,000 kms.

Pakistan's Hatf-I has a payload of 500 kgs and a maximum range of 80 kms. The figures for Hatf-IA are 500 kgs and 100 kms; for Hatf-II (M-11), 500 kgs and 300 kms; for Haft-III, 500 kgs and 600 kms; for Ghauri I (Nodong I), 600 kgs and 1,000 kms; Ghauri II (Nodong II), 700 kgs and 1,500 kms; and for Shaheen-I, 1,000 kgs and 700 kms.

All the above missiles can deliver nuclear warheads. Pakistan has already conducted the third test of its Ghauri missile, primarily for the benefit of its domestic audience. Its programme is dependent on China and North Korea. All solid propellant ballistic missiles have come from China, while those with liquid propellant owe their existence to the North Korean Nodong missile. In a fusion of interests, Pakistan provided North Korea many of the designs for gas centrifuges and much of the machinery it needed to make highly enriched uranium for its nuclear weapons project.

The United States's Central Intelligence Agency told members of US Congress that North Korea's uranium enrichment programme-which it discovered only in the summer of 2001-will produce enough material to make nuclear weapons in two to three years. Previously, the CIA had estimated that North Korea had probably extracted enough plutonium from a nuclear reactor to build one or two weapons, until that programme was halted in 1994 in a confrontation with the US. It is strange one of the world's poorest and most isolated nations could put together a new, complex uranium project. It is time to face up to the fact the relationship between North Korea and Pakistan is much deeper and more dangerous than the US and India have ever suspected.

Even after General Musharraf sided with the US in ousting the Taliban in Afghanistan and hunting down Al Qaeda leaders post-9/11, Pakistan has continued its murky relationship with the North Korean military. It is a partnership involving an insecure Islamic Pakistan and a failing and poor communist country, both in need of each other.

Due to years of US-imposed sanctions, Pakistan- in its desperate desire to counter India's superior military force -turned to North Korea. As the latter too was increasingly cut off from Russia and China, it tried to develop uranium-based nuclear weapons. Incidentally, North Korea has plentiful supplies of uranium. The US had put tremendous diplomatic pressure on it to abandon the project, and also cut off oil supplies.

The US has never publicly discussed the role of Pakistan or North Korea with regard to nuclear proliferation. The Bush Administration, in its wisdom, has decided (at least by implication) that Pakistan's cooperation in the search for the Al Qaeda is so critical that it had better ignore the federal statues that require President George W Bush to impose stiff economic penalties on any country involved in nuclear proliferation. Or, alternatively, to issue a public waiver of those penalties in the interest of national security. Mr Bush earlier removed sanctions and penalties that were imposed on Pakistan, after it set off a series of nuclear tests in 1998.

Evidence suggests that Osama bin Laden is still alive, perhaps on Pakistani soil. So Mr Bush has turned a blind eye to what is going within that country. Where India and Pakistan are concerned, war is a very costly proposition. Both countries have similar problems and similar burdens-the legacy of their traditions, history and economy. More than 1.4 billion people live in the Asian subcontinent. More than 50 per cent of them live in abject poverty with no immediate prospect of escaping their precarious conditions in the foreseeable future.

Any move that will bring the two nuclearised neighbours closer, reducing tensions, is welcome. Both India and Pakistan are bound by history and geography. They have waged war on several occasions and engaged in border skirmishes. India was not on talking terms with Pakistan after the ouster of Mr Sharif in a coup. It did not recognise the legitimacy of the military regime. It also tried its best to have Pakistan expelled from the Commonwealth. Finally, a dialogue between General Musharraf and Prime Minister Atal Bihari Vajpayee in Agra ended that period of hostilities. Tensions flared again last year, with troops mobilisation at the border, till finally Operation Parakram was called off.

The fact is that we do not know what will or can end Pakistan's pathological hatred of India. Like the rest of the world, our neighbour too respects only those nations that are economically and militarily stronger than it is. The only way to deal with Pakistan is to be stronger than it in all ways, which we are in any case at present. It is equally important to remember that it is force and money power that rule the world. Power will come to us if we are determined to be powerful. While we should stick to the doctrine of no first use, let us not be caught unaware by a wily General. We should not allow his bluff to get better of us. In the view of North Korea's Kim Jong Il, the difference between North Korea and Iraq is that Mr Saddam Hussein does not have nuclear weapons-and look what is happening to him. As Mao Zedong rightly said, power flows out of the barrel of a gun.

2.2. The Mystery Deepens

Benazir Bhutto was assassinated on December 27, 2007, when she popped up through the sunroof of her armoured black SUV to wave to a crowd of supporters cheering her and waving flags as she left Rawalpindi's Liaquat Bagh minutes after addressing an election rally. A number of questions have been raised as to who killed the former Pakistan Prime Minister and what was the motive behind this dastardly act.

While other Pakistani leaders hesitated, Bhutto spoke eloquently against radical Islamism, saying more than once that Islamist extremism had struck deep roots in Pakistan. She returned to Pakistan following a reported power-sharing agreement with President Pervez Musharraf. Mr. Musharraf has maintained in an interview that he had personally told Bhutto that she was under threat and that under the circumstances, the PPP leader should not have done the things she did on that fateful day in December. About the allegation that the Pakistan Government had a hand in her killing, he said, 'This is unfortunately a very baseless allegation,' adding that there is 'no real protection against a suicide bomber'.

Mr. Musharraf has blamed Al Qaeda, particularly Beitullah Mehsud, who operates from Pakistan's lawless tribal region, for Bhutto's assassination. He has also claimed that Bhutto made a mistake by ignoring warnings that 'there's a likelihood of a suicide attempt'.

Italian news agency 'Adnkronos International' was the first to report that an Al Qaeda spokesperson had telephoned to claim responsibility for the killing of Bhutto. The agency also said that the decision to kill Bhutto was made by Al Qaeda's No 2, Ayman al-Zawahiri, in October 2007. Death squads were allegedly constituted for the mission and ultimately one cell comprising a Punjabi volunteer of the defunct Lashkar-i-Jhangvi succeeded in carrying it out.

Pakistan's Interior Minister Aftab Sherpao said, 'We have the evidence that Al Qaeda and the Taliban were behind the suicide attack on Benazir Bhutto.' Pakistan's Interior Ministry spokesman claimed that the Government had recorded an 'intelligence intercept' in which Baitullah Mehsud congratulated his people for carrying out this cowardly act. The Al Qaeda leader was also responsible for the Karachi bombing in October 2007 that killed more than 140; incidentally, Bhutto was lucky that time.

Pakistan had earlier refused any international assistance in the investigations into Bhutto's assassination. Now under pressure for an international investigation, Pakistan's Government has called Scotland Yard to help in unravelling the mystery behind the murder. A six-member team of Scotland Yard investigators has already arrived and a second team, comprising technical staff, will join soon.

The investigation of the Bhutto case is going to run into legal difficulties because no post-mortem was done to establish the exact reason for her death. Pakistan's Prime Minister Mohammedmian Soomro says that it was Bhutto's husband, Mr Asif Ali Zardari, who did not allow doctors to perform autopsy. In the case of unnatural death, it is the medical examination and post-mortem of the dead body that can pin point the cause of death. Even otherwise the cause of death has been attributed to different factors.

While one report said that Bhutto died as a result of bullet injury, another forwarded the theory that a suicide bomber blew himself next to her bullet-proof vehicle. However, a day after Bhutto's assassination, Pakistan's Interior Ministry claimed at a Press conference that she died due to injury to her skull caused by the lever of the sunroof of her car, and not because of bullet injuries. Later, a video recording showed a young man in dark glasses firing bullets at her. The Deputy Superintendent of Police of Rawalpindi, too, confirmed that Bhutto was targeted by that man.

The truth behind every political assassination in Pakistan has been elusive and ambiguous. In Pakistan, the best means of defeating one's enemies is to kill them or send them into exile. Gen Zia-ul Haq did the same to Zulfiqar Bhutto, father of Benazir Bhutto, when he got him hanged through a so-called judicial process in 1979. Mr Musharraf did not go that far, but exiles his opponents — real or perceived.

This brings us to the question: Will there be any let up in the war against terrorism in Pakistan? What will be the consequences of Benazir Bhutto's assassination on India? When any Pakistani leader is out of power, he or she makes pro-peace noises vis-?-vis India. But the moment he or she comes to power, everything changes. In 1990, it was Benazir Bhutto who called on Kashmiris to cut the then Governor of Jammu & Kashmir, Mr Jagmohan, into pieces for his strong anti-terrorism stand. She actively supported the Taliban's military takeover of Afghanistan, with the objective of provide Pakistan 'strategic depth'. While paying tribute to her, we need to keep in mind her anti-India stance, particularly in fuelling the Khalistani movement in Punjab, and role in transferring nuclear technology to North Korea.

Bhutto was not a paragon of virtue and integrity. There were several corruption charges against her and Mr Zardari. In order to evade such charges, she moved to Dubai and London with her family. She returned from self-exile on October 18, 2007, after a 'deal' was struck with Mr Musharraf. For Bhutto, the 'deal' had two components: One, it would pave the way for her to become Prime Minister again; and, two, the Musharraf Administration would drop corruption cases against her. In turn, she was expected to support Pakistan's role in the US's 'war on terror' and accept Mr Musharraf as President.

The Pakistan Government must understand that it should properly investigate the reasons behind the assassination of Benazir Bhutto. It is for the state to take revenge of this kind of dastardly crime. To take revenge half-heartedly is to court disaster.

2.3. Mafia, Cricket and Woolmer

Pakistan's cricket coach Bob Woolmer was found dead in his room in Hotel Pegasus in Jamaica on March 19 after his team's defeat at the hands of Ireland. Woolmer had played Test cricket for

England in the mid-1970s. Before taking over as Pakistan's coach in 2004, he coached South Africa in the 1990s when its captain Hansie Cronje admitted to accepting money to 'fix' matches and was banned from playing for life.

That fateful day, an attendant staff of the hotel found Woolmer lying on the floor in boxer shorts, with half his body out of the bathroom. One witness, who reported having seen blood and vomit splattered in the room said, "Whoever killed the coach, gained access to his room without forcing the door open and attacked Woolmer, without people in the adjacent rooms noticing anything amiss." In the said hotel, access to guest floors is restricted; a card key is required to operate the elevators.

A post-mortem examination has established that Woolmer died as a result of "manual strangulation", and so Jamaican Police is treating the case as one of murder. The police said that none of his possessions were missing. Woolmer was a large man. It must have taken a lot of strength to subdue him.

Mr Nasim Ashraf, chairman of the Pakistan Cricket Board, who resigned in the wake of his team's loss to Ireland, said that he had received an e-mail sent the previous Saturday evening from Woolmer in which the coach had expressed disappointment over the defeat. The e-mail read: "I would like to praise my association with the Pakistan team, but now I would like to announce my retirement after the World Cup to live the rest of my life in Cape Town."

Pakistan team spokesman Pervez Jamil Mir said Woolmer was upset that parts of the manuscript of the book he had been writing had disappeared. To add to this, former Pakistani fast bowler Sarfaraz Nawaz has claimed that Woolmer was killed because he was writing a book that would have exposed illegal gambling in cricket.

This murder is a complex case for Jamaican Police that has probably never handled any similar case before with more than one angle to it - revenge and/or match fixing. But a few inferences have emerged. One, somebody who either knew Woolmer or was somehow linked to him murdered him as he had let his assailants into his hotel room. Woolmer would normally not let anybody in to his 12th-floor hotel room, unless he knew who the person was.

One or more people could be involved in the murder. Authorities are studying the footage captured by closed circuit television cameras in and around the Pegasus Hotel. No allegation of any sexual escapades by the coach or any team member has surfaced. But it will be worth investigating this aspect.

For further investigations, Jamaican Police has sought the help of a toxicologist and a histologist (examiner of body tissues) to pinpoint the method of death. The pathologist involved in the investigation has attributed the cause of death to "asphyxia as a result of manual strangulation". Separately, the International Cricket Council's anti-corruption unit will investigate if match fixing had a role to play in the death. The fact that Woolmer had expressed his desire to retire after the match with Ireland shows that there is more than what meets the eye.

Woolmer's murder has again raised the apprehension of the involvement of betting rackets which are infamous for amassing fortunes at any cost, be it match fixing in cricket, horse racing or boxing. If you do not accept bribe in doing the biddings of the underworld, you die. In Woolmer's case, he might have uncovered some nasty, unpalatable evidence that expose such rackets. But the keys to the match fixing angle and its linkage with gambling cartels lies in Pakistan and not Jamaica. Of course, the entire Pakistani team has been questioned and their fingerprints registered.

Any investigation into the world of violent crimes, such as the murder of Bob Woolmer, must follow the established procedures of analysis and reconstruction of the entire crime. A good rule to follow is to arrest the suspects within the first 72 hours of the execution of the crime, failing which cracking the case becomes difficult. That was not done for whatever reasons. Now it is important for Jamaican Police to examine mobile phones and telephone records, mails, emails, food in Woolmer's refrigerator, his meetings, appointments, work and recreation habits.

They should also look into who Bob Woolmer's possible enemies from his business, political and personal circles could be. It would be equally helpful to find out Woolmer's medical history. Establishing the motive of the case will help develop a viable theory about what happened. The usual motives in murder are anger, love, revenge, jealousy and profit.

Jamaican Police can perhaps learn from the relevant CBI inquiries. The CBI report on cricket match fixing in India had this to say: "The romanticism associated with the game is perhaps gone forever. Increasingly, in the playing fields around the world, the music of sweetly timed strokes is being replaced by the harsh cacophony of ringing cell phones. Both inducements and threats to players are bound to increase in view of the big money involved in gambling on cricket and the entry of the underworld. Major corrective steps need to be taken to put cricket back on rails."

The inquiry also showed that small-scale betting on cricket matches has been taking place in India for a long time. Betting on a major scale started only after India won the World Cup in 1983. Betting increased further when live telecast of cricket matches became regular. It attained sophistication and spread across the length and breadth of the country, as the use of computer and mobile phone gave a major fillip to betting.

In this country, betting on cricket is perhaps the biggest organised racket. According to rough estimates, the turnover in betting on any one-day international match being played anywhere in the world runs into hundreds of crores of rupees. It is now suspected to be worth around Rs 30,000 crore.

There are clear signals that the underworld mafia has started taking interest in betting and is expected to take this activity under its control if the malaise is not checked immediately. What was once small-time wagering, which is inevitable, has now been replaced by an organised syndicate run by the underworld mafia that has started interfering with the purity of the sport. And this has happened because of the negligence of police and other regulatory authorities. The game has lost a considerable degree of its credibility already. It will be a national shame if the problems, apparent from the evidence gathered by the CBI, are not immediately and decisively solved.

With a large amount of money at stake, it makes sense for both bookies and punters to manipulate results of cricket matches. This has resulted in their developing a close and unholy relationship with cricketers. It is for society to accept this challenges so that it can feel the exhilaration of genuine victory.

3. Of Iraq

3.1. Iraq Needs More Concern

No war proceeds exactly as planned or anticipated. And no side tells the actual or whole truth about any war. The US and the

UK expected to finish the Iraq war in a few days. The conflict took 21 days to end. After the Saddam International Airport, renamed Baghdad International Airport, fell to US forces, the capture of Baghdad was easy, with hardly any sign of the much-touted Republican Guard. Some people rejoiced at the fall of Sad-dam Hussein by pulling down his statues and later looting his palaces, the houses of his close aides and government offices.

The coalition victory did come sooner than expected by the rest of the world. The 1991 war had started on March 20, with simultaneous bombing of Baghdad and other targets. The action lasted more than 40 days, the last two days reserved for action on the ground. The present war saw closure in a little over three weeks. As in 1991, the enemy was Saddam Hussein, who has either been killed or disappeared without leaving any trace. In 1991, the Americans had virtually the entire world behind them. Many countries at the time had felt that Iraq had unjustifiably attacked Kuwait with a view to annexing it. This time, the Americans stood on their own, with only the UK and Australia as active coalition partners.

People in many countries, including in Europe, and even many American and British citizens opposed the war. The Indian Government, due to its own compulsions, did not formally condemn the US attack. But Indian legal luminaries said that, after failing to secure the second UN Resolution to justify the use of military force, the US and the British Governments unilaterally attacked a sovereign country, after debilitating it with 12 years of comprehensive economic sanctions. Parliament passed a resolution deploring the war-but only on the day Baghdad fell. Former British Foreign Secretary Robin Cook, who resigned from the Government on the issue of the war, said at one stage, "I have had my fill of this bloody and unjust war. I want our troops home ... before more of them are killed."

A vast majority of Muslims all over the world also disapproved of the war. In India, Darul Uloom, Deoband, one of the oldest and most prestigious religious schools of the Sunni Muslims around the world reissued a fatwa, asking Indians in general and Indian Muslims in particular to boycott American and British manufactured products in protest against the US-led attack on Iraq.

The same institution had earlier issued a fatwa against US companies during the American attack on Afghanistan. In contrast, a Shia cleric in the holy city of Najaf, issued an edict on April 3, 2003, asking the Iraqis to remain calm and not hinder the invading US forces. Pushed to the wall, a few suicide attacks were launched by a few members of the Iraqi forces, with the unfulfilled promise of more suicide attacks against the Anglo-American forces. The determination of Iraqis to fight or resist the invaders with all their might, daily proclaimed to the world, ended as mere verbal bombast. So far, the coalition forces have suffered less than 149 casualties, whereas the estimates-albeit unconfirmed-of Iraqi casualties stand at 7,500, with as many as 20 times of that figure surrendering.

In 1991, evicting Iraqi forces from Kuwait was the clear war objective. Iraq's territory was bombed only to humble its military machine and to force it to withdraw its troops from Kuwait. The war aim of 2003 was less categorical, combining regime change, installation of democracy and the locating and destruction of weapons of mass destruction. Only the first has been accomplished; the second and the third are still to be realised. America had committed a huge ground force of around 300,000 personnel. Incidentally, the US army-which has not undertaken any major action since the infamous Vietnam war-has acquitted itself as a first rate war machine, with excellent coordination between air and ground forces. There have, of course, been a few cases of bombings taking out wrong targets and friendly fire incidents.

Meanwhile, US special ground forces are still scouting the hills and caves of Afghanistan, in search of Taliban leaders and Al Qaeda chief Osama bin Laden. The US Army was nicknamed Christmas Pudding Army during the Vietnam war. Some soldiers had reportedly refused to fight unless Christmas puddings were airdropped, which they eventually were. In Afghanistan, they are branded the mineral water army. Suspicious of local water, they carry heavy water loads. In Iraq, they had a tougher time, since even ordinary water was difficult to obtain, let alone mineral water.

In Gulf War II, causality-wise, fire power-wise and military might-wise, it has been an unequal battle. Modern warfare is computerised and fought with deadly long-range missiles, bombers, aircraft carriers and other gadgets that can be fired from a safe distance. Its most spectacular casualty has been Saddam Hussein, who has alternated between being America's tactical ally and an evil tyrant, depending on how he served US interests. In the 1980s, when Iran's spiritual leader, Ayatollah Khomeini, was the US's main enemy, it suited America to finance Saddam to foil Iranian expansionism. The US's explanation is that you must adapt your policies to the nature of the threat. In many cases such as that of even bin Laden, it has been US policy to demonise its erstwhile friends and allies.

Until 1990, when Iraq invaded Kuwait, hefty US agricultural loan guarantees and trade credits flowed to Iraq, despite evidence of grave human rights abuses. George Bush Sr, then President, signed a waiver on grounds of national interest in January 1990, overriding a congressional bar on trade credits to Iraq that lawmakers had imposed after Saddam used poison gas against the Kurds.

With Saddam gone, it is time to start the work of Iraq's reconstruction. In this context, the US House of Representatives had passed a resolution on April 4, 2003, excluding France, Germany, Russia, and Syria from any post-war reconstruction contracts on the grounds they had opposed the war. This would even bar them access to information on reconstruction bids. The US Senate had already voted $ 78.7 billion for the war and related needs. French Prime Minister Jean-Pierre Raffarin had said on April 3: "The Americans made a triple mistake; first of all, a moral mistake and, I think we have to say this, there was an alternative to war. We could have disarmed Iraq differently. Also, they made a political mistake, because we know very well the difficulties of this region. It is a serious political error to start trouble in this region. And then, there is a strategic mistake (to think) that today one country can lead the world."

The US, wherever possible, has been purchasing cooperation. Pakistan was rewarded with a waiver of a one billion dollar debt and rescheduling of the remaining $ 2.3 billion to be paid in easy instalments over the next 38 years through an agreement signed on April 5. The US thus fulfilled a promise of a financial reward to Pakistan in exchange for bases and logistic support for fighting the Taliban in 2002.

The US President and British Prime Minister are now seeking to calm the Iraqi and Arab fears, saying the coalition is not an occupying force and that they will help build a representative government that protects the rights of all Iraqi citizens. British Premier Tony Blair has said: "Our forces are friends and liberators of the Iraqi people, not conquerors." This claim should be taken with a pinch of salt. Experience has shown that wherever Americans have gone, whether Pakistan, Kuwait, Philippines, Afghanis-tan, or any South American country, they have stayed there, ostensibly in the name of serving democratic values but actually to maintain hegemony.

Let us not merely hope to see the Americans do not reduce Iraq to a colony due to their interest in its oil. Let us work towards ensuring this. True, India can only play a marginal role, since it does not have much influence with the Arabs or the West. But whatever little we can do for Iraq, let us not hesitate to do it.

15

Hinduism and Threats

1. Of Perversion

1.1. Dressed for Cheap Thrills

An IPS officer of the rank of Inspector General of Police, Uttar Pradesh, proclaimed that he is "doosri Radha". He has changed his stand now and says that he is Rukmini, Lord Krishna's wife (Radha is Krishna's consort, not wife, according to folk lore).

He wore a nose pin since 1992 and followed it up by wearing lipstick, nail enamel and women's clothes. The Central Government has asked the Uttar Pradesh Government to take action against him for a conduct which was 'unbecoming of a civil servant'. The Government felt that the officer has brought disrepute to the civil services by his 'deviant' behaviour. The officer has applied for voluntary retirement from service and it has reportedly been granted.

What a person does in his or her private life is his affair but when he or she holds a position of responsibility in Government he has to fulfill certain expectations of both the public and the Government. India is a secular country and has no state religion. Everybody is free to practice and pursue his or her faith. But in case a person is a Government official, he is obliged to follow Government rules. This is especially true of services that require their personnel to be in uniform like the IPS. In such services the officials and their subordinates are expected to follow a code of conduct. There are All India Services Conduct Rules, as well as IPS Uniform Rules to guide these Government servants.

In fact, there are 'dress rules' not only for police and other uniformed officers but also airhostesses, cabin crews, pilots, doctors, nurses, advocates, watchmen, bus conductors, drivers, railway officials. Even the judges follow a dress code when sitting on the benches to deliver justice. Women are not debarred from joining the Indian Police Service. There are many women in the Indian Police Service, and one of them has become the State Police Chief. But so far there has been no man in the Indian Police Service who, by proclaiming himself as a woman has become the head of police force.

Whatever may be people's views about the claim of the officer, that he is the female consort of Lord Krishna, neither the police force nor the public in general is gullible. Lord Krishna is above all such antics. In fact, I personally think he would not have approved of a male Radha.

The biggest problem that the officer has created is for his family which finds itself in a quandary. In fact, at the time of vacating his official residence, there were heated arguments between him and his wife, Veena. The situation took an ugly turn when his wife reportedly ripped off his nose ring and pushed him aside leaving him badly bruised. On the complaint of his wife, the police arrived at the IG's residence and prevented the officer from taking the refrigerator and washing machine with him. The IG has been married for 33 years and has two sons.

His wife says that he has been spending his time embracing a peepal or holy fig tree in his garden and chanting mantras to his beloved lord Krishna. One room in his house is kept sacred and secret. The officer says, "That is my private bed room. Only Krishna can enter there." The IG believes himself to be the reincarnation of the lady consort of the Hindu god. However, he claims that he is merely exercising his freedom of religion. But his wife, who is suing him, says he is no woman at heart - just a womaniser. According to a senior officer, "It is a real embarrassment for (the) police force if its senior officer behaves in such manner."

Close on the heels of Inspector General of Police, Lucknow, projecting himself as "Radha", came another incident in which a mother of four children in neighbouring Burhanpur district declared herself as wife of former Pakistani cricket captain Wasim Akram. A lady clerk in the commercial tax department, called Krishna, claims to have accepted Akram as her husband since she saw his performance on television during an India-Pakistan cricket ODI in 1999. She has broken her marriage with a retired Government servant.

She now considers the former Pakistani cricketer as her husband. She says, "I am yet to meet him (Akram). Whether he accepts me or not, I will spend the rest of my life as his wife." She claims that "a godly figure clad in white clothes had shown her Akram's face in her dreams telling her that it was that of her husband." In another case in November this year a teenage boy bedecked himself as a bride and married an idol of Lord Shiva in the presence of hundreds of guests in Orissa's Balasore district.

Sixteen-year-old Bhawani Das, a resident of Barabati claims to be an incarnation of Goddess Bhagawati. On November 24 he dressed up in bridal finery donated by local businessmen, wore makeup with the help of beauticians from the town's best beauty parlour and married the idol of Lord Shiva. He said, "I always felt I am the wife of Lord Shiva. God also asked me in my dreams to perform the marriage ceremony."

Various theories have been put forward to explain such actions. Some people believe that such behaviour, which includes cross-dressing, is nothing more than an attention-grabbing exercise. Religion, mysticism and self-induced hallucination all combine to give an excuse to validate such myths. Cross dressing does not turn men into women or change their sex. Another official of UP Government, who ran up a telephone bill of Rs. 25,000, claims that it was due to his talking directly to Lord Shiva. He has not clarified as to what is the telephone number of the god or whether the deity has a VSNL connection or some other company.

There have been cases in the past where Government officials have incurred huge telephone bills. On inquiries, it has been discovered that the telephone was used for a chat on sexual subjects with people abroad. This officer's wife as well as the one of retired IPS officer posing first as Radha and now as Rukmini have been left exasperated by their husbands' antics. In fact, the tendency to be close to god, like the tendency to be close to the power centre, seems to be the trend. You can always sell a ticket to heaven for earthly gains or for forgiveness as the Christian priests did in 16th century which led to the birth of Protestantism.

A psychologist says, "There is no particular reason for cross-dressing. Some individuals are dissatisfied with their biological sex and hence, they think they are trapped in the body of the opposite sex." Another psychiatrist adds, "Some individuals cross dress purely for sexual arousal, this is called fetishist transvestism. These individuals have no illusions about their gender and rid themselves of the clothes and make-up shortly after they masturbate."

Another male cross dresser says, "Many cross-dressers (including myself) cannot fully articulate why we have a need to dress up and present ourselves as women. Essentially we have a strong need to express feminine feelings." Another writer says, "For some, the desire to cross-dress is to reject the very norms that dictate society. Why should some clothes be 'only for women'", he asks.

Whatever people may say, there is nothing like dressing with dignity. While people are free to flaunt their divine connections, they are not free to bring ridicule, and humiliation to all those including their families and public who are affected by their antics. It is time to recall what William Hazlitt said, "Those who make their dress a principal part of themselves will in general become of no more value than their dress."

2. Of Conspiracy

2.1. Washing the Ganges Water: A Willful Conspiracy

There is an old saying: Cleanliness is next to godliness. Rivers are the greatest cleaning agents this world has. But unfortunately in our country, they are treated as extensions of drainage systems, where the rubbish and refuse of cities are dumped. Most of the Indian rivers find mentions in the scriptures. They are believed to be so holy that if the dead are cremated on their banks, they get absolved of all sins.

For ages, the Ganga has not only been considered holy, but is believed to have healing powers. In fact, when a Hindu is about to die, Gangajal - the water of the river is administered to him.

Thousands of sadhus who travelled hundreds of miles for the Ardh Kumbh Mela last month expressed their unhappiness with the pollution levels, and even threatened to boycott the ceremonies this year. They expressed their anguish on the state of the Ganga and Yamuna that have been reduced to a big drain carrying filth, toxins and diseases. But then why should administration listen to sadhus who do not constitute a vote-bank?

There are many reasons for this sorry state of affairs. Pollution in the rivers is attributable to human and industrial factors. Professionals dealing with such projects assert that the practice of dumping untreated sewage from cities and consigning dead bodies in the river are the major causes of its high pollution levels.

River water is today badly polluted because industries use rivers as waste disposal sites. A typical comment is that though lakhs of people come to bathe in the rivers, they are actually taking a dip not in the river water but in the effluents from factories along with dirt and refuse from the city drains. The problem is compounded by the use of riverbeds and banks as open-air lavatories, as civic bodies do no provide sufficient public utility services even for pilgrims. The normal biological oxygen (BOD) level in the Ganga is five; but ideally, it should not exceed three if it is to be fit for bathing.

The BOD level in the Ganga now stands at six, making it unfit not only for drinking but even bathing. Ganga receives a pollutant effluents to the tune of about 29 MLD (million litres daily). They were being poured into the river through the Salori drain till recently, which is now being trapped. The Mori dam contributes 20 MLD of effluents while nearly 150 small drains account for another five MLD. Tanneries and paper mills in Kanpur, too, make their contribution to the worsening of the situation.

According to a World Bank report, the Ganga water is now the reason for nine to 12 per cent of the total disease affliction in Uttar Pradesh because of a very high level of pollution. The report testifies that pollution levels in the holy river are the biggest contributor to water-borne diseases among the population residing close. As for the aquatic life, it is seriously endangered.

The Ministry of Environment and Forests initiated the Ganga Action Plan to clean critical areas of the Ganga in its course from Hardwar onwards to make it fit for bathing. Since 1980, about Rs

1,000 crore has been spent on GAP without any worthwhile improvement in the quality of water.

The Public Accounts Committee of Parliament report of 2006 says that the work of GAP-I that was to be finished in 1990 is yet to be completed and the deadline has been extended from 2001 to 2008. The committee has held that the Government did not tackle the problem promptly and handled the project in a casual manner. As a result, 149 schemes are still incomplete in UP and Bihar. According to its report, Ganga is the way it is today not because of paucity of funds but because of slow pace of work.

The river passing through Delhi, Yamuna, which joins the Ganga, is in no better condition. It has been reduced to a putrid mess. It has a sluggish flow, further burdened with plastic, solid waste, untreated sewer and corpses. The Yamuna enters Delhi at Wazirabad Barrage, flows 22 km through the National Capital Region till the Okhla barrage before it enters Haryana. In this stretch, 17 major drains empty untreated sewage into the river. Besides, plastic, garbage and solid wastes are tossed into it. The money spent on cleaning the Ganga and Yamuna has gone into the pockets of the corrupt. No other reason can explain this apathy.

The administrative indifference is almost reminiscent of the fodder scam, in which crores of rupees were pocketed in the name of animal husbandry. Here, the difference is the projects involve holy rivers. As the rivers flow through various States that are supposed to implement the projects with Central Government funding, it becomes impossible to monitor and check the claims on the progress in cleaning the rivers. The latest Union Government affidavit filed in the Supreme Court is a pathetic tale of total failure of cleaning the Ganga and Yamuna. As the cleaning of Ganga had to be done in different States, 59 towns were identified in the Ganga basin.

In the second phase of the GAP, 270 projects were sanctioned at a cost of Rs 615 crore. Only 111 projects (less than 50 per cent) have been completed. In UP alone, only 17 of the 43 sanctioned schemes have reportedly been completed, while in Uttaranchal, only 16 out of 37 sanctioned projects are in various stages of operation. West Bengal has completed only 56 projects out of its allocated share of 170.

The figures submitted by the Government to the Supreme Court indicate that, barring a few exceptions, the pollution level has either remained the same or has increased since the first phase of the GAP was initiated. However, in the same breath, the affidavit says: "In terms of both the cost and the time taken, the Ganga Action Plan compares favourably with similar initiatives taken to restore rivers like the Thames, the Rhine and the Danube."

The Centre also said before the Supreme Court that the Rs 1,000 crore plan to check pollution is a grand success. At the same time, it says that the cleaning of the Ganga was a mammoth task as pollution levels were continuously increasing due to the pressure of population on urban centres located on the banks. To underplay the gravity of situation at the time of Ardh Kumbh Mela and the protests of the sadhus, the affidavit says, "Except for small stretches near Kanpur, Allahabad and Varanasi, which remain problem areas, the rest of the river from Rishikesh to Patna carries potable water." Obviously in the contradictory affidavit, facts, tales, and wishful thinking have been mixed. Nobody who has seen the state of the river believe the observations made in the affidavit.

The real problem in the case of non-completion or substandard work lies with errant officials, private contractors, middlemen and other beneficiaries who would not hesitate to embezzle of public money through forgeries. Cleaning the rivers is almost like desilting of drains in municipal areas where crores of rupees are spent without any improvement in the situation.

Index

C

J

K

M

O

Q

R

S

U

V

W

Y

Z